The Forthcoming EC Directive on Unfair Commercial Practices

Private Law in European Context Series

VOLUME 5

Series Editors:
Martijn Hesselink
Ugo Mattei
Horatia Muir Watt

**For the
Society of European Contract Law (SECOLA)**

*Massimo Bianca   Hugh Collins   Stefan Grundman (President)
Ewoud Hondius   Sophie Stiijns*

Contract law is probably the most dynamic area of European Private Law and also the fundamental private law discipline in all national legal systems. SECOLA was founded to assist the study of European contract law and to enhance its quality. SECOLA organises an open, interdisciplinary, truly international and interdisciplinary discussion platform. The focus of the Society is upon newly enacted European Community legal measures, on core concepts in the field of European contract law, and on proposals for further legislation. The Society organises one or two international conferences each year, arranges for the publication of scholarly discussions in the field including books to be published in this series, and assists with other network activities. In addition, SECOLA is building up an information platform, systematically structured, containing all relevant European legal measures in full text in all official languages of the Community, together with their transposition into national laws and with reference to the pertinent scholarly literature (see www. secola.org).

This volume in this series was realised jointly by SECOLA with the London School of Economics and the British Institute of International and Comparative Law. It builds on the papers delivered at a conference held in London in May 2002, sponsored additionally by Allen & Overy, solicitors.

A list of previous titles in the series may be found at the end of this volume.

Private Law in European Context Series

The Forthcoming EC Directive on Unfair Commercial Practices

Edited by H. Collins

KLUWER LAW INTERNATIONAL
THE HAGUE / LONDON / NEW YORK

A C.I.P. catalogue record for this book is available from the Library of Congress.

ISBN 90 411 22249

Published by:
Kluwer Law International
P.O. Box 85889
2508 CN The Hague
The Netherlands

Sold and distributed in North, Central and South America by:
Aspen Publishers, Inc.
7201 McKinney Circle
Frederick, MD 21704
USA

Sold and distributed in all other countries by:
Extenza-Turpin Distribution Services
Stratton Business Park
Pegasus Drive
Biggleswade
Bedfordshire SG18 8QB
United Kingdom

Printed on acid-free paper

Printed in the Netherlands

Preface

Bringing with them sunshine and hot weather, delegates to the second annual conference of the Society of European Contract Law (SECOLA) convened in London in May 2002 to discuss aspects of the progress towards European Union contract law. The focus of the meeting was on the law governing marketing, an emphasis prompted not only by the European Commission's recent Green Paper on Consumer Protection in October 2001 (Com (2001) 531), but also on the ground that this field was of particular interest because it investigated some of the most contested ground in the project of negative integration to complete the Internal Market. The meeting was conscious that if the Commission succeeded in justifying EC regulation of marketing practices and implemented a uniform legal regime in this area, it would constitute a major step towards the creation of an European Union law of contract more generally, not merely because this field is important in any system of law, but also because it might demonstrate by an example that uniform laws in relation to contracts are an essential ingredient in the aim of dismantling barriers to cross-border trade.

As ever, Professor Grundmann, as the President of the Society, provided the driving force behind the agenda for the meeting, and facilitated a fascinating discussion over the two days of the conference. The topic compelled a productive dialogue to open up between lawyers approaching the issue of unfair commercial practices from three perspectives: consumer protection regulation, competition law, and general contract law. Nor was the conference confined to purely legal analysis: perhaps the most intensive debates concerned the economic analysis of legal regulation, particularly with respect to the efficiency of consumer protection regulation and its compatibility with the agenda of promoting the competitiveness of markets. Hence, the essays collected in this volume, which represent revised versions of some of the papers presented at the conference, range over the fields of consumer law, competition law, and general contract law, and engage not only with legal problems, but also discuss the economic implications of different proposals for legal regulation of unfair commercial practices.

After the contributions for this book went to press, the Commission took a further step towards the realisation of its proposal to regulate unfair commercial practices. It published a draft Directive concerning business-to-consumer commercial practices in the Internal Market.[1] The proposed Directive follows closely the ideas presented in the earlier consultation documents discussed in this volume. The central principle of the draft Directive is that 'unfair commercial practices are prohibited'.[2] The draft then proceeds to define commercial practices as unfair if (a) the practice is 'contrary to the requirements of professional diligence' and (b) it materially distorts the economic behaviour of the average consumer (or the average member of the particular group at which the practice is targeted). Without diminishing the generality of this principle, the Directive uses two further methods to give greater specificity to the concept of unfair commercial practices. It defines in general terms two types of unfair commercial practices: 'misleading commercial practices' and 'aggressive commercial practices'. In addition, the draft Directive proposes a 'black list' of commercial practices, which shall in all circumstances be regarded as unfair. Although this preface is not the place to discuss the details of these provisions for their substance is considered in the essays in this volume, it is worth highlighting here some of the major features of the draft Directive.

Perhaps most controversially, the Commission proposes that the Directive should be a measure of 'maximum harmonisation'. In other words, the Commission intends that the Directive should set both minimum and maximum standards for consumer protection against unfair commercial practices. Thus Member States cannot restrict the freedom to provide services nor restrict the free movement of goods for the reason that the marketing practices employed are regarded as unfair commercial practices by reference to standards other than those established by the Directive. There is also a 'mutual recognition' clause, which has the effect that traders engaged in cross-border activity need only comply with national laws of the Member State in which they are established. For example, if a business trading out of Belgium uses marketing techniques for selling goods in Italy that the Italian authorities regard as unfair to consumers, even if the commercial practices appear unlawful under Italian domestic law, any sanctions against the business can only be taken under Belgian law, and furthermore the applicable standards must only be those which serve to implement this draft Directive in Belgium.

This proposal for maximum harmonisation is likely to be highly contro-

---

[1] Brussels, 18.6.2003 COM(2003) 356 final; 20003/0134 (COD) (Draft Directive).
[2] Draft Directive, Article 5.1.

versial in those countries with high levels of consumer protection, which go beyond the standards contained in the Directive. Under this draft Directive Member States will not be able to enforce those added protections for consumers in so far as they deal with matters within the field approximated by the Directive. Thus the fear, discussed by several contributors in this volume, that the Commission, for the sake of completing the internal market, will insist on a levelling down of consumer protection as well as a levelling up, is fully realised. It would be ironical, to say the least, if a measure initially welcomed as a path-breaking initiative to protect consumers and to promote the internal market should turn out to be one that in fact diminishes the legal protection afforded to many consumers in Europe.

The precise extent to which Member States might be required to reduce levels of consumer protection if this draft Directive is implemented as it stands remains extremely difficult to establish. Harmonisation is only required within the field of unfair commercial practices in business-to-consumer transactions. It follows that strict harmonisation is not required for commercial practices which fall outside the scope of what is meant by 'unfair commercial practices' in the Directive. It is true that the scope of the Directive is extremely broad owing to its 'general clause' described above. This width is expanded, because a further clarification explains that the Directive applied to practices both before and after a commercial transaction has been made. Nevertheless, there are bound to be borderline cases where it can be contested whether a consumer protection measure in national law concerns an unfair commercial practice. For example, suppose that a German law requires a trader to provide a consumer with information about the environmental impact of a product, and that a French trader marketing products in Germany fails to comply with this requirement. Does the draft Directive pre-empt this German standard and prevent its enforcement? The answer depends on whether this disclosure requirement falls within either the scope of a 'misleading commercial practice', which includes misleading omissions to provide consumers with material information that they require to take an informed transactional decision,[3] or falls under the general clause defining unfair commercial practices described above. The emphasis of the draft Directive is upon consumers' economic interests, so perhaps their environmental concerns will not be covered. If, however, the German disclosure

---

[3] Draft Directive Art. 7.

requirement falls within the scope of the Directive it will be unenforceable against the French trader.

The precise impact of the Directive is further complicated by its focus on consumer protection. As the essays in this volume make abundantly clear, it is not straightforward to distinguish between, on the one hand, consumer protection measures, and on the other hand, laws designed to protect traders against unfair competition by other traders. Indeed most laws in this area have a double effect: they both protect the consumer and also prevent unscrupulous traders from obtaining a competitive advantage against rival businesses. For example, misleading claims that goods have been reduced in price ('sale', 'great bargains', 'prices slashed') both protect consumers against deception and protect rival businesses against unfair competition. Because this Directive has been proposed by the directorate of the Commission concerned with consumer protection, it only purports to harmonise the law governing commercial practices directed by traders towards consumers, and not to affect unfair competition between traders. Yet this dividing line is plainly an untenable distinction in practice. Many national legal systems make no such distinction, but rather have a unified consumer and competition law in this area. The European Community encountered this problem before in the context of comparative advertising, where one business denigrates by unfavourable comparisons the products of another. Is the requirement of truthfulness in such comparative advertising designed to protect consumers or to protect businesses?[4] The answer, of course, is both. But the proposed Directive is only intended to harmonise the law governing unfair commercial practices with respect to consumer protection not competition. How this distinction will be drawn is unclear. But it is an important distinction, because national laws that do not approximate to the standards of the Directive in the field of consumer protection will be unenforceable, whereas those that concern competition between businesses will be valid (provided, of course, that they comply with other European requirements of the internal market).

One further matter regarding the scope of the draft Directive should be noted here. The proposal is to preserve existing more specific Directives in so far as they provide specific requirements for traders to follow, such as a duty to disclose certain types of information. But the draft Directive is perceived to be a 'framework directive', by which is meant that the general clause is applicable to any unfair commercial practices, even if those practices have

---

[4] Directive 84/450, as amended by Directive 97/55.

been previously regulated in general terms. For example, the e-commerce Directive requires disclosure of certain types of information by the trader on the Internet, and the proposed Directive will add to this requirement by prohibiting the supply of this information in a misleading way.[5] An exception to this pattern is the replacement of the misleading advertising Directive by the proposed directive, except, of course, with respect to misleading advertising that harms other businesses.[6]

By these measures the proposed Directive seeks to avoid conflicts between it and existing or future Directives. But this purported reconciliation does not highlight the point that many previous Directives were minimum standards, so that Member States could preserve superior protection in national law for consumers. For example, the package travel Directive permits Member States to adopt more stringent consumer protection measures.[7] This permission must now be read in the light of the maximum harmonisation of the proposed directive on unfair commercial practices. Any more stringent measures for consumer protection with respect to package travel must not exceed the legal requirements of the general clause on unfair commercial practices. Again there seems to be the prospect of EC law compelling the levelling down of national measures of consumer protection.

The precise implications of this potential levelling-down effect are hard to predict, but it is worth noting here that they may affect not only trading standards but also measures designed to achieve effective enforcement. For example, where the burden of proof is placed can seriously affect the chances of successful enforcement against rogue traders. In the general clause that defines the concept of unfair commercial practices, there are two difficult matters to prove: that the trader has deviated from the requirements of professional diligence, and that the conduct is likely to distort the economic behaviour of consumers. One can predict that traders who may be challenged under this provision will insist that any claimant or enforcement body should prove deviation from professional diligence and distortion of consumers' economic behaviour, which may prove difficult. Under UK law this problem is

---

[5] Directive 2000/31, OJ L 178, 17/07/2000, p.1.

[6] It is proposed to re-enact slightly altered provisions: Draft Directive, Art.14. There is also a proposal for a new Directive on consumer credit to replace Directive 87/102, OJ L278, 11/10/1988, p.33, which will be a maximal harmonisation Directive: COM (2002) 443 final, 2002/0222 (COD).

[7] Directive 90/314. OJ L 158/59, 23.6.90.

often addressed by the use of strict liability in criminal statues combined with a defence available to the trader that it had exercised 'due diligence'.[8] The effect of this provision is that the trader must demonstrate that it was careful to comply with the relevant standards, thereby imposing the burden of proof on the trader. It seems possible that the proposed Directive is inconsistent with such a reversal of the normal burden of proof, which would require UK law to be altered, thereby reducing the chances of successful prosecution.

This issue of effective enforcement is always a matter of prime concern in connection with the regulation of unfair commercial practices. Rogue traders have a habit of disappearing, changing their methods rapidly, and operating from remote locations. The proposed draft Directive adopts the now standard provisions of EC law to enhance enforcement possibilities including the use of consumer organisations and administrative enforcement agencies to bring complaints, and the availability of injunctions against unfair commercial practices.[9] Since the proposed draft Directive adopts the rule of 'mutual recognition', under which each Member State has exclusive control over traders established within their own territory, effective enforcement of the standard is plainly at risk where a trader operates out of one country, but harms the interests of consumers exclusively in other countries. The option canvassed earlier of dealing with this problem by a 'federal' or EU enforcement authority seems to have been silently dropped. It has been recognised for a long time, however, that if 'mutual recognition' is used, there needs to be effective co-operation in enforcement by national authorities.

Although the proposed draft Directive does not tackle this problem, the Commission has also proposed a Regulation on cooperation between national authorities responsible for the enforcement of consumer protection laws.[10] In short the proposed Regulation requires 'mutual recognition' to be accompanied by 'mutual assistance' by designated competent authorities in each Member State. Mutual assistance includes a duty to supply information on request to a competent authority of another Member State, a duty to notify the competent authorities of other Member States when a competent authority becomes aware of infringements of Community consumer protection laws,

---

[8] E.g. Trade Descriptions Act 1968, s. 24.

[9] There is a separate proposal for a consolidated or codified version of the Directive on injunctions for the protection of consumers' interests: COM (2003) 241 final, 2003/0099 (COD), 12.5.2003.

[10] COM(2003) 443 final, 2003/0162 (COD), 18.7.2003.

and a duty on request to take all necessary measures to bring about the cessation or prohibition of an infringement of EC consumer law. It is clear that without this mutual assistance envisaged in the draft Regulation, the enforcement of the proposed draft Directive on unfair commercial practices will be severely hampered. The two instruments need to be seen as a package, even though they have been separated into distinct legislative measures.

Finally, with respect to the content of the proposed draft Directive, considerable interest and concern, as reflected in the essays in this volume, was generated by the Commission's earlier reflections on the possible use of other non-legislative governance mechanisms such as 'soft law', 'co-regulation', codes of practice, and the like. In particular, voluntary codes of conduct are used in some countries both to help specify the legal requirements and also to ratchet up consumer protection standards. The proposed draft Directive permits national trade associations to enforce their own codes of conduct against their own members, provided that these rules do not exclude the application of the legislative standards.[11] It is also an automatically unfair commercial practice on the 'black list' to claim falsely either to be a signatory to a code or that the code has an endorsement from a public or other body.[12] But more concretely, it is also a misleading unfair commercial practice where a trader fails to comply with commitments contained in a code of conduct by which the trader has undertaken to be bound, provided that the commitment was firm and that the list of signatories to the code is publicly verifiable information.[13] Beyond these points, however, the Commission seems to have withdrawn, at least for the time being, from its more ambitious proposal to promote the use of European-wide codes of conduct in order to help specify the standard of unfair commercial practices. As a consequence, the criticism that the general clause governing unfair commercial practices is too vague to provide adequate guidance to businesses may be voiced again as an objection to the proposed Draft Directive.

Authors in this volume also raise questions about the implications of the proposed draft Directive for the evolution of general contract law. Although the scope of the draft Directive is confined to business-to-consumer transac-

---

[11] Draft Directive Art. 10. This replicates the provision contained in the existing misleading advertising Directive.

[12] Draft Directive, Annex 1, paragraphs (1) and (2).

[13] Draft Directive Art.6(2).

tions, it sets a new standard for pre- and post-contractual dealings, which may have an impact, or at least an irritating effect, on general contract law in national legal systems. It may also indirectly lay the foundations for general standards in any evolving European general contract law. The proposed draft Directive declares that it is without prejudice to the rules on the validity, formation or effect of a contract.[14] Yet one wonders what national courts will do when faced with a purported contract which has been secured by the use of an unfair commercial practice: will they simply apply traditional national laws on the formation and validity of contracts, or will they strive to invalidate the contract? If the latter, which seems distinctly likely, they may be indirectly modifying the applicable national standards. This modification of national law may operate, however, either to improve or to weaken the protection of the victims of unfair commercial practices according to the prior position of national law.

The proposed draft Directive on unfair commercial practices is subject to the co-decision procedure, so that both the European Parliament and the Council must agree the final text. Although that process may prove lengthy, it seems from the rapid progress made with this Directive and its widespread support in both Council and Parliament that it fair for us to describe it in the title to this book as not merely a proposal but a forthcoming Directive.

Hugh Collins
London School of Economics
December 2003.

---

[14] Draft Directive Art.3(2).

List of Contributors

Guido Alpa, Professor, Rome University, 'La Sapienza'
Luisa Antoniolli, Professor, Trento University
Hugh Collins, Professor of English Law, London School of Economics
Fernando Gomez, Professor of Law and Economics Universitat Pompeu Fabra, Barcelona, Spain
Stefan Grundman, Professor of European Private and Business Law Friedrich-Alexander-University Erlangen-Nürnberg
Geraint Howells, Professor, Sheffield University
Hans-W Micklitz, Bamberg University
Georgio de Nova, Professor, Milan University
Jules Stuyck, Professor, K. Leuven University
Tom Van Dyck, K. Leuven University
Thomas Willhelmsson, Professor, Helsinki University

Contents

1. EC Regulation of Unfair Commercial Practices

Hugh Collins

I am a sucker for special offers. The sign 'buy one get one free' attracts me like a politician to a microphone. The sticker 'low price' convinces me that I have a bargain. Yet once the shopping frenzy of the weekly supermarket trip has subsided, doubts creep into my mind. If I bought two for the price of one, perhaps the price was so elevated that in fact I paid the normal market price for both. No real harm done, except now I have an unnecessary second bag of rotting fruit. And how low was that price in fact? My local supermarket distributes this label 'low price' liberally around its products, and indeed its prices are usually lower than corner shops. But I suspect that the real purpose of these notices is to distract my attention from the fact that the price in the supermarket has gone up this week.[1] Oh well, no harm done, because prices do go up from time to time. I can console myself by calling that special telephone hotline on the scratch card in my magazine to discover whether I have won one of the 'fabulous prizes' such as the holiday to Paradise Island;[2] it seems not, but I have won a free copy of the tour company's brochure and a £10 discount voucher, so at least I can peruse glossy pictures of palm fringed golden sands and fantasize about the question of on which holiday should I spend my discount of 0.00025%.

Is any harm done during this contemporary tale of a consumer's exposure to modern marketing techniques? Nothing very significant, perhaps, because I ended up paying approximately the normal market price for all the goods purchased. But we need to think about the cumulative effect of misleading and deceptive practices. One of the central purposes of the law should be to help to construct a competitive market in goods and services, and to protect it

---

[1] This practice may be contrary to the 'soft law' of the Consumer Protection (Code of Practice for Traders on Price Indications) Approval Order 1988 SI 1988/2078, paragraph 1.1.1, which is practical guidance offered by the UK government on the effect of Consumer Protection Act 1987 and best practice.

[2] Prior to an audacious instance of re-branding, this location was known as Hog Island, The Bahamas.

H. Collins (ed.) The Forthcoming EC Directive on Unfair and Commercial Practices, 1-42.
©2004. Kluwer Law International. Printed in the Netherlands.

against attempts to destroy the integrity of the market. The law may only play a minor role in helping to build the necessary trust and confidence for people to take the risks of disappointment and betrayal incurred in every market transaction. But the law can help to combat a variant of Gresham's law: just as bad money drives out good money, so too bad marketing practices drive out good practices. A seller who can increase its market share by misleading and deceptive practices can obtain an advantage over competitors who stick to the unvarnished truth. The competitors will therefore quickly emulate those misleading and deceptive practices in order to restore their market position. This race to the bottom endangers the operation of a competitive market by inducing the production of misleading information and as a consequence by distorting preferences. The law can discourage this race by prohibiting such behaviour by traders as wrongful marketing practices.

Yet how can we tell right from wrong? The law needs to discourage marketing practices that damage the market in the long run, whilst permitting businesses to use all their ingenuity to reach consumers and other traders in order to persuade them to purchase their products. The law has to construct rules and procedures that amount to a duty to trade or deal fairly, or at least not to use unfair trade practices. But how should we define fair trading? The notion is hard to pin down in the abstract. In the context of a consumer transaction, Lord Bingham has offered the following, rather open-textured definition of fair dealing, viewed as an aspect of good faith in contract law.

> Fair dealing requires that a supplier should not, whether deliberately or unconsciously, take advantage of the consumer's necessity, indigence, lack of experience, unfamiliarity with the subject matter of the contract, weak bargaining position or any other factor listed in or analogous to those listed in Schedule 2 to [the Unfair Terms in Consumer Contracts Regulations 1994; i.e., the strength of the bargaining positions, any inducements to agree to the contract, whether the goods were a special order, and 'the extent to which the seller or supplier has dealt fairly and equitably with the consumer'.][3]

Does this definition, or rather concept, of fair dealing in consumer contracts elucidate whether my experiences of 'buy one get one free', or 'low

---

[3] *Director General of Fair Trading v First National Bank plc* [2001] UKHL 52, [2001] 3 WLR 1297, 1308.

price', or my 'fabulous prize' of a 'free brochure' and 'discount' amount to unfair marketing practices? Though perhaps pointing in the direction of the conclusion that all those marketing practices are fair, in the end the answer given by Lord Bingham is that it depends upon the extent to which the seller has dealt fairly and equitably with the consumer, a matter of degree rather than any sharp boundary.

When we alter the focus to transactions between two businesses, the question of the content of the duty to trade fairly may have to be answered in many instances in much the same way. Many small businesses may be in the same position as consumers in terms of their relevant expertise and bargaining power. A shopkeeper, a craftsman, or small family hotelier may be subject to all kinds of scams. Other businesses try to sell them services, such as apparently cheap advertising or advice on regulatory compliance, but it turns out that these services have no real substance or value. Like consumers, these small traders with only a few employees can be subject to misleading practices, unfair pressure, and taking advantage of another's necessity, particularly when the transaction concerns matters outside the normal business concerns of the small trader.[4] But in addition to this similar application of the duty to trade fairly to small businesses, the duty to trade fairly has to cope with the way that two businesses may construct their long-term trading relationship.

Unlike discrete consumer transactions, business to business relations often persist over a long period of time. The parties structure this relationship between supplier and purchaser in various ways. Sometimes they will reach no formal agreement – there is just a pattern of repeated orders for the same product. But often the parties to a commercial relationship establish a framework agreement to govern their transactions. The framework establishes the terms on which they will deal with each other for the future. The framework may take the form of a distributorship, a franchise, or some kind of requirements contract. Although the framework agreement may or may not be legally enforceable in itself, the intention of the parties is to construct their own rules for how they will trade with each other in the future. By agreement, the parties set their own standards that give content to the duty to trade fairly between themselves.

What is important to notice, however, is that there is nothing in this pro-

---

4   The Federation of Small Business and European Small Business Alliance, *Response to the European Commission on the Follow-up Communication to the Green Paper on Consumer Protection* (London/Brussels, 2002).

cess of reaching a framework agreement that ensures that this private code corresponds with any objective or public concept of fair dealing. For example, if a supermarket agrees with its supplier under a requirements contract that the supermarket can retrospectively insist upon a price reduction payable to the supplier in order to fund a promotional offer, such as 'buy one get one free', the supplier may feel compelled to accept such a term in order to obtain access to the retail market. The private code permits the supermarket to renegotiate prices unilaterally after the goods have been delivered, which hardly seems to comprise a fair commercial practice. Consumers obtain a real benefit from this practice, however, since they may in this instance actually receive an extra item free. But the supplier has to pay for this largesse by the supermarket under the terms of the requirements contract. The bargaining power of the supermarket, derived from its control over access to the consumer retail market, permits it to negotiate a private code of dealing with its suppliers that may be replete with the potential for what would be regarded in other contexts as unfair commercial practices. A duty to trade fairly, once extended beyond the scope of consumer transactions, has to address the question of whether framework agreements need to be regulated to prevent them from becoming an opportunity for oppressive and unfair trading practices.

None of these issues about fair trading or fair dealing are new. No doubt scams have existed for as long as the market economy itself. The ingenuity of business leads to the constant discovery of new marketing methods, often by seizing upon recent technological developments such as the Internet and harnessing them to the purposes of growing markets for their products. New techniques may pose fresh difficulties for the application of existing rules about unfair commercial practices in these novel contexts, but this cat and mouse game will continue forever. What sets the backdrop for this volume of essays on this theme is not the emergence of a new social problem, but rather the potential for addressing it in Europe at a transnational level.

The advent of the European Single Market, with its legal framework of the European Community (EC), and its government agency the European Commission, creates the space for a new regulatory order to govern fair trading in the marketplace. The EC has as one of its central activities the construction of an internal market with the free movement of foods, persons, services and capital, together with the development of a common commercial policy, and systems for ensuring that competition is not distorted.[5] It is within the

---

[5]   Treaty Establishing the European Community, Article 3 (as amended).

competence of the EC, at least in some instances, to seek to regulate unfair trading practices in this internal market, which will extend before long to the territory of 25 nation states. Indeed, the EC has already intervened on many occasions with legislative initiatives designed to establish some common rules about marketing practices, from the selling of package holidays to the purchase of goods and services on the Internet.[6] Granted the existing presence and competence of the EC in this field, known as the 'acquis communitaire',[7] the question becomes whether nation states should retain their existing laws governing unfair commercial practices or whether the EC should attempt to harmonise those laws into a uniform or closely approximate body of regulations that would apply throughout the internal market.

A more immediate provocation for this volume of essays is the European Commission's Green Paper on Consumer Protection in October 2001.[8] This document argues that further harmonisation of law in the field of trade practices is required in order to assist the evolution of a smooth functioning market with high levels of consumer protection. New EC legislation is required, argues the Commission, as part of its central agenda of 'negative integration' for the purpose of completing the internal market. Negative integration requires the dismantling of legal barriers to cross-border trade, with a view to constructing an open transnational market. The Commission proposes not only to enact improvements to existing EC legislation, but also to create a new 'framework' Directive about unfair commercial practices. Though limited to contracts with consumers, the Green Paper envisages the creation of transnational framework legislation that will supersede and harmonise national laws on fair trading. In addition, the Commission envisages fresh initiatives to support high levels of compliance with the standards throughout the EC. These proposals, which will be considered in greater detail shortly, provoke a number of questions that permeate this volume of essays.

Yet our themes in these essays are broader than those raised by the Commission in this particular Green Paper. We endeavour to examine the topic of the law of marketing in Europe in the round, without being confined by considerations either of the competence of the EC under the current Treaty provisions, or of the artificial divisions and complicated rivalries between

---

6   Respectively Directives 90/314 of 13 June 1990 and 2000/31/EC, of 8 June 2000.

7   The full range of the *acquis communitaire* with respect to contracts and marketing is out lined in *Communication from the Commission on European Contract Law*, 11 July 2001, COM(2001) 398 final, appendix 1.

8   Com (2001) 531 2 October 2001 'Green Paper'..

the Directorates of the Commission. The field of enquiry encompasses unfair trading practices between businesses to the extent that they pose different issues from those arising in business to consumer transactions. It also incorporates the perspective of competition law, which in addition to consumer protection measures, has a profound influence on the law of marketing at EC level.

The central questions addressed by this collection of essays include:

- Why is the Commission confident that EC legislation is necessary to govern marketing practices with respect to consumers? Or, to put the same issue the other way around, what is wrong with the existing system of national level regulation, and how will an intervention by the EC remedy the problem? Does the EC and the internal market require uniform laws for controlling unfair marketing practices, or can it proceed by securing the approximation of national laws, or is any harmonisation an unnecessary and confusing re-regulation that duplicates adequate national systems of law?
- In view of the cultural differences and diversity in market practices between Member States, can the EC devise a uniform standard that is acceptable throughout Europe? For example, if door-step selling is completely banned in some countries but tolerated in others, which rule should be preferred? Or is it sufficient for the EC to adopt a minimum standard, such as safeguards for consumers against the abuses of door-step selling, leaving Member States to set higher standards in conformity with their established market practices?
- Even if agreement can be reached on particular instances about whether certain market practices should be forbidden because they are unfair, how can these conclusions be adequately expressed through general laws? In particular, can the EC legislation give determinate meaning to a legal duty to deal fairly? Can we articulate a conception of fair dealing that has the potential to cover all instances of abuse, or must we limit legal regulation to particular instances of deceptive trading?
- From a more practical point of view, how could such general transnational legislation ever become effective in deterring unfair trading practices? It is hard enough for national authorities to police and enforce their own standards in the market place. The problem of ensuring compliance only becomes magnified as the size of the market is increased. Can we rely upon national enforcement authorities to police common standards of fair dealing, or will this system prove ineffective to deal

with unscrupulous cross-border traders? Can the institutions of the EC add significantly to the levels of enforcement and compliance with the standards. Would new institutions at EC level be required, in order to provide both a uniform and effective system for policing standards and to enable and assist cooperation between national enforcement authorities?

- The Commission's immediate proposal is limited to consumer contracts, but it can hardly be denied that small businesses also suffer similar detriment from unfair commercial practices. We have also observed that quite large businesses may be locked into framework agreements that enable the exploitation of a dominant market relationship. Does it make sense for any transnational regulation to be confined to consumer transactions, or should the principle of fair trading also be applied to business to business contracts?

- Regulation of fair trading seems to be inevitably linked to issues of competition between businesses. Prohibitions on unfair commercial practices restrict the ways in which businesses may compete for market share with each other. The question becomes to what extent should the law accept restrictions on competition in the marketplace established by framework agreements that seek to structure and control trading relationships in the view of the likelihood that these framework agree-ments were themselves constructed in order to facilitate the exploitation of markets and to improve competitiveness. In short, does the duty to trade fairly require legal regulation of framework agreements and similar arrangements in order to prevent oppressive trading relation-ships between businesses?

- Finally, would the introduction of a duty to trade fairly as part of EC law have an impact on the private law systems of Member States? Many of the issues arising in cases of unfair commercial practices are forbidden by the ordinary law of contract in national legal systems. Rules against coercion and misrepresentation catch many of the worst abuses. Consumer regulation both extends the scope of prohibitions and also introduces different regulatory techniques in order to become more effective. Instead of simply invalidating a contract, for instance, consumer law may impose a criminal penalty or permit official actions to obtain an injunction against future use of a deceptive market prac-tice. The question is whether the introduction of a duty to trade fairly would have implications for the evolution of private law systems, and in particular whether it might lay the foundations for principles of a

European law of contract that may evolve or even be enacted.

In this particular essay, no attempt will be made to answer all these questions. These themes are explored more fully in the subsequent essays. My contribution concentrates on both the potential and the difficulties for European or transnational regulation of this field of fair trading. How can the EC best make a valuable regulatory initiative with respect to unfair commercial practices, and what might be the implications of such an initiative for the evolution of European contract and commercial law? My discussion is divided into four parts. The first provides a review of the Green Paper and subsequent elaborations and discussions of its proposals. The second part examines critically the rationale for transnational regulation of the field of unfair commercial practices in Europe. The third section considers, as problem of regulatory technique, the task of devising standards that adequately express what may be meant by unfair trading practices. The final section considers the implications of EC regulation of unfair commercial practices for the evolution of contract and commercial law as a whole in Europe.

I.   THE GREEN PAPER

A useful place to commence an answer to these questions is an examination of the proposals in the Green Paper on Consumer Protection itself. This document has to be read in the light of a subsequent 'Follow-up' to that Green Paper in June 2002.[9] This follow-up document was produced after a consideration of responses from businesses, consumer organisations and national governments, though prior to any response by the European Parliament. In the follow-up document, the Commission broadly reaffirmed its proposals, but added clarifications and an action plan involving further research and consultation about the details of its proposals. The Commission had pressed forward rapidly because twelve Member States had supported the idea of a framework directive, and a large majority of respondents favoured a proposal for the Commission to assist in enforcement co-operation between agencies in Member States.

At the heart of these proposals is a 'framework directive'. This Directive would create an obligation not to trade unfairly, which would include but

---

[9]   *Follow-up Communication to the Green Paper on EU Consumer Protection*, 11 June 2002 Com(2002) 289, 'Follow-up'.

extend beyond the narrower concept of 'misleading practices'. The general clause would comprise two elements: a concept of unfair commercial practice combined with a consumer detriment test. The risk of detriment or actual detriment to a consumer would be measured against the standard often used by the ECJ, that is a consumer of average intelligence, reasonably well informed and reasonably circumspect.[10] But this general clause, according to the Commission's proposals, would be substantiated by an 'exhaustive' number of specific provisions that further defined notion of fairness.[11] The proposal is to include specific rules that would deal with at least four types of unfair commercial practices: misleading information, a duty to disclose material information, prohibitions on coercion and undue influence, and a requirement of fair complaint handling in the after-sales period. These specific rules, though still at a high level of generality, would specify the scope of the general clause, and therefore would apparently detract from its broad sweep. Trade practices that might be regarded by some consumers as unfair but which fell outside the scope of the specific rules would not be covered by the framework Directive. It is clear, however, that the Commission envisages that the specific rules would cover all the different stages of the business to consumer relationship, and that few, if any, gaps in coverage would emerge.

In particular, it is important to notice that the proposed concept of unfair commercial practices includes conduct during and after the performance of the main substantive obligations under the contract. The framework directive would not be merely aimed at pre-contractual behaviour. The Commission emphasises that a duty to trade fairly would require businesses to have adequate complaint-handling procedures. Businesses would be required to respond quickly and effectively to any complaint and to make full redress when justified. These requirements might also encourage the development of the availability of alternative dispute handling procedures, and the provision of information and assistance to consumers in using such third party resolution mechanisms. The Commission is also considering whether the duty to trade fairly should also require further obligations with respect to after-sales service, such as a duty on businesses to provide information about the ser-

---

[10] *Estee Lauder v Lancaster*, C-220/98 ECR I-117; *Gut Springenheide*, C-210/96 [1998] ECR I-4657; *Commission v Germany "Sauce Hollandaise"*, C-51/94 [1995] ECR I-3299; *Mars*, C-470/93 [1995] ECR 1923.

[11] 'Follow-up' p.16.

vicing of a complex product, to maintain an adequate supply of spare parts, and an obligation not to charge excessive prices for the parts or labour to fix defective or unsatisfactory goods.

This emphasis on complaint-handling mechanisms is highly appropriate in the context of consumer contracts. Empirical evidence in Britain and the USA suggests that at most half of consumers who perceive a problem with a product or service go to a third party such as a lawyer or consumer advice agency for assistance, and of course only a tiny minority ever take formal legal proceedings.[12] Instead consumers typically make a complaint, and if the business does not respond, they tend to give up. Indeed, lawyers, public officials, and advisors are likely to encourage consumers to use the trader's complaint-handling mechanism in order to negotiate a settlement rather than to pursue a legal claim.[13] Since businesses are usually concerned about their reputation and often want to keep their customers for future sales, the complaint-handling mechanisms of businesses seem to provide consumers more often than not with a superior remedy to that provided by the law.[14] Of course, legal regulation of unfair commercial practices would not really be addressing those businesses where the prevailing ethos is that the 'customer is always right', but rather the minority of businesses, which reject any complaint, no matter how well founded. Regulation of complaint-handling mechanisms might help to reduce the number of traders in the latter category, by adding to the market incentives to put the customer first.

The framework directive would be enforceable in national legal systems by the established collective enforcement mechanism of injunctions sought by official agencies and consumer organisations.[15] In order to help deal with

---

[12] A. Best and A.R. Andreasen, 'Consumer Response to Unsatisfactory Purchase: A Survey of Perceiving Defects, Voicing Complaints, and Obtaining Redress' (1976-77) 11 *Law and Society Review* 701; R. Miller and A. Sarat, 'Grievances, Claims and Disputes: Assessing the Adversary Culture' (1980-81) 15 *Law and Society Review* 525; R. Cranston, *Regulating Business: Law and Consumer Agencies* (London: MacMillan, 1979) 60; National Consumer Council, *Seeking Civil Justice – A Survey of People's needs and Experiences* (London: National Consumer Council, 1995) 25,41.

[13] S. Macaulay, 'Lawyers and Consumer Protection Laws' (1979) 14 *Law and Society Review* 115; R. Cranston, *Consumers and the Law*, 2nd edn (London: Weidenfeld and Nicholson, 1984) 85.

[14] H. Collins, *Regulating Contracts* (Oxford: Oxford University Press, 1999) 341.

[15] Directive 98/27/EC, 19 May 1998, on injunctions for the protection of consumers' interests.

unfair commercial practices that operate across a number of states, the Commission proposes that it should develop a second legal instrument on enforcement co-operation. This proposal envisages the creation of the establishment of a central national liaison point in each Member state, the construction of mechanisms for mutual assistance between national authorities, and a common enforcement action. The aim of this aspect of the proposals is to improve the intelligence of national enforcement authorities by sharing information about developments in unfair commercial practices. To some extent this imitates the procedures in general product safety, which permits the Commission to promote and take part in the operation of a European network of the authorities in Member States for the purpose of exchanging information on risk assessment, best practices, and for collaboration on product recalls.[16] With such an information network in place for unfair commercial practices, once new scams have been identified, it may then become possible to enable a collective enforcement action for an injunction to prohibit the use of this unfair commercial practice throughout the EC, without the need for each Member State to act independently.

In addition to the framework directive on unfair commercial practices, the Commission proposes to proceed with sector specific Directives, and to develop a Regulation on sales promotions. This proposal for a 'mixed approach', that is a combination of a general duty and sector-specific Directives, is slightly surprising given that the idea of a framework directive is to provide an over-arching regulatory regime. Presumably the sector specific Directives can address more clearly particular problems that may be arising in the market, such as difficulties of knowing the identity of the trader in e-commerce or the precise information that must be disclosed prior to the formation of a consumer credit transaction. An alternative justification for sector-specific Directives may be that they can provide a formal reconciliation of competing policy objectives in relation to a particular market activity, such as the tension between competition and internal market law, on the one hand, and protection of public health, on the other, that arose in the context of tobacco advertising. The proposal for a Regulation on sales promotions is presumably motivated by the desire to have uniform rules or maximum harmonisation wherever it is possible to reach agreement in the Council of

---

[16] Directive 2001/95, Article 10; this builds on the RAPEX system of Council Decision 84/133, OJ 1984 L70/16, sees. S. Weatherill, *EC Consumer Law and Policy* (London: Longman, 1997) 132.

Ministers. Some of the existing Directives, however, could be reformed and included under the umbrella of the framework Directive as part of a proposed comprehensive review by the Commission of the existing consumer legislation, to be carried out with a view to consolidating and simplifying this *'acquis communitaire'*.

Perhaps the greatest innovation in terms of regulatory technique is the proposal in the Green Paper to try to establish mechanisms for the agreement of voluntary codes of conduct for business sectors at a European level. The central idea is that businesses in a particular sector may agree standards of conduct relating to unfair commercial practices. Non-compliance with those standards by a particular enterprise that has previously made a commitment to that code would be regarded as an unfair commercial practice. These codes would not be applied to non-signatories, and nor would it be necessary for business sectors to create codes at EC level. Instead, the incentive to develop codes is that by following a code, which has been established by the appropriate EC mechanism for the industrial sector, the trader would create a 'presumption of conformity' to the general duty not to trade unfairly. A further incentive to adopt a code is that it would probably avoid consideration by the Commission of sector specific legislation. The Green Paper leaves for further deliberation whether or not a public authority should play a role in the endorsement of codes with a view to ensuring that such codes conform to Community law and the general duty to refrain from unfair commercial practices. If a technique for endorsement of codes could be developed, the certification would presumably create a very strong presumption that compliance with the code amounts to conformity with fair trading rules. These codes would not have to be EU-wide, but clearly the Commission would like to encourage such transnational developments in business sectors, in order to promote harmonisation of standards.

Beyond the use of formal, if voluntary codes, the Commission proposes that a mechanism should be developed for providing further, more detailed guidance on the meaning of unfair commercial practices. This mechanism would involve extensive participation by 'stakeholders', that is representatives of business and consumers, and should result in non-binding guidance on the meaning of unfair commercial practices. The purpose of this mechanism is perhaps rather more to do with building a greater consensus within Europe about the meaning of unfair trade practices than with clarifying the meaning of the legal obligation itself. This consensus is particularly important to build between those national public authorities which have the duty to enforce the standards contained in the framework directive. If these national public authorities could evolve a shared perception of what should count as an unfair trading practice, the standards applied in practice to traders would become approximately the same across Europe.

Although the Green Paper and its follow-up are exclusively focussed on business to consumer contracts, the introduction of a general principle along the lines of a duty to trade fairly has implications for the evolution of commercial and contract law more generally. It is evident, for example, that rules against misleading advertising are as much concerned with unfair competition between businesses as with consumer protection, since, as we have already noted, many of these unfair commercial practices have the effect of giving one business an unfair advantage over others in the market place. Indeed, in some Member States the rules of competition and consumer law are integrated. Commercial and Competition law cannot therefore be excluded from the picture. The Commission recognises, for instance, that voluntary business sector codes, even if established with the endorsement of public authorities, could not provide an exemption from Community provisions on competition law.[17] Furthermore, the proposals in the Green Paper will have to be fitted into the parallel Commission consideration of proposals for gradual (or perhaps even rapid) harmonisation of the law of contract as a whole.[18] It is hard to imagine, for instance, that extensive EC regulation of topics such as duress and undue influence in consumer contracts will not be regarded as having implications for the more general principles of private law.

II. The Rationale for EC Regulation

Perhaps the first question that anyone new to this field of enquiry might ask is why is the European Community involved in the regulation of marketing practices at all? After all, the Member States already have elaborate private law systems of contract law, supplemented by consumer protection and competition law measures, so that the field can hardly be presented as one requiring regulation. The response of the Commission is that its purpose is to remove obstructions to cross-border trade whilst ensuring a high level of consumer protection. These purposes are, of course, accepted objectives of EC law.

---

[17] 'Follow-up', para. 29.

[18] Above note 7; S. Grundmann and J. Stuyck (eds), *An Academic Green Paper on European Contract Law* (The Hague: Kluwer Law International, 2002).

The removal of direct and indirect obstacles to trade constitutes the central objective of Internal Market policy. The protection of consumers within this Single Market is a subsidiary but important goal of community law. Using regulatory diversity as its crutch, the Commission in this Green Paper, as in its previous discussions of initiatives in relation to contract law and consumer protection, constructs its standard argument for regulation in the Internal Market. Regulatory diversity creates legal risk and transaction costs. Businesses may be discouraged from entering foreign markets either by the difficulty of estimating the magnitude of the risk that they may violate regulatory standards or by the costs of reducing that risk. Harmonisation of regulation throughout the market should reduce legal risk and transaction costs, thus removing the deterrent effect of regulatory diversity on cross-border trade. It is also argued that harmonisation is a species of deregulation in the context of consumer contracts, for at present under the rules of private international law a consumer is protected by mandatory rules of her place of residence in cross-border transactions

We can ask three questions about the Commission's assertion of the need for European regulation in this field: What exactly are the regulatory obstructions to cross-border trade that need to be removed, and in particular do these obstructions include the diverse national regulations on unfair commercial practices? How will EC law, and in particular a framework Directive, serve to reduce or remove obstructions? And, finally, how high is the level of consumer protection that we should aim for, given the diversity in standards between national regimes?

1. Obstructions to Trade

The Commission is confident that obstructions to cross-border trade exist, and this claim cannot seriously be doubted. The Commission points to compelling evidence. A recent Commission survey of prices found, for example, price differences of 30% or 40% for branded consumer electronics goods in different countries, a disparity that could not be explained by variations in indirect taxes.[19] Similarly, English consumers know that they can purchase a new German car far more cheaply in Germany than in the high street in Britain. Obstructions clearly exist, and the question is rather what is the nature of those obstructions?

---

[19] 'Green Paper', para.3.1; Com 2001(736) of 7 December 2001.

Most of the obstructions to cross-border trade between businesses and consumers are obvious and apply to any market. Consumers face increasing search costs in discovering better prices in a wider market, and businesses encounter increased costs in seeking to market, distribute, and service their products over a larger geographical space. Legal regulation neither creates these obstructions, nor can it reduce them. The question that must be confronted by proposals for EC regulation is whether the existing national regulation of markets itself contributes to the obstruction of cross-border trade. If so, then a case can be made for harmonisation or uniformity of laws.

In its response to the Commission's Green Paper on *European Union Consumer Protection,* the UK Department of Trade and Industry asks first and foremost for evidence that regulatory diversity in national legal systems creates an obstruction to cross-border trade.[20] The Commission is always asking for similar information, which suggests that this evidence is hard to discover. The Commission has built up research data that supports the view that there is considerable diversity in regulatory standards and techniques governing marketing practices in the Member States.[21] This information is hardly surprising. Laws regulating marketing have typically developed in a piecemeal fashion in response to perceived problems of deceptive and unfair practices. Many regulatory techniques may be used to attempt to counter these practices. The choice of regulatory technique often turns on the degree of political pressure supporting the measure. Consumer law is littered with ineffective regulation because business interests have succeeded in blunting the teeth of the proposals. These regulatory interventions also have to be fitted into each national legal system, where diverse traditions of private law impose different demands for retaining the coherence of the legal system as a whole.

As the Commission suggests, it is possible that this diversity of regulation may significantly discourage businesses from engaging on cross-border trade. Businesses may be concerned that the standard marketing techniques, though permitted in their home state, infringe a regulatory provision in

---

[20] Department of Trade and Industry, *Green Paper on EU Consumer Protection: UK Government Response* (2002) para.4.

[21] http://europa.eu.int/comm/consumers/policy/developments/fair_comm_pract/. There is an enormous wealth of information and critical reflection in the study by the team led by Prof. H. Micklitz concerning the Proposal for a General Legislative Framework on Fair Trading with its accompanying national reports.

another Member State where they may wish to enter the retail market. The European Financial Services Round Table has commissioned a report which argues that regulatory diversity renders a pan-European marketing strategy and standardised financial products impossible.[22] The cost of ascertaining whether these standard marketing techniques infringe a national regulatory provision may deter entry into foreign markets, especially if the legal advice is ultimately equivocal. Perhaps more persuasive evidence of obstacles to trade is to be found in 'Eurobarometer' survey or public opinion polls. One survey demonstrated that consumers have significantly lower confidence in making purchases across borders, which is to be expected given the different languages and conventions in the market place. But more significantly, the report showed that only about one third of consumers felt that their interests were well protected when in dispute with a business in another Member State, which compares unfavourably with the evidence that more than a half of consumers felt well protected by the law in their dealings with a local or national business.[23] It may be that it is not so much that actual differences between national laws discourage cross-border trade, as that consumers' perceptions of possible differences create obstructions to the functioning of the internal market.

I am not, myself, wholly convinced about this alleged obstruction to cross-border trade. It seems to me that most cross-border trade is likely to be initiated in some way by a business rather than a consumer. Although some consumers may surf the Internet in an unspecific way or just go off for a shopping binge at a foreign destination, most consumers will encounter the possibility of cross-border transactions, I suggest, by having the opportunity deliberately created by a business trying to enter a foreign market. When entering foreign markets, however, it seems to me that businesses are likely to have other considerations at the forefront of their minds, such as the costs of transport and distribution. For example, if a manufacturer of washing-machines in the UK wants to enter the French market, the pressing problems are likely to be the need to find ways of making their products accessible to French consumers through retail outlets, distribution systems, distance selling, service arrangements, and consumer financing. Worries about the legality of standard marketing techniques, such as promising in a misleading way that there may be a free holiday for purchasers of washing-machines,

---

[22] www.zew.de/erfstudyresults/ ; 'Follow-up', para. 24.
[23] FLASH BE 117 'Consumer Study' January 2002; 'Follow-up', para. 25.

16

will not be at the top of the agenda. The problem of regulatory diversity is undoubtedly present, but it is likely to be a low priority for business and swept up in an unspecific and general concern about legal risk that extends to many other considerations such as taxation and compliance with other regulatory measures.

Regulatory diversity is likely to present the greatest problem in those fields such as financial services that are already intensively regulated by national laws.[24] In that sector as well, the contract itself represents the product being sold, so that the precise legal incidents of the document and the legal framework in which it can be validly negotiated become crucial. Rules about marketing techniques may also create substantial obstacles to trade, though not so clearly in the context of simply consumer purchases, but rather in the framework agreements through which the business is likely to operate in a foreign market.[25] With regard to simple sales to consumers, it is true that businesses will have to acquire information about local legal requirements, and this requirement imposes a transaction cost on the business in paying for professional advice. Except in a few instances, however, the trader is unlikely to have to alter its marketing practices substantially to achieve compliance with these local regulations. Diversity in national regulation of advertising can prevent the use of the same advertising campaign in different countries, though in practice the advertisements may have to be adjusted in any case to suit local taste. Nor do all marketing practices have the potential to encounter obstacles to cross-border trade: whilst misleading advertising can promote trade unfairly across borders, door-step sales are by definition invariably within a single jurisdiction. In contrast, the accommodation of business to business marketing techniques through framework agreements into national legal systems may impose more insuperable obstacles to cross-border trade. In the case of franchising, for instance, different national rules may prevent a uniform approach to the use of franchising as a marketing and distribution technique, though it must be said, looking at the surprising uniformity of the names of retail shops in the high streets of Europe, this constraint may not in practice place a significant brake on expansion into foreign markets.

With further research, it may become possible to identify more clearly

---

[24] H. Beale, 'Finding the Remaining Traps Instead of Unifying Contract Law' in Grundmann and Stuyck, above note 18, 67.

[25] H. Collins, 'Transaction Costs and Subsidiarity in European Contract Law' in Grundmann and Stuyck, above note 18, (eds), 269, 271.

some genuine obstructions to cross-border trade created by regulatory diversity. Within those obstructions, we may discover instances that fall within the scope of the proposed framework directive. One has to agree at least in part with the UK government's affirmation that 'This evidence must be appropriate, comprehensive, and should not only be undertaken to support a policy direction that has already been decided.'[26] The Achilles heel in the Commission's justification for legislation in this field of marketing is that they have been unable so far to find the evidence base for their chosen policy. What the Commission can demonstrate, however, is that cross-border sales to consumers have stagnated between 1991 and 2002, and that a majority of businesses in a large opinion survey believe that harmonisation of the law of marketing would facilitate and stimulate cross-border sales.[27]

2.   Reduction of obstacles by EC Laws

Nor is it clear that European legislation can remedy the (alleged) problems for the operation of a competitive market created by regulatory diversity. Two problems arise in seeking to eliminate or reduce barriers caused by differences in national laws. The first is essentially a political problem, and the second a matter of regulatory technique.

Directives often merely set minimum standards, thereby permitting Member States to preserve superior measures of consumer protection. This technique of minimum harmonisation is necessary to secure consent to EC initiatives from those Member States where elaborate and well-developed measures of consumer protection already exist and function effectively. Furthermore, the Commission hardly wants to present itself as a body seeking to reduce levels of consumer protection in some Member States. The result of the minimum harmonisation Directives is therefore not harmonisation at all, but merely different, though perhaps less significant, regulatory divergences. National prohibitions on door-step selling can be valid, for instance, even though the Directive merely insists on certain procedural safeguards.[28] For

---

[26] Department of Trade and Industry, *Response of the UK Government to the European Commission's consultation on the Follow-up Communication to the Green Paper on EU Consumer Protection* (London: October 2002) para. 4.

[27] D. Byrne, Commissioner for Health and Consumer Protection, *From National Legislation to a Framework Directive on Fair Commercial Practices: Workshop on Unfair Commercial Practices* (Brussels, 22/1/2003) http://europa.eu.int/rapid/start/cgi.

[28] *Buet v Ministere Public* C-328/87 [1989] ECR 1235.

this reason, the Commission is likely to try to insist that the proposed framework Directive should impose full harmonisation, or pre-emption of national legal systems, so that uniform principles apply across the EC. Therefore the proposals are likely to court political unpopularity with those Member States that will not be able to conserve superior measures of consumer protection.

But this need for maximum harmonisation may leave EC law in a rather puzzling situation. The framework Directive may impose uniform standards, but sector specific directives that merely impose minimum standards may govern particular market sectors. National laws that set standards in those sectors governed by specific Directives can usually exceed the EC standards for the purpose of consumer protection. But will this national legislation be permitted any longer, if those national standards exceed the requirements of the framework Directive on unfair commercial practices? The logic of the proposed full harmonisation framework Directive is surely that everything related to unfair trading practices must be eventually subsumed within its standards, so that higher levels of consumer protection, even if tolerated by sector-specific directives, should not be permitted. The Commission, it seems to me, cannot escape eventually from putting itself in the uncomfortable position of insisting on the reduction of levels of consumer protection in some Member States, if it is to achieve its goal of eliminating barriers to trade created by regulatory diversity.

Turning to the second problem of regulatory technique, the method of using Directives establishes common or uniform general standards, but each Member State has to integrate them into its domestic legal system. During this process, it seems likely that fresh divergences emerge as the requirements of the Directive are understood in different ways by each legal system.[29] To some extent this divergence can be suppressed by the interpretation of Directives under the reference procedure to the European Court of Justice (ECJ).[30] But the reference procedure seems a haphazard method to secure uniformity in the sense that it depends upon national courts deciding that the criteria for a reference have been satisfied. If the national court takes the view that the Directive in question supplies a perfectly clear standard that requires no further interpretation, it is unlikely to make a reference, even if another court in a different Member State might reach a different view on the meaning of the Directive. For example, in the earlier quotation from Lord Bingham, he

---

[29] G. Teubner, 'Legal Irritants: Good Faith in British Law or How Unifying Law Ends Up in New Divergences' (1998) 61 *Modern Law Review* 11.

[30] Treaty of EC Article 234.

was explaining and justifying his view that the meaning of good faith in the unfair terms in consumer contracts Directive and the implementing national Regulations was perfectly clear and not reasonably capable of differing interpretations.[31] He asserted that the good faith and fairness standard could be applied straightforwardly in the case before him, with the implication that any reference to the European Court of Justice was unnecessary. But this argument seems less persuasive when one learns that the inferior Court of Appeal had reached precisely the opposite conclusion about the meaning and application of the good faith standard to the particular case before the court.[32] It is also well known that interpretations of the concept of good faith differ between national legal systems.[33] The problem of interpretation of good faith therefore seems to raise the kind of issue where the same decision would not have been obvious to the ECJ and other national courts, in which case the House of Lords was under an obligation to refer the question to the ECJ.[34] Although the dialogue between national courts and the ECJ permitted by the reference procedure sometimes produces fascinating conversations,[35] it seems to me that the dialogue is too intermittent and subject to the idiosyncratic controls of national courts to serve as a reliable basis for establishing uniform interpretations of the standards set by Directives. To achieve that goal, the EC would have to evolve some kind of federal court structure that ensured uniform interpretation.[36]

In response to the problem of securing uniform interpretation of the proposed framework Directive, the Commission proposes some novel regulatory techniques. One possible justification for the use of the 'soft law' techniques in the form of non-binding guidance proposed in the Green Paper is their

---

[31] Director General of Fair Trading v First National Bank [2002] 1 All ER 97, HL,107; Directive 93/13, OJ 1993 L95 p. 29, implemented by SI 1994/3159 (now amended by SI 1999/2083).

[32] *Director General of Fair Trading v First National Bank* [2000] QB 672, CA.

[33] R. Zimmerman and S. Whittaker, *Good Faith in European Contract Law* (Cambridge: Cambridge University Press, 2000).

[34] Treaty of the EC, Article 243(3); *CILFT* C-283/81 [1982] ECR 3415; M. Dean, 'Defining Unfair Terms in Consumer Contracts – Crystal Ball Gazing?' (2002) 65 *Modern Law Review* 773.

[35] C. Kilpatrick, 'Gender Equality: A Fundamental Dialogue' in S. Sciarra (ed), *Labour Law in the Courts* (Oxford: Hart, 2001) 31.

[36] H. Collins, 'Transnational Private Law Regulation of Markets' (1998) 4 *Europa E Diritto Privato* 967.

potential contribution to securing a more harmonious interpretation of the general standards. The Commission suggests that non-binding guidance would minimise the risk of differing interpretations of the framework directive from arising.[37] The proposals remain unclear, however, on how such soft law might be developed. The Commission suggests that it might present formal recommendations, after having consulted representatives of governments, business associations, and consumer organisations. It would be necessary to establish criteria for the selection of these representatives or stakeholders, for the purpose of ensuring that the groups are properly representative of different interests. To overcome the potential obstacle that a meeting of stakeholders might be unable to agree upon non-binding guidance, the Commission suggests that it should have the right to produce guidance itself if the negotiations fail within a clear deadline.[38]

This last point perhaps reveals the Commission's hand rather more than it might wish. It becomes clear that a framework Directive only becomes a viable instrument for the harmonisation of law, if it is supplemented by further guidance, for otherwise the general clauses of the Directive will merely produce new divergences. Although stakeholders will be given the opportunity to develop this guidance for themselves, the Commission's patience cannot be taxed for too long, because to make its project successful, it requires the further guidance to be in place. The Commission may also be sceptical about the likelihood of the stakeholders being able to agree on guidance. As well as the normal problems of serious disagreements between consumer and business associations, and within business associations between large and small enterprises, the negotiations are likely to become complicated by the need to achieve agreement across all the Member States in which different conventions and opinions are likely to present a major obstruction to consensus.

Because the idea of developing non-binding guidance is inextricably linked to the problem of securing uniform standards across the EC, the proposed use of this technique involves a distortion of its normal use. The advantage of non-binding standards negotiated by stakeholders should normally be that it achieves high levels of compliance. If the parties can agree a set of standards or guidelines, they are likely to prove reflexive in the sense that they accommodate the needs of the parties subject to the regulation and will be expressed in terms which they understand and can implement. These

---

[37] 'Follow-up', para.32.
[38] 'Follow-up' p.19.

advantages of achieving reflexivity in regulation lead to the development of procedural regulation, which abstains from setting mandatory standards, but rather initiates a structured dialogue between stakeholders, with a view to inducing them to produce their own standards that they regard as acceptable and practicable norms of behaviour. Although the Commission's proposals in the Green Paper look at first sight as if they include this procedural and reflexive element, it becomes clear that the Commission is in fact unwilling to relinquish completely the standard-setting role to negotiations between stakeholders. The stakeholders will only be permitted to agree non-binding guidance, and if they fail to do so, the Commission will provide this guidance itself. The process is driven not by a concern to establish reflexive regulation, but rather by the need to secure a uniform interpretation of the standards set by the proposed framework directive.

Viewed in this light, the resort to non-binding guidance signals that the Commission views the prospects of securing actual agreement by Member States to detailed legal regulation of marketing practices as fairly unlikely. The soft law technique becomes a method by which the Commission, when unable to obtain sufficient political agreement in the Council, in effect assumes regulatory powers. It is true, of course, that the guidance remains 'non-binding', and thus the Commission would not be making law. But if the earlier point is correct that, without this guidance, the framework Directive would not achieve harmonisation to any significant degree, it becomes clear that the Commission needs this non-binding guidance to become accepted as in practice authoritative by national officials and courts. No doubt the Commission will take considerable steps to publicise and encourage conformity to its standards in this non-binding guidance, so that in practice it will become indistinguishable in its legal effects from a legal instrument.

3.   The Level of Consumer Protection

Recall that the original rationale for EC regulation of unfair commercial practices combines the need for negative integration of the market with ensuring high levels of consumer protection Throughout the Green Paper, in addressing the issue of the justification for a framework Directive, the Commission constantly returns to the question whether new regulation is required to promote the operation of the internal market by means of harmonising laws and improving measures of consumer protection and market competition. Notice that the fundamental thrust of this question is to ask how to improve the competitiveness of the Single Market rather than how to improve protection of consumers. It is true as a generalization, of course, that increased cross-border demand from consumers raises competitive pressures within the internal market, which should in turn lead to more efficient and competitively priced supplies of goods and services. It is assumed that consumers will benefit from a more competitive market by a reduction of prices as competitors enter the market. Although that economic prediction is not always borne out by experience, I think we can accept that consumers should benefit on the whole from price reductions caused by increased cross-border trade. But is this ambition of price reduction all that we mean when we speak of ensuring a high level of consumer protection? Is there a problem here that we are losing sight of the original double objective that encompassed both competitiveness and a high level of consumer protection?

To a considerable extent it can be argued that the pursuit of competitiveness entails a high level of consumer protection. Competitiveness can be promoted by measures directed against market failures, particularly those concerning the availability of reliable information. For instance, a prohibition against the dissemination of misleading information protects both consumers and rival traders who do not resort to such tactics. Furthermore, businesses and consumers are only willing to enter transactions, if they have a high degree of confidence that they will not be disappointed. Consumer protection laws can serve to enhance trust, and thus can improve competitiveness by providing some guarantee against disappointment. For example, protections for consumer privacy in the context of internet trading may not directly improve competition, since the measures restrict the flow of information, but they may encourage consumers to purchase goods and services through this relatively novel medium for the regulation may lessen their fear of unwelcome intrusions. This encouragement to enter internet transactions may therefore indirectly increase the competitiveness of markets by increasing the amount of distance and cross-border transactions. Thus any consumer protection measure may have the effect of encouraging consumer confidence, that is to increase the willingness to enter into a transaction involving unfamiliar products, by unfamiliar means, with unfamiliar businesses. 'Confident consumers' are an essential ingredient in the strategy of enhancing competition.

Yet there must remain a doubt whether the measures required by the confident consumer are equal to the measures required by the protected consumer. Are there examples of regulation that protect consumers against unfair marketing practices, yet which do not even indirectly promote the competitiveness of the market? I do not think any clear answer can be given to this question. Nevertheless, some consumer protection measures are extremely difficult to justify on the basis that they also serve the end of improving the competitiveness of markets. The absolute prohibition of doorstep selling in Denmark, for instance, may be a desirable consumer protection measure, but it is hard to see how it improves competitiveness.

Examining the Commission's Green Paper with these distinctions and possible justifications in mind, it becomes clear that the rationale based upon competitiveness is the dominant, and perhaps ultimately the only, justification proposed for EC regulation. It is perhaps significant that in the section headed 'the need for action',[39] the justifications for EC regulation are couched entirely in terms of competitiveness, that is improving the functioning of the internal market. The benefits to consumers are described as having access to greater choice and better prices. There is no mention of improving consumer protection beyond the dictates of improving competitiveness. This sets us out on a search for regulatory principles that should directly or indirectly serve the goal of increasing cross-border trade, rather than a search for principles that protect consumers more systematically against bad bargains arising from unfair commercial practices.

The reason for this emphasis on competition is, I think, not merely governed by the need to find a secure basis in the Treaty of European Union for legislation. My impression is that the Commission believes that the promotion of living standards is the key strategy for endearing the European Community to its citizens. If this goal of increased prosperity can be achieved, argues the Commission, European citizens will come to appreciate that the internal market matters and benefits them, and is not simply a project designed to serve the interests of business. Cheaper goods and services thus become a vital strand in Brussels' strategy for persuading an increasingly sceptical European public that the European Community provides real benefits for all its citizens. The Commission is perhaps unusually frank about its political motives:

> 'a fully functioning consumer internal market could play an important part in the strategy to bring the EU closer to its citizens, by dispelling the myth that internal market is a corporate business project and delivering tangible economic benefits to their daily life.'[40]

Is the Commission's strategy correct? Can European citizens be persuaded to believe in the virtues of the institutions of the EC by a policy for regulation of markets that pursues solely the objective of competitiveness? Or should

---

[39] 'Green Paper' para.3.1.
[40] 'Green Paper' para. 3.1.

the Commission present itself as the champion of the consumer by proposing levels of protection that exceed the demands of supporting competitiveness? Should the Commission, if it wants to justify transnational regulation, reach beyond the goal of creating the confident consumer towards the ambition of ensuring the satisfied consumer? Unless the Commission is prepared to act as the champion of the consumer, it seems likely that some national legislators will insist upon keeping the higher standards of domestic law, so that EC regulation will have to remain a minimum standards form of harmonisation, with the consequence that regulatory diversity is preserved and this possible obstruction to cross-border trade left partially in place.

III. THE PROBLEM OF REGULATING MARKETING PRACTICES

My second topic commences from the one certainty in this field of regulating market practices: the devising of adequate and effective regulation is extraordinarily difficult. The underlying problem is that marketing practices are constantly evolving as businesses seek new ways to tempt consumers to purchase their wares. As soon as one deceptive practice is expurgated, another springs up like the weeds in a garden. And to continue the metaphor, each new growth has to be inspected closely before it can be determined whether it is an unwelcome weed or a splendid innovation.

1. General Clauses

Acknowledging this frustrating truth about the regulation of marketing practices, the Commission observes that Directives with a high degree of specificity quickly become obsolete as rogue traders find new methods.[41] Indeed, given the time that elapses between conception and implementation of EC Directives, the legislation may be largely irrelevant before it comes into effect. For example, as soon as the content of the Directive on timeshare contracts was known, sellers were able to develop similar marketing techniques such as 'holiday clubs' that avoided the application of the EC rules. The rules can be avoided if the offer does not refer to a specified building or involves a period of less than three years. Indeed, businesses that run such 'holiday clubs' make a point of explaining that they are not selling 'timeshares', which, they say, are unsatisfactory for their customers owing to excessive EC regulation. Similarly, the cooling-off period required by the

---

[41] 'Green Paper' para. 2.2.

Directive on contracts concluded away from business premises has provoked marketing techniques for the avoidance of its requirements. The trick is to obtain an express request from the consumer on the telephone for a visit to the consumer's home. Once in the house, subtle techniques of pressurised selling are used, such as walking around the house and not leaving when requested to do so, in order to engineer a sale of product that the consumer may indeed want but at an inflated price.[42] The sobering conclusion is that effective regulation of deceptive market practices will always prove one of the hardest tasks for governments.

It is in this context that proposals are put forward for general principles or general clauses. If particular rules can be evaded, the response is to raise the level of generality or abstraction. General standards such as a duty to trade fairly will be applicable to any kind of marketing practice, so at least the law will not become irrelevant or obsolete before it is even implemented. But of course general clauses tell us nothing useful. Whatever the words employed, the clause merely says that weeds are forbidden and flowers permitted, but does not tell us how to classify the plants as we inspect them. We will have to rely on the expertise of the gardener, which in this instance will be the judges and officials who deal with claims. A general clause merely delegates the law-making power to the decision-maker, with no guarantee that the objective will be pursued.

For these reasons, it is difficult to contest the logic of the Commission's argument when it proposes that what is needed to cover future developments in marketing practices is a general framework Directive based upon a general clause. Even the UK response from the Department of Trade and Industry (DTI) is unable to find plausible grounds for rejecting this logic, even though it wants to reject the conclusion that a general clause is needed.[43] Where the DTI is on much firmer ground, of course, is when it takes issue with the remarkable claim made by the Commission that a general clause 'would provide a high degree of legal certainty for business and consumers'.[44] When proposals for a general clause were considered before in Britain, it was eventually concluded that such a legislative framework would generate many disputes about the meaning and application of the clause to particular marketing practices, with the result that enforcement would become bogged

---

[42] In the UK, the National Consumer Council keeps a dossier of such examples.

[43] DTI, above note 20, para.4.

[44] 'Green Paper', para.4.5.

down in litigation and become impracticable.[45] Evidence supporting this conclusion was found in the extensive litigation around the comparable provision in the USA concerning 'unfair or deceptive act or practice'.[46] I will not devote space to making the argument that general clauses on their own do not promote legal certainty and simple enforcement. What seems to me to be the crucial issue and the interesting regulatory problem is how to construct more determinative and effective guidance for sorting the weeds from the flowers. In other words, how can we give precision to the general standard without returning to the problem encountered by specific regulation that it is always under-inclusive? The Commission implicitly acknowledges that what is required realistically is a mixed strategy: a combination of a general clause as 'sweeper', together with more precise guidance.

Yet the more precise the guidance that is provided, the less the regulation will have the potential to adapt to market circumstances. To meet the objection that the term unfair commercial practices is far too vague to be practicable, the Commission in the Follow-up appears to offer two further ways of tightening the definition in the Directive itself. One that has already been mentioned is the idea the 'the general clauses would have to be substantiated by a number of specific rules (the "fairness/unfairness categories")'.[47] The second technique that would be included in a framework Directive would be a non-exhaustive list of examples of unfair commercial practices, a technique that was used in the Directive on unfair terms in consumer contracts.[48]

2. Unfairness Categories

The four categories proposed by the Commission concern misleading information, a duty to disclose material information, a prohibition on coercion and similar marketing techniques, and fair complaint-handling. This method for promoting certainty clearly detracts from the utility of a general clause. In practice it deprives the general clause against unfair commercial practices of any legal weight, if it is intended that its meaning should be confined to the four categories of unfairness. Legal reasoning and official action against

---

[45] Office of Fair Trading, *A General Duty to Trade Fairly* (London, 1986); Office of Fair Trading, *Trading Malpractices* (London: 1990); D. Oughton and J. Lowry, *Textbook on Consumer Law* 2nd edn (London: Blackstone, 2002) 40.

[46] Federal Trade Commission Act, 15 USCA s. 45 (a)(1)

[47] 'Follow-up', p. 8.

[48] Directive 93/13 of 5 April 1993, OJL 95, 21 April 1993, p. 29.

unfair commercial practices will always have to be justified by reference to one of the categories, thereby rendering the general clause redundant.

Whether or not this approach will reduce the flexibility of the regulation to cope with shifting marketing practices is unclear. The categories of unfairness may be stated at a sufficient level of generality that they can accommodate any marketing practices that officials regard as unfair. If the categories are framed at a sufficient level of generality, they may deal with three of the main sources of distorted preferences: informational asymmetry, coercive bargaining techniques, and post-breach of contract deception. That leaves the remaining problem of monopolies that distort preferences under the aegis of Competition law.

3.   Examples of Unfair Commercial Practices

As for the second method to be contained in the proposed framework directive, a list of examples of unfair commercial practices, this technique has proven to provide useful regulatory guidance. Officials can use the examples on a day-to-day basis, without the need for complex legal advice on the interpretation of the law. There is a danger that the examples might be regarded by officials as an exhaustive list of unfair commercial practices, which would inhibit the potential of the Directive to cope with new marketing practices. To counter that danger, the Directive would have to make it clear that the list is non-exhaustive and that unfair commercial practices might be identified by analogy with those examples.

A further problem with lists of examples is that if the list identifies marketing practices that are always automatically unfair, it seems likely that they will have to be defined tightly and the list may become extremely long. For this reason, it seems advisable to use a 'grey list', that is examples that raise a strong presumption of unfairness, rather than a 'black list' in which every example is automatically unlawful.

4.   Sector-specific Directives

Beyond these techniques for achieving a balance between legal certainty and adaptability in the framework Directive itself, we have already noted further strategies proposed by the Commission. The 'mixed strategy', which preserves independently of the framework directive further directives addressed to particular market sectors can be justified as contributing to greater certainty in fields where the precise requirements of unfair commercial practices might prove unclear or especially contested. This mixed strategy, however, does pose some further difficulties for legal interpretation of the relevant standard. We have noted already the potential problem of the hierarchy of rules presented by the mixed strategy. A trader who consciously complies with the detailed regulation still cannot be sure whether the activity might be prohibited under the framework directive, unless the particularistic regulation is given priority even though it might set a lower standard than the general clause.

5. Injunctions

In a sense, the use of the procedure to secure injunctions against unfair marketing practices could serve an equivalent function to sector specific directives.[49] At present the use of injunctions is envisaged to involve an order to a particular business to desist from an unfair marketing practice. Before an injunction can be issued, it is usually necessary to consult the business concerned with a view to achieving the cessation of the unfair marketing practice without the need for legal action. The injunction must be issued by a court against a named person or business. But the injunction procedure could be harnessed so that orders might be addressed not only to a particular trader but more generally to traders in a particular market sector.

For such an evolution of the injunctions method of enforcement, it would be necessary to ensure that the businesses concerned were alerted adequately to the order, or alternatively, once an unwitting breach of the injunction had been discovered, that the business should have the opportunity to rectify the position quickly without further penalty. An outline of such a procedure known as 'super-complaints' has recently been enacted in the UK.[50] The idea is that designated consumer bodies will be empowered to complain to the official agency, the Office of Fair Trading (OFT), that any feature or combination of features of a market for goods or services is or appears to be significantly harming the interests of consumers. The OFT is then required to investigate and publish what action, if any, it proposes to make. The advantage of this procedure is that pressure from a consumer association can lead to an investigation of a whole trading sector or a particular trading practice used widely, rather than being confined to the investigation of a particular rogue trader.

---

[49] Directive 98/27/EC of 19 May 1998, OJL 166, 11 June 1998, p. 51; implemented now in the UK by Enterprise Act 2002 Part 8.

[50] Enterprise Act 2002 s. 11.

6.   Safe Harbours and Co-regulation.

In a speech giving support to the proposed framework Directive the EC Commissioner for Health and Consumer Protection appears to support another regulatory technique that might achieve a better balance between legal certainty and changes in marketing practices.[51] This regulatory technique is the method of creating safe harbours. Here the idea is that rules describe permitted behaviour or conduct for traders in the market. Provided that the trader complies with those rules, the trader is virtually immune from legal challenge, even under the general clause. The main advantages of safe harbours are that they provide determinate guidance to participants in the market and give an incentive to comply with the law. Instead of playing the eternal game of cat and mouse with rogue traders who comply with the letter but not the spirit of the regulation of trading practices, we provide an incentive for compliance, which may outweigh the potential advantages to traders of finding a route around the rules.

The technique of safe harbours is usually, though not necessarily, linked to mechanisms for self-regulation. In order to create a safe harbour that is practicable and attractive to traders in a market sector, it is helpful to allow that industry to have a major role in fixing the location of the safe harbour. For this reason, in so far as the Commission pursues the strategy of creating harbours, this method is connected to the creation of codes of conduct. The Commission seeks to encourage the development of EU-wide codes by business sectors or trade associations. If a particular trader signs up to comply with one of these codes, however, the Commission envisages that compliance will only create a 'presumption of conformity' with the legal standard. This does not amount to a complete safe harbour, for it remains possible for the public authorities to contest the code's interpretation of the legal standard of unfair commercial practice. But following the analogy drawn with the 'New Approach' to technical standards, just as following a technical standard provides a strong presumption of compliance with product safety rules,[52] so too would compliance with a code provide strong evidence of compliance with a duty to trade fairly.

Under the proposals so far advanced by the Commission, however, not

---

[51] Speech/01/620 Mr David Byrne, The EU Consumer Protection Green Paper Public Hearing on the Commission's Green paper on Consumer Protection, Brussels, 7 December 2001: http://europa.eu.int/rapid/start/cgi/guesten.

[52] Directive 2001/95 of 3/12/2001, Article 3.

only is there no safe harbour obtained by compliance with a voluntary code, but also there appears to be a disincentive for voluntarily subscribing to a code. Under the Commission's proposals, a business that has signed up to a code and then breaches it would be automatically regarded as having committed an unfair commercial practice. The logic here is plainly that the misleading statement of membership of a voluntary code is itself an unfair commercial practice, which is certainly a necessary ingredient of an effective system of self-regulation. But the problem this logic causes is that a business may be better off not subscribing to any code at all rather than taking the risk that a challenge to its marketing practices could be successful on a technical non-compliance with some detailed provision of a code.[53]

One understands the reluctance of the Commission to permit conformity to voluntary codes to provide a safe harbour, if there is no guarantee that the business sector will devise a code that complies with legal standards. The problem can be solved in principle by prior approval of codes by a relevant public authority, perhaps after consultation with consumer organisation. The Commission has proposed that it should consult further on the possibility that a mechanism for public endorsement should be created, which would create a stronger and perhaps irrebutable presumption that conduct in conformity with the code did not violate the unfair commercial practices standard, though without prejudice to other regulatory requirements. In the UK, recent legislation reflects the government's view that sector specific codes function better by improving consumers' and businesses' perceptions of the value of a code by giving the relevant public authority, the Office of Fair trading, specific powers to approve codes that meet core criteria.[54]

An alternative measure for giving greater credence to voluntary codes whilst not loosing their reflexive qualities is to grant an individual trader which complies with a code an immunity against the charge of unfair commercial practice, but hold the business or trade association that devised the code responsible for its failure to require conformity to the standards set in the framework directive. The problem with this alternative is that trade associations might become reluctant to devise codes if that initiative might lead to legal responsibilities. Much might depend on whether this legal responsi-

---

[53] Department of Trade and Industry, *The European Commission's Consultation on the Follow-up Communication to the Green paper on EU Consumer Protection: Response of the UK Government* (London: October 2002) para. 28.

[54] Enterprise Act 2002, s. 8(2).

bility was simply confined to a requirement to revise the code, or whether it might extend to some kind of financial compensation or fine. If the remedy were confined to the former, trade associations should not be deterred from promulgating codes.

Yet a further technique for supporting the safe harbours method of regulation might be to require trade associations to consult with consumer organisations before promulgating a code. If the code could be agreed after negotiations with consumer organisations, it might then be granted the status of a safe harbour for traders that conform to its requirements. We can perhaps plot in advance the trajectory of this negotiation, assuming that it could ever lead to an agreement. It seems clear that whatever consumer protection measures might be proposed by consumer organisations, only those which might improve consumers' confidence and therefore competition would be acceptable to representatives of business. The process thus seems to determine the outcome that competitiveness rather than consumer protection becomes the goal of the code. Furthermore, for the process to produce the most competitive solution, it depends upon businesses regarding fair competition in the market as more desirable than having minimal regulation which imposes few costs. For instance, for the self-regulation process to produce a competitive market, the representatives of business must want to eliminate 'rogue traders', that is businesses that employ deceptive practices in order to win customers. But if there are few rogue traders and they make little dent in the consumer market, the business side of the negotiations may prefer to have a relaxed regulatory regime that minimises costs of compliance. In predicting the probable outcome of such deliberations, it is important to recognise that business will have to weigh up the certain cost of compliance with the uncertain and possibly negligible benefits of fair competition. These arguments explain why there should be serious doubts about whether a self-regulatory process will produce determinate regulations that implement the objective of a general duty to trade fairly.

Despite these concerns about the potential outcome of 'co-regulation' through codes of conduct, the Commission is evidently keen in general to promote techniques of self-regulation by stakeholders. The White Paper on Governance expresses the hope that a more participatory mechanism for regulation in the EC will serve both to reduce the democratic deficit in Community institutions and to speed up the integration process. Some scepticism has been expressed about whether the process of 'co-regulation' within the context of framework directives is likely to achieve these objectives.[55] It is not immediately apparent, for instance, how the process of negotiating deals between business organisations and consumers groups in some system of committees that meet in private will ensure that citizens of the Community will feel that there is democratic accountability in EC institutions. The participants or 'stakeholders' would not be elected or accountable to anyone but themselves, and would be selected by invitation from the Commission. Nor is it immediately apparent why this process of negotiation is more likely to produce expeditious, clear outcomes than the alternative method of council Directives. Some stakeholders, particularly on the side of business may see advantage in prolonging discussions for as long as possible. In labour law, which is the field where co-regulation has been most successful through the 'Social Dialogue', for instance, there is reason to think that self-regulation has only been agreed under the credible threat of imminent action by the Council.

Leaving these sceptical comments aside, however, the Commission, despite its desire for a 'co-regulation' solution, is compelled to recognise that at present there are no institutional mechanisms for establishing an appropriate community level dialogue. What is required is European level organisations of business and consumers, which can be presented as sufficiently representative groups to have the authority to negotiate binding regulations for all businesses. These organisations might have to be specific to industrial sectors, in order to reflect the national level organisation of business or trade associations.

In my view, sector level negotiations at national level are probably the most effective way of producing determinate guidance on the meaning of general standards, but whether or not this method could work at a transnational level must be open to question. At the transnational level, the motivation for business must be questionable. It must be tempting for businesses to preserve the insulation of their domestic markets by keeping regulatory diversity, even though they might wish to open up other markets through harmonisation. But an alternative reading of the prospects suggests that larger businesses may be prepared to combine together to impose standards with which they already comply on smaller traders and new entrants to markets,

---

[55] P. Magnette, 'European Governance and Civic Participation: Can the European Union be Politicised?', in C. Joerges, Yves Meny & J.H.H. Weiler (eds), *Responses to the European Commission's White Paper on Governance* (Florence: European University Institute, 2001) 23.

some of which may be prepared to engage in dubious market practices in order to break into a lucrative market. Again there is a parallel with the Social Dialogue in labour law, where larger employers may have been prepared to endorse regulation containing standards that they already accepted as a result of collective bargaining or for other reasons, in order to impose similar costs on smaller employers. The Court of First Instance has insisted that such co-regulation institutions should ensure the 'representativity' of the parties to the dialogue,[56] which may prove a valuable safeguard.

The potential anti-competitive motivation for the adoption of self-regulation at a transnational level is implicitly acknowledged by the Commission in the Green Paper. It is observed that as the Commission has the task of enforcing competition rules, it cannot participate in the process of self-regulation in case its position on competition policy is compromised.[57] That observation leads to the case for the establishment of some other competent authority to assist, steer, and help to enforce self-regulation – a federal trading standards authority, an idea which seems to have been dropped.

Whether or not the Commission must take a back seat with respect to trading standards seems to me to be less clear in terms of policy. If the Commission were in a position to offer a safe harbour not only with respect to fair trading laws but also with respect to competition laws, the attraction to business of agreeing to binding codes of practice might become irresistible. Furthermore, we cannot divorce consumer protection measures from competition rules. The general principles on fair trading have to address the problems of when the consumer receives inadequate or deficient information, misleading information in the sense that it creates a false impression about the quality of products or prices, and distracting information in the sense that the information diverts the consumer's attention away from key issues such as price and quality comparisons. Legal rules about these issues, however, may have the effect of presenting an obstacle to competition by excluding business competitors,[58] or by forcing them to alter their marketing strate-

---

[56] *UEAPME v Council* Case T-135/96 [1998] ECR II-2335; J. Scott and D.M. Trubek, 'Mind the Gap: Law and New Approaches to Governance in the European Union' (2002) 8 *European Law Journal* 1.

[57] 'Green Paper', para. 4.4.

[58] *E.g.* Case C-315/92 *Verband Sozialer Wettbewerb eV v Clinique Laboratories SNC* [1994] ECR I-317 (the brand name Clinique misleading consumers to believe in medicinal properties of cosmetics).

gies.[59] The task of devising general principles on fair trading thus indirectly determines crucial aspects of the policy of promoting competition in the internal market. Another way in which to express this connection is to say that the extent to which the general principles of fair trading rely upon the sophistication of consumers to process information also governs the intensity of competition through marketing techniques. The Commission cannot therefore distance itself from the problem of resolving the potential tension between competition rules and consumer protection rules, and the mechanism of safe harbours may provide a technique for a practical resolution.

When self-regulation is combined with a safe harbour, some further problems seem destined to arise. A safe harbour in the proper sense of the word provides an immunity against claims of violation of the regulation. Often legislators are reluctant to confer such an immunity. They prefer instead to attempt to construct commercial advantages for those who comply with the rules of the safe harbour. For instance, some kind of certification procedure can be adopted, so that a firm can claim that its goods are safe and of satisfactory quality and obtain a commercial advantage from displaying a particular logo or certification. Although this employment of commercial incentives to encourage compliance with regulatory standards is certainly a technique worth considering, I doubt whether in relation to the problem that we are addressing the technique would bear much fruit. These rogue traders who are willing to engage in deceptive practices would not, one surmises, be averse to including in their deceptive practices false claims about their certification or achievement of certain regulatory standards. Nor am I convinced that consumers would respond to this mechanism by, for example, demanding proof of certification before continuing a phone conversation or an internet transaction. My view is that if we go down the route of safe harbours, we will have to combine the incentive of legal immunity with some kind of punitive sanction against those who falsely claim compliance. Anything less than this, and safe harbours would not work to encourage compliance.

Nevertheless, the possibility of the creation of safe harbours is plainly on the agenda, at least to the extent that compliance with a code of practice might achieve a 'presumption of conformity' with the general standard of fair trading. I think we should welcome this development. As a regulatory technique, safe harbours combine the virtues of determinate guidance

---

[59] *E.g.* Case C-286/81 *Oosthoek's Uitgeversmaatschappij* [1982] ECR 4575 ('free' gifts as an inducement to purchase encyclopaedias).

with incentives for compliance. Provided the codes of practice are created through self-regulation, they will have the reflexive quality of being tailored to the needs of particular business sectors. Given the possible bargaining strategies in co-regulation described above, however, it seems essential that some regulatory oversight in the public interest should place restraints on the outcomes of self-regulation. This oversight is necessary to achieve even the Commission's goal of improving competitiveness, let alone the goal of improving consumer protection.

IV. GENERAL CONTRACT LAW

As my third topic, I raise a matter not mentioned explicitly in the Commission's Green Paper, but one of deep concern to SECOLA. This topic concerns the relation between proposals for regulation of marketing practices and the general laws governing contracts. In particular, I am interested in the evolutionary trajectory of the mutual interference between systems. Let me explain that slightly mysterious remark.

One can view private law, including the general law of contract, as a particular regulatory technique. The purpose of this regulation is, broadly speaking, to assist the construction and operation of markets, which is achieved in part by seeking to deter practices such as fraud and coercion that tend to reduce confidence in markets. The regulatory technique of private law has many distinctive features, not least the method of self-enforcement in which private parties must assert their rights under the rules. Nevertheless, the codes and systems of private law all tackle through mandatory rules a wide range of unfair market practices. The standards set by most private law systems were, however, fairly low, since the rules had to be applied across the whole of the market without any differentiation between the types of contracting parties involved. There is, for instance, in private law systems one law of fraud for both businesses and private individuals.

During the twentieth century, legislation typically added another layer of regulation of market practices. This legislation differentiated between types of parties to contracts, and selectively increased the standards required in the market. For example, in the UK, the standard imposed on business through consumer regulation became one to refrain from misleading statements, not merely ones that were deliberate incorrect statements of fact. Furthermore, the legislation typically involved the introduction of new enforcement techniques where public authorities or collective organisations performed a monitoring and enforcement role. As EC Directives have entered this field, they have also adopted these regulatory techniques, as for example promoting collective enforcement mechanisms.

Although lawyers are often tempted to consider general contract law and consumer protection law in isolation from each other, the boundaries of these two systems are permeable in practice. In other words, the concepts, standards, and methods of reasoning in the two systems influence each other. Private law discourses influence the interpretation of consumer protection measures, and more crucially consumer protection measures serve as an irritant to the settled ways of private law. For this reason, those interested in general private law cannot ignore the presence of consumer regulation. Nor do they, as we have seen in relation to the Unfair Terms in Consumer Contracts Directive. The question posed by that Directive for private law systems is whether its foundational concepts of transparency of terms, good faith, and substantial imbalance, may influence the evolution of private law systems beyond the strict confines of the application of the Directive and its implementing legislation.

The same potential for mutual interference arises in the context of the proposal for a general clause concerning fair trading. For example, if the general clause is interpreted to mean (amongst other things) 'putting your cards on the table', in the sense of requiring the disclosure of material information, this standard may influence the evolution of private law with respect to pre-contractual disclosure of information. The degree of interference is likely to be enhanced to the extent that the framework Directive has horizontal effects in the sense that individual consumers and business may rely upon it in claims against businesses for unfair pre-contractual conduct.[60] The insertion of a general clause regarding fair trading would provide support for proposals for EC contract law of the kind put forward in the *Principles of European Contract Law*, in which nearly all the difficult borderline issues would be resolved by granting judges a discretion under the general clause that the parties are under a duty to act in accordance with good faith and fair dealing.[61] Or, to put the point the other way round, the presence of a general clause

---

[60] As under the Australian Trade Practices Act 1974 s. 52; D.J. Harland, 'The Statutory Prohibition of Misleading or Deceptive Conduct in Australia and Its Impact on the Law of Contract (1995) 111 *Law Quarterly Review* 100.

[61] O. Lando and H. Beale (eds), *Principles of European Contract Law Parts 1 and II*, (The Hague: Kluwer Law International, 2000) Article 1:201.

concerning unfair market practices would weaken the position of those who contend that, if the EC is to proceed with harmonisation of general contract law, it should do so not in the tradition of the grand sweeping principles of nineteenth century codes of private law, but in a more detailed, nuanced, regulatory framework, that distinguishes between market sectors and the types of parties to contracts.

Of course, this potential for mutual interference has a special resonance in common law Member States, because uniquely we lack any general provision with respect to fair trading. It is the possibility of a general clause with its potential spill-over effects into general contractual law that both alarms and excites lawyers interested in private law. But, unusually for a common lawyer, I am not concerned about the generality or abstraction of a general clause. I am much more interested in the normative value or principle contained in any consumer regulation, because it may have a spill-over effect into private law reasoning. A duty to trade fairly might shape or interfere with established patterns of private law with respect to pre-contractual obligations, performance obligations, and possible enforcement mechanisms. A new general principle might serve as an 'irritant' in all national contract law systems,[62] leading to the evolution of new doctrinal standards.

Consider for instance the proposal to include as one category of unfair commercial practice a failure to disclose material information to a consumer. General private law systems do not have an equivalent general requirement, though duties of disclosure may arises with respect to particular contracts such as insurance, and between parties with certain types of relationship such as partners and agents. The Directive might need to give further specificity to what information should be regarded as material to the consumer. This list might include the nature of the goods and services provided, the price inclusive of taxes, delivery charges, the arrangements for delivery or performance, the conditions for exchange or refund, the identity and address of the supplier, the conditions of after-sales service, the membership of a code of conduct, and the availability of alternative dispute resolution mechanisms. An equivalent list has already been set by EC Directives for consumer credit transactions,[63] and contracts of employment and consumer credit transactions.[64] An analo-

---

[62] Teubner, above note 28.

[63] Directive 87/102 of 22 December 1986, OJ L 1987 42/48, as amended in 1990 OJL 61/14 and 1998 OJL 101/17.

[64] Directive 91/533 of 14 October 1991, OJ L 1991 288/32; S. Deakin, 'The Written Statement

gous duty to provide material information as an incident of a duty of loyalty between financial service providers and their clients is also required in investment services,[65] and insurance.[66] If something like this list were included in a specification of the requirements of the framework directive, together with the other Directives mentioned, it would set a model for a limited duty of disclosure of material information that might influence the evolution of private law in its application to other kinds of contracts. This general principle might follow the standard that a person who holds himself as having a degree of specialist expertise assumes a responsibility to disclose such information that the other party would reasonably regard as material.[67] In addition to this 'shingle' principle based upon professional expertise, a duty of disclosure of material information might arise in particular circumstances when the course of the negotiations has given rise to a reasonable expectation that if some relevant facts were to exist, they would be disclosed to the other party.[68]

This prospect of the evolution of private law systems directs out attention to the precise formulation of the general clause and the normative values that it contains. The Green Paper does not venture an articulation of these principles or values. It indicates that the principles would draw on both existing EC legal concepts and national legal concepts in order to flesh out a general standard of unfairness. But those sources provide a wide variety of possible standards or principles. In thinking about the principles of fairness in trading practices, we are therefore simultaneously considering the evolutionary trajectory of national private law systems, not merely the details of consumer protection laws. We are also potentially laying the foundations for a general and uniform law of contract throughout Europe.

Directive – Social Norms, Information, and the Employment Relationship' in S. Grundmann, W. Kerber, and S. Weatherill (eds), *Party Autonomy and the Role of Information in the Internal Market* (Berlin: de Gruyter, 2001) 371.

[65] Directive 93/22 of 10 May 1993, OJL 1993 L 141/27, amended in 1995 OJL 168/7; S. Grundmann and W. Kerber, 'Information Intermediaries and Party Autonomy – The Example of Securities and Insurance Markets' in Grundmann, Kerber, and Weatherill, above note 59, 264.

[66] Directives 92/49, of 18 June 1992; 92/96 of 10 November 1990.

[67] K.J. Hopt, 'Disclosure Rules as a Primary Tool for Fostering Party Autonomy – Observations from a Functional and Comparative Legal Perspective', in Grundmann, Kerber, and Weatherill, above notes 59, 246, 257.

[68] Harlan, above note 60 , 115.

V. Conclusion

The preceding observations have essentially been directed towards issues of regulatory technique. One reason for considering this question of technique so closely is that this field of unfair commercial practices is notoriously difficult to regulate with an optimal level of precision. General clauses provide insufficient guidance for honest traders and law enforcement authorities; detailed and particularistic clauses are an invitation to rogue traders to steer around the prohibitions by means of a slightly different marketing device. But this problem applies to all national legal systems, and the EC has to grapple with it in the same way as other legal systems have done before. The difference is that the EC can learn from the experiences of Member States in order to devise better, more effective regulation.

Similarly, the mutual interference of regulatory systems has a long history in national legal systems. The advent of consumer protection laws and other distinct branches of contract law such as employment law has had an impact on the evolution of private law systems in all Member States. But in every case there remains the problem of determining how autonomous the particular consumer regulation should be regarded, and how much it should be permitted to influence the general background principles of law. This issue recurs in EC law, but with this significant difference, that the EC lacks a general private law system as a co-ordinating point of reference for particularistic regulation. Thus the EC Directives dealing with particular types of transactions such as consumer purchases, contracts of employment, and unfair terms in contracts, may have the special significance that they provide the primary source for the development of principles of EC private law.

Where EC regulation of marketing practices poses a relatively novel problem is in the attempt to harmonise 15 or more national legal systems, which already possess extensive regulation of unfair commercial practices. The challenge for the EC lies in both finding a consensus about the appropriate standards and in devising enforcement mechanisms that ensure high levels of compliance in all Member States. No doubt there is much common ground between the different jurisdictions, but at the boundaries of permitted trading behaviour there are likely to be many disagreements about how to draw the line between unfair sharp practice and merely efficient marketing techniques. It is for this reason, I suggest, that of cultural diversity as much as regulatory diversity, that the EC will need to experiment with varieties of techniques of soft law in order to build consensus.

Indeed, even if the framework Directive is enacted, it seems to me that this will in fact only initiate a process of mutual learning between Member States. What will be required in this field of unfair marketing practices is something analogous to the Open Method of Co-ordination, proposed by the Commission in its White Paper on European Governance.[69] Under such a mechanism each Member States would be required to prepare annual reports on the problems occurring in trading practices and how national regulation including soft law such as voluntary codes of practice is combating them. The Commission might identify various heads under which reports should be made, and devise some indicators of success in regulatory control. The outcome would be national reports that would expose new methods of deceptive trading, the variety of techniques being employed across the Member States for dealing with them, the content of codes of practice and guides, and some kind of estimate of their effectiveness. It would then be open to the members of the Council and the Commission to draw conclusions or recommendations, such as advising Member States to take action against a particular unfair trading practice, to note the ineffectiveness of measures in particular Member States, and to advocate best practice.

Before lawyers dismiss this method of harmonisation out of hand as wholly ineffective in addressing the problems confronting cross-border trade, they should consider again the difficulties facing comprehensive regulation. In our earlier metaphor, new weeds are springing up all the time, and there is great uncertainly about how best to cope with them. We could describe this as a problem of information deficit: regulators do not know what has to be controlled and how best to achieve this goal. The Open Method of Co-ordination is designed primarily to address these twin aspects of the problem of information deficit. Harmonisation of laws emerges indirectly as the Member States learn from each other common methods for identifying undesirable marketing practices and how best to combat them through regulatory measures. I think we should be modest in our claims with respect to knowing what kinds of consumer laws are effective. Consider, for example, the case of 'cooling-off' periods. Do these provisions that permit consumers to cancel contracts increase or decrease the number of transactions that consumers regret? On the one hand the ability to cancel the contract does provide an opportunity to act on that regret. On the other hand, the possibility of cancellation may encourage the consumer to act rashly in the first place. The consumer may then be too embarrassed or simply too slow to act to cancel the contract. It

---

[69] Com (2001) 428.

seems possible, though I don't think we know the answer, that cooling-off periods in practice increase the number of transactions that consumers regret and provide an excuse for the use of high-pressure sales techniques. This kind of regulatory back-firing is a common problem in all business regulation, and warns us to be cautious in our prescriptions for measures of consumer protection.

An Open Method of Co-ordination of the kind described above is a technique for addressing these puzzles of regulation. In the long run it is likely to produce better regulation in the sense that it is more effective and more efficient. The adoption of the Open Method of Co-ordination does not rule out interim measures of the kind adumbrated by the Commission, but it does urge humility about our ability to harmonise legal rules in this area successfully.

2. A General Framework Directive on Fair Trading

Hans-W. Micklitz

I. INTRODUCTION

The paper intends to discuss the feasibility of a general legislative framework on fair trading.[1] The major deficit of fair trading legislation results from the constant neglect of consumer protection. Whilst it will be necessary to bring a revised concept of fair trading into line with intellectual property rights legislation, the following paper is based on the premise that a European legislative framework has to pay tribute to the rise of consumer protection in recent decades. It starts by recounting the different efforts of the European Commission to get to grips with fair trading, which resulted in piecemeal legislation (II). Any new initiative has to be based on a thorough comparative analysis of the legal position in the Member States, and it has to justify the need for action by the European Community (EC) before it is possible and feasible to define the elements of a general legislative framework (III). It is suggested that a general framework directive must reach beyond mandatory legislation and has to take into account softer forms of regulation. The new approach on technical standards and regulations deserves particular attention as it may, though in a revised form, structure the development of non-binding standards on marketing practices (IV). A general legislative framework has to give shape to the ways and means in which the rules will have to be enforced, and who will be in charge of their enforcement (V). The paper will not discuss the question of competences in the aftermath of the tobacco-judgment.[2]

---

[1] It is largely based on the feasibility study, the Institut für Europäisches Wirtschafts- und Verbraucherrrecht has conducted on behalf Sanco in 2000. The study is available on the Internet http://europa.eu.int/commm/consumers/policy/developments/fair-comm-pract/. The paper, however, integrates recent reactions and tries to duly reflect the critique raised so far.

[2] Case C-376/98 *Federal Republic of Germany v European Parliament and Council* and Case C-74/99 *The Queen v. Secretary for Health ex parte Imperial Tobacco Ltd* (2000) ECR I-8599.

H. Collins (ed.) The Forthcoming EC Directive on Unfair and Commercial Practices, 43-90.
©2004. Kluwer Law International. Printed in the Netherlands.

II. A new initiative on an old issue – an EC regulation on fair trading

The Treaty of Rome did not set up a regulatory framework on fair trading. Right from the beginning, however, there was a strong impetus towards the establishment of such a regulatory framework, initially as a means to complement the competition policy, today as an instrument to promote consumer protection. The policy shift is widely seen and has become common ground. A modern law on fair trading is in essence focussed on marketing practices paying due regard to the interests of consumers.[3] Today EC regulation on fair trading seems to have arrived at its crossroads: either the recent initiative will lead to a general legislative framework, or the issue might vanish in the haze for the next decades.

1. The Mandate of the Commission

The efforts to establish a general duty to trade fairly are of a fairly long history.[4] In the 1960s, the Commission had already begun to consider the problems concerned with the observance of unfair competition within the Common Market. At that time, it asked the *Max-Planck-Institut*[5] to undertake a comparative analysis of the Member States' trade laws, in order to ascertain the differences between the national rules that were liable to affect the development of the then Common Market. This investigation led to series of country reports, and a comparative analysis under the editorship of *Eugen Ulmer*.[6] A more consumer-orientated view was developed in a study made

---

[3] See the recent initiatives undertaken by the German Ministry of Economics to foster the modernisation of the German UWG. The two studies demonstrate unanimity here, see K-H Fezer, 'Modernisierung des deutschen Rechts gegen den unlauteren Wettbewerb auf der Grundlage der Europäiserung des Wettbewerbsrechts', wrp 2001, 989; G. Schricker and F, Henning-Bodewig, 'Elemente einer Harmonisierung des Rechts des unlauteren Wettbewerbs in der EU', wrp 2001, 1367; the *latter* have presented the essence of their analysis in an English version, published in eipr 2002, 271.

[4] A. Ohly, 'Die Bemühungen um eine Rechtsvereinheitlichung auf EU-Ebene von den Anfängen bis zur Richtlinie über irreführende Werbung von 1984', in G. Schricker and F. Henning-Bodewig (Hrsg.), *Neuordnung des Wettbewerbsrechts*, (1999) 69.

[5] Max-Planck-Institut für ausländisches und internationales Patent-, Urheber- und Wettbewerbsrecht in Munich, Germany.

[6] E. Ulmer (ed.), *Das Recht des unlauteren Wettbewerbs in den Mitgliedstaaten der Europäischen Wirtschaftsgemeinschaft: Gutachten erstattet im Auftrag der Kommission der*

by later *Gerhard Schricker,* the successor of *Eugen Ulmer* in the *Max-Planck Institut.*[7]

(a) The first step – the adoption of a directive on fair trading

After years of preparatory work, the Commission presented its Proposal[8] for a Council Directive relating to the approximation of the laws, regulations and administrative provisions of the Member States concerning misleading and unfair advertising submitted to the Council on March 1, 1978. The objective of the Directive, as articulated in Art. 1 of the Proposal, was 'to protect consumers, persons carrying on a trade, business or profession, and the interests of the public in general against unfair and misleading advertising'. The recitals left no doubt that the harmonisation of the laws against unfair advertising were considered to be prerequisite for the proper functioning of the Common Market and the protection of the consumer (esp. recitals 2 and 3).

However, the Proposal did not meet unanimous approval. The Member States cancelled the "unfairness section" – i.e. also comparative advertising, which was understood as a component of unfair advertising – and finally adopted the Directive 84/450/EEC[9] relating to the approximation of the laws, regulations and administrative provisions of the Member States concerning misleading advertising, which was the sole common denominator at that time. Yet, it is this piece of Community legislation that provides the most outspoken mandate for further legislative measures in the unfair advertising sector. Its recitals reveal that the harmonisation of misleading advertising and of unfair advertising (and of comparative advertising 'as far as necessary') is understood as being two stages of the same project: namely to comply with the 'interests of the public in general, that of consumers and all those who, in competition with one another, carry on a trade, business, craft or profession, in the common market' (recital 6). The second stage has partially been realised in Directive 97/55/EEC[10] amending Directive 84/450/EEC, so as to

---

Europäischen Wirtschaftsgemeinschaft vom Institut für Ausländisches und Internationales Patent-, Urheber- und Markenrecht der Universität München, (1965) 7 Volumes.

7   G. Schricker, *Unfair Advertising – Comparative Advertising, Definition of the terms and survey of the practice in Belgium, Holland, Luxembourg, Germany, France and other Member States of the EEC with a view to a harmonisation* (unpublished manuscript, 1985).

8   OJ C 70, 21 March 1978, 4.

9   OJ L 250, 19 September 1984, 17.

10   OJ L 290, 23 October 1997, 18.

include comparative advertising; whereas the "pure unfair part" is still awaiting its realisation.

(b) Intermediary steps – piecemeal legislation

The European Commission did not take up the overall issue of a fair trading directive for more than a decade. However, there was no standstill in the regulation of marketing practices. A considerable number of legislative measures document a change in policy, away from a broad concept of fair trading, towards the regulation of particular issues of major importance for the Common Market, later the Internal Market. The original idea of a general concept of fair trading was kept alive, by being laid down in recitals or particular provisions. One may refer to Directive 85/577/EEC[11] to protect the consumer in respect of contracts negotiated away from business premises, which was intended as a measure 'to protect consumers against *unfair commercial practices* in respect of doorstep selling' (recital 3). Also the Television Directive 89/522/EEC[12] ('Television without frontiers'), as amended by Directive 97/36/EC,[13] was intended to 'preserve free and *fair competition*' (recital 16 of Directive 97/36/EC) and protects the consumer by various advertising provisions, such as requirements for teleshopping (Art. 10 *et seq.*), a ban on tobacco advertising (Art. 13) and several rules on the protection of minors (*e.g.* Art. 15 lit. a, Art. 22). Directive 97/7/EC[14] on the protection of consumers in respect of distance contracts aims at providing information to consumers in connection with entry into such contracts with due regard, in particular, to "*the principles of good faith in commercial transactions*" (*cf. e.g.* Art. 4). Finally, the Directive 2000/31/EC,[15] (Directive on electronic commerce) recognises that commercial communications must meet a number of transparency requirements 'in the interests of consumer protection and *fair trading*' (recital 29).

These directives are only examples of a much larger catalogue of legislative measures on marketing practices. The policy shift has led to the 'piecemeal' regulation which exists at present. A variety of fair trading rules on the Community level exist, but they neither cover the whole spectrum of trade

---

[11] OJ L 372, 31 December 1985, 31.
[12] OJ L 298, 17 October 1989, 23.
[13] OJ L 202, 30 July 1997, 60.
[14] OJ L 144, 04 June 1997, 19.
[15] OJ L 178, 17 July 2000, 1.

practices, nor interlink or constitute a consistent approach in their regulatory techniques.

(c)　The Green Paper on Consumer Protection, the Proposal for a Regulation on Sales Promotion and the Follow-up Communication

On the very same day, the 2nd October 2001, the Commission published two important documents: the Green Paper on Consumer Protection[16] – which is in fact a Green Paper on Fair Trading – and the Proposal for a Regulation on Sales Promotion in the Internal Market.[17] The future of both papers is uncertain. The Green Paper on Consumer Protection was subject to a public hearing in December 2001, the Commission intends to sum up the findings of the hearing and integrate them in a communication on fair trading. The Proposal for a Regulation on Sales Promotion has already been channelled into the legislative pipeline. The first bears the handwriting of DG SANCO; the second of DG Market. It is not haphazard event that the papers were published on the same day. They document a compromise forged in the Commission.

The first one, the Green Paper on Consumer Protection is the long awaited initiative to get to grips with a coherent concept of fair trading. On the basis of three studies which have been conducted on behalf of DG Sanco, the Commission now presents various options on the regulation of fair trading in the European Community. The Green Paper on Consumer Protection advocates the development of a comprehensive framework on fair trading, in which the present directives as well as the proposed regulation on sales promotion can be integrated, be it in the form of a general clause on fair trading or misleading advertising.[18] Whilst the Commission discusses the options jointly under the false premise that they are to some extent equivalent,[19] the Commission seems to favour a general clause on fair trading as the broader concept. If, however, agreement on a general clause on fair trading cannot be reached,

---

16　COM (2001) 531 final. 'Green paper'

17　COM (2001) 546 final, from a German point of view the two documents are presented by S. Göhre, *wrp*, 2002, 26, for a deeper analysis: A. Wiebe, *wrp* 2002, 283, the position paper of the *Max-Planck-Institut*, GRUR Int. 2002, 319 as well as F. Henning-Bodewig, *GRUR Int.* 2002, 389.

18　Green Paper 15, 16.

19　Green Paper, 7 with reference to the UK.

the Commission intends to broaden the notion of misleading advertising.[20] Reaching far beyond the existing approaches, the Green Paper on Consumer Protection then discusses the possible choice between a 'special' i.e. a sector specific and a 'mixed approach', *i.e.* a comprehensive legislative framework directive, supplemented by targeted directives. Implicitly the Commission seems to favour a mixed or combined approach. The Green Paper on Consumer Protection provides little help, however, in answering the question what such a framework could and should look like, as the issue of how the different regulatory pieces might be merged remains unclear. The Commission refers to some vague idea of a 'framework directive', and leaves it open whether it should be a directive in the proper sense, a regulation, some sort of a new approach type regulation, or something inspired by the concept of co-regulation.[21]

The regulatory philosophy of the draft Regulation is completely different. The draft is based on a problem-related approach, thereby heavily relying on the Green Paper on Commercial Communication.[22] Eight forms of sales promotion are subject to regulation:[23] (i) simple price reductions; (ii) quantity discounts; (iii) coupons and vouchers; (iv) free gifts; *i.e.* gifts offered unconditional on sale; (v) premiums considered to be offers other than discounts which are provided to the consumer once the latter has ordered or bought the promoted product or service; (vi) promotional contests involving questions to consumers, the answer to which requires certain skills; (vii) promotional games, where the winner is designated by chance and where no payment is required to participate; and (viii) promotional games, where the winner is designated by chance and where no payment nor obligation to buy is required to participate. The Communication starts from the idea that three types of provisions are necessary: (1) *harmonisation of certain provisions concerning the use and communication of sales promotions*; (2) *the replacement of certain disproportionate restrictions*, and (3) *the application of mutual recognition*. In the first area full harmonisation is needed, it is argued, in order to ensure effective protection of European consumers.[24] The second area is closely linked to the first. Bans and restrictions shall be lifted in the name of an increased freedom to import services, the freedom of establish-

---

[20] Green Paper, 16.
[21] Green Paper, 15 and 16.
[22] COM (96) 192 final.
[23] Communication on Sales Promotion, (COM (2001) 546 final, 4.
[24] Id, 7.

48

ment, the export of services, and the removal of appreciable distortions of competition.[25] The remaining national requirements on sales promotions shall be eliminated by reference to the principal of mutual recognition.[26]

The Follow-up Communication to the Green Paper on EU Consumer Protection from the 11. June 2002[27] underlines the Commission's understanding that the proposed framework directive does not contradict its other draft proposal on sales promotions.[28] The Commission sticks to the idea of a framework directive whose major elements are laid down in the Annex I to the Communication.[29] Further research shall be undertaken with respect to issues left open, including the concept of fair trading, the necessity for establishing a regulatory committee, and on the role and function of consumer organisations.[30] An expert committee composed of national governmental experts is expected to provide pressure towards the further development of the initiative. Its final results will be made public.[31] Perhaps in order to counterbalance the force of this body comprised of governmental expertise, a working group of independent academics is envisaged.[32] Quite surprisingly, the Follow-up Communication announces the publication of a proposal for a legal instrument on enforcement co-operation by the end of 2002, following consultation with national governments and enforcement authorities that are most concerned.[33] The previous research undertaken, as well as the Communication on Consumer Protection, have not discussed enforcement issues.

2.   The Prevailing EC Approach – Chances and Limits of
      Harmonisation and Country of Origin Principle in Marketing
      Practices Regulation

So far the European Community has relied on harmonisation as the appropriate means to set a framework on fair trading. The idea behind it is that harmonisation is needed to unite two objectives, freedom of trade and services

---

[25] Id, 8.

[26] Id, 8.

[27] COM (2002) 289 final, Communication from the Commission, Follow-up Communication to the Green Paper on EU Consumer Protection: 'Follow-up'

[28] Follow-up, 12.

[29] Follow-up, 18.

[30] Follow-up, 8, 14, 15.

[31] Follow-up, 16.

[32] Follow-up, 16.

[33] Follow-up, 3, 14.

as well as consumer protection. Only such a tight regulatory framework is expected to guarantee the overall objective, which is to realise the Common and later to complete the Internal Market. Little attention has been devoted so far to the second basic principle already enshrined in the Single European Act, although it has not really been applied: the concept of mutual recognition of Member States' fair trading rules. It seems as if the European Community is reluctant because of uncertainty on the point whether or not the Member States have the same or equivalent standards in the field of marketing. However, two important exceptions have been made, in directive 89/522/EEC on television without frontiers and directive 2000/31/EC on e-commerce. At first glance the two recent initiatives of the Commission do not fit very well into the bifurcation between harmonisation and mutual recognition, though it may appear that the initiatives may be related to the still prevailing concept of harmonisation in the case of the Green Paper on Consumer Protection and mutual recognition in the case of the Draft Proposal for a Regulation on Sales Promotion.[34]

A deeper look at the prevailing approaches demonstrates that the European Community has rendered both concepts more flexible, as they seem of limited value for the integration process, at least in their proper form. Both concepts, however, trust in mandatory regulation alone. They do not consider the combination of mandatory and voluntary regulation, which might be of particular importance in the field of marketing practices. This is likewise true for the idea, to combine harmonisation and the country of origin principle, a proposal which has remained confined to academic writing so far.

(a)   The heterogeneous picture of harmonisation

According to the general competence norm in Art. 94 of the Treaty, the Community 'shall issue directives for the approximation of such laws, regulations or administrative provisions of the Member States as directly affect the establishment or functioning of the common market'. This approximation of laws is commonly known under the term harmonisation. The Community has pursued different harmonisation approaches within the context of fair-trading directives. One can classify the approaches according to the degree of harmonisation and the scope of harmonisation.

With regard to the degree of harmonisation, one can fundamentally distin-

---

[34]   See under III.

guish between full harmonisation and minimum harmonisation. Both types oblige the Member States to completely implement the standards required by the directive. But whereas full harmonisation directives do not provide for any national deviation from those standards, minimum-harmonisation directives confer the freedom on the Member States to adopt more detailed or stricter rules in the areas covered by the respective directive. As a combined type there are directives following basically a full harmonisation approach, but allowing national variations in explicitly specified matters.

- Full harmonisation Directives: Directive 84/450/EEC[35] on misleading and comparative advertising as amended by Directive 97/55/EEC,[36] as far as comparative advertising is concerned (Art. 7 paragraph 2); Directive 92/28/EEC[37] on medicinal products for human use; Directive 95/46/EC[38] on data protection; Directive 2000/13/EC[39] on advertising for foodstuffs; Directive 2000/31/EC[40] on E-Commerce; Common Position of a Directive concerning the distance marketing of consumer financial services.[41]
- Full harmonisation Directives allowing national deviation: The articles in brackets indicate deviation provision; Directive 93/22/EEC[42] on

---

[35] Council Directive 84/450/EEC of 10 September 1984 relating to the approximation of the laws, regulations and administrative provisions of the Member States concerning misleading advertising, OJ L 250, 19 September 1984, 17.

[36] Directive 97/55/EC of European Parliament and of the Council of 6 October 1997 amending Directive 84/450/EEC concerning misleading advertising so as to include comparative advertising, OJ L 290, 23 October 1997, 18.

[37] Council Directive 92/28/EEC of 31 March 1992 on the advertising of medicinal products for human use, OJ L 113, 30 April 1992, 13.

[38] Directive 95/46/EC of the European Parliament and of the Council of 24 October 1995 on the protection of individuals with regard to the processing of personal data and on the free movement of such data, OJ L 281, 23 November 1995, 31.

[39] OJ L 109, 06.05.2000, p. 29 (ex Council Directive 79/112/EEC of 18 December 1978 on the approximation of the laws of the Member States relating to the labelling, presentation and advertising of foodstuffs for sale to the ultimate consumer, OJ L 33, 08 February 1979, 1.

[40] Directive 2000/31/EC of the European Parliament and of the Council of 8 June 2000 on certain legal aspects of information society services, in particular electronic commerce, in the Internal Market (Directive on electronic commerce), OJ L 178, 17 July 2000, 1.

[41] Amended proposal for a European Parliament and Council Directive concerning the distance marketing of consumer financial services and amending Directives 97/7/EC and 98/27/EC, (2000/C 177 E/04), COM(1999) 385 final, OJ C 177 E, 26 June 2000, 21.

[42] Council Directive 93/22/EEC of 10 May 1993 on investment services in the securities field, OJ L 141, 11 June 1993, 27.

investment services in the securities field (Art. 20 paragraph 5; Art. 21 paragraph 3).

- Minimum harmonisation Directives: The articles in brackets indicate the minimum harmonisation approach: Directive 84/450/EEC[43] on misleading and comparative advertising as amended by Directive 97/55/EEC,[44] as far as misleading advertising is concerned (Art. 7 paragraph 1); Directive 85/577/EEC[45] on door-to-door sales (Art. 8); Directive 87/102/EEC[46] on consumer credits as amended by Directive 98/7/EC[47] (Art. 15);Directive 89/552/EEC[48] – "Television without frontiers" – as amended by Directive 97/36/EC[49] (Art. 3 paragraph 1); Directive 97/7/EC[50] on distance selling (Art. 14); Directive 98/43/EC[51] on tobacco advertising (Art. 5).

With regard to the scope of harmonisation, there exist: (1) horizontal har-

---

[43] Council Directive 84/450/EEC of 10 September 1984 relating to the approximation of the laws, regulations and administrative provisions of the Member States concerning misleading advertising, OJ L 250, 19 September 1984, 17.

[44] Directive 97/55/EC of European Parliament and of the Council of 6 October 1997 amending Directive 84/450/EEC concerning misleading advertising so as to include comparative advertising, OJ L 290, 23 October 1997, 18.

[45] Council Directive 85/577/EEC of 20 December 1985 to protect the consumer in respect of contracts negotiated away from business premises, OJ L 372, 31 December 1985, 31.

[46] Council Directive 87/102/EEC of 22 December 1986 for the approximation of the laws, regulations and administrative provisions of the Member States concerning consumer credit, OJ L 42, 12 February 1987, 48.

[47] Directive 98/7/EC of the European Parliament and of the Council of 16 February 1998 amending Directive 87/102/EEC for the approximation of the laws, regulations and administrative provisions of the Member States concerning consumer credit, OJ L 101, 01 April 1998, 17.

[48] Council Directive (89/552/EEC) of 3 October 1989 on the co-ordination of certain provisions laid down by law, regulation or administrative action in Member States concerning the pursuit of television broadcasting activities, OJ L 298, 17 October 1989, 23.

[49] Directive 97/36/EC of the European Parliament and of the Council amending Council Directive 89/552/EEC on the co-ordination of certain provisions laid down by law, regulation or administrative action in Member States concerning the pursuit of television broadcasting activities, OJ L 202, 30 July 1997, 60.

[50] Directive 97/7/EC of the European Parliament and of the Council of 20 May 1997 on the protection of consumers in respect of distance contracts, OJ L 144, 04 June 1997, 19.

[51] Directive 98/43/EC of the European Parliament and of the Council of 6 July 1998 on the approximation of the laws, regulations and administrative provisions of the Member States relating to the advertising and sponsorship of tobacco products, OJ L 213, 30 July 1998, 9.

monisation and (2) vertical harmonisation. Whereas horizontal harmonisation approximates the national advertising laws in general, vertical harmonisation is more restrained and approximates the laws according to a specific object of reference.

- Horizontal-harmonisation Directives: Directive 84/450/EEC on misleading and comparative advertising as amended by Directive 97/55/EEC.
- Vertical-harmonisation Directives: (a) According to the trade practice: Directive 85/577/EEC on door-to-door sales; Directive 97/7/EC on distance selling; Common Position of a Directive concerning the distance marketing of consumer financial services. (b) According to the medium: Directive 89/552/EEC – "Television without frontiers" – as amended by Directive 97/36/EC; Directive 2000/31/EC on E-Commerce.(c) According to the product: Directive 87/102/EEC on consumer credit as amended by Directive 98/7/EC; Directive 92/28/EEC on medicinal products for human use; Directive 93/22/EEC on investment services in the securities field; Directive 98/43/EC on tobacco advertising; Common Position of a Directive concerning the distance marketing of consumer financial services; Directive 2000/13/EC on advertising for foodstuffs. (d) According to the purpose: Directive 95/46/EC on data protection.

(b)   The half-hearted implementation of the country of origin principle

The Community introduced the country of origin principle in the Television-without-frontiers Directive as well as in the E-Commerce Directive. Both of the Directives concern so-called 'multi-state acts of advertising', i.e. the single advertising act emanating from one country has an effect on the markets of several other countries simultaneously, as is generally the case in cross-border media (as in all kinds of commercial-communications media) and in Europe-wide marketing concepts. If the alternative principle of country of determination applied in such instances, advertisers would be obliged to know the advertising and competition-law rules in every country where their advertising had any perceptible effects. The larger the number of legal systems referred to, the less practicable it becomes to assess the lawfulness of advertising for each place of business separately. The use of the principle of the country of determination raises particular difficulties in cases where the accessibility of the advertisement may no longer be controlled (e.g. advertising on the Internet, where advertisers cannot prevent users from a specific country from accessing their websites).[52] On the other hand, one has to consider the risk to consumers of a so-called 'race to the bottom'. As Directives predominantly provide for minimum harmonisation, companies might try to launch their advertising from the Member States that do not go beyond the minimum standard. As, in turn, the Member States have a strong interest in commercial activity in their countries, they might in addition be incited even to lower their legal requirements (to the limit of the minimum). One may wonder whether this would be detrimental to consumers.[53] The concept of the country of origin principle is likely to foster minimum harmonisation or at least does not do very much to encourage full harmonisation.[54] The effects of the country of origin principle are even more far reaching in areas where there is no harmonisation at all. Here there is not even a minimum level of rules available and the race to the bottom might become a plummet to the bottom.

(aa) The Television without frontiers Directive

The country of origin principle was first introduced in the *Television without frontiers* Directive (Directive 89/522/EEC[55] as amended by Directive 97/36/EC[56]) known as 'transmission-state principle'. The key provision of the transmission-state principle is Art. 2a paragraph 1, according to which 'Member States shall ensure freedom of reception and shall not restrict re-transmissions on their territory of television broadcasts from other Member States for reasons which fall within the fields co-ordinated by this Directive'. The scope of the transmission-state principle is linked to Art. 2 paragraph 1, according to which 'each Member State shall ensure that all television broadcasts transmitted by broadcasters under its jurisdiction comply with the rules of the system of law applicable to broadcasts intended for the public in that Member State'.

The impact of the transmission-state principle becomes clear in combination with the minimum standard principle (Art. 3 paragraph 1).[57] The Direc-

---

[52] N. Dethloff, *Commercial Communications* (Issue 22, December 1999), 2, 4.

[53] P. Mankowski, GRUR Int. 1999, 909, 914.

[54] G. Bender and C. Sommer, RIW 2000, 260 , 262.

[55] OJ L 298, 17 October 1989, 23.

[56] OJ L 202, 30 July 1997, 60.

[57] T. Bodewig, GRUR Int. 2000, 475 (478).

tive 89/522/EEC regulates how much, when, under which circumstances, and which kind of television advertising (including sponsoring and Tele-shopping) is allowed. Member States have to implement these minimum standards into their national law. They may, however, adopt stricter rules.[58] It is the possible divergence of rules which gives the transmission-state principle its specific importance: on the one hand, the transmission-state principle intends to ensure free movement of broadcasts without secondary control on the same grounds in the receiving Member States;[59] on the other hand, the divergent Member States' regulations represent incentives for secondary control to the receiving Member States. In *De Agostini and TV-Shop*[60] the Court held that the Directive did not in principle preclude the application of national rules with the general aim of consumer protection, provided that they did not involve secondary control of television broadcasts in addition to the control which the broadcasting Member State must carry out.[61]

Although the co-ordinated fields are restrained, the transmission-state principle is of a comprehensive nature. It applies unconditionally to broadcasts from other Member States. There is only one exception to this rule, namely the ability of a Member State to provisionally suspend broadcasts emanating from another Member State, if these broadcasts 'manifestly, seriously and gravely' infringe one of the rules on protection of minors (Art. 2a paragraph 2 in connection with Art. 22 and Art. 22a).

(bb) The E-Commerce Directive

Directive 2000/31/EC applies to all information society services within the meaning of Art. 1 Nr. 2 Directive 98/34/EC, as amended by Directive 98/48/EC according to Art. 2 a) Directive 2000/31/EC, which means basically to all online-services, such as the sale of goods and services, electronic newspapers, search-engines, discussion-groups and so forth.[62] However, the Directive does not apply to tax-issues; protection of personal data and privacy as covered by Directive 95/46/EC and 97/66/EC; cartel-law; the services of

---

[58] Cf. N. Reich and A. Rosenboom, *Verbraucher und Recht im elektronischen Rechtsverkehr*, 2000, 7.

[59] Cf. recital 15 of Directive 89/522/EEC.

[60] ECJ, 9 July 1997, Joined cases C-34/95, C-35/95 and C-36/95 – *Konsumentenombudsmannen vs. Agostini Förlag and TV-Shop i Sverige*, (1997) ECR, I-3843.

[61] ECJ, 9 July 1997, Joined cases C-34/95, C-35/95 and C-36/95 – *Konsumentenombudsmannen vs. Agostini Förlag and TV-Shop i Sverige*, (1997) ECR, I-3843, at 32 to 34.

[62] A. Waldenberger, EuZW 1999, 296.

notaries and similar professions, as long as they have a direct or indirect connection to the exercise of public authority; the representation of a client and defence of his interests in front of the courts; and gambling activities which involve wagering a stake with monetary value in games of chance according to Art. 1 (5) d Directive 2000/31/EC.

In order to remove the obstacles hampering the free exchange of information services, the Directive provides a country of origin principle, which resembles the one provided for in the Directive Television without frontiers. The applicability of the country of origin principle to information society services including commercial communication[63] is laid down in Art 3 para 1 and 2 of Directive 2000/31/EC. Every Member State is obliged according to Art. 3 para 1 to ensure that information society services established on its territory comply with the national provisions applicable in the Member States in question, provided that they come under the notion of the so-called 'co-ordinated field'. This term is defined in Art. 2 lit g Directive 2000/31/EC. Member States in which the service provider is not established are basically not entitled to take any actions against the information society service or the commercial communication according to Art. 3 (2) Directive 2000/31/EC. The provision is governed by the basic concept to keep Member States, including their courts,[64] in which the service provider is not located, away from taking any action due to a violation of the Member State's legislation in the co-ordinated field against a service provider who is established in another Member State.

The 'co-ordinated field' to which the country of origin principle applies is determined as the 'requirements laid down in Member States' legal systems applicable to Information Society Service Providers or Information Society services, regardless of whether they are of a general nature or specifically designed for them' (Art. 2 lit. g). The co-ordinated field concerns requirements with which the service provider has to comply in respect of the taking up and the pursuit of an information society service. It must be noted that the co-ordinated field is very broad. It incorporates all Member State legislation applicable to information society services or service providers directly or non-specifically, except requirements applicable to the goods as such, their delivery, or to services not provided via electronic means according to Art. 2 (h) ii) Directive 2000/31/EC. Therefore, the country of origin principle is far reaching. It is not only the Member State legislation as harmonised through

---

[63] A. Waldenberger, EuZW 1999, 298; P. Mankowski, GRUR Int. 1999, 912.
[64] G. Spindler, MMR 1999, 206; Appel and Grapperhaus, WRP 1999, 1252.

Directive 2000/31/EC, which is subject to the country of origin principle, but also all other Member State legislation applicable to information society service providers in general, such as price regulations, especially rebates, gifts, premiums etc. Its far-reaching effect has to be kept in mind when applying the rules developed in *De Agostini*. Due to the fact that a second control should be excluded in the "co-ordinated field", other States than the one in which the service provider is established basically are excluded from taking any actions against the information society service or the commercial communication.

As far as consumer protection is concerned, the exclusion of contractual obligations from the country of origin principle as enshrined in the annex of the Directive is of the utmost importance. However, it is not clearly recognisable what is meant by "obligations resulting out of consumer contracts". According to recital 56 the Directive "cannot have the result of depriving the consumer of the protection afforded to him by the mandatory rules relating to contractual obligations of the law of the Member State in which he has his habitual residence". Contractual obligations here are defined to include the information on the essential elements of the content of the contract including consumer rights. The entire law applicable to contractual obligations resulting out of consumer contracts is to be determined through the Member State in which the consumer is habitually resident.

(c) Harmonisation and country of origin principle combined

Strictly speaking directives 89/522/EEC and 2000/31/EC combine harmonisation and the country of origin principle. However, combining means that both approaches exist side-by-side. The concept which has been proposed differs from existing approaches in that the country of origin principle should be based upon a set of harmonised rules.[65] The advantage seems to be obvious. A set of rules guarantees a common standard of Community law. The country of origin, however, is and remains responsible for the execution and enforcement of the harmonised Community standards. In the case of multi-state advertising or more broadly speaking of transborder advertising, the

---

[65] To my knowledge, the first discussion of such a concept was N. Reich, 'Rechtsprobleme grenzüberschreitender irreführender Werbung im Binnenmarkt' RabelsZ 56 (1992) S. 444. The idea was re-introduced by F. Henning-Bodewig, 'E-Commerce und Irreführende Werbung – Auswirkungen des Herkunftslandsprinzips auf das europäische und deutsche Irreführungsrecht', wrp 2001, 771.

responsibilities are clearly shaped. The whole debate over whether the country of origin or the country of determination has to observe the Community standards becomes superfluous. Whilst the idea is fascinating, the limits of the concept are likewise evident. It is bound to mandatory regulation alone. There is no space for non-binding rules or for the combination of binding and non-binding rules. However, it seems to be as if a new initiative has to fully consider the possible means of integrating non-binding rules into a general legislative framework.

3.   The Urgent Need for a New Approach – Beyond Harmonisation and Country of Origin Principle

The driving force in the recent debate on a general legislative framework is consumer protection and the growing quest for consistency and coherence in Community legislation. The two recent initiatives, the Green Paper on Consumer Protection and the Proposal for a Regulation on Sales Promotion largely reflect the prevailing regulatory options; the country of origin principle is to be found in the Proposal for a Regulation on Sales Promotion and the harmonisation in the Green Paper on Consumer Protection. The papers and the strategies behind them are linked to different political options enshrined in different directorates within the European Commission. The Green Paper on Consumer Protection has been developed by DG SANCO, and it bears a strong consumer impetus. The contrary is true for the Proposal. It is DG Market who is behind it, and which tries to link the Proposal for a Regulation on Sales Promotion to the successful policy based on the Green Paper on Commercial Communications. Whilst it is true that the Green Paper on Consumer Protection opens up a new debate over new forms and methods of regulation, it does not really push the development forcefully ahead. There is more needed than a political declaration to seek new forms of regulation. A general legislative framework on fair trading has to be shaped along the line of the New Approach on Technical Standards and Harmonisation. At least, this is the hypothesis that I would like to defend.

(a)   The first option – the legitimating basis of the country of origin
principle in commercial communications

The Green Paper on Commercial Communications in the Internal Market[66] adopted in 1996 paved the way for the elaboration of the Communication

---

[66] COM (96) 192 final; cf. the follow-up to the Green paper COM (98) 121 final.

on the Proposal for a Regulation of the European Parliament and the Council concerning Sales Promotion in the Internal Market.[67] The Proposal for a Regulation on Sales Promotion is the second strike after the adoption of the E-Commerce Directive in 2000. The Green Paper on Commercial Communications comprehends by 'commercial communications' all forms of advertising, direct marketing, sponsorship, sales promotions and public relations promoting products and services (without packaging). It deals to a considerable extent with issues and features that might ideally characterise a general approach towards fair trading. The Green Paper on Consumer Protection devotes Part II to an evaluation of the need for Community action. The topic is considered to constitute an area where there is a high-ranking need for action, since the Internal Market objective for commercial communications might not be met at the current time, because national measures – in the relevant fields of unfair competition law, consumer protection law and specific legislation for the protection of the wider public interest – diverge substantially from each other and are regarded as potential barriers to cross-frontier activity. As a follow-up the Commission established a Commercial Communications Expert Group, in order to identify harmonisation needs, which has elaborated upon Directive 2000/31/EC on e-commerce and the Proposal for a Regulation on Sales Promotion. When the E-Commerce directive had been adopted under the flag of the country of origin principle, at least in the field of marketing practices, rumours were going around that the Commission would favour the country of origin principle as a general rule to overcome divergences in the Member States' regulations on marketing practices as well. However, the Proposal for a Regulation on Sales Promotion, whilst breathing the regulatory philosophy of the country of origin principle, relies mainly on harmonisation, the country of origin principle being reduced to a means of last resort with an unclear scope of application.[68]

(b)   The second option – the legitimating basis for harmonisation in consumer protection

The Council Resolution[69] of 19 January 1999 on the Consumer Dimension of the Information Society has strengthened the Commission's commitment.

---

67   COM (2001), 546 final.
68   See S. Göhre, 'Frischer Wind aus Brüssel', wrp 2002, 36, 42.
69   OJ C 23, 28 January 1999, 1.

The Council recognises that consumers are 'particularly concerned by issues related to fair marketing practices' (recital 4 lit. d). It considers it necessary to establish consumer confidence by the 'protection of consumers from unsolicited, misleading and unfair marketing practices, including advertising' (recital 6 lit. c). Therefore, the Council invites the Commission 'to examine existing Community consumer-related legislation in the new circumstances arising from the information society, to identify possible loopholes in this legislation concerning specific problems in the context of the information society and to identify possible areas where additional regulatory action may be necessary' (No. I 1).[70]

The idea of a general legislative framework on fair trading in transactions between consumers and businesses was highlighted in the Commission's Consumer Policy Action Plan 1999-2001.[71] The Action Plan commits itself *inter alia* to grant full respect for consumers' economic and legal interests (Section 5). It recognises that a substantial regulatory framework is already in place, but that a more up-to-date regulatory framework is necessary. It recognises that the recent developments in product and service markets and the adoption of the Amsterdam Treaty call for a consolidation of existing legislation and its updating where necessary. The Plan becomes fairly concrete as it states that the 'Commission will also examine the feasibility of a general legislative framework on fair trading' (Section 5.2).

The Action Plan's commitments gain still more weight, since the Council welcomed the Plan in its Resolution of June 28, 1999.[72] Here, the Council requires consistency of and complementarity between the different Community activities and puts specific emphasis on economic and legal interests (as well as on health and safety; No. II 1). The Council asks the Commission to continue its active policy aiming at the maintenance of market transparency and market balance in the interests of the consumer, and to review in this context existing Community consumer protection legislation and propose new provisions where necessary (No. II 4).

The adoption of the Green Paper of Consumer Protection must be seen as the direct result of the EC's policy in the field of consumer protection. The Council Regulation of 19th January 1999 served as a starter for DG SANCO

---

[70] The Commission has launched a study, see PriceWaterhouseCoopers/University of Utrecht/ University of Tilburg, *Final Report Study on Consumer Law and the Information Society*, 17 August 2000.

[71] COM (98) 696.

[72] OJ C 206, 21 July 1999, 1.

to step into the field of fair trading. Therefore, it is no surprise that the Green Paper on Consumer Protection expresses the intention to develop a general legislative framework with particular emphasis on consumer protection alone. DG SANCO remains within the ambit of its competences when it narrows down the scope of application of the envisaged general legislative framework to consumer protection.[73] German commentators advocate a general legislative framework on fair trading, which is not bound to the protection of consumers, and which covers the interests of the competitors as well.[74] The most recently adopted Communication on the Consumer Policy Strategy 2002-2006,[75] reiterates DG SANCO's intention to come up with a follow up Communication to the Green Paper on Consumer Protection. It is by no means clear how the Communication will look like and what approach might be chosen. The Commission sticks to harmonisation as the appropriate means, though mutual recognition might suffice if a sufficient degree of harmonisation has been achieved.

(c) The third option – the feasibility of the new approach on technical standards and regulations in marketing practices regulation

Any effort to develop a general legislative framework on fair trading can certainly not be restricted to a reiteration of the old arguments pro and con harmonisation and country of origin principle. It has to take into account changes in the legal, economic and social environment. The European Community today is hardly comparable to the European Community of the early sixties. The integration process is far advanced, and the regulatory network in the regulation of marketing practices has become dense and sophisticated. The Single European Act has pushed the European Community into action, and paved the way for the adoption of a whole set of regulatory measures, quite a number of them dealing with marketing practices. Globalisation and the new economy raise new challenges to a supranational though regional legal order. Forty years later major upheavals have taken place. If anything, solid reasons are needed more than ever to justify further Community regulation.

The hypothesis defended here is that the country of origin principle is not

---

[73] COM (2001) 531 final, 11.

[74] See Max-Planck-Institut, Stellungnahme zum EU-Grünbuch zum Verbraucherschutz, GRUR Int. 2002, 319, 322; Fezer, above note 3, 991; Schricker and Henning-Bodewig, above note 3, 1367

[75] COM (2002), 208 final, under 3.1.2.1.

the appropriate means to guarantee that fairness is established in the marketing of products and services in the European Community. However, harmonisation alone does not suffice to overcome different Member States' marketing practices regulation. A joint approach is needed, which combines mandatory legislation with new forms of self-regulation. The European Community has developed in the New Approach on harmonisation of technical standards and regulation a regulatory technique whose feasibility might and should be tested to get to grips with the development of an appropriate legislative framework on fair trading. The philosophy behind the New Approach led to the adoption of the Single European Act, still the most powerful amendment of the Treaty of Rome. One may even conclude that the legal principles enshrined in the New Approach have gained quasi-constitutional character, at least as long as the European legal order is interpreted together with the ECJ as a constitutional charter.[76] It will have to be demonstrated that the New Approach might not be transferred 'tel quel' to fair trading, but that a modified new approach on fair trading allows to set new incentives in the long lasting debate. The Green Paper on Consumer Protection does not request such an option; however, its open-minded spirit permits us to look for new solutions in the thorny field of marketing practices regulation.

III.   A General Clause on Fair Trading – Justification and Proposal for Action

There is a growing concern in the European Commission and the Member States on the consistency of European rules on marketing practices. The striving for consistency and coherence, however, does not suffice to build up a fully fledged regulatory framework on fair trading. The classical debate results from differing Member States' legislation. This is still the case, as the common law Member States remain resistant to the introduction of broad principles in their national legal orders. The major impetus may be derived from the need to improve consumer protection. If such reasoning is correct, the 'burden of proof' for the need for a general legislative framework on fair trading lies with consumer protection.

---

[76] H-W. Micklitz, *Internationales Produktsicherheitsrecht*, 1995, 144.

1.   General Concepts in the Member States

Thirteen out of the fifteen Member States rely on a general clause to regulate fair trading. Five different legal instruments are on the table: *bonos mores* (Austria, Germany, Greece and Portugal); *fair commercial practices* (Belgium, Italy, Luxembourg and Spain), *good marketing practices* (Denmark, Finland and Sweden), *unlawfulness* (Netherlands) and *fault* (France). It seems as if the choice of the appropriate wording is still very much influenced by the circle of law to which the country belongs. None of the countries, however, refers to the prevailing concept of the control of unfair terms along the line of Directive 93/13/EEC – *good faith*.[77] The idea of *bonos mores* in Austria, Greece and Portugal is derived from the German civil law tradition; *fair commercial practices* in Belgium, Italy, Luxembourg and Spain seems to unite the countries with a code civile tradition – this might even be true for France, at least in the way Article 1382 CC is applied by the courts;. *good marketing practices* demonstrates the compactness of the Scandinavian countries. Only the Netherlands seems to follow its own way. The situation is different again in United Kingdom and Ireland. The UK Fair Trading Act is under revision. The government's position is essentially to give the OFT the role of developing *core principles* which the codes should comply with. Thereby, the UK seems to recognise the need of some sort of general guidelines that will bind suppliers and traders. This overall objective becomes clear from the proposed core principles: *truthful adverts, clear helpful and adequate pre-contractual information, clear, and fair contracts.*

The simple finding whether there is a general clause or not in the Member States is of limited value. Of greater importance is the concept of competition, which lies behind the respective legislation. It becomes clear in the relationship between fair trading legislation and consumer protection legislation. There are Member States that rely on one and the same legislation to cope with the protection of both competitors and consumers against unfair marketing practices. Here consumer protection is not explicitly mentioned as a policy objective. The origins of the Acts may be found in early legislation at the beginning of last century where consumer protection was not yet an issue. Unfair trading legislation should avoid 'aggressive' competition between competitors alone. When consumer protection arrived on the agenda, the scope and reach of these Acts were simply enlarged without substantially

---

[77]   The wording appears once in Article 5 of the Spanish Ley de Competencia Disleal.

altering the policy direction of the legislation. This approach may be found in Austria, Germany, and Portugal. Somewhat more complicated is the situation in countries in which consumer protection may even be condensed in a separate piece of legislation, where unfair trading, however, is not regarded as being a subject of consumer concern (France, Ireland, Portugal, Spain). Here protection of consumers against unfair marketing practices may only be achieved either through the application of general legislation that aims at the protection of competitors or through separate legislative rules. The third group concerns countries that have adopted rules about marketing practices which aim *inter alia* explicitly at the protection of consumers. This is true for the Scandinavian countries as well as for Belgium. Finland is the only country which adopted separate fair trading acts on consumer protection and on unfair trade practices.

2.   The Added Value of a General Legislative Framework for Consumers

There is a real economic and consumer policy problem which calls for action. The economic dimension of fair trading rules can best be demonstrated by the growing importance of electronic commerce.[78] Consumers and consumer transactions are at the forefront of the development here. Business and business transactions might follow suit and bypass the turnover via the internet in the years to come. However, for the time being, most transactions on the internet are taken by consumers, here understood as final consumers in the EC legal terminology. They need a uniform legal basis on which they can rely once they contact suppliers via the internet. Directive 2000/31/EC tries to overcome divergences between the Member States by relying on the country of origin principle. Whilst this principle might help to challenge outdated and burdensome rules on prices in the Member States, it cannot cover those consumer issues where common rules are needed. This might explain why the Directive 2000/31/EC contains numerous exemptions, most prominently with regard to consumer protection. Globalisation via the internet underlines the necessity of a legislative framework which pays due regard to consumer protection.[79] However, binding rules are needed, which set mandatory rules.

---

[78] See PriceWaterhouseCoopers *et al*, above note 70.

[79] The OECD Guidelines for Consumer Protection in the Context of Electronic Commerce fit well into such an overall picture, reprinted in Reich and Nordhausen, *Verbraucher und Recht im elektronischen Rechtsverkehr*, (2000) 195.

These cannot be developed at the international level. Here there is room for the European Community to step in and to initiate the elaboration of a tight regulatory framework on fair trading.

The added value of a general legislative framework on fair trading is obvious. It could take the role and function of an *'umbrella'* and a *'safety net'*,[80] – an umbrella to cover all the piecemeal regulations and put them under a common regime, and safety net to get to grips with issues that are not subject to special rules. European directives dealing with fair trading neither provide for an umbrella nor for a safety net. Their lack has become abundantly clear in *Direct Shopping*, the well-known litigation on trans-border advertising.[81] The subsequent political debate turned very much around the lack of appropriate and enforceable judicial and administrative remedies in the Member States, thereby paving the way for the adoption of Directive 98/27/EC. Less attention was attributed to the difficulties that French and German courts met in finding out whether consumers were misled or not. At the heart of the matter were the rules on the burden of proof, where German and French laws differ, and where Directive 84/450/EEC on misleading advertising is of little help. As long as conflicts have no trans-border dimension, Member States' courts and administrative authorities overcome these difficulties by referring to the general clause[82] – in so far as there is one!

There is an area where both dimensions are coming together, globalisation via the internet and unsolved issues of consumer protection: *sweepstakes*. Consumer organisations all over Europe might report endless stories concerning sweepstakes, where consumers were cheated and where the organisers managed to escape legal sanctions.[83] Globalisation and the internet have increased the sheer number of sweepstakes, and made it even easier to hide

---

[80] The description is taken from A-D Bruun Nielsen, *Analysis of the possibility of introducing a general clause on good market behaviour into Community law*, – Report prepared for the Nordic Council of Ministers, TemaNord, February 2000.

[81] See H-W. Micklitz, 'Cross-Border Consumer Conflicts – A French-German Experience', JCP Special Issue, *European Consumer Policy After Maastricht, (1993), 411.*

[82] This is true for the Scandinavian countries, cf. Nielsen, above note 80, as well as for Germany, see the careful analysis of the German law on sweepstakes, F. Bultmann, 'Gewinnspielwerbung in Wettbewerbsverfahren des Verbraucherschutzvereins – eine rechtliche Analyse', in H-W. Micklitz (ed.), *Rechtseinheit oder Rechtsvielfalt in Europa?*, VIEW Schriftenreihe Band 1, 1996, 299.

[83] For the German law see, F. Bultmann, above note 82; for the European dimension Bob Schmitz, 'Gewinnspielwerbung in Deutschland – Kommentar zu Fritz Bultmann', in Micklitz, above note 82., 321.

the companies' identity in an inaccessible post box.[84] There seems to be no advert without a sweepstake on the internet. Globalisation of the economy makes law enforcement even harder and even more complicated. In theory only a global solution could set an end to unfair sweepstakes. In practice, delegating the problem to the international level and waiting for a global rule will easily end in never having any regulatory framework at all. The European Community has the chance to set standards which might gain importance even beyond the territory of the Member States, mainly in the Eastern European countries.[85] A European rule on sweepstakes could not be more than just a first step. Sweepstakes are in a process of constant change. That is why sweepstakes strongly support the idea of having a general legislative framework, – a safety net to guarantee effective trans-border consumer protection.

3. Possible Elements of a General Legislative Framework

The general legislative framework should be composed of three elements: the general clause, the duty to supply information, and a list of prohibited marketing practices. By and large the Green Paper on Consumer Protection underpins such a three-pronged approach. Early comments on the Green Paper on Consumer Protection point in the same direction.[86] So far, however, it is very much a German academic debate. The Green Paper on Consumer Protection has pushed all parties concerned into action. The responses are available on the Internet.[87] The reactions are far from being homogenous. This diversity is true for the Member States, but also for business.

---

[84] The German consumer organisation, the Verbraucherschutzverein in Berlin, encountered until September 2000 more than hundred transborder consumer complaints on sweepstakes offered and sent out from Member States territory to Germany. Redress in more than 50% failed, as competent authorities refused to disclose the companies identity hidden under a post box address.

[85] Bultmann, above note 83, and in the very same context, J. Franck, *Lotteries and Sweepstakes: A Common Problem to Western and Eastern Consumers,* 327.

[86] See Max-Planck-Institut, Stellungnahme zum EU-Grünbuch zum Verbraucherschutz, GRUR Int. 2002, 319, 322; Fezer, above note 3; Schricker and Henning-Bodewig, above note 3.

[87] http://europa.eu.int/comm/consumers/policy/developments/fair_comm_pract/responses/responses_en.html.

(a)   Proposal for a general clause on fair trading

> *Unfair commercial communication is prohibited; particularly unfair is commercial communication, which unduly interferes with the freedom and autonomy of market participants be they competitors or final consumers and which impedes market transparency; particularly unfair is commercial communication which is not recognisable as such, in particular through subliminal advertising*

The *general clause* should reflect the concept of workable competition.[88] The way in which suppliers are competing with each other and for customers is at its core based upon an exchange of information between the market participants, especially between suppliers and private consumers. There is no competition without communication between the supply and the demand side of the market in respect of the terms of a potential trade, like price and quality. Fair communication in the market presupposes autonomy on the side of the market participants and market transparency. Autonomy and transparency are of particular importance for consumers. Consumer orientated market transparency is the indispensable pre-condition to secure the autonomy and the sovereignty of the decision-making process. Information comes into a prominent position. That is why the general legislative framework must contain *a duty to provide information.*

The concept of fair communication does not and cannot fully explain why certain forms of commercial communication are unwanted for political reasons. It might justify public policy decisions as long as there is a link to communication, mainly with regard to the requirement of fair communications with consumers. However, outside and beyond such a linkage, Member States should keep the power to decide public policy issues. Deeply rooted moral and ethical implications come into play here, which have to be taken seriously and which do not require total harmonisation.

There is no uniform terminology on the types of commercial communication which should be prohibited. International rules refer *to honest practices*

---

[88] See Clark, *Competition as a Dynamic Process* (1961); Bartling, *Leitbilder der Wettbewerbspolitik* (1980) 20; Clark, 'Competition: Static Models and Dynamic Aspect' (1955) 45 *American Economic Review* 460; Kantzenbach, *Die Funktionsfähigkeit des Wettbewerbs*, 2nd ed. (1977) 32; Säcker, *Zielkonflikte und Koordinationsprobleme im deutschen und europäischen Kartellrecht* (1971) 32.

(Paris Convention, TRIPS and WIPO), *or legal, decent, honest and truthful advertising* (ICC); national rules range from *bonos mores*, over *good* or *fair marketing practices,* to *fault* or *unlawful behaviour.*[89] The situation in the European Community is quite specific, as there is no codified general legislative framework. However, the ECJ and secondary community law rules refer most prominently to the existence of some sort of *'fairness'.* Despite such homogeneity, there is ample evidence that the difficulty of selecting wording for a general legislative framework should not be underestimated.[90] First of all, there is the language dimension which has to be taken into account. At the international and European level, relevant regulation is officially translated. Whenever legal terms imply moral, cultural and ethical questions, literal translation is nearly impossible. Even where translation is possible, the same wording may be based on substantially different legal concepts. So there is a strong need in any effort to unify, to harmonise or to approximate legislation, to use terms which match comparable value-driven judgements. Secondly, comparative legal analysis has underlined the limited importance of the wording of the general clause in contrast to the outstanding role of the concept of competition behind it.[91] That is why the concept presented here relies on 'fair' communication. The term has a legal and a social connotation nearly worldwide, and its use might pave the way for the development of a common understanding of where to draw the borderline between legally acceptable commercial communication and those forms which might be prohibited.

The specifications in the general clause must convert the concept of competition into a concrete formula. Ideally the specifications should therefore fully reflect the basics of the concept of competition. At the heart of the

---

[89] See G.H.C: Bodenhausen, Pariser Verbandsübereinkunft zum Schutz des gewerblichen Eigentums, Köln and others, 1968, Wolfgang Fikentscher, Wettbewerbsrecht im TRIPS-Agreement der Welthandelsorganisation, GRURInt. 1995, 229; A. Heinemann, Das Kartellrecht des geistigen Eigentums im TRIPS-Übereinkommen der Welthandelsorganisation, GRURInt 1995, 535; R. Knaack, 'The Protection of Geographical Indications according to the TRIPs Agreement', in K. Beier and G. Schricker (eds), *From GATT to TRIPs*, (Weinheim and others, 1996) 117; R. Krasser, 'The Protection of Trade Secrets in the TRIPs Agreement', in *ibid*, 216; A. Kur, ' TRIPs and Trademark Law,' in ibid, 93; G. Schricker, 'Bemerkungen zum internationalen Schutz gegen unlauteren Wettbewerb', in B. Großfeld, (ed), *Festschrift für Wolfgang Fikentscher zum 70. Geburtstag*, (Tübingen: 1998) 985.

[90] In the same sense, Max-Planck-Institut, *Stellungnahme zum EU-Grünbuch zum Verbraucherschutz*, GRUR Int. 2002, 319, 322; Fezer, above note 3, 991.

[91] See Ulmer, above note 6.

matter of the concept is fair communication. Fair communication presupposes autonomy and market transparency of the market participants in the decision-making process. These two elements are given shape in the *first* specification. Autonomy and market transparency permit the realisation of a high degree of market rationality. If taken seriously, autonomy and market transparency might become powerful instruments in the realisation of fair communication all over Europe, all the more so in connection with a general duty to supply information.

Commercial communication has to be clearly separated from non-commercial communication. This distinction is behind the *second* specification. It is largely inspired by the wording of Art. 6 a) Directive 2000/31/EC. According to Art. 6 (1), 7 (1) Directive 2000/31/EC and Art. 10 (1) Directive 97/36/EC (Television without frontiers), commercial communication must be identifiable as such. According to Art. 3 (2) Common Position on Financial Services and Art. 4 (2) and (3) Directive 97/7/EC, the commercial character of any information issued for commercial purposes must be revealed. A comparison of these directives shows that the principle of 'recognisability' in commercial communication is not only laid down in the directives on E-commerce and Television without frontiers, but can be found in the directives on distance selling and financial services as well. All Member States have transferred this principle into national legislation, at least with respect to advertising on television. Some have even extended the scope of its applicability to advertising in general (Denmark, Belgium, Ireland, Portugal and Greece), as being misleading if advertising fails to clearly announce that it is advertising, or to other forms of commercial communication (Spain for distance-selling and France for the Internet). This survey suggests that the principle of recognisability represents a general principle.

There should be separate rules on duties to supply information, conformity to public policy, and breach of law. The concept of workable competition is based on the existence of reliable information. That is why duties to supply information belong to the core of the general clause. The situation is different with regard to public policy issues. They may be integrated into the concept of competition as far as there is a link to fair communication. If there is no such link, they are largely outside the concept of competition presented here. The third possible element kept outside the general clause is 'breach of law'. Again one might consider having a specification which makes clear that a violation of existing EC rules on marketing practices must be regarded as unfair within in the meaning of the general clause.

There might be arguments for and against the integration of these three elements into a general clause. The major reason to keep these issues separate stem from the need to ensure that each element receives the attention that it deserves. This is particularly true for the duty to supply information. The complexity of public policy issues is widely known. The problem is where to draw the correct borderline between those issues which should come under the scope of the proposed framework and those which should remain outside. Breach of law issues have already been subject to regulation in the EC. The point is how to link the envisaged general legislative framework to Directive 98/27 even in a revised form. Therefore all three elements raise complicated and controversial questions. At the present stage of Community law possible answers might overload the general clause and water down its leading message.

(a)   Proposal for information duties

> *Commercial Communication is deemed unfair, if it does not contain the information final consumers may legitimately expect; such as inter alia, consumer-related information requirements in existing EC regulations and EC directives, or consumer-related information on health, safety and environmental protection.*

In a concept of competition which is based on fair communication, information and market transparency are essential for consumers. Without information, they are unable to take autonomous and responsible decisions. This point is self-evident and commonplace. The crucial question concerns the quality of the information. The Treaty of Amsterdam has granted consumers a right to information. Even if the right to information is not given shape in Art. 153, its sheer existence underlines the constitutional importance of information for the completion of the Internal Market and even for integration beyond the market. Information therefore has received a prominent role in the European constitutional charter. Any legislative framework on fair trading has to be checked against the constitutional implications. The Green Paper on Consumer Protection therefore relies on Art. 153 as well to justify the need for appropriate duties to supply information.[92] *Caveat emptor* can no longer be the solution to the problem of overcoming deficits in informa-

---

[92]   COM (2001) 531 final, under 4.3., 14.

tion. The duty to supply information is placed on the business competitor in the marketplace. He has to supply the consumer with the information that he needs. More specifically, he has to *disclose all information* that the consumer may *legitimately expect* in order to be capable to fulfil his role and function in the *constitutional charter*. 'Legitimate expectations of consumers' is a well-established concept in EC law, which is employed to balance the conflicting interests between consumers and competitors.[93] It might be used to contribute to a determination of the scope and quality of the information which has to be integrated into commercial communication with consumers. Non-disclosure of such information would be regarded as unfair commercial communication.

The duty to supply information is not yet well established in the legal systems of the Member States. Duties to supply information duties are usually limited to specific media of communication or reflect the restricted scope of the relevant EC directives. In addition, one can regularly find duties to supply information in connection with price-related trade practices. A *general* duty to inform, however, is not yet established. Sweden has taken the lead in the Scandinavian countries and has introduced a duty to provide information to consumers.[94] Germany may follow suit, if the government decides to follow the proposal presented by the working group.[95] Outside the European Community, reference should be made to the United States, where disclosure of information has become a powerful instrument of the Federal Trade Commission to fight unfair marketing practices.[96] The European Community has not established such a principle, neither through primary law via the ECJ, nor

---

[93] H-W. Micklitz, 'Legitime Erwartungen als Gerechtigkeitsprinzip des europäischen Privatrechts', in L. Krämer, H-W. Micklitz, K.Tonner (eds), *Law and diffuse Interests in the European Legal Order*, (1997) 245, quite critical on the notion of legitimate expectations W-H Roth, 'Berechtigte Verbrauchererwartungen im Europäischen Gemeinschaftsrecht', in H. Schulte-Nölke and R. Schulze (eds.), *Europäische Rechtsangleichung und nationale Privatrechte*, Nomos Verlagsgesellschaft, Baden-Baden, 1999, 45.

[94] See A-D Bruun Nielsen, *Analysis of the possibility of introducing a general clause on good market behaviour into Community law, – Report prepared for the Nordic Council of Ministers*, TemaNord, February 2000.

[95] See on the background of the German reform debate, reluctant, Fezer, above note 3; in favour of a duty to provide information, Schricker and Henning-Bodewig, above note 3.

[96] In *Budget Rent-a-Car*, 113 FTC 1109 (1990) the unfairness consisted in renting cars without informing consumers about prior recall actions. In all these cases, the common element of unfairness consists in consumers not being adequately informed about the risks involved in the transaction and therefore being unable to avoid it.

through secondary Community law. However, a number of directives impose duties to supply information on the supplier before the contract is concluded, thereby deeply intervening in the contract law of the Member States.[97] These heterogeneous rules do not start from a common concept and they cannot be condensed to a single legal principle. If any conclusion might be drawn from an examination of these directives, it might be that, if there is an obligation to inform, the information must be provided clearly, comprehensibly and unambiguously[98] or briefly and accurately.[99]

The duty to supply information defined here provides for a general obligation which sets a certain framework but which needs further clarification. One option would be to define positively the information which must be made available to consumers, in an attempt to generalise from the content of the existing directives. Such an approach would lead to a very comprehensive and perhaps even overloaded rule, which might suffer from the disadvantage that it is hard to foresee all the types of information that might become relevant. That is why a general duty to supply information seems to be more appropriate. Without further specification, however, the general obligation might lack impetus. Connecting the general obligation to existing duties to supply information in directives related to consumer protection serves a twofold purpose: the general obligation is given shape through its references to other directives that indicate the direction in which the wind blows, and the existing directives would become integrated into a general legislative framework.

Duties to supply information might be related to the *content of the contract*,[100] to the *means of communication,*[101] or a combination of both.[102] The Directives resemble each other in respect of duties regarding the *contents of commercial communication*. Except for Directive 87/102/EEC on consumer credit, they all require commercial communication to indicate

---

[97] See most of all Directive 97/7 on Distant Selling, Micklitz in Grabitz and Wolf, *Fernabsatz-richtlinie*, A 3 Rdnr. 34.

[98] Art. 5 (2), Art. 7 (1) and Art. 10 (1) Dir. 2000/31; Art. 4 (2) Dir. 97/7/EC; Art. 3 (2) Draft Directive on Financial Services. The principle of transparency is enshrined in Art. 4 Dir. 93/13 as well.

[99] Art. 3 Dir. 94/47.

[100] Directive 87/102 on Consumer Credit, Directive 94/47 on Timesharing and directive 89/522 on television without frontiers with regard to teleshopping.

[101] Directive 97/7 Distant Selling, Dir. 2000/31 on E-Commerce.

[102] Common Position on Financial Services.

the identity of the supplier.[103] Except for Directive 2000/31/EC, the supplier is obliged to indicate the counter-performance for advertised goods or services,[104] and the price indication must contain all additional charges and costs.[105] Directive 97/7/EC on distance selling, Directive 2000/31/EC on e-commerce, the common position on Financial Services, Directive 94/47/EC on time-sharing and Directive 87/102/EC on consumer credit establish further information requirements. So, there is a recognised list of a broad range of types of information which should be available and which serves to illustrate what the legitimate expectations of the consumer might be. Therefore, the first specification contributes to the task of giving shape to a general duty to supply information.

Comprehensive information on health, safety and the environment are of outstanding importance for consumers, as recognised in the ICC Code of Environmental Advertising.[106] These three issues might become a major field of application for the general duty to supply information. There is a strong link here between unfair advertising resulting from non-disclosure of information and misleading advertising resulting from incomplete or false information. This linkage is also backed up by the laws of the Member States, where unfairness in connection with environmental advertising is seen to result mostly from incomplete or false information.[107] The existing rules on misleading advertising, at least in so far as they are based on Directive 84/450/EC, do not reach beyond the lacunae the ECJ refused to close up. A general duty to supply information, which makes clear that it requires disclosure of information on health, safety and environmental matters, could contribute to overcome the deficiencies of the directive on misleading advertising. This is exactly the task and function of a general legislative framework

---

[103] Art. 4 No. 1 a) Dir. 97/7/EC; Art. 5 No. 1 a) Dir. 2000/31/EC; Art. 3 (1) in combination with Annex I a) Dir. 94/47; Art. 3 (1) a) Common Position on Financial Services.

[104] Art. 4 (1) c) Dir. 97/7/EC; Art. 3 (1) c) Common Position on Financial Services; Art. 3 (1) in combination with Annex 1 i) Dir. 94/47; Art. 6 (1) second indent Dir. 87/102

[105] Art. 4 (1) c) d) g) Dir. 97/7/EC; Art. 3 c) Common Position on Financial Services; Art. 3 (1) in combination with Annex I i); Art. 6 Dir. 87/102. According to Art. 5 (2) Dir. 2000/31, it suffices to indicate whether or not an indication of prices is inclusive or exclusive of tax and delivery costs. This can be seen as a minimum requirement to be met regarding the indication of additional costs to the consumer.

[106] See details in the Code of Environmental Advertising of the International Chamber of Commerce, 1991.

[107] See N. Reich and R. Heine-Mernik (eds), *Umweltverfassung und nachhaltige Entwicklung in der Europäischen Union*, 1997.

as a safety net. If the more specific and narrower directive on misleading advertising does not apply for whatever reason, there is still the general clause on fair trading, here combined with the duty to supply information, to guarantee effective protection of consumers against selective information policies within commercial communication.

(c)   A possible list of prohibited marketing practices

There seems to be a growing preparedness, within the Commission and at least in the academic environment, to complement a general clause of fair trading with a list of prohibited marketing practices.[108] The Green Paper on Consumer Protection discusses such a list as an integral part of the so-called combined approach along the lines of the indicative list established in the Directive 93/13/EC on unfair terms in consumer contracts. However, any such list of prohibited marketing practices should not be merely indicative but mandatory. Litigation on the nature of this list, especially with regard to whether Member States are obliged to implement the list into their legal order, should be avoided.[109] The scope and reach of such a blacklist could be developed on the basis of a comparison of the respective Member States' legislation and/or established case-law. All Member States have in common rules that rohibit particular marketing practices which they deem to be 'unfair'. Marketing methods were and are a subject of particular concern for primary and secondary Community law. Where appropriate, the ECJ's decisions might be considered, and, even more importantly, secondary Community laws should be relied upon, as they define European standards – maximum and/or minimum – with regard to particular products or particular means of communication. These European rules have to be tested for their appropriateness and feasibility in order for them to become true horizontal European standards.

Without going into details,[110] the list of prohibited marketing practices

---

[108] See especially, Fezer, above n 3; but also Schricker and Henning-Bodewig, above note 3.

[109] The European Commission initiated proceedings against Sweden for the non-implementation of the indicative list in directive 93/13 on unfair terms in consumer contracts. AG *Geelhoed*, 31 January 2002, Case C-478/99 did not follow the Commission, although the ECJ seems to be prepared to use the list as a yardstick without deciding over its legal quality, ECJ, 27 June 2000, Joint Cases C-240/98 to C-244/98 – *Océano*, ECR I-4941.

[110] There would have been a lot to say on the different issues, on whether the list is complete or not. However, an in depth discussion would go far beyond the purpose of the paper.

should deal with the following issues: (1) distant and direct communication: commercial communication should not unduly interfere with the private sphere of the recipient, and it should be prohibited to supply goods or services to a consumer without their being ordered by the consumer beforehand, where such supply involves a demand for payment, (2) price: the selling price and the unit price of a good or service must be unambiguous, easily identifiable, and clearly legible. If the good or service is offered to a consumer, the price has to include all taxes; – additional rules on rebates, free gifts, sweepstakes and sales at a loss might also be considered; (3) public policy: as far as consumer interests are concerned, commercial communication should not a) prejudice respect for human dignity; b) discriminate on the grounds of race, sex or nationality; c) be offensive to religious or political beliefs, d) encourage behaviour prejudicial to health or to safety; e) encourage behaviour prejudicial to the protection of the environment and the protection of children; (4) Breach of law (Rechtsbruch): any breach of an EC regulation, EC directive or EC provision aiming at the protection of the interests of consumers, should be deemed to be unfair.[111] The Green Paper on Consumer Protection seems inclined to put non-binding marketing rules on an equal footing with binding EC law.[112]

(d)   Total vs. minimum harmonisation

The degree of harmonisation is certainly one of the most sensitive issues in the law-making procedure. This is particularly true in contract law.[113] One may wonder whether the situation in marketing practices law is different. Marketing all over Europe follows more and more the same standards. Such considerations may lie behind the European Commission's preparedness to favour full harmonisation in marketing practices regulation.[114] At first glance, the idea of a general framework directive which is shaped along the lines of the new approach seems to underpin the availability of a single fully-fledged

---

[111] However, already *de lege lata* any breach might be regarded as misleading advertising, at least if directive 84/450/EEC is read together with Art. 153 Treaty of Rome.

[112] COM (2001) 531 final, under 4.4., see for a critical comment, Max-Planck-Institut, GRUR Int. 2002, 319, 322.

[113] T. Wilhelmsson, 'Private Law in the EU: Harmonised or Fragmented Europeanisation', (2002) ERPL 77.

[114] COM (2002), 208 final, under 3.1.2.1, and COM (2002) 289 final, Follow-up Communication, 5.

concept of a general clause, supplemented by a list of prohibited marketing practices, which set common standards for all market participants. The safeguard procedure would then have to balance out conflicting interests between the Member States, in order to adapt the list of prohibited marketing practices to their actual needs. Member States would remain free within the logic of the new approach to prohibit other marketing practices, which are not blacklisted. They would then have to notify their regulatory action to the safeguard committee.

However, one may wonder, whether the new approach procedure really meets the needs of a dynamic law on fair trading which is still deeply grounded in national traditions, or whether ways and means have to be found, which enlarge the freedom of the Member States beyond the new approach-type regulation, or to put it bluntly, whether it might be better renounce the program of full harmonisation and to stick to the well-established policy of minimum harmonisation. The ample differences between technical standards and marketing practices seem to confirm such a reading. Technical standards are laid down for mass production, i.e. to solve technical issues of general importance, whereas marketing standards have always to deal with particular practices of the respective business. Marketing practices law is inherently bound to its context of application to individual cases. The whole comitology is meant to deal with conflict over general – legislative or technical – standards. That is why the parallel between technical standards and marketing practices should not be over-stretched. Technical regulation and marketing regulation have to meet different challenges. These differences have to be fully considered in the shaping of a general legislative framework. However, as far as implementation by Member States is concerned, be it through their legislative powers or by their executive branch adopting general standards on marketing practices, the new approach type regulation may well serve as a regulatory pattern. Outside and beyond this, new regulatory means have to be found – on the basis of minimum harmonisation.

IV.   SELF-REGULATION, CO-REGULATION AND CONSUMERS –
       JUSTIFICATION AND PROPOSAL FOR ACTION

A directive alone does not suffice to get to grips with fair trading. Additional instruments are needed to supplement the general clause, the duty to supply information, and the list of prohibited marketing practices. Any initiative has to consider seriously the existing self-regulation in the field of advertising and integrate it into a coherent regulatory framework. At the heart of the matter will be the proposal for a revised 'New Approach.' The Green Paper on Consumer Protection, although leaving space for non-binding rules, does not even define the possible options in soft-law making.[115] However, it quite strongly advocates the need to allow for the participation of stake-holders in the elaboration of non-binding marketing standards.[116]

1. The Situation in the Member States

The availability or non-availability of self-regulation in the Member States provides little guidance on the degree to which self-regulation serves as a means to cope with marketing practices. From a systematic point of view, it seems possible to distinguish between countries in which the promotion of self-regulation is bound to certain legal requirements and those in which self-regulation is not even explicitly mentioned as a means to foster the development of fair marketing practices. UK and Ireland are the countries in which self-regulation constitutes an integral part of the governmental policy in its striving for fair marketing standards. The enforcement authorities are requested to set incentives for trade and industry to elaborate self-regula-tion and the authorities may even have powers to approve self-regulatory measures. There seems to exist a coincidence between the lack of a general clause and a strong position on the advantages of self-regulation. However, at least two other Member States have to be mentioned in which self-regulation contributes to the implementation of fair marketing practices, though without legislative support: Italy and the Netherlands. The Scandinavian countries have their own legal culture which entrusts the ombudsman to develop guide-lines and recommendations. These are, however, state induced rules, although they are not legally binding. The lack of an official governmental policy does not mean that all the other countries do not recognise self-regulatory measures in the field of marketing practices. They exist and are the subject of analysis here, as far as is relevant. However, these codes fulfil a rather complementary function. Courts are usually not prepared to take them into account in cases of conflict.

---

[115] Green paper, 4.4.
[116] Green paper, 4.6.

2. Growing Awareness of Self-Regulation in the European Community

The large range of EC directives on marketing practices demonstrates a growing awareness of the role and function of self-regulation. Attention may be drawn to self-regulatory mechanisms in Directive 93/22/EC on investment services in the securities field; in Directive 97/7/EC on distance selling, and to Directive 2000/31/EC on e-commerce. The approaches chosen differ widely. The directive 93/22/EC lays down mandatory requirements for the development of appropriate information and advice schemes;[117] Directive 97/7/EC on distance selling must be read together with recommendation 92/295/EC on codes of practice. The latter formulates a set of principles, which might guide the elaboration of codes of practices. Some of the issues here mentioned result from unsolved problems in the legislative process.[118] The most recent and perhaps the most prominent initiative has been undertaken in the e-commerce directive. The original proposal for the promotion of self-regulation came near to the New Approach-type directives. The final adopted version is less ambitious, but it still encourages the elaboration of codes of practice with the participation of consumer organisations.[119] Of course, a number of issues have not been addressed: whether there should be binding requirements to guide the content of the codes, whether consumer organisations have a right to participate, and last but not least whether codes which comply with Community rules benefit from a privileged status. All these open issues have to be taken on board in the envisaged general legislative framework on fair trading.

At the heart of the matter is the feasibility of the New Approach for the regulation of marketing practices. The elaboration of marketing standards on multi-level marketing under the New Approach has been proposed in a study conducted for the European Commission on 'Door to Door Selling – Pyramid Selling – Multi Level Markeing'.[120] This proposal was subject to

---

[117] See N. Horn, 'Die Aufklärungs- und Beratungspflichten der Banken' ZBB 1997, 139; D. Weber-Rey and C. Baltzer, 'Neueste Entwicklungen zu den Verhaltensregeln für Wertpapierdienstleistungs-unternehmen,' WiB 1997, 1283.

[118] See Micklitz in Grabitz and Wolf II, *Fernabsatzrichtlinie* A 3, Rdnr. 183-184.

[119] There are some initiatives to be reported from the European Commission to lay down principles which may guide the elaboration of such codes.

[120] H.-W. Micklitz, B. Monazzahian, Ch. Rößler, *Door to Door Selling – Pyramid Selling – Multilevel-Marketing, A Study Commissioned by the European Commission*, Volume I and II, November 1999, published in the internet http://europa.eu.int/comm/dg24/library/surveys/sur10_en.html.

a Hearing held by the European Commission on the 15/16 March 2000.[121] The former experience and especially the statements and submissions made at the Hearing have considerably enriched the analysis of the feasibility of the New Approach for the regulation of marketing practices and deepened the understanding of similarities and deviations between technical standard making and the making of marketing practices. Therefore it seems impossible to understand a New Approach type directive on fair trading as an alternative to the traditional directive under which mandatory standards of fair trading would have to be defined. The New Approach can only be used as an instrument to *supplement* traditional secondary law-making, or more specifically, to *supplement* the general clause and the list of prohibited marketing practices. It is therefore necessary to define clearly the role and function of the New Approach within a general legislative framework.

3.   A Modified New Approach to Supplement the General Clause?

(a)   The new approach on technical harmonisation revisited

One possible option could be to understand the New Approach mechanism as a means of giving shape to the general requirement of trading fairly; another option might be to formulate legally binding 'core principles' for the elaboration of marketing standards. These legally binding 'core principles' would then make concrete the general clause and may be understood as the equivalent to the essential requirements under the New Approach. They might be laid down in the general legislative framework on fair trading so as to ensure their binding nature.

However, even in such a modified form the standard setting procedure of the New Approach cannot be transferred '*tel quel*' to the development of marketing standards, neither at the European nor at the national level. The necessary procedural requirements which should guide the elaboration of marketing standards under a modified New Approach need to be reconsidered. Under the traditional New Approach, standardisation institutions hold the monopoly on the elaboration of technical standards. In the field of marketing practices, national enforcement authorities with experience and skill in the development of self-regulatory measures, guidelines and recommendations should

---

[121] A summary of the written submissions and the statements at the hearing are available on the internet, http://europa.eu.int/comm/consumers/policy/developments/door_sale/door02.

be given a more prominent role. There is considerable concern that the standardisation institutions do not have the skills to develop marketing standards. The integration of national enforcement authorities might help to overcome these reservations. This is all the more so, as marketing standards might also be developed within the national legal and economic context. The role and function of consumer organisations is another field of conflict. Although they participate in the process of making standards, they do so without any legal status. Any proposal in the field of marketing practices should promote the role of consumer organisations in the formulating of marketing practices. This has already been recognised by the directive on e-commerce, though in a rather smooth form. The Green Paper on Consumer Protection definitely goes one decisive step further in the promotion of stakeholders.

The most difficult and perhaps the most important issue may be the granting of privileges to those who decide to comply voluntarily with the non-binding marketing standards. Trade and industry favour a 'safe harbour approach', a concept which is not yet established either in the EC nor in the United States of America. There is certainly a need to set positive incentives for those who are willing to subscribe to standards which reach beyond the binding law, be it a 'simple' obligation to trade fairly or 'only' core principles. The appropriate solution might be found in the granting of a 'fair communication' logo. Such a logo, however, has to be monitored. Then the question arises as to who shall be responsible for the monitoring – business and industry or national authorities – and what the sanctions might be in case of non-compliance. The proposal on the feasibility of a general framework on fair trading presented here will pick up the issue and try to propose a coherent concept in which self-regulation is given a prominent role.

The process envisaged is no longer self-regulation in the traditional sense, as trade and industry are no longer free in what they may do. They have to comply with binding standards and they have to integrate consumer organisations in the standard making process. On the other hand, marketing standards may not be the correct term anymore, as the procedure under which the rules are developed is no longer comparable to the New Approach. Here there might be room to talk *of co-regulation*, a term which is currently under consideration in the EC.[122] Co-regulation involves the legislator, the enforcement authorities, trade, industry and consumers.

---

[122] See Erik Liikanen, Member of the European Commission responsible for Enterprise and

(b)   Possible elements of co-regulation in marketing practices

Trade, industry and consumer organisations shall be encouraged by the European Commission and by the Member States to develop marketing standards in order to give shape to the general clause. The standards shall be developed for the European Community as a whole. However, they may cover the national markets only in so far as the rules are deemed necessary due to specific linguistic, social and cultural conditions.[123]

If trade, industry and consumer organisations so decide, marketing standards have to comply with the following mandatory requirements; legal, decent, honest, truthful commercial communication; clear, helpful and adequate pre-contractual information; clear, fair contracts, including a right to withdrawal where appropriate; a dispute settlement procedure along the line of recommendation 98/257/EC;[124] *a mechanism to supervise and monitor marketing standards; an obligation to report on compliance with the marketing standards and complaints about its operation.*

Marketing standards may be elaborated by national or European organisations of trade, industry or consumers, by national enforcement authorities or by national and/or European standardisation organisations. Trade, Industry and consumer organisations have a right to participate in the rule-making.

The marketing standards shall be notified to the competent national enforcement authorities. The authorities may grant the 'fair communication logo' if the marketing standards comply with the mandatory requirements. National authorities remain responsible for the supervision of compliance of marketing standards with the mandatory requirements. In case of violation, the authorities may revoke the logo on fair communication.

Information Society, *Co-Regulation: a modern approach to regulation*, Speech on the Meeting of Association of the European Mechanical, Electrical, Electronic and Metalworking Indusrtries (Orgalime) Council, Brussels, 4 May 2000.

[123] The formula is taken literally from ECJ, 13.01.2000, Case C-220/98 – *Estée Lauder Cosmetics GmbH vs. Lancaster Group GmbH*, not yet reported, at 29.

[124] OJ 1998 L 115, 31.

> *These rules are established for a test period of three years. In order to further develop co-regulation, a working group composed of government experts and/or qualified specialists from other interest bodies should be set up, in order to come up inter alia with proposals on the following issues: responsibilities for supervision and monitoring of co-regulatory measures; feasibility of safeguard and complaint committees for co-regulatory measures; the development of a European fair communication logo: specification of the legal effects of a fair communication logo; responsibilities for compliance with the fair communication logo; judicial review and legal redress with regard to co-regulation.*
>
> *12 months before expiry of the test period, the Commission shall present a progress report, together with possible proposals for amendments, if necessary.*

The development of these marketing standards should not be left to trade and commerce alone. There is ample evidence even in countries which heavily rely on voluntary codes of practices as a means to guarantee 'fair trading' that these rules suffer from major deficiencies.[125] A legal framework is needed to secure a high quality of marketing standards meant to give shape to the general clause and to guide trade and industry in their commercial communication. The solution proposed here is largely inspired by the New Approach on technical standards on harmonisation and follows recent political initiatives of the European Commission to promote co-regulation.[126]

The traditional New Approach on technical harmonisation and standards is based on the idea that European technical standards should be developed, which can then be transformed into national standards. Deviations between European and national standards are in principle not permitted, though exemptions may be granted under very restricted conditions, and if they are given, they are bound to narrow time limits.[127] The situation is different with regard to commercial communication.[128] The overall objective might be and should remain to elaborate European marketing standards. However, in

---

[125] See, Office of Fair Trading, *Raising Standards of Consumer Care*, (London, 1998).

[126] See.Liikanen, above note 122.

[127] See CEN/CENELEC, Internal Regulations under 3. General provisions – 3.1.9; 3.1.10 and 4.4. Deviations and special national conditions.

[128] Due to the different nature of commercial communication and technical standards.

82

commercial communication more flexibility is needed to cope with different legal cultures and traditions. On the other hand, national rule-making should not be completely released from the European legal order. That is why the national initiatives should be bound to a formula the ECJ has developed in relation to '*lifting*',[129] in order to balance out the overall objective of common marketing rules against the national need for deviations.

The overall objective of achieving European standards can only be kept alive if there is a common framework that governs the elaboration of marketing standards at the national and the European level, and which applies irrespective of who is actually taking responsibility to get the rule-making going. The proposal relies on the regulatory technique developed in the New Approach on Technical Harmonisation and Standards. Marketing standards have to comply with so-called *mandatory requirements*. These mandatory requirements must be understood as specification of the general clause on fair communication. The mechanism governing the elaboration of technical standards has to be adapted to the needs of fair trading regulation. *Therefore* the responsibility cannot remain in the hands of the national and/or European standardisation bodies alone, but must be shared with competent national authorities; and *therefore* consumer organisations must be given an active role in the development process. Marketing standards may be developed, however, without prejudice to Art. 81.[130]

Voluntary rule-making under the auspices of a statutory authority may not work without incentives which encourage trade and industry to engage in this business. The most promising solution seems to lie in the development of a 'fair communication' logo, which may be given to those who subscribe to the voluntary rules. The idea here, which is widely supported, is to compensate business and industry for their efforts, to increase compliance, and even to develop 'better' rules than the law requires. The New Approach on Technical Harmonisation and Standards has turned compliance into a presumption rule – those companies which comply with the technical standards are supposed to comply with the mandatory requirements. They are given a passport to the Internal Market, pending proof to the contrary. The visual sign which documents free access is the CE mark.

However, the presumption of conformity rule, which has turned out to be a

---

[129] See ECJ, 13 January 2000, Case C-220/98 – *Estée Lauder Cosmetics GmbH vs. Lancaster Group GmbH* (2000) ECR I-0000 at 29.

[130] The point has been stressed in the position paper of the Max-Planck-Institut, GRUR Int. 2002, 319, 323.

powerful instrument in the completion of the Internal Market, is not feasible for co-regulation of marketing standards. Compliance of products or services with technical standards can easily be measured and controlled. The point of departure is different with regard to commercial communication, where 'behaviour' would have to be supervised and checked against marketing standards. Subscription to marketing standards may document the good will of the party to respect the rules, but does not indicate how the party behaves in commercial intercourse. If trades and industries that adhere to the co-regulation are in no way privileged for their engagement, or do not benefit from a competitive advantage, they will hardly be prepared to co-operate in the elaboration of marketing standards. In the Netherlands, business, consumers and national authorities have developed a voluntary code on e-commerce,[131] which provides for a standstill period during which mainly consumer organisations are not allowed to go to court. Perhaps such a mechanism might help to set incentives for co-operation.

Test period – there is a need to test the feasibility of the proposed regulatory model on the elaboration of marketing standards.[132] There are a number of details which need further inquiry and where a working group should be installed to come up with appropriate proposals. Moreover, during three years all parties concerned should benefit from some leeway in the way the rules are applied and in the search for better and even more appropriate rules. It will be incumbent on the European Commission to prepare after the end of the test period a progress report which gives a full and critical analysis of the regulatory initiatives taken at the national and at the European level and to come up with proposals for revision, if necessary.

(c) Critique on the feasibility of new approach type of regulation

New Approach type regulation on marketing standards is alien to the Member States' legal systems. The arguments brought forward may be grouped around three major issues:[133] (1) the role and function of self-regulation as such in

---

[131] Electronic Commerce Platform Nederland (ECP.NL), *Model Code of Conduct for Electronic Commerce*, Draft version 3.0.

[132] The same might be true for the regulation of multi level marketing, Micklitz, et al, above n 120.

[133] See A. Wiebe, 'Die guten Sitten im Wettbewerb – eine europäische Regelungsaufgabe?' Wrp 2002, 283, 290; Max-Planck-Institut, GRUR Int. 2002, 319, 323.

whatever form, (2) the responsibilities in the law-making procedure, and (3) responsibilities in the enforcement procedure.

Member States which are not familiar with self-regulation demonstrate reluctance towards any form of self-regulation. However, I will not argue in favour of self-regulation, but in favour of non-binding marketing standards, which are elaborated within a tight legislative framework. Without any guidance in the form of mandatory rules, voluntary marketing standards will not be a feasible method of regulation within a general legislative framework. The second argument goes very much to way in which marketing practices are administered and monitored in the Member States. Thirteen out of fifteen Member States have put the supervision and monitoring of marketing practices into the hands of statutory agencies. Only Austria and Germany rely on the judiciary, which is set into motion by trade and consumer organisations as the sole stakeholders of the parties' and the public interest. Secondary Community law can only be addressed to the Member States. Therefore a solution must be found to make sure that an EC marketing standard-making procedure can benefit from the skill and knowledge of the sole stakeholders. Last but not least, the most fundamental reservation about self-regulation may concern the shift in responsibility, away from the judiciary to the executive branch of government. A general legislative framework on fair trading will have to address the need to set appropriate means of judicial review and legal redress. Unfortunately, the Green Paper on Consumer Protection remains quite reluctant to address enforcement and redress mechanisms. In essence it relies on enhanced and intensified co-operation between statutory agencies.[134]

V.   The Remaining Issues – Enforcement And Revision

1.   Judicial Review and Legal Redress Against Regulatory Actions and Decisions

The Directive 84/450/EC on misleading advertising has set the tone, which was hardly modified in Directive 93/13/EC on unfair terms, Directive 97/7/EC on distant selling and Directive 98/27/EC on trans-border consumer complaints. Whenever secondary community law sets binding legal requirements on marketing practices (unfair terms included), the directives oblige Member States to take appropriate measures to ensure compliance either through

---

[134] Green paper, para 5.2.

national administrative authorities or through national courts on the request of consumer and/or trade organisations. The general framework on fair trading may therefore rely on a well-settled body of EC rules, which needs to be given greater specification only in so far as consumer organisations should be clearly given standing in legal proceedings, in order to overcome possible conflicts that may result out of the somewhat opaque wording of the respective provisions in the directives concerned.

The feasibility test of a general legislative framework on fair trading raises questions of larger and more problematic dimensions: *should there be some sort of European enforcement mechanism*? And if so, what should be its scope of activities? Should a European body be competent for the control of enforcement of the general clause and the non-binding standards relating to marketing practices? And what should then be the role of the national enforcement authorities?

Information exchange and consultation should be the lowest common denominator of European enforcement. Some information exchange and some co-ordination in the field of unfair trading already takes place in the International Network of Market Surveillance, hosted by the OECD. This seems to be exactly the policy of the Commission as laid down in the Green Paper on Consumer Protection.[135] The establishment of any such mechanism would therefore only upgrade the European Community to the 'enforcement structures' already available in quite a number of international organisations. The appropriate forum for such *information exchange and co-ordination* could be a European Agency on Fair Trading.[136] It might be supplemented by a database on national decisions on fair trading. The 'CLAB' database might serve as a model here.[137] Such a European Agency on Fair Trading would not

---

[135] Ibid.

[136] The European Community has already established a whole set of agencies which could serve as a model for regulation, such as, for instance the European Environment Agency (Council Regulation 1290/90, OJ L 120, 11 May 1990, 1, amended by Council Regulation 933/1999, OJ L 117, 1999, 1), European Agency for the Evaluation of Medicinal Products (Council Regulation 2309/93, OJ L 214, 24 August 1993, 1), European Agency for Safety and Health at Work (Council Regulation 2062/94, OJ L 216, 20 August 1994, 1), European Monitoring Centre for Drugs and Drug Addiction (Council Regulation 302/93, OJ L 36, 12 February 1993, 1).

[137] For five years now contractors in each Member State have collected and analysed court decisions and dispute settlement decisions under a common scheme. The data is available on the internet, http://europa.eu.int/clab. Cf. also the report from the Commission on the implementation of Council Directive 93/13/EEC of 5 April 1993 on unfair terms in con-

have decision-making powers. If such a firm structure in the form of a European Agency on Fair Trading meets insurmountable resistance, a committee in which all the enforcement authorities are united and where information is exchanged and where enforcement is co-ordinated might constitute the lowest common denominator. Such a committee should allow for some flexibility in the way in which it is composed, in order to take care of the differences in law enforcement at the national level. It should be open to national authorities as well as to those consumer and trade organisations which play an active part in the protection of consumers against unfair trade practices.

2. Safeguard Committee on Fair Trading Regulations

A general legislative framework would seriously affect the sovereignty of the Member States. The sole legal basis for such a Community measure seems to be Art. 95. The procedure envisaged under Article 95 IV should compensate Member States for the loss of their sovereignty. However, in the aftermath of the Single European Act, the EC has developed a well-established policy to pin down the rights of Member States under Article 95 IV into a separate legal mechanism – the so-called safeguard committee.[138] This committee confirms the rights of Member States' to adopt deviating rules even in areas which are fully harmonised. If they do so, however, they are bound to respect a procedure which should lead to a uniform application of EC law. The Green Paper on Consumer Protection softly opts for the introduction of such a committee.[139]

The list of prohibited marketing practices touches upon quite sensitive policy fields. The Member States' legitimate interests in maintaining or adopting deviating rules might either be based on Article 95 IV directly, or might be bound to a safeguard procedure, which would then have to be written down in the general legislative framework. So far, Member States have demonstrated a preparedness to rely on the safeguard procedure as the appropriate means to balance conflicting interests. However, the experience of the safeguard procedure is largely based on policy fields which are gov-

---

sumer contracts at http://europa.eu.int/comm/dg24/policy/developments/unfa_cont_term/uct03_en.pdf

[138] See with regard to product safety, E. Vos, *Institutional Frameworks of Community Health and Safety Regulation, Committees, Agencies and Private Bodies*, (1999).

[139] Green paper, 5.2.

erned by administrative law. The recent initiative of the European Commission to extend the safeguard procedure to the e-commerce failed. It might nevertheless be worthwhile considering the introduction of a safeguard clause into the general legislative framework.[140] This is all the more true as the list of prohibited marketing practices, as presented, is not governed by clear-cut rules but much more by general formulae which need to be specified. Public policy issues are of a particular importance as the legislative framework covers only consumer-related commercial communication. There remains a grey area which deserves closer inspection. If the advertising or marketing practice in question is outside the proposed framework, the Member States still hold the power; if it comes under the notion of the prohibited practice, Member States are no longer free in their decision-making process, they are bound to Community law, at least under the safeguard clause.

VI. THE APPROPRIATE REGULATORY TECHNIQUE

Eugen Ulmer proposed in 1965 to establish a uniform legal body on fair trading by way of a *convention*.[141] The legal political trend seems to work the other way round as the envisaged transformation of the Brussels Convention into a regulation demonstrates.[142] So far, the European Community has only used directives as its method for harmonising marketing practices. There might be a need, however, to re-consider the feasibility of a Regulation instead of a Directive as the appropriate means. Such a choice might be justifiable under a common concept of competition which unites competition law, fair trading law and consumer protection law. A similar approach has been proposed with regard to the harmonisation of European private law.[143] The project of a general legislative framework deserves more attention than a piecemeal approach on the harmonisation of certain marketing practices.

The nature of the regulatory methods, Directive or Regulation, will largely

---

[140] See Article 60 in Directive 2000/12/EC of the European Parliament and of the Council of 20 March 2000 relating to the taking up and pursuit of the business of credit institutions, OJ L 126, 26 May 2000, 1.

[141] See Ulmer, above note 6 , 232.

[142] See Council Regulation (EC) No. 44/2001 on jurisdiction and the recognition and enforcement of judgments in civil and commercial matters, OJ L 12, 16 January 2001, 1.

[143] Jürgen Basedow argues in favour of the application of Art. 235 (Art. 308) to adopt a European Civil Code in form of a regulation. J. Basedow, 'A common contract law for the Common Market' (1997) 33 CMLR 1169. The author is director of the Max-Planck Institut für ausländisches und internationales Privatrecht in Hamburg.

determine the degree to which existing secondary law rules on marketing practices may be integrated or not. If a Regulation is chosen, coherence is required more than ever. A Regulation would have to cover all existing rules, as far as possible. A Directive would provide more flexibility. The general legislative framework could be realised through the form of a directive as well. Such a choice would put less pressure on the Commission. It might be feasible to start harmonising fair trading via a Directive and then later develop a coherent body of marketing practice rules which might be realised via a Regulation. Any legislative framework on fair trading in whatever form has, however, to be made compatible with directives on marketing practices already in existence.

3. Rules on Competition and Fair Trading

Guido Alpa

If we choose a perspective of consumer protection, and consider the impact of EC regulations or EC directives on the national systems (e.g. the Italian legal system), the idea of introducing general rules on fair trading into the common market should be highly recommended. The aim of the following pages is indeed to give evidence for the fact that these rules are already in existence in some national legal systems and cope very well with the rules provided by the Charter of Fundamental Rights. When a European Civil Code (a "model" code, or a set of general principles) will be enacted, those rules could cope with the other rules there provided and those concerning the economic relationships between professionals and between professionals and consumers.

I.   Freedom to Conduct a Business and the Limits Thereto

"The freedom to conduct a business in accordance with Community law and national practices is recognised": thus Article 16 of the Charter of Fundamental Rights of the European Union.

The limits to this freedom seem to stem solely from the need for compliance of the economic activity with: (i) the rules of community law, namely the rules of the Treaty of Rome, regulations and directives, and the other sources of Community law, (ii) the rules envisaged in the national systems, and (iii) the rules that the professionals have imposed upon themselves in as much as they derive from the "practices", i.e. from the uses, from repeated and accepted conduct, which have therefore been codified into models of reference contained in codes of self-regulation.

These are, in substance, rules of action, of control, and of supervision, which are intrinsic to the market, and that, therefore, translate into an equal number of limits dictated by the workings of the market to ensure the better competition of operators.

Taken out of its context, and read in accordance with the canons of literal interpretation, this provision seems to legitimize any conduct held by the

H. Collins (ed.) The Forthcoming EC Directive on Unfair and Commercial Practices, 91-110.
©2004. Kluwer Law International. Printed in the Netherlands.

operators that is kept within these sole limits, limits that are, so to speak, *internal* to the market.

But, as is the case with any provision of law, even Article 16 must be interpreted in context, and according to the canons of systematic interpretation and interpretation according to the goals of the law (so called teleological interpretation).

In the body of the same Charter we find rules that conflict with freedom to conduct a business and constitute an equal number of limits to the same: human dignity (art. 1), the physical and legal integrity of the person (art. 3), individual liberty and security (art. 6), protection of private life (art. 7) and of personal data (art. 8), environmental protection (art. 37), consumer protection (art. 38), and, of course, the rights of workers (arts. 27–32).

The overall picture of the values that have to be reconciled with freedom to conduct a business is therefore vast and articulate. In brief, it is already summed up in a provision of the Italian Constitution (of 1948), which, in art. 41, in addition to recognising and guaranteeing private economic freedom, envisages that the same cannot take place "in contrast with social usefulness or in such a way as to damage human security, liberty or dignity".

In general terms, we can therefore distinguish two main categories of limits to freedom to conduct a business: in addition to those deriving from the market, the *internal* ones we have already mentioned, there are other limits, which we could call *external,* because they relate to values which must be reconciled with economic freedom, values which, as they concern the individual, should by nature *prevail* over economic freedom.

When we speak of economic freedom, we cannot therefore ignore this great division: on the one hand we have the dynamics internal to the system of economic relations, *i.e.* to the market, on the other hand we have the limits to economic freedom which derive from fundamental values. If we mix the two levels, we risk mediating between economic interests and higher-level interests, debasing the latter.

The relevance of external limits to economic activity is not new to Community law. If we read the provisions of the Treaty of Rome, we immediately understand that economic freedom is tempered by the provisions concerning workers, consumers and the environment. However, art. 16 of the Charter, read in connection with the other provisions contained therein, clarifies in marked terms the overall picture of values that business activity must comply with. The fact that in the text of the Charter the values of the individual are placed before those relating to economic activity is an unequivocal sign that the Charter intends to underline more markedly the external limits, compared to their emergence already in the Treaty.

But the time has come to re-think also the internal limits.

First and foremost among the "constitutional" provisions of the Union – as Mario Monti, the Commissioner for competition policy has recently reiterated – "is the fundamental principle according to which the Union's economic policy is implemented" in accordance with the principle of an open market economy in free competition. The promotion of a competitive environment by no means excludes public interventions aimed at objectives of general interest, rather these are often necessary for the protection of consumers, of operators, of the workers, in short for the whole of society. But they must be proportionate to the realization of the public good they intend to pursue and must never be motivated by the will (in most cases disguised) to protect vested interests, with the result of harming precisely that common good that we claim to pursue".[1]

Usually it is held that if the consumer is placed in a position to choose on the basis of correct information the goods and services he requires, it is not necessary to go beyond this position.

Now, can we assume that from an economic viewpoint, i.e. looking inside economic relationships, consumer protection merely requires balanced information?

It has been said, by an authority on the subject, that the competitive method is designed in accordance with consumer choices; that protection must be devoid of paternalism, as it is pointless to erect the consumer as an autonomous legal entity and a repository of good feelings and human solidarity; the consumer's dignity derives from his right to information. Economic freedom and risk of enterprise correspond to freedom of preference and risk of choice'.[2] I do not share these opinions.

It is not paternalism, but acknowledgment of the objective disparity of economic and legal position between consumers and entrepreneurs which is at the basis of the Community directives which protect the consumers from untruthful advertising, from business practices which encroach on their privacy, from the abuse of standard terms of business, from the lack of sub-

---

[1] Tesauro and D'Alberti (eds), Concorrenza e regolazione nell'Unione Europea, in Regolazione e concorrenza (Bologna: 2000) 74.

[2] Irti, 'La concorrenza come statuto normativo' in Amorosino, Morbidelli, Morisi (eds), *Istituzioni, mercato e democrazia, Liber Amicorum for the eightieth birthday of Alberto Predieri*, (Turin: 2002) 340.

stantial binding content in contracts, from the circulation of products that are harmful because they are defective, from the sale of products which do not conform to the contract. Accurate information and freedom of choice would not by themselves be sufficient to place consumers and professionals on a level of parity.

We should ask ourselves then if it is not necessary or desirable to take a step further.

Again in full observance of the principle of subsidiarity, and without resorting to the introduction of new rules, it is appropriate to proceed as the Charter has done, for external limits, i.e. making clear the values which are already contained in the fabric of Community law and which, however, given its very nature, are present in a widely fragmented context.

I refer to the fairness of conduct of professionals.

Fairness of conduct is one of the factors of competition, but normally the concept of competition itself concerns relations between competitors, *i.e.* between professionals that are on the same plane. Nowadays, fairness, precisely taking into account the Community directives that protect consumers' interests, cannot be evaluated by only considering the homologous interests of operators, but it must be appraised also taking into account the interests of consumers. In real terms, we must ensure that the conduct of professionals complies with a principle of *fairness* to be abided by also vis-à-vis the consumers.

In this we may recognise a further merit of the Community *acquis*. The building of a single integrated market is also useful moment in which to modernise the rules of the legal systems of the Member States, often left to nineteenth century codes, or to rules of self-discipline, which end up by alienating or not considering at all the interests of subjects regarded as foreign to the professional category, such as the interests of consumers.

II. COMPETITION AND FAIR TRADING AMONG PROFESSIONALS: IN QUEST FOR A GENERAL CLAUSE

The models of a Civil Code or a Commercial code of Continental Europe offer interesting issues for our purposes, because the regulation of competition, where it is envisaged, is aimed at pursuing merely a balance between the conflicting interests of competitors, rather than to *directly* protect the interests of consumers.

This assumption, borne out by massive literature, is not without exceptions, which are due to eminent scholars, concerned with modernising the rules of trade in accordance with the new requirements of dynamic market, not devoted exclusively to profit.

In one of the first important works regarding the regulation of competition, *Teoria della concorrenza e dei beni immateriali* (The theory of competition and of incorporeal rights), published by Tullio Ascarelli in Milan in 1955, the theory of the freedom of competition is put forth, and it is claimed that competition also protects the interests of consumers, but it is acknowledged that this protection is only *indirect*.

Even the Italian Civil Code, which is one of the most original and recent (having been promulgated in 1942) among the Codes of Continental Europe, is mainly concerned with ensuring equality of treatment in the event of contracts by the monopolist, and to repress *unfair* competition, but legitimated non-competition covenants (art. 2595 *et seq.*).

Hence the conclusion that, as it is possible to renounce freedom of competition, competition 'is not conceived as a guarantee for consumers or, in general as a guarantee of collective prosperity – which would entail its inalienability, as the individual cannot dispose of the public interest – but it is conceived as an instrument which achieves an individual interest and, therefore, a freedom which the individual, who is the bearer, can in fact dispose of'. In other words, 'by recognising... the validity of these covenants, the Civil Code demonstrates that it considers the interests related to freedom of competition as entirely private interests of entrepreneurs'. We should also underline the fact that the same limits imposed on the validity of the covenants 'are envisaged to protect the said entrepreneurs: they are inspired by the need to avoid that entrepreneurs should divest themselves of their freedom, forfeiting all economic activity or forfeiting the same perpetually, and not by the appropriateness of protecting consumers from agreements entered into, to their detriment, by entrepreneurs'. These tendencies can be found in the entire regulation of the enterprise, and are confirmed on the subject of consortiums (art. 2602 *et seq.* of the Civil Code), of exclusivity agreements, of sales concessions, and so on.[3]

Similar indications can be drawn from the regulation of the legal limits on competition: art. 2595, according to which 'competition shall go on in such a way as not to harm the interests of the national economy, and within the limits provided by law and by corporative norms', at the time of its introduction constitutionalised the protection of the interests of entrepreneurs

---

[3] Ghidini, *Monopolio e concorrenza*, in *Enc. dir.*, vol. xxvi, (Milan: 1976) p. 818.

(and thus corporate interests); nowadays, in conjunction with art. 41 of the Constitution, it sets forth indicative guidelines, which, nevertheless, by no means imply consistent support for freedom of competition.

The rules of the civil Code appear decidedly 'pro-monopolistic': *a)* the rules admit, without discrimination, restrictive covenants on any 'subject' whatsoever; *b)* as the extreme consequence of this 'permissiveness', the rules admit covenants of entire abstention from competition, and therefore the formation of entirely monopolistic situations, which may go as far, in substance, as actual *(de facto)* monopolies by sector. We can deduce, therefore, that the rules of the Italian Civil Code by no means defend freedom of competition.

The resulting legislative picture is one that inevitably favours the interests of business, and neglects those of consumers. This trend emerges more evidently from the rules on unfair competition.

In the articles of the Code that provide for the regulation of unfair competition, consumer protection does not appear as the ultimate goal of such rules. Consumers, in other words, are not identified in their position as the addressees of a body of rules introduced in their favour; on the contrary the role assigned to consumers is merely *instrumental,* for two main reasons.

On the one hand, because the *parameter*, the yardstick used to outline the 'rules of the game', i.e. to define the guidelines relating to competition, is the interest of competitors; competition, in fact, is unfair (*ex* art. 2598 of the Civil Code) when it is likely to create *confusion* among the products of various entrepreneurs, or when it is likely to *discredit* the products of others, or again when it does not conform to the principles of correct behaviour in the trade and is likely to injure another's *business*. As we can see from reading the provisions of the law, this legal framework does not contemplate the consumer, who appears not as a subject to be protected, but as the simple receiver of the messages, the distinctive signs, the words, the statements and the activities which are deemed unfair. The consumer remains in the shadows, because what matters, in the definition of the balance of the interests at play, is the protection of the entrepreneur who is the victim of the unfair competition. But there is more. The *loss* that is considered legally relevant is not that sustained by the consumer, deceived by advertising that confounds his criteria for choice among products; it is instead the injury to another's business, for the discredit of his products or activities, for the diversion of his clientele, and so forth.

On the other hand, this exploitation appears more indirect and covert. There is an attempt, in fact, to try to give the rules on unfair competition a justification which highlights the specific intent of protection of the public, while, as a consequence of the simple reading of the text of the laws, the interests directly protected are exclusively those of the entrepreneurs. Unfair competition means nothing if not competition conducted in a way that is contrary to the rules (of law or of custom) through the means of persuasion used to solicit the demand of consumers. And the design that results from the rules on the subject is ordered from a rather limited perspective. As Francesco Galgano warns, the law 'does not concern itself from the point of view of protection of the consumers; it concerns itself, instead, from the point of view of protection, in the mutual relations among entrepreneurs, with the freedom of competition of each one of them'. Therefore, there is no legislative consideration given to

> Those techniques of persuasion, even more widely used, which are directed at creating or at spreading , in the public of consumers the need for always new industrial products and which are the cause (...) of deep social imbalances (economic resources are diverted from investment in the production of essential goods and services and devoted to the satisfaction of artificial needs, created by the organization of production itself), in addition to posing, by their very nature (for instance as regards techniques of hidden persuasion), problems of protection of human freedom itself.[4]

The subject matter of unfair competition has given rise to an immense series of problems, which here we can mention in a merely cursory way. All of these problems, however, relate to the regulation of economic relations among competitors who operate in the same market sector, and make no reference to the issue of consumer protection. Court decisions, in general, develop restrictive guidelines, circumscribing the scope of application of art. 2598. In other words, the issue is whether these rules are applicable to those who are not entrepreneurs, whether the act of competition carried out through a third party is unlawful, whether the competitive practice carried out in violation of rules of public policy is unlawful.

More significant is a problem, of a general nature, posed by the interpretation of art. 2598 of the Italian civil Code. It regards the meaning of the *general clause* of Para. 3 of this article, which qualifies as an act of unfair competition the conduct of an entrepreneur who 'avails himself directly or indirectly of any (...) means which do not conform with the principles of correct behaviour in the trade and are likely to injure another's business'.

---

[4] Galgano, *L'imprenditore*, (Bologna: 1998).

On that issue it is not necessary to dwell extensively. It is a typical general clause that, precisely because of its indeterminacy has been construed in various ways. Some have identified 'correct behaviour in the trade' with commercial practices, others with the rules of 'custom'; in both cases reference is made to evaluation parameters which place the issues of compliance or not with 'fairness' under a decidedly 'corporative' perspective; in other words, the lawfulness or otherwise of a given competitive practice is inferred by the rules, by the conduct observed in practice, by the trade usages in force in the same entrepreneurial world. Correct behaviour in the trade therefore means, in this sense correct behaviour in the defence of the 'interests of the trade'. The clear result is that the interests of consumers are not included among them. Even those who propose a different interpretation of the rule and, instead of referring to a code of practice, or to meta-legal parameters of judgment, propose to engage in a 'comparative evaluation' of the interests involved, and then to establish whether a certain competitive practice is lawful or unlawful, do not greatly distance themselves from the logic that has been mentioned. It is obvious, therefore, that 'the interests of the public at large are not immediately protected' by that provision.

As to the techniques of protection, the Code offers to professionals the traditional remedies of injunction and damages; the case law offers now the injunction also to the consumers' associations.

III. Competition and Consumer Protection

Even from an economic point of view, the concept of competition has changed in time.

"Competition is the consumer's best friend", heralds the report prepared by a commission of experts around the nineteen fifties in the U.K. which was entrusted with the task of making a complete review of the problems concerning capitalist societies, with particular reference to consumer protection.[5]

---

[5] The regulation of production activities does not include, obviously, only the regulation of relations between competing producers, but a very thick network of laws, decrees, regulations, which set forth the ways, the forms, the techniques which enterprises in the various sectors must comply with for the production, packaging, labelling of their products. Many of the provisions are established for safety reasons, how often goods produced or services offered can harm the users' or employees' health; recently, certain facts which have impressed public opinion (relating to the marketing of seed oil of unknown origin, or products coloured with toxic chemicals) have set open the question of the lack, in the Italian

This consideration is certainly not new; starting with Adam Smith, down to Guido De Ruggiero, all the backers of *laissez-faire* economics have always maintained it to be the case, thereby justifying, at the same time, the case for giving free reign to entrepreneurial activities, and letting entrepreneurs free to take possession of the product of those activities. This assumption is no longer sustainable in the current reality. There is no longer a place, in affluent societies, for a perfect competitive market, for the free inter-play of economic forces ranged against each other, as there is no longer a place for the theory of the sovereignty of the consumer.

Perfect competition, as the balance which represents the optimal allocation of resources, as in the neo-classical model, has given way to 'possible competition', inspired by principles of functionality, reality and 'graduality'.[6]

Hence the great change brought about by the Community rules, which take into account, among the internal limits of the market, the interests of third parties relating to labour, consumption, and the environment.[7]

But we can ask ourselves how these principles have been accepted within the legal systems of the Member States.

If we read the regulation of the internal market, we find that the principles that were the starting point of our discussion have been totally neglected, or only partially taken into consideration.

The Italian model gives a clear example of this state of affairs.

The modern rules on competition were introduced in Italy, on the model of the Community rules, only in 1990. That was the year, in fact, in which Law 10.10.1990 note 287 was enacted. In reality, a number of attempts were made by scholars and legislators to introduce more adequate rules on the subject, but each attempt was doomed to frustration. The title of Law 10.10.1990, note 287 concerns the protection of *competition* and of the *market*; as the two terms are joined by the word 'and', 'competition' and 'the market' may

---

legal system, of adequate legislation to avoid the manufacture of harmful products: these are, in any case, issues which relate to the criminal liability of enterprise, which we cannot deal with in these pages. On this item, however, see Ghidini, *Per i consumatori*, (Bologna: 1977) pages 55 *et seq.*. See further the numerous contributions and analyses of cases collected in the R. Piccinino (ed), *Rassegna di Diritto e Tecnica dell'Alimentazione*, published by F. Angeli.

[6] D. Young and S. Metcalfe, 'The Economics of the European Union', in M. Artis and N. Lee (eds), *Competition Policy* (Oxford: Oxford University Press, 1994).

[7] A. Tizzano, *Diritto comunitario e sviluppo del principio di libera concorrenza in Italia*, in *Dir. dell'Unione europea*, 1996, pages 745 *et seq.*

constitute a hendiadys (two terms that define a single concept), or hint at two different phenomena. According to logic, the second is the correct alternative, in this context: whilst there can be a market without competition (the so-called monopolistic or oligopolistic market), there can be no competition without a market; therefore, it is logical to believe that we are not faced with a hendiadys, but with two different phenomena, even if not in opposition. Given, however, that competition is a mode of the market (the so-called free market), it may have been simpler to refer exclusively to the protection of competition. If the words 'and the market' were added, it was to forewarn the reader that the range of interests involved is greater than that to which we normally refer when we speak of competition, *i.e.* the interests of competing entrepreneurs, making reference to the interests of third parties, such as the public good, the interests of competing entrepreneurs who purchase goods and services, the interests of consumers. In short, it comprises all the interests that normally conflict, and then come together again, within the market.

If we were to assume that the title of the law represents a synthesis of the aims pursued by the legislator, we would immediately reach the conclusion that these rules are aimed *a)* at the protection of values or rights (competition, the market) and therefore *b)* at the interests involved with those values or those rights, that is *c)* the public good and individual interests; thus *d)* the public good – in this context – would identify with competition and the market, and that individual interests would be protected in so far as they be compatible with the public good and with the market; *e)* individual interests might be diversified, as the bearers would be both economic operators who produce goods and services (offering entrepreneurs) and economic operators who are the receivers of goods and services (acquiring entrepreneurs), and also consumers considered as operators (*homines oeconomici*) or as simple users.

It has been observed that the discipline of competition and of anti-competition phenomena (antitrust) reflects terms, concepts, orientations of the economic thought, that antitrust law proceeds by cycles, that it moves with the varying of the underlying economic theories, and with their predominance within the decision-making processes.[8] However, once the term has come

---

[8] Van den Bergh, 'L'analisi economica del diritto della concorrenza', in AA. VV., *Diritto Antitrust italiano*, Bologna, 1993, p. 2. And see now the green paper on Community policy and the vertical restrictions of the Commission of the European Communities dated 22 January 1997 (COM 96,721 final). See also G. Amato, *Il potere e l'Antitrust*, (Bologna: 1998)

into a legislative provision, it acquires an added value, it becomes a legal term, even if derived from the language of economics. Whether the terms mentioned above have, in the Italian legal system, a sole and accepted meaning, or whether, not having been legislatively defined, they should be read with economic meanings, is still an open question.[9]

The commentators advise, therefore, that we should refer to the legal notions of competition and the market, as referenced: *a*) in the rules under review; *b*) in Community rules, recalled by Para.4 of art. 1 *sub specie* 'principles of the system of the European Communities on the subject of rules on competition'.

In the construction of the commentators, the legal notion of the market remains vague, as the market is the ideal meeting place of demand and supply, which varies according to goods and services, regions, political systems, and therefore the economic systems.

The notion of competition also varies, with regard to unfair competition, consortiums, non-competition covenants, etc..

On their part, the principles are understood, in the analysis of the writers, as legal rules of the second degree, derived by the inductive process from the written provisions, and expressed in general terms. A systematic reconstruction of the general principles in the Italian legal system is still under way; the historical and legal-political profile of the general principles and an attempt at analysis by sectors has revealed the evanescence of the notion and the arbitrariness of its employment in judicial decisions.[10] The principles of Community law emphasise freedom of competition;[11] however, if this subject matter involves also the interests of consumers, they will also relate to consumer protection. It is accepted, in fact, that consumer protection is now a general principle of law (both at national and Community level). Nevertheless, the principles are conflicting and need to be reconciled. In any

---

pp. 12 *et seq.*; H. Micklitz and S. Weatherill, *European Economic Law*, (Dartmouth: 1997); AA. VV. *Per una nuova costituzione economica,* edited by G. della Cananea and G. Napolitano, (Bologna: 1998).

9   G. Donativi 'Introduzione storica' in della Cananea and Napolitano, above note 8, pp. 49 et seq., and above all G. Bernini, *La tutela della libera concorrenza e i monopoli. Studio di diritto comparato*, (Milan: 1963).

10   See G. Alpa, *I principi generali*, (Milan: 1993).

11   See V. Toriello, in *Nuova Giur. civ. comm.*, 1993, II, pages 1 et seq.; Guntner, quoted by Donativi, above note 9, p. 79, note 107; F. Munari, *Commento all'art. 1 L. cit..*, edited by V. Afferni, (Padova: 1994).

case, reference to the principles of Community law considerably enlarges the scope of intervention for commentators, because the principles are the origin not only of the interpretation of provisions, but also of the trends of the courts and of the guidelines of legal scholars, not to mention – for whoever does not have a restrictive concept of the notion – the values underlying interpretation. In this sense, competition and the market have been referred to as 'values'.

In the text under review, the term "consumer" is recurrent, in particular:

a) in article 3, Para. 1, where in relation to abuse of predominant position, it is specified that it is forbidden "to hinder or limit the production, outlet or access to the market, the technical development or technological process to the detriment of consumers";

b) in article 4, Para. 1, where on the subject matter of derogations to the ban on agreements restricting freedom of competition, these agreements are held to be lawful if, having been authorised by the administrative agency (the authority established by the same law) they give rise "to improvements in the conditions of supply in the market, the effects of which are such as to ensure a substantial benefit for consumers";

c) in article 12, where, within the description of the authority's powers, those elements are considered relevant which are brought to its attention "by public administrations or by whoever has a vested interest, including the associations representing consumers".

With the introduction of rules on competition 'and the market', the interests of consumers are necessarily directly involved: not therefore *sub specie* of the protection of competition, but *sub specie* of the protection of the market. This, because consumers too operate in the market, not as *domini* of the situation, nor as *subiecti*. If the market is the ideal place for the conflict and the reconciliation of the different interests at stake, also the interests of consumers – both from an economic-social and from a legal point of view – must have the right of citizenship.[12]

The same way of considering the market can be found in the rules on securities, where the protection of savings does not imply merely the protection of the individual interests of banking and financial operators, but also implies the protection of the clients of banks and financial brokerage companies, be they institutional investors or occasional investors, i.e. savers.

---

[12] On the ample notion of citizenship see G. Alpa, *La persona. Tra cittadinanza e mercato*, (Milan: 1992).

Now, what relevance do we give to such interests in the rules set forth in Law n. 287 of 1990? The interests of consumers are given some attention; and the Authority charged of the application of the statute has frequently allowed (through its 'decisions') associations of consumers to take part in the proceedings against violation of competitions rules.

IV. Competition and General Fairness Clauses in the "Principles of Contracts in International Trade" and in the "Principles of European Contract Law"

If we are to assume the principle of competition as one of the linch-pins of the market economy, we must acknowledge that the carrying out of economic activity must be entrusted to rules of fairness that are valid vis-à-vis both the professionals and the consumer. This opinion is so widespread as to be accredited in the drafting of principles recognised either at universal level (for instance the Principles set forth by Unidroit) or at European level (for example the Principles set forth by the Commission coordinated by Ole Lando and Hugh Beale).

As for the former, art. 17 is actually entitled 'good faith and fair dealing', conjugating two concepts which are not homologous: good faith (in the sense of fairness and protection of the interests of the counter-party) and "fair dealing" in the sense of fairness of conduct in trading, and therefore in the actions which are functional to economic activity.

As regards the latter, art 1.201 states, in a similar way: 'each party must act in accordance with good faith and fair dealing'.

Now, it is actually true that in both texts reference is made to contractual behaviour, in the first case by economic operators dealing in international trade, in the second by the parties to any contract, regardless of their status. But it is equally true that contractual behaviour is one of the segments in which the professional's activity is borne out.

V. Techniques of Consumer Protection

Beyond the expressions of intent, beyond the rhetoric of economists, the techniques with which to pursue the protection of consumers within the rules applicable to the market (and therefore to competition) propose various initiatives, but two in particular are highlighted:

a) representation (the so-called right to be heard and the right to take part in the offices or bodies which administer the interests of consumers);

b) the actionability of the injured interests.

Now, neither one of these two techniques have been contemplated in Italian antitrust regulations.

Not the first, because consumers are not represented in the identification of the members of the supervising Authority. One could object that the Authority protects the market, and that therefore, in the same way as there are no representatives of the operators, it could not include consumers' representatives. In addition, because the Authority is independent of representative groups, it is equally able to protect consumers. This is not so, because if you protect competition, the protection of consumers' interests is mediated and indirect; if you protect the market, you must take into consideration all the interests at stake; the same reasoning applies to the regulation of securities and the composition of CONSOB which, the commentators point out, protects the market and not savers *tout court*.

This means that the objective of the legislator, that is the *mens legis,* in this as in the other provisions regarding the market in general, is not to protect the consumers, but the interests of the consumers *together with* the interests of the entrepreneurs. This arrangement leads inevitably on the path of mediation of interests by the legislator, and therefore by the *lobbies* that operate in Parliament; mediation occurs, however, also on the judicial level and on that of *moral suasion* for CONSOB and on the level of anti-competition syndicates effected by the *antitrust* Authority. This may appear balanced, in a democratic system; but the balance is only *apparent*, in as much as the interests of entrepreneurs are solid, firm, assisted by a historically relevant protection, and, above all, always present in legislative rules (in terms of special laws and, obviously of a codified nature); on the contrary, the interests of consumers are not class interests, are not firm but fragmented, are not strong but weak, being entrusted to associations which are as yet hardly present on the institutional scene, and above all only very recently present in legislative texts. We cannot, therefore, speak of a perfect balance.

Not even the second technique has been contemplated in *antitrust* regulations, because actions in defence of the interests of consumers in the rules on the protection of competition and of the market are considered only marginally.

First of all, associations only have the power to inform the Authority (art. 12), that is to bring to its attention the anti-competition phenomena that are to be repressed. It is quite a bland way of implementing the right to be heard.

The associations, therefore, have been given quite a lesser role than has been recognised within the scope of environmental protection regulations and the rules on misleading advertising. They appear *in limine* in the ascertainment procedure, but can neither follow-up the same, nor take an active part.

As regards legal capacity to sue on the subject matter of damages, associations are ignored, the only possible action being a claim by an individual. There is in fact a legal capacity to sue on the part of the final consumer for losses incurred as a consequence of anti-competitive actions.[13] However, the attention of legal writers has focused on the nature and on the extent of losses; but on the subject matter of torts deriving from violations of antitrust rules, the most delicate problem is posed neither by the identification of the criterion for the apportionment of liability, nor by the evidence or the quantification of losses, but by the proof of the *causal link*. We find ourselves facing a problem that is also relevant to losses attributable to *insider trading*: how to demonstrate that loss sustained at the individual level is directly linked to the breach of *antitrust* rules?

Only by admitting the capacity to sue on the part of consumer associations, that is with the introduction of *class actions*, could we have ensured an effective protection of consumers; an advantage which – given the current state of regulation – has not been deemed worthy of appreciation.

In the Green Paper on consumer protection dated 2. 10. 2001, the European Commission asks whether it is useful to prepare a unified text preceded by some general rules on fair trading. The solution to the problem might seem easy, if only we consider that there are many cases in which – again using the method of *fragmentation* – the Community has intervened to prevent unfair practices towards consumers; in as much as intervention by the supervising authority may be promoted also by a professional or by a professional body these interventions may be considered as aiming at ensuring general fairness, also in the relations between competitors. On the other hand, the increasing number of cross-border exchanges implies not only the transfer of goods and services from one Member State to another, but also the use of promotional techniques, advertising messages, sales procedures that reach beyond national borders. This situation is accentuated when- as is normal

---

[13] Nivarra, 'La tutela civile: profili sostanziali', in *Diritto antitrust italiano*, (Bologna: 1993) 1455; but see also V. Affernit (ed), *Concorrenza e mercato*, (Padova: 1994), and the contributions of numerous authors in *Econ. e dir. del terziario*, 1994, n.1. On consumer protection by the Antitrust Authority, see Amato, *Il potere e l'Antitrust*, (Bologna: 1998); F. Gobbo, *Il mercato e la tutela della concorrenza*, (Bologna: 1997).

nowadays -the market is globalized. The problem might be easily resolved if each country were equipped with rules on fair trading, and if these rules were of the same tenor. But this is not the case, and thus the solution is far from simple. In the international arena, an understanding has been reached in several specific sectors.[14]

In the European context, according to the results of a recent survey, as many as thirteen States envisage in their legal systems a general clause on fair trading, even if inspired by different models. In fact, there is the model which refers to *bonos mores*, one to fair commercial practices, and others that refer to unlawfulness or to *culpa*. The terminology varies, but each formula appears on the one hand tied to a general clause, and on the other hand to subjective criteria. It has been maintained that no model refers to *bona fide*, but if we deem applicable to our case, in addition to art. 2595, which must now be interpreted in the light of Italian constitutional and Community values, also art. 1175, the expression "fairness" becomes synonymous with objective "*bona fides*".

The major contrast among the various legal systems is not, however, so much on the formulae, as in the juxtaposition (which is nowadays typical in so many other sectors) between the legal systems of continental Europe and those of *common law*. In the latter, in fact, though we may envisage the highlighting of general principles of fair trading, the accepted model is based on self-regulation.

Now, as Hans Micklitz has highlighted, the general rules on which the single European market is based must coordinate, that is ensure the mutual compatibility of, three principles: competition, fairness in trading, consumer protection. These principles are not all placed on the same level, nor are they known as such, in the legal systems of the Member States. And prior to the approval of the Single Act, only competition, together with the four freedoms constituted the backbone of Community law, as the rights and interests of consumers were protected only indirectly. After the Single Act, but, I would add, above all after the Amsterdam Treaty, the protection of the rights and interests of consumers has become one of the immediate objectives of the Union. Thus not only must the three principles find a unified solution of reconciliation (hence the notion of 'practicable competition'), but, given their immediate relevance also in the national legal systems, they must also be applicable in the national legal systems.

---

[14] See PriceWaterhouseCoopers, Universiteit Utrecht, Tilburg University, *Final report. Study on Consumer law and the Information Society*, (Amsterdam, August, 2000).

In each system the three principles are combined differently. In the Italian system they are separated from each other and carry differing "weights". The strongest, by and large the absorbing principle, is the one which guarantees freedom of competition; its new legal format, consolidated since 1990 with a strong policy of awareness and defence of its prerogatives by the antitrust Authority, together with a strong power of intervention and results which have been appreciated both by the operators and by experts, has caused it to be considered also as inclusive of the principle of consumer protection. This, as several attempts have tried to clarify, is not possible either from a conceptual, practical, or formal point of view. From a conceptual viewpoint, because consumer protection would be merely an indirect and mediated effect of its application; from a practical viewpoint, because the aim of consumer protection might even be in conflict with competition; from a formal viewpoint, because consumer protection requires *ad hoc* interventions regarding pre-contractual information, the procedures for contract execution, and the myriad of adequate provisions of law bent on the requirements borne out of the individual regulations. The principle of fair trading is the weakest of the three, because it is not supported by an apparatus of clear and incisive rules.

This evolutionary path, which at the same time constitutes a possible solution to the fragmentation of the Community system and to the coordination of the three principles, should constitute the response to the well-founded uncertainties on the future of Community regulations, in these sectors, raised by the Green Paper on the subject of consumer protection.

But how should we proceed? Through the imposition of a number of general rules identical for everybody? Or through the process of harmonisation?

There are, as already mentioned, different levels of harmonisation depending on the subject matter of the individual directives, depending on the time and the context in which the directive was approved, depending on the objectives which the directives aim to achieve.

Observers believe that even if the harmonisation process does not achieve the level of uniformity, the current policy of the Union is aimed at achieving advanced harmonisation, and therefore approximation of laws at the highest level.

The drafting of a number of general rules that might be the epigraph of the single text on provisions relating to consumers, and at the same time providing the guiding reference for commentators, might be the premise for the process of total harmonisation. Commentators are, however, divided as to how this project could be achieved.

According to the Italian technique of drafting single texts, which do not constitute the simple juxtaposition of fragmented provisions, but their systematic organization, it would suffice to envisage one or more general rules which might expressly clarify, in the sector of trade, the principle of fairness. After all, we already have some clues in the legal fabric, especially in the more recent laws, from the fundamental law on the rights of consumers to the antitrust law. But we may welcome even more detailed models, bearing in mind the possible resolutions of Community law. That is, it would be possible to draft a list of practices considered unfair, which would serve to integrate the general rules and also serve as closure provisions.

The list, at Community level, might be integrated, in the individual countries, into list of further practices deemed to be unfair, as for the list of terms deemed unfair by way of presumption in the Directive on unfair terms in consumer contracts.

With the binding rules for all the Member States, with the minimal list of unfair practices, and with the recognition of self-regulatory Codes of conduct, we would start to achieve a uniform model, though neither a unified, nor an authoritarian model, which might respect both the principle of subsidiarity and the principle of autonomy of the individual national legal systems.

The alternative, at Community level (as it is not desirable to choose non-intervention, that is leaving things as they are), might be the introduction of a Community regulation, instead of a single text for the coordination of the directives. Formally, this I believe to be the preferable solution,[15] for many reasons. We could obviate the slowness brought on by the implementation of directives, which also imply different time-schedules for the approval of the same by the Member States. We could also obviate the discrepancies in the implementation of directives and even the divergences in the national implementation laws. Given the ever-increasing and ever more rapid cross-border circulation of goods and services, which is made simpler also by the introduction of the Euro, the fact of being able to count on the same rules in every corner of Europe would provide the consumer with more confidence and peace of mind, so as to overcome the barriers (also of a psychological nature) to *freedom of purchase*.

The Regulation model could also support those legal systems in which

---

[15] *Contra,* H-W. Micklitz, in this volume, Chapter 2.

a single text has not yet been approved, by supplying a coordinated body of laws on the rules concerning consumers. And thus it could constitute an instrument of progress and adjustment to the new requirements with more rapid effects that could be more easily envisaged by the same economic operators.

The problem still remains as to the level of consumer protection, a problem that must be addressed by the model that relies on directives and the general rules of the epigraph, and on the minimal list of unfair practices, and the regulatory model. How should we operate with those States that have already achieved very high standards of protection and could find them reduced, and how to deal with those States that do not envisage any protection except for the minimal protection afforded by Community law?

The solution is not legal but political and involves both aspects of national identity and aspects of the so-called European "citizenship" in the meaning given by T. Marshall.

VI. UNFAIR TRADING PRACTICES

On several occasions, while commenting on aspects of trading, it has been highlighted how domestic regulations are ridden with loopholes. Hence the desirability of the introduction, at Community level, as the issues under review have not yet been brought to the attention of the Italian Parliament or Government, of a general body of rules which imposes fair practices upon traders. The European Consumer Law Group, thanks to the dedication of its two major leaders, the Dutchman Ewoud Hondius and the German Hans W. Micklitz, has examined the issue of the so-called 'pyramid systems' and of multi-level marketing to verify how this may affect the interests of consumers. This is one of the most aggressive sales techniques, because contact with the consumer is not made by an employee of the distributor but by a subject who acts on behalf of the distributor, on an *ad hoc* basis, and may present himself under the guise of a neighbour, of a friend, of an acquaintance, and so forth; it is difficult even to distinguish, in this case, between a sales proposal and a simple advice to purchase.

A more careful examination can highlight many of the aggressive techniques through which this economic activity is pursued: techniques which fair competition, by itself, would not harm, because they do not reflect on the interests of other professionals, but concern only the relationship between the professional and the consumer. Thus it is not sufficient to reason in terms of 'fair competition' in order to achieve a satisfactory level of protection for consumers. Instead, it is necessary to place before the fragmented regulation that concerns, on a sector by sector basis, the individual economic relations between professionals and consumers, certain rules of a general nature which relate not to individual actions (messages, promises, techniques of Contract execution, agreements, registrations, etc.), but activities considered in general, the practices of professionals.

The general 'fairness' clause (which can be deemed similar to the "objective *bona fides*") or fair trading clause, may be sufficient to strike at those practices which harm the consumer, because they take advantage of his good faith, because they are needlessly aggressive, because they have "surprise" effects, and because they are basically deceitful.

Correct conduct is one of the models that inspire the codes of conduct, of self-regulation, of moral suasion adopted by almost all sectors of trade.

But the general rules which may be placed before special regulations are not in conflict with those codes, rather they support and reinforce them.

First, they operate where the self-regulating codes have not yet been adopted.

Secondly, they operate in those cases in which self-regulatory codes do not take a stand.

Thirdly, legal rules being superior or super-ordained with respect to the codes, which are in any case merely an expression of contractual freedom, though, in most instances, they are also merely the expression of corporate interests of the professionals of that sector, they can amend the self-regulatory codes where the latter are lacking or restrictive.

We should therefore add to the soft law rules of a general nature that allow the interpreter to adjust them to the most diverse (and often unforeseeable) circumstances, given that we cannot codify a comprehensive inventory of all the possible cases of unfair practices.

This is in the interest of consumers, but also of the professionals, who, by behaving fairly, would compete 'on equal terms' with consumers.

4. Conflict of Interests and the Fair Dealing Duty

Giorgio De Nova

I. INTRODUCTION

In 1877, in his work *Der Zweck im Recht,* Rudolf von Jhering wrote:

> Until there will be one's own interest at the helm of rights, it is clear that it will avoid to damage itself. But the guaranty inborn in one's own interest falls when the helm is assigned to a stranger's arms: it creates the risk that the helmsman follows the route appearing better to him, not on the basis of the others' interest, but on the basis of its own interest.[1]

This is the problem of the conflict of interests.

I fully agree with the proposition that a framework directive on unfair trading would need to be more specific then simply supplying a general clause. The aim of this paper is to verify whether to act in conflict of interests could be considered as a particular illustration of unfair dealing. With the expression 'conflict of interests', I will refer to the case in which two interests belonging to different individuals are incompatible, because to pursue one's interest means to affect, wholly or partially, the another's interest.

II. THE NOTION OF "CONFLICT OF INTERESTS"

1. Conflict of Interests and the Conclusion of Contracts in the Name of a Principal

The Unidroit Convention on Agency in the International Sale of Goods undersigned in Geneva in 1983 does not deal with conflict of interests. Nor does the Unidroit principles of International Commercial Contracts dated 1994, which deliberately do not cover agency problems.

---

[1] R. Jhering, *Der Zweck im Recht*, Breitkopf und Härtel, 1877, I, 7, 8.

H. Collins (ed.) The Forthcoming EC Directive on Unfair and Commercial Practices, 111-130.
©2004. Kluwer Law International. Printed in the Netherlands.

The Principles of European Contract Law (PECL) dedicates Article 3: 205 to the 'conflict of interests'.[2] It is the first international text to do so. Article 3: 205 governs the case of an agent who acts in the name of the principal (and not the case of an intermediary who acts on behalf of a principal, but not in the name of the principal). Art. 3: 205 PECL states that 'if a contract concluded by an agent involves the agent in a conflict of interest of which the third party knew or could not have been unaware, the principal may avoid the contract'. In this context, the conflict of interests can be considered to be a reason for invalidity of the contract concluded by the agent with the third party. In the case in which the agent acted also as agent for a third party or when the agent in its personal capacity contracted with himself, it is presumed that the interest of the principal has been neglected.

The presumption can be rebutted. The principal may not avoid the contract if he consented to the agent to act in such a way (or could not have been unaware of it), and if the agent has disclosed the conflict of interests and he did not object. The rationale of such a rule is that a principal cannot be bound to a contract which is different from the contract that he himself would have executed, or (which is the same thing) that would have been concluded by an agent exclusively pursuing the principal's interest.

2. Conflict of Interests and Fiduciary Duties

Thus far the discussion of the concept of conflict of interests could not be used to specify any notion of fair dealing, because the focus was on the validity of the contract and not on the party's behaviour. In the following section I will suggest a use of the notion as a way to give normative content to fair dealing. The problem of conflict of interests should not be seen only when a party acts in the name of another party: it arises also when a party acts on behalf of another, and not in its name.[3] If we consider the substantive relationship principal – agent, and not the authority to act in the name of the principal (the power of attorney), we can see anyway that 'an agent does, because the principal places confidence in him, owe a fiduciary duty to the principal'.[4]

---

[2]　O. Lando and H. Beale (eds), *Principles of European Contract Law Parts I and II* (The Hague: Kluwer, 2000).

[3]　De Nova, *La rappresentanza: nozione e disciplina*, in Visintini (ed.), *Rappresentanza e gestione*, (Padova: 1992) 17; Sacco and Graziadei, *Sostituzione e rappresentanza*, in Digesto IV ed., UTET 1998, 619.

[4]　G. Treitel, *The Law of Contract,* 10th edn, (London: Sweet and Maxwell, 1999) 690.

As has been stressed, "the core idea is that a fiduciary is a person who is held to duties positively to promote another person's interests even at the costs of his own'.[5] In the United States, the Restatement of the Law of Agency, 2nd, § 1 defines agency as a fiduciary relationship, and in §§ 387 and the following sections reference is made to 'duties of loyalty'. Independently from the fact that the agent specifies that he is acting on behalf of the principal, it nevertheless constitutes a breach of the fiduciary duty by the agent 'to put himself into a position where his interest and duties conflict'.[6]

With regard to the principal – agent relationship, the EEC Directive 86/653/EEC on the coordination of laws of the Member States relating to self – employed commercial agents in art. 3.1 does not expressly deal with conflict of interests. But it states that, 'In performing his activity a commercial agent *must look after his principal's interest* and act dutifully and in *good faith*'.

The conflict of interests, as unfair dealing, is nevertheless expressly considered in Community law involving a theme related to consumer: investment services. The English model provided the basis for this area of community law protection.

Article 10 of the Directive 93/22/EEC on investment services in securities states that investment firms 'shall be structured and organized in such a way as to minimize the risk of clients' interests being prejudiced by conflict of interest between the firm and its clients or between one of its clients and another'. And article 11.1 states that an investment firm shall "try to avoid conflict of interests and, where they cannot be avoided, ensure that its clients are fairly treated".

In this case, the rule that forbids a person to act in a "conflict of interests" situation applies to the investment firm, even if it acts just on behalf of the client but not in his name (as can happen according to Italian law, see art. 21, Dlgs 24.02.1998, n. 58). The duty exists even before the investment activity: the investor's organization shall be structured and organized in order to avoid a conflict of interests.

I briefly refer to how the Directive 93/22 has been executed in Italy. This should offer some more precise indications regarding the suitability of the

---

[5] S. Whittaker and R. Zimmermann, '*Good* faith in European contract law: surveying the legal landscape' , in S. Whittaker and R. Zimmermann (eds), *Good faith in European contract law*, (Cambridge: Cambridge University Press, 2000) 46 (Bussani e Mattei gen. eds.)

[6] Treitel, above note 4, 690.

notion of "conflict of interests" to work as a parameter of unfair dealing.

Art. 21, lett. C) Italian statute provides that an 'intermediary shall organize itself to reduce to the minimum the risk of conflict of interests and, in situation of conflict, shall act anyway to secure transparency and fair treatment of its clients'.

With regard to regulations of the Authority of control, art. 27 of the Consob regulation 11522/1998 provides that: 'authorized intermediaries shall not act with or on behalf of clients in cases where they have – directly or indirectly – an interest in conflict, even if deriving from group relationships, from joint execution of more services or from other business relationship both regarding themselves or any company of the group. Such prohibition is valid unless intermediaries have previously informed, by written notice, the investor on the nature and the extension of his interest in the business and unless the investor expressly consented the execution by written notice. In cases where the transaction is executed by phone, the fulfilment of the mentioned duties of information and the release of the relevant authorization by the investor shall be registered on a magnetic tape or using another equivalent instrument'.

Regarding the organization's aspects of the discipline, the Consob has acted with the communications n. DIN./20844 dated 16th March 2000 and n. DIN./1011290 dated 15th February 2001, through which Consob suggested to authorized intermediaries not to insert into contracts clauses providing commissions quantified according to the number and the quality of the transactions entered into. This step was taken in order to avoid the so called *churning* practice, i.e. to multiply transactions on behalf of the client, not because every single transaction fulfils the client's interest, but because the volume and the quantity of transactions satisfies its own interest in obtaining commissions.

Some comments are in order: a) it is accepted that the conflict of interests cannot be removed, because it is embedded in the performance of investment services, and above all by multifunctional subjects. The concept of avoiding a conflict of interests provides a standard for the discipline of the activity.

b) The requirement of transparency involves duties the supply information. But informing investors of the existence of the conflict of interests is not enough: it is necessary for the investor to have expressly authorized the conclusion of any transaction where there is a conflict of interest.

c) The investor's authorisation does not exclude the obligation that the intermediary should act in any case according to a standard of fair treatment, i.e. in the client's interest.[7] It has to be stressed that § 31 par. 1 n. 2 Wp.HG has translated the expression 'fairly treated' mentioned in the EEC directive with the phrase 'due observance of the client's interest'.

d) 'Fair treatment' means that the intermediary shall act pursuing the interest of the client, and not pursuing his own interest or the interest of subjects connected to him, and not forwarding other clients' interests.[8]

At the moment, a revision to the EEC Directive on the investment services is being undertaken. A proposal for a directive may be approved by the end of 2002 by the Council of Ministry of the EEC and by the European Parliament. In the most recent document prepared by DG Internal Market, the Commission stresses how it proposes to revise the orientation of the law. The proposal suggests that it is necessary 'to introduce different dispositions concerning the management of conflicts of interests, considering the great and increasing importance that they have to the aim of safeguarding the clients' interests – especially when authorized intermediaries carry on different basic activities such as the dealing on own account and the execution of orders on behalf of clients'.

It is important to notice that acting in conflict of interests constitutes a breach of the fiduciary duty, and that this requirement goes beyond the non fulfilment of the duty of diligence or care, but "connotes disloyalty or infidelity".[9]

The consequence of acting in conflict of interests is a breach of the fiduciary duty that carries – rather than the invalidity of the contract with the third party – the duty to pay damages.[10]

Regarding the quantification of damages, the client should be entitled to the difference between the sum that would have obtained from an investment not vitiated by the conflict of interests and the sum actually obtained.

The principle in force in Italian law, under which the client who has suffered damages cannot obtain a restoration greater than the actual damage suffered, seems to exclude the possibility that such a client might be entitled to recover the enrichment that has been obtained, at his detriment, from the transaction in conflict.

---

[7] Sartori, 'Il conflitto di interessi tra intermediari e clienti nello svolgimento dei servizi di investimento e accessori: un problema risolto?' Riv. Dir. Civ. 2001, I, 206.

[8] Sartori, above note 7.

[9] *Bristol & West B.S. v Motyhen* [1998] Ch. 1 at 18: Treitel, above note 4, 690.

[10] Roppo, 'Le varie tipologie di conflitto di interessi e i rimedi', and Afferni, *Rappresentanza e conflitto di interessi nell'ambito dell'impresa*, in G. Visintini, *Rappresentanza e gestione*, Cedam, 1992, 188 and following and 201 and following.

In case the intermediary acts pursuing the interest of another client, the damaged client shall be entitled to the difference between the return obtained by the preferred client and his own return.[11]

3. Conflict of Interests and Sale Contracts

It has been said that 'a conflict of interests is imbedded in the structure of bargain because in such case the typical profit pursued through the execution of the business shall be obtained by each party against the other'.[12] Therefore, in bargaining situations one party will pursue its own interest and the so too will the other party seek to further its own interests. The only limit on the pursuit of self-interest is provided by the general duty to act in good faith.

As for Italian law, it can be remembered that in 1983 Professor Bianca made a proposal to give greater specificity the general clause of good faith. He suggested that it could be identified as 'the duty of each party to secure the utility of the other party up to the limit that it does not imply for it a considerable sacrifice'.[13] Prof. Bianca's proposal has been accepted by the Italian Supreme Court, which has stated that good faith implies that 'each of the parties is obliged to secure the interest of the other party in cases where such duty does not imply a considerable sacrifice of its own interest'.[14]

One party can therefore pursue its own interest even if, as a consequence, the other party's interest will be prejudiced. But one party must secure the interest of the other party if it can do so without a significant sacrifice of its own interest.

A question that in my opinion has been neglected is whether a subject, who is a party in two contractual relations, can act in conflict of interest in the sense that it can prefer the interest of one contractual party to the interests of the other contractual party.

Let us take the case of a chain sale. The seller has a contractual relation with the producer and another contractual relation with the purchaser. If the seller provides a clause in the sale contract that excludes the producer's liability, he is acting in the interest of the producer and against the interest of the purchaser.

---

[11] Maffeis, *Contratto in conflitto di interessi e rimedi*, in press, cap. VI, par. 4, note 48.

[12] P. Ferro Luzzi, *I contratti associativi*, Giuffrè, 1971, 112.

[13] C.M. Bianca, 'La nozione di buona fede quale regola di comportamento contrattuale', Riv.dir.civ., 1983, I, 210.

[14] Cass. 20 aprile 1994, n. 3775, in Corr. Giur. 1994, 566, and many other subsequent decisions.

A second example reverses the priority accorded to the different interests. According to art. 2.5 of the Directive 99/44 on the sale of consumer goods, the seller is liable if the goods do not conform to the characteristics stated by the producer in advertising or on labelling. But the seller is not liable if the statement has been corrected by the time of conclusion of the contract. The seller could therefore correct by itself the statement, thereby avoiding its potential liability. In so doing, the seller acts in its own interest and in the consumer's interest, but against the producer's interest, because the consumer could refrain from purchasing the goods.

A third example is the case of the seller applying an extraordinary low price. Supermarkets, being advantaged by the high discount applied over all its products, can sell some goods below cost. In so doing, the seller acts in the interest of the consumer who obtains benefits from low prices and simultaneously in its own interests, because the supermarket is likely to attract more customers. But the supermarket can be seen to be acting against the interest of the producer, whose trade mark or brand is devalued. Recently, Italy has enacted a discipline ruling on the issue of below cost selling (d.p.r. 6 aprile 2001, n. 218 which applies art. 15 d.lg. 1993 n. 114): such selling is permitted, within certain limits, and on condition of an obligation to supply certain information.

III.   CONCLUSIONS

A)   It is unduly restrictive to regard the prohibition of conflict of interests as an issue that arises only in connection with a contract entered into by an agent in the name of a principal;

B)   A prohibition on acting in conflict of interests becomes important in order to identify the content of the duty of fair dealing in the broader range of cases of contracts characterized by a fiduciary relationship;

C)   Beyond this, when considering contracts involving exchanges such as sales, the prohibition on acting in a way that involves a conflict of interests can give some indication of the meaning of the concept of fair dealing.

5. Co-Regulation's Role in the Development of European Fair Trading Laws

Geraint Howells

The promotion of 'soft law' techniques of regulation has for a long time been on the Community's consumer protection agenda.[1] More recently the phrase soft law has been replaced by co-regulation.[2] These developments have taken a variety of guises. The most sophisticated integration of soft law has been in the context of product safety and can be dated back to the new approach to technical harmonisation in 1985.[3] This used the standardisation process as a mechanism for involving stakeholders in concretising legislative aspirations of safety. To date the role of standards in the sphere of economic consumer protection has been less developed and has generally involved free-standing efforts to produce codes that have not directly integrated with the legal framework. In other words, they have been a substitute and not a complement to legal regulation.

The recent Green Paper on European Union Consumer Protection[4] and the subsequent Follow-Up Communication[5] both call for the greater development of Codes of Conduct and the use of non-binding guidance with greater stakeholder involvement. Neither of these techniques, as mapped out in embryonic form in those documents, seems as advantageous as the role which standardisation has played in the 'New Approach' to technical standardisation. Although the Follow-Up Communication does hint at some similarities with the New Approach and the introduction of a presumption of conformity, the main differences are that Code development is still seen as an essentially private pursuit. Stakeholder involvement is only mentioned in the

---

[1] For a discussion of its development see, G. Howells and T. Wilhelmsson, *EC Consumer Law*, (Dartmouth, 1997) at 327, and in more detail G. Howells, 'The Function of Soft Law in EC Consumer law' in P. Craig and C. Harlow (eds), *Law-making in the European Union* (Kluwer, 1998).

[2] See White Paper, *European Governance*, COM (2001) 428

[3] OJ 1985 C 136/1.

[4] COM (2001) 531: 'Green Paper'.

[5] COM (2002) 289: 'Follow-up'.

H. Collins (ed.) The Forthcoming EC Directive on Unfair and Commercial Practices, 119-129.
©2004. Kluwer Law International. Printed in the Netherlands.

context of guidance, which is to be non-binding. Therefore what is missing is an attempt to involve stakeholders in ways which produce soft law rules that have some validity within the legal regime and are firmly integrated into a legal framework. However, the use of soft law is a relatively new concept which has taken on a variety of forms, and one detects that even the Commission is unsure of exactly what the contours of soft law regulation in fair trading law ought to be. This paper will try to raise some questions that need to be addressed if soft and co-regulatory techniques are to have a meaningful role within European fair trading laws.

This paper will argue that standardisation can have an important role to play in the development of European fair trading laws. However, it will also suggest that the New Approach to technical standardisation cannot simply be transplanted as a model to the fair trading context. The points of distinction from technical harmonisation include the fact that the basic values at stake are more contestable; consumers are less well organised to engage in the process and government; and the courts have traditionally had a stronger role to play in this area. Whilst it is possible, and probably desirable, for legislation to fix the parameters of fair trading more firmly and for consumer involvement to be enhanced, nevertheless traditions of state and court involvement in the development of fair trading laws need to be taken into account. That said, some key elements of the New Approach could usefully be adopted for fair trading law. In particular it is crucial that standardisation not be viewed as a stand-alone activity, but rather be integrated into the legislative framework. The practise of standardisation should no longer be viewed as a purely private function controlled by business. The inclusion of consumers must be seen as an important aspect of the process.

I.   Co-regulation

Recently co-regulation seems to be in vogue. The term, 'co-regulation' is a much bandied about concept in governance discussions. This paper argues that co-regulation should mean 'co' in a double sense of (i) integrating voluntary standards into the legal framework, as well as, (ii) involving all stakeholders in the development of those standards. This is not dissimilar to the use of the term by the European Commission in the White Paper on European Governance.[6]

---

[6]   COM (2001) 428.

The White Paper says: 'Co-regulation combines legislative and regulatory action with actions taken by the actors most concerned, drawing on their practical expertise.'[7] The White Paper makes some sensible suggestions about co-regulation. It needs a sound legislative framework. It should only be used where it adds value and serves the general interest. It should involve organisations that are representative, accountable and capable of following open procedures. And co-regulation should be compatible with competition rules. However, the White Paper also makes some more contestable comments.

For instance, the White Paper says that co-regulation should not be used in situations where rules need to apply in a uniform way in every state. This seems strange. If uniform laws really are not needed then one might suggest that the legal basis for any form of binding legislation on to which the soft law might combine would be hard to defend. Soft law would certainly not be suited to fair trade legislation where the aim, as required by Art. 95, is to harmonise trading conditions. It also says soft law is only suited to cases where fundamental rights and major political choices are not called into question. As human rights legislation increasing is being used in the commercial law context, how does one decide what is so unimportant that it can be satisfied by co-regulation? It would probably have been better to have not put this point in that form, but rather to have restricted its comment to the point that the exact shape of co-regulation will vary from sector to sector.

The introduction of soft law into the legal framework can take on many forms. Indeed, the Green Paper invoked at least two – Codes which bind traders who claim to adhere to them, and guidelines that may assist harmonising enforcement but have no binding force in their own right. Nevertheless, it seems the Commission is as yet uncertain about what co-regulation is, and how it should be introduced into the governance landscape of Europe.

II.   THE NEW APPROACH TO TECHNICAL HARMONISATION

At this stage it might be useful to explain the principles behind the New Approach to technical harmonisation. Then the Commission's proposals in the area of fair trading will be described and critiqued.

New Approach directives deal with broad product sectors, and establish the general obligation only to supply safe products. The concept of safety is fleshed out in an Annex containing essential safety requirements. Producers can either find their own way of satisfying these requirements, or else comply

---

[7]   *Ibid* at p. 21.

with standards developed to assist compliance and which benefit from a presumption of conformity. Compliant products bear the CE marking. The CE marking is not in fact a consumer safety mark to inform consumers, but rather a passport to relatively unhindered circulation in Europe, which is addressed to national enforcement authorities. However, these New Approach directives may not be the proper comparator for a general fair trading directive.

The correct comparator perhaps ought to be the General Product Safety Directive.[8] Interestingly, the revised version of that Directive also foresees a greater role for standardisation in establishing compliance with the general safety requirement. Art. 3(2) now provides that:

> 'A product shall be presumed safe as far as the risks and risk categories covered by relevant national standards transposing European standards, the references of which have been published by the Commission in the Official Journal of the European Communities in accordance with Article 4.'

III.   Co-regulation and the Green Paper

The Green Paper on Consumer Protection made three important points about its approach to self- and co-regulation.[9] First, any general duty would define non-compliance with a voluntary commitment made by business in respect of consumers as either a misleading or unfair trading practice. Although this is a positive step forward, nevertheless this may be too limited a development, if codes of conduct are to be a co-regulatory tool for fleshing out the general standard. Second, this obligation would extend to trade associations. Presumably all that this proposal means is that trade associations could be brought to book, if their codes breached the law. It is highly unlikely that codes would actually breach the law. Codes sometimes have an educative role in reinforcing what the law states, but few code drafters would seek to offer less protection than required by the law. More often they are seen as engines for voluntarily forcing up standards beyond the legal minimum, especially in areas where legal norms may not be well suited. Finally, the Green Paper concluded that it would not be appropriate for the Commission to endorse or approve codes because of the potential for abuse of competition rules. I shall

---

[8]   OJ 2002 L11/4.
[9]   Green Paper', 14-15.

argue that this is problematic, if consumers are to have confidence in codes across Europe. Thankfully, in the Follow-Up Communication there are signs that the Commission is willing to rethink this position.[10]

The Green Paper also floated the idea of practical guidance.[11] User-friendly language would be used to benefit consumers, businesses, judges, and enforcement officials. It was rather vague about the form of the proposed guidance, stating that it could either take the form of Commission recommendations or, as in the unfair terms legislation, indicative lists of general and sector specific examples of commercial practices. The Commission seemed to favour the latter, slightly, stating it had the advantage of formally linking the guidance to the underlying legislation. This practical guidance was seen as a way of increasing stakeholder participation, but it was said that a structure for it would have to be established in the framework directive, and that EU wide bodes would have to be better organised than at present. It was also suggested that a regulatory committee might be set up to keep the guidance under review.

IV.   THE FOLLOW-UP COMMUNICATION

The consultation following from the Green Paper found that the issue of Codes caused the most controversy and don't knows, but still the majority of business and consumer respondents favoured the development of EU-wide codes. However, a large majority of those businesses, which expressed a view, opposed making voluntary commitments to code legally binding.[12] The issue of non-binding guidance also provoked questions. Whilst there was broad support of the use of EU level guidance, there was clearly some unease about its value and the structures for establishing it. Although for some respondents the proposed guidance would add certainty and clarity, others feared that it would not solve the problem of fragmentation.[13]

The Follow-Up Communication then goes on to set out criteria to be followed in the development of codes at the EU level. These include:

- Codes should be voluntary and not bind non-signatories;
- Non-compliance with voluntary commitments should be considered as

---

[10] 'Follow-up' 11.

[11] 'Green Paper', 15

[12] 'Follow-up', 5.

[13] 'Follow-up', 6.

misleading and therefore an unfair commercial practice;

- Only business -consumer commercial practices would be covered;
- Only non-compliance with firm commitments (i.e. to follow certain 'good practices') would be misleading and not non-compliance with aspirational commitment ('Best efforts');
- Code owners should be responsible for conformity of codes with legislation, but not legally liable for compliance of their members;
- Encouragement of EU-wide codes providing an implicit 'presumption of conformity' equivalent to standards under the New Approach;
- Further consideration to be given to the public endorsement of codes.

Whilst the Commission continues to stress the need for non-binding guidance and stakeholder involvement, the Follow-up Communication is vague on its content and form, and simply says there is a need for further research.

V.   CRITIQUE OF CO-REGULATION IN THE FAIR TRADING CONTEXT

1.   Core Concepts

One sharp difference between the product safety field and the fair trading arena is that the central objective of safety law is obvious. Admittedly safety is in itself a polycentric concept, and there may be debates as to the appropriate level,[14] but at least there is some consensus on the scope and objective of the law. In the fair trading field, that cannot be said.

Concepts such as *bonos mores*, fair commercial practices, good marketing practices, unlawfulness, and fault are found in the law of Member States, and they are aimed at a wide variety of potentially unfair practices. The Green Paper even hints that it may be more practical to have a directive that simply deals with deceptive and misleading practices.[15] Micklitz has also noted in a report to the Commission that this even hides the true extent of the disparity. Differences between labels is one thing, but the content behind the label is even more significant.[16]

---

[14] See J. Henderson , 'Judicial Review of Manufacturers' Conscious Design Choices: The Limits of Adjudication' (1973) 73 *Columbia Law Review* 1531.

[15] 'Green Paper', 13.

[16] See VIEW, *Study on the feasibility of a general legislative framework on fair trading*, http://europa.eu.int/comm/consumers

The problem is that, whilst we all have a fairly common sense ability to determine which product design is safer (we may quibble over some trade-offs or there may be the occasional difference of approach), in contrast the issue as to what trading practices are fair or good or moral is far more open to debate. Different people have different views on the ability of the consumer to protect herself, the need for traders to have concern for consumer welfare, and indeed will have different reactions to whether the dissatisfaction of consumers to a 'freely' struck bargain should be relevant. This is really a topic for other papers to explore in more detail.

It may be possible to agree a general clause that reflects a consensus view of what should be regulated, at least at the European level.[17] The problem for standardisation is that if the outcome of the standardisation process is uncertain, it is harder for those mechanisms to work effectively. Whilst there is always some room for discussion at the margins when generating standards following a New Approach mandate, the standardisation process works in the safety field exactly because those discussions are at the margins. If the central objective of the controls is still up for debate, then the standardisation process may struggle to bring about consensus solutions.

2.   Soft Law and an Integrated Approach

The most striking feature of soft law across the European Community is how it is treated differently within different cultures. It is most developed in the UK and Ireland. In Scandinavia it is known in the context of public authority negotiation with industry. In the Netherlands it is a feature of their consumer law. But in many other parts of Europe, it is hardly known of, and in some countries it is even openly derided. A framework directive which does not integrate soft law and still views standardisation as a private function will perpetuate the imbalances of the impact of Community law.

Those countries which lack a history of using soft law techniques are only likely to take it seriously if it forms part of the legal regime, whilst those countries where it is already well developed normally have a place for it within their legal architecture. A stand needs to be taken, so that consumer representatives will be enabled to participate with industry to create stan-

---

[17] But the preference for a maximal harmonisation directive, i.e. fettering the ability of Member States to have national rules, and mutual recognition and the country of origin principle means that the task is likely to be the complicated one of finding a formula that Member States are happy with covering all the practices they want to regulate.

dards which are meaningful and yet leave room for flexibility and innovation. These standards must be arrived at through a procedure which is open to all stakeholders.

However, this is a debate which must be capable of influencing the content of the general clause. One incentive for industry to engage in the question of what is fair trading would be for compliance with the codes to be a passport to compliance with general fair trading laws. Another might be if guidance was generated, which though formally non-binding had some persuasive force within the legal regime, so that it could be taken account of by enforcement officials and courts as indicative of fair trading practice. There is clearly a debate to be had about the respective roles of the guidance and codes. Do they both contribute to our understanding of the interpretation of the general clause or are Codes stand-alone concepts?

3. Codes as Stand-Alone Concepts

The Green Paper does not see Codes as being integrated into the framework directive. Codes would only be brought into this framework by a trader reneging on a voluntary commitment and that being deemed a misleading or deceptive practice. This might, however, seem too cautious.

Under the New Approach, standardisation should give content to the general clause and in that way at least influence court's application of the general clause. This is one way to mitigate the free rider problem often associated with standardisation or following codes. If codes are to be stand-alone concepts, then compliance with them has to add real value, or else businesses will simply not sign up to them or be diligent in compliance. Also, if codes are to be a stand-alone concept, it is even more important that there should be non-binding guidance to flesh out any general clause.

Unfortunately, the Green Paper still seems to think in terms of self-regulation rather than co-regulation, despite a nod and a wink in the direction of stakeholder involvement. These terms are much debated, but it has already been argued that co-regulation should be 'co' in the double sense both of integrating the codes into the legislative framework and of fully involving stakeholders. The Green Paper clearly sees the prime developers of codes as private bodies such as trade associations (and indeed it says the general duty should apply to trade association bodies). Standardisation under the New Approach is quite different, and crucially involves stakeholders in the development of the standards.

4. The Forum for Generating Codes

Technical standards are developed by standardisation bodies – CEN at the European level, and bodies such as DIN, AFNOR and BSI at the national level. Although admittedly industry dominated, these bodies have the potential to provide a neutral forum for debate, and indeed most such bodies have mechanisms for the involvement of consumers. Indeed, this involvement of consumers is supported by the EU through ANEC.[18] There are of course some problems with co-ordinating consumer representation in the safety field, given that for the representation to have an impact, the consumer bodies need technical expertise, which they only possess in a few countries.

The question of fair trading seems, if anything, more appropriate for resolving by a proper dialogue between consumers and industry than technical safety harmonisation, because it is of a less scientific character. Yet consumers seem less willing to engage in it, and equally industry seems less willing to engage with consumers. The standardisation model used in safety matters does not seem to work. In large part this failure is because trade associations have a strong self-interest in keeping control of the process for fear of members seeing little value if conduct standards are determined in another forum. Certainly, the suggestion of the OFT in the UK that the BSI should be involved in setting trading standards was given a cold shoulder by industry. Also the standardisation process seems to be too technical to deal with fair trading matters, or at least that is some of the anecdotal evidence from the experience of developing standards for complaints handling.

Many government bodies have had a lot of experience in promoting good trade practices, and this has been enhanced by the unfair contract terms directive. If standards bodies are not the appropriate forum for developing Codes, perhaps government bodies need to take a stronger lead in establishing standards. The UK model is for approval of Codes by the OFT, and this is currently being strengthened so that following the Enterprise Act 2002, only those Codes that really prove themselves to be effective in practice will obtain a logo signifying approval. This will be judged against a set of core criteria laid down by the OFT. The actual setting of the standards again, however, remains in private hands.

Is there not a role for the state to be more proactive at the European level? Even if individual industry standards are also needed, could certain guide-

---

[18]   B. Farquhar, 'Consumer Representation in Standardisation' [1995] *Consumer Law Journal* 56.

lines not be established at a national or Community level. The Commission initially set itself against even approving codes, let alone establishing criteria or fixing horizontal codes. This position was supported by arguments based on competition law, which one might suspect to be more theoretical that real, at least if one adopts the technique of the New Approach of always allowing other means of meeting the general standard as well as compliance with standards.

Perhaps some parallels might be drawn from the approach with regard to conformity assessment.[19] In this area Europe establishes standards, which national governments have to check are met by conformity assessment bodies and the Member States then notify the names of conforming bodies to Brussels. Could Europe not set out minimum criteria for fair trading codes? National governments could test codes against these criteria, and then allow them to use a logo demonstrating conformity to minimum European standards. At the risk of imposing yet another potential source of confusion, on an already sometimes over informed consuming public, there could perhaps be some sort of logo, which not only signifies compliance to consumers, but also can act as a passport for trading practices around Europe in much the same way as the CE marking does. Consumers shopping abroad would then know whether a Code at least met certain minimum standards. It would be important that this logo was awarded only when Codes had proven they were effective in practice.

One might question, whether, if Codes develop in this way, there is a need for both Codes and non-binding guidance. Certainly there would be if Codes only bound those who voluntarily committed to following them, for there would be a significant free rider problem. One way to resolve the guidance/Code conundrum might be to consider a hierarchy whereby the non-binding guidance is at a lower level and seeks to establish what amounts to unfair, deceptive and misleading practices. The Codes would be at a higher level and seek to go further and promote fair practices. In this model, the non-binding guidance would be the important safety net for consumers, and one would have to consider carefully the forum for generating this guidance and also question just how non-binding it should be. The Follow-Up Communication noted some scepticism amongst the business community about the establishment of yet another regulatory committee at the EU level charged with this task.[20] In relation to the guidance one might want to reflect the different

---

[19] See Council Resolution, *A Global Approach to Conformity Assessment*: OJ 1990 C 10/1.
[20] 'Follow-up', 5.

national traditions whereby some states have left the development of fair trading practices to the courts and others have had more state involvement.

VI. Conclusions

It seems clear that co-regulatory instruments will have an important role to play in developing European fair trading laws. This seems positive, for many of the service levels implied by fair trading are unsuited to legislative determination and are best fixed by a dialogue between traders and consumers within a legislative framework. It is important that the legal effects of any resulting rules are both tangible and well defined. This is particularly important within Europe where soft law has a varied take-up and different degrees of respect within Europe. Central to the effectiveness of any co-regulatory rules will be a clear framework within which they can operate. There will have to have a clear central concept that is expanded upon within the framework directive, so that the co-regulatory structures can give content to agreed rules, rather than simply become another site for debate as to what the appropriate standards should be. The functions of non-binding guidance and Codes need to be carefully thought out. Their relationship to one another and to the general standard needs careful consideration.

The success of the introduction of co-regulatory techniques into European fair trading laws may largely depend upon working out these details. There should be caution before moving to adopt a framework directive that leaves a lot to be decided by co-regulatory procedures, which have yet to be fully developed and thought through. There are many ways in which soft law techniques can be integrated; it is important to know just what is being proposed. Any proposals should seek to involve all stakeholders in open discussion and ensure that the resulting rules have a clear basis in the legal structure, albeit that they may not be formally binding or only binding if voluntarily agreed to. These elements of stakeholder involvement and integration into the legal regime are features which can distinguish 'co'-regulation from 'self'-regulation and make it more palatable to consumers.

6. EC Competition Rules on Vertical Restrictions and the Realities of a Changing Retail Sector on National Contract Laws

Jules Stuyck and Tom Van Dyck

I. INTRODUCTION AND LIMITATIONS

In the present text, we shall focus on the changing and changed realities of vertical arrangements, and critically examine from this perspective the Commission Regulation No 2790/1999 of 22 December 1999 on the application of Article 81(3) of the Treaty of the European Community to categories of vertical agreements and concerted practices (the "Block Exemption Regulation"),[1] as well as the accompanying Guidelines on Vertical Restraints (the "Guidelines").[2]

In particular, in section II, we shall attempt to show that, although vertical relationships often are believed to involve a manufacturer drawing on vertical restraints to control retailers, the relationship between retailers and manufacturers is actually a dynamic one rather than a static one. Their mutual relationship, it will be argued, is more subtle than it appears to be at first sight. More specifically, the text will show that, since the 1950s in the US and later also on the European markets, a shift of power towards a certain category of large retailers (i.e. the superstore or supermarket chains) has occurred. Moreover, in the course of the 1990s, this shift of power may have been further facilitated by innovations in information technology. Technological developments may have provided large – or more precisely: sophisticated – retail stores with a cost-efficient capability to obtain an enormous mass of data and information on customer behavior. Such data and information, it will be further argued in the text, may serve as leverage for the bargaining power of those sophisticated retail stores not only in their downward relation with consumers, but also in their upward relation with wholesalers, distributors or manufacturers. This leverage results in a changed and changing

---

[1] OJ 1999 L-336/21.
[2] 2000/C 291/01, OJ 2000 C-291/1

H. Collins (ed.) The Forthcoming EC Directive on Unfair and Commercial Practices, 131-186.
©2004. Kluwer Law International. Printed in the Netherlands.

manufacturer-retailer relationship. For this reason, the text comes up with the notion of the *'dynamics of the (changed or changing) manufacturer-retailer relationship'*. The text illustrates this notion with three instances which we believe are indicative of the shift in power towards large and sophisticated retailers and exemplify the impact of their 'buying power' on the upward distribution chain: (i) the use of 'loyalty schemes', (ii) the deployment of 'category management', and (iii) the occurrence of 'slotting allowances'. The discussion in section II concludes with the introduction of a second notion – the notion of a *'vertical cooperative information-based structure'*, – which results from an initial analysis based on the dynamism of the particular relationship between manufacturers and large and sophisticated retailers.

In section III, a set of important questions will be deduced from this economic analysis. One of those questions relates to how the Block Exemption Regulation takes into account the dynamics of the (changed or changing) manufacturer-retailer relationship, as reflected in buying power. One other question deals with how the Block Exemption Regulation applies to a vertical cooperative information-based structure. In addition to these questions, stemming from the changing world of retail business, the following question, stemming from the reality that contract law in this area is (still) national, is deduced: what are the contract law consequences, in the light of the nullity sanction of Article 81(2), of a system of a block exemption with a series of exclusions of the benefit of the exemption for certain clauses (or for distribution contracts containing certain clauses)?

In order to be able to come up with a reasoned answer to the questions posed in section III, the text then discusses, in section IV, first, the particularities and policy underpinning of the Block Exemption Regulation and the Guidelines. Specific attention will be devoted to the economic approach towards vertical arrangements, which replaces a regulation that has provided the market players with a mechanical white-list approach. The scope of the Block Exemption Regulation, its definitions, and the hardcore and 'severable' restrictions will briefly be considered as well. The second part of section IV attempts to provide an analysis of the specific provisions in the Block Exemption Regulation and the Guidelines that concern buying power.

As section IV provides a solid but necessary theoretical background to tackle the important questions that were set out in section III, section V will attempt to answer those questions posed earlier in section III. The analysis will lead us to the stand that the Guidelines seem to fail to appreciate correctly buying power in its complex meaning, the actual substance of which will depend on the particulars of a dynamic manufacturer-retailer relationship. Moreover, it will be argued that the Block Exemption Regulation embodies a static and what we will call 'manufacturer-centric' approach, to which is added, perhaps incorrectly, the assumption that buying forces are unilateral, or at best, countervailing. Such a manufacturer-retailer relationship is, as we called it, perceived as dynamic rather than static. Hence, it will be argued that the buying power provisions set out in section IV seem to be corrective nuances to such manufacturer-centric approach rather than a useful analysis. Section V continues to argue that this could lead in turn to an inaccurate appreciation of potentially anti-competitive effects of so-called 'co-operative vertical arrangements', which can be structured in such way that they fall within the scope of the exemption of the Block Exemption Regulation. The section concludes with a plea for empirical economic research in order to measure the extent of the changed and changing relationship between that type of large retailers and manufacturers and the extent of the impact thereof on the current economic view on vertical restraints.

In addition to the questions tentatively answered in section V, stemming from the changing world of retail business, further important questions, stemming from the reality that contract law in this area is (still) national, shall be addressed in section VI, *i.e.* what are the contract law consequences, in the light of the nullity sanction of Article 81(2) EC Treaty, of a system of a block exemption with a series of exclusions of the benefit of the exemption for certain clauses (or for distribution contracts containing certain clauses)? The final section VI will attempt to provide a subtle and careful analysis of this complex question, taking into account the preceding discussion.

From the outset it must be underlined that this text merely focuses on large and sophisticated retail chains such as a grocery retailer operating throughout the EU through a network of about 300 hypermarkets, and is limited to an analysis of what influence or power such retailer, by virtue of its sophistication and size, may possibly have on the manufacturers producing grocery products. In our analysis, we do not examine deviating fact patterns, such as instances whereby a manufacturer supplies the retailer its private label products, a manufacturer is 'captivated' (i.e. manufacturer whose sunk costs, switching costs and transaction costs make him subject to the buying power of the retailer),[3] a government that acts as a buyer, and instances of monopolistic behaviour etc.

---

[3] OECD, "Buying Power of Multiproduct Retailers", DAFFE/CLP(99), 1999, Background Paper at 20. This report (the "OECD Report") is also available on the website of the OECD at http://www.oecd.org/pdf/M00007000/M00007735.pdf [last visited on 1 September 2002].

Other limitations to the discussion exist. Although the text attempts to give impulses for a multi-layered (as we will call it 'dynamic') economic analysis of this matter, the text itself does not present such full-scale analysis. Consequently, at least in part reference can be made to the OECD Background Paper, published in 1999, which contains a useful summary of many economic factors and implications involved.[4] Also, for the purposes of the present analysis, the effect of large superstores on end-consumers will not be considered, since the Block Exemption Regulation is not applicable to sales to final consumers.[5] In addition, the text does not discuss the impact – and power – that is developed by associations of retailers. It may be noted, however, that Article 2(2) of the Block Exemption Regulation includes in its application vertical agreements entered into by such associations.[6]

II.   THE CENTRAL NOTION OF 'THE DYNAMICS OF A (CHANGED OR CHANGING) RETAILER-MANUFACTURER RELATIONSHIP' AND THE RESULTING NOTION OF 'THE VERTICAL COOPERATIVE INFORMATION-BASED STRUCTURE'

1.   Framework of Analysis

Vertical relationships are often believed to involve a manufacturer drawing on a mechanism of vertical arrangements – such as franchise fees, royalties, resale price maintenance, territorial restrictions, tying or exclusive dealing – in an attempt to take control of, or steer the behavior and underlying incentives of, its distributors or its retailers (as will be elaborated in section V, this belief may be illustrative of what can be called a *"manufacturer-centric"* approach).[7] This might indeed be true for certain categories of manufacturers

---

[4]   *Idem,* at 15-68.

[5]   Agreements with final consumers do not fall under Article 81(1) EC Treaty, as that Article only applies to agreements between undertakings, decisions by associations of undertakings and concerted practices. See the Guidelines, at para. 24 as well as the definition of "vertical agreements" in Article 2(1) of the Block Exemption Regulation.

[6]   See the Guidelines, at paras. 28/9.

[7]   See, typically, the Commission Notice concerning Commission Regulations (EEC) No 1983/83 and (EEC) No. 1984/83 of 22 June 1983, published in OJ C 101, 2, as replaced by the Block Exemption Regulation. See also the critical notes by A. Chen and K. Hylton, 'Procompetitive Theories of Vertical Control', (1999) 50 *Hastings Law Journal*, 573 at 579; J. W. Burns, 'Rethinking the "Agreement" Element in Vertical Antitrust Restraints', (1990) 51 *Ohio State Law Journal* 1, 14 ('the imposition of vertical restraints is seen as a decision

134

which, in a particular market, given their size, financial resources, maintenance of continuous flows of market information or constant product development, have amalgamated a significant amount of reward and/or coercive
power.[8] The manufacturer need not necessarily be large. For instance, retail
ers may have become dependent on the product output by manufacturers,
irrespective of their size, when they offer a 'unique' good or service – such
as a patented innovation or trademarked content.[9]

Notwithstanding the fact that many vertical relationships still reflect this
archetypical structure, certain categories of large buyers-retailers (such as
supra-national superstore chains, large buyer associations, etc.) do not really
fit into the traditional concept. Increasingly, economists – followed by legal
scholars[10] and policy makers[11] – have looked into the substance of the relationship between powerful retailers and manufacturers. For instance, during
the 2000 Fordham conference several interesting contributions discussed
retailer buyer power issues (which partially served as starting point for the
discussion of this text).[12]

Let us consider the supra-national superstore chains, which are probably
prime illustrations of the large, powerful and sophisticated buyer. Typically, a
superstore combines the characteristics of a grocery store with the characteristics of a merchandise store, creating what has been described as a kind of
'powerful cross-shopping vehicle using logistical efficiencies and economies
of scale to cut costs and sell food products to increase customer traffic in
view of attaining higher margins in the general merchandise section of the

---

    resting principally and ultimately with the manufacturer rather than a 'joint manufacturer-
    dealer' endeavor'); J.W. Burns, 'Vertical Restraints, Efficiency, and the Real World',
    (1993) *Fordham Law Review*.

8   L. Stern and A. El-Ansary, *Marketing Channels*, (New Jersey: Prentice-Hall, Inc., 1977) at
    433.

9   *Idem.* See also R. Little, 'The Marketing Channel: Who Should Lead This Extracorporate
    Organization', (1979) 34 *Journal of Marketing* 34.

10 See for instance J. C. Fourgoux, 'La grande distribution et le contrôle de la puissance
    d'achat dans l'union européenne', in E. A. Raffaelli (ed.), *Antitrust between EC Law and
    National Law – Antitrust Fra Diritto Nazionale E Diritto Comunitario*, (Brussels : Bruy-
    lant/ Milan : Giuffrè, 2000) 381.

11 Examples of the cautious steps taken by policy makers will be examined in the various sec-
    tions of this text.

12 B. Hawk (ed), *International Antitrust Law & Policy*, (Fordham Corporate Law Institute,
    2001) Chapters 23 – 29.

store'.[13] Superstore chains may indeed couple their position as a significant – possibly the largest or even the only – customer of a particular supplier, thus establishing a certain kind of power, which may be referred to as 'buying power'.[14]

Although it appears from the economic literature that amongst scholars no general consensus exists on the exact nature of power and influence presently held by retailers in their relationship with manufacturers, it is worth stressing that the position of retailers and their relationship with manufacturers should not be seen as a 'static' fact.[15] In particular, what seems to have developed since the 1950s in the US and later also on the European markets is a slow but continuous trend towards a shift of market power away from manufacturers to a certain category of retailers.

As early as 1962, Gerald Tallman and Bruce Blokstrom noted a change in the influence of retailers due to the fact that on the US market from around 1954 a new kind of store – the 'discount department store' – emerged.[16] The appearance of such large retailers and the related phenomena of relocation and of (product and services) reorientation challenged the traditional powerful position of the manufacturers. The authors described this as follows:

Traditionally, the manufacturer has taken the lead in getting products designed, manufactured, distributed, and sold across retail outlets. [...] By contrast, two retailing institutions – i.e., mail-order houses and, to

---

[13] W. Borhesani, P, de la Cruz and D. Berry, 'Food For Thought : The Emergence of Power Buyers and Its Challenge To Competition Analysis', (1998) 4 *Stanford Journal of Law, Business and Finance* 39, 47.

[14] The concept 'buying power' will be further explored in the next sections of this text, especially in section IV.2.

[15] See for instance B. Kahn and L. McAlister, *Grocery Revolution* (Addison-Wesley, 1997.) 56-7. The authors discuss gross margin, expense ratio, operating margin and sales increases of the chain Toys "R" Us in the years 1985-89. It may be noted in this context that this chain has been the subject of an administrative proceeding in which the FTC found (largely affirmed by the Seventh Circuit), amongst other things, that Toys "R" Us used pressure on manufacturers to enter into unlawful vertical agreements. See *Toys "R" Us, Inc. v Fed. Trade Comm'n*, 221 F.3d 928 (7th Cir. 2000) and the detailed discussion of the proceedings in the OECD Report, *National Contribution: United States*, 227-232. See also D. A. Valentine, 'Retailer Buyer Power: Abusive Behavior and Mergers/Acquisitions Roundtable', in Hawk, above note 12, Chapter 28, at p. 529-530. As this case concerns US antitrust law, further analysis is beyond the scope of the present text.

[16] G. Tallman and B. Blokstrom, 'Retail Innovations Challenge Manufacturers', (1962) *Harvard Business Review* 130.

136

a lesser extent, chain stores – have frequently taken this leadership role away from the manufacturer. [...] The contest between manufacturers and large retailers for the dominant role in the marketing sequence becomes more intense as retailer buying power is increasingly concentrated in large organizations.[17]

Since then, a continuous development seems to have occurred that shifts power to the large retail chains.[18] According to a 1987 study, the shift of market power may have become apparent at three different levels. First, the shift of power goes along with changes in the relative sizes of manufacturers and retailers.[19] Second, retailers seem to have seized control over a variety of functions traditionally assumed by manufacturers.[20] Third, on the basis of the information examined in this study it was plausible that a growth in the profitability of retailing companies occurred.

This proposition has not remained uncontested among economists, however. In a 1992 study, it was considered that even if retailers had at that time achieved a certain degree of power over manufacturers, they were not able to convert such power into profits.[21] However, even according to this study, if retailers colluded or became large enough, then perhaps they could force manufacturers to provide concessions that would not be immediately competed away (by competing retailers).[22]

Also, the mere possibility of the occurrence or development of 'buying power' obviously also depends on the nature of the market concerned. Our typical fact pattern involves a grocery retailer versus a grocery manufacturer. This choice has been made quite deliberately, since in most other sectors little or even no 'buying power' exists. A perfect example of how little power

---

[17] *Idem*, at 135.

[18] One author, citing the OECD Report, above note 3, states that large retail chains ("la grande distribution") have acquired more than 50% of the market share in Europe and account for about 45% of the world market: Fourgoux, above note 10, 384.

[19] Rapid internal growth and external mergers and acquisitions have resulted in creating retail groups exceeding the sizes of their suppliers in terms of sales, assets and equity: R. Grant, 'Manufacturer-Retailer Relations: the Shifting Balance of Power', in G. Johnson (ed), *Business Strategy and Retailing* (John Wiley & Sons, 1987) at 43.

[20] Such as the physical distribution, advertising or product design: Grant, above note 19. 43. Other recent examples might involve the set-up of e-commerce retail sites.

[21] See P. Farris and K. Ailawadi, 'Retail Power: Monster or Mouse?', Marketing Science Institute, Technical Working Paper, Report number 92-129, October 1992, at 23.

[22] *Idem,* at 22.

some retailers have can be found in the motor vehicle distribution where the recent Commission Regulation (EC) No 1400/2002 of 31 July 2002 (the 'Block Exemption for the Motor Vehicle Industry')[23] aims amongst others things – roughly speaking – to assure sufficient access to technical information for independent retailers[24] and sufficient access to dealers for spare part producers[25] and, in general, to strengthen the dealers' independence.[26] The new Commission Regulation can be seen as an attempt to offer increased protection to the weaker market players.[27]

This notwithstanding, economic theory seems to suggest several scenarios in which a (grocery) retailer may become powerful. Consider for instance the case where a small manufacturer is unable to develop a brand image.[28] It can be noted in this respect that this scenario may prove to be problematic, because the notion of 'market power', as it has been defined and developed in the Block Exemption Regulation, may be inadequate to measure the real 'buying power' of large retailers (see sections V.1 and V.2). Consider also

---

[23] Commission Regulation (EC) No 1400/2002 of 31 July 2002 on the Application of Article 81(3) of the Treaty to Categories of Vertical Agreement and Concerted Practices in the Motor Vehicle Industry, OJ 2002 L 203/30. See also the Draft Commission Regulation on the Application of Article 81(3) of the Treaty to Categories of Vertical Agreements and Concerted Practices in the Motor Vehicle Industry, published on 16 March 2002 in OJ 2002 C 67/2 (the 'Draft Block Exemption for the Motor Vehicle Industry')

[24] See Article 4, 2. (and Preamble 26) of the Block Exemption for the Motor Vehicle Industry.

[25] See Article 4, 1. (h)-(l) of the Block Exemption for the Motor Vehicle Industry, above note 23.

[26] This stems from the rationale behind (many of) the provisions of the Block Exemption for the Motor Vehicle Industry. See e.g. Preamble 9 as well as Articles 4 and 5 of the Block Exemption for the Motor Vehicle Industry, above note 23.

[27] See Annex 1 ("Reasons for a New BER for Motor Vehicle Distribution") of the Draft Block Exemption for the Motor Vehicle Industry, above note 23. Note that the Block Exemption for the Motor Vehicle Industry, above note 23, in its Preamble 32 refers to cases *where the buyer has significant market power on the relevant market on which it resells the goods or provides the services or where parallel networks of vertical agreements have similar effects which significantly restrict access to a relevant market or competition thereon; such cumulative effects may for example arise in the case of selective distribution*'. In our view this kind of power represents in fact downstream '(re)selling power' (i.e. the power a buyer/reseller has vis-à-vis the subsequent buyers), which is not to be mistaken with the (upstream) "buying power" that forms the study object of the present text. This view is consistent with the wording and scope of Article 6, 1.of the Block Exemption for the Motor Vehicle Industry.

[28] L. Stern and A. El-Ansary, above note 8, 444.

the case where a retailer, irrespective of its size, provides significant sales assistance and retail outlets are selectively rather than densely located.[29] Generally, if a retailer's influence on product differentiation increases (for instance if the retailer offers a certain reputation, image or services like payment facilities or extended warranty, selling presentations, advice etc.) the bargaining power of such retailer in his relation with the manufacturer increases.[30]

Similar views were expressed in a 1999 study for D.G. Competition on 'buying power' and its impact on competition in the food retail distribution sector within the European Union.[31]

> In practice, the power of the retailer in buying comes from the sheer range and diversity of the products it stocks. Even for a supplier that may have considerable market share (bringing it close to being classified as dominant on normal Article 86 principles) may not be in a position to resist a key retailer's demands. For the supplier, the retailer may represent a significant proportion of its overall sales (say 15%), but for the retailer that 15% may represent say only 1% or 2% of turnover, and thus the real power may lie with the purchaser and not the supplier.[32]

In a similar way, several studies suggest that a certain category of (large) retailers thus resemble 'gatekeepers'.[33] We have nonetheless decided not to use this term in this text, since we believe the term is somewhat misleading in the sense that in many cases it does not completely reflect the boundaries in

---

[29] *Idem.*

[30] *Idem*, 445. Warren Grimes interestingly observed that 'As long as brand loyalty was low, consumers would freely switch amongst brands in any retail store to obtain the best price [...] The retailer could pick the highest margin brands to stock its shelves. Producers had to reduce their prices or institute vertical price fixing [under the US rules] to assure the retailer this high margin.'. See W. Grimes, 'The Seven Myths of Vertical Price Fixing: The Politics and Economics of a Century Long Debate, (1992) *Southwestern University Law Review* 1285, 1305.

[31] Report produced by Dobson Consulting on buyer power and its impact on competition in the food retail distribution sector of the European Union of 13 October 1999, published at the Commission D.G. Competition website, at http://europa.eu.int/comm/competition/ publications/studies/bpifrs/ [last visited on 1 September 2002]

[32] *Idem*, at 34/5.

[33] See for instance the Report on the Federal Trade Commission Workshop on Slotting Allowances and Other Marketing Practices in the Grocery Industry of February 2001, available on the website of the FTC, "Introduction and Executive Summary" at 8.

which a so-called gatekeeper-buyer must act, and thus can have a misleading effect (see in this context the discussion about the uneasy concept of 'buying power in section V.1).

2.   The Notion of the 'Dynamics of the (Changed or Changing) Relationship Between Retailers and Manufacturers'

All such indications of 'buying power' resulting from a shift in the power may have one underlying basic thought in common: the fact that the relationship between manufacturers and retailers is not to be perceived as a 'static' relationship or a 'one-way' (i.e. top-bottom) relationship. On the contrary, we believe that it is important, not to say imperative, to get to understand the dynamics of the relationship (in time, in space, in quality, in quantity, upstream as well as downstream, and probably on a game-theoretic level etc.), and to appreciate that a typical analysis starting from the manufacturer's viewpoint may need to be adapted in order to reflect the truth of a particular distribution relationship.

Hence we introduce the notion of the *'dynamics of the (changed or changing) relationship between retailers and manufacturers'*. A correct legal analysis in this matter starts with a correct appreciation of the true dynamics of all kinds of vertical relationships. Simple maxims like 'vertical good, horizontal bad' are two-way oversimplifications.[34] We believe that the relationship between retailers and manufacturers should be perceived dynamic rather than static. The 'dynamism' of the retailer-manufacturer relationship embraces at least three views. First, relationships between the retailer and manufacturer may substantially diverge depending on the identity and the characteristics of a particular retailer, manufacturer, product and market. In other words, the relationship between a large retailer A and a manufacturer B in a market C should not be assumed to be identical to the relationship between a retailer X and a manufacturer Y in a market Z. Second, even when considering a particular relationship (e.g. the relationship between a retailer A and a manufacturer B in a market C), it must be borne in mind that this relationship itself may be changing, subject to market fluctuations, historic evolution, expectations about the future, etc. A third, related (because necessarily intertwined with the former) view exists. As we will further point out,

---

[34]   J. Baker, 'Vertical Restraints with Horizontal Consequences: Competitive Effects of 'Most-Favored-Customer' Clauses', (1996) 64 *Antitrust Law Journal* 517, 518.

in each manufacturer-retailer an inherent dynamism exists that (at least in the vertical relationships that form the object of this study) is potentially transposed into special kinds of interrelation between manufacturers and retailers that go well beyond stereotypes of countervailing power.

The generality of this notion notwithstanding, we believe in particular that the tendency set out in the paragraphs above should be examined from such a 'dynamic' interpretation of vertical relationships – rather than from a 'manufacturer-centric' approach – which needs to take into account not only the particularities of a certain market, but, among other things, the realities of a changing economic environment and the precise upstream or indirect (anti- or pro-) competitive effects of a particular vertical arrangement (see also section V.2).

We believe that the current legal and economic literature on this topic, or at least some parts thereof, misses this rather important point. Often, we believe, it is too quickly assumed that the relationship between manufacturer and retailer is *adverserial*. The upstream and downstream powers are assumed to collide or, at best, to counterbalance (see for instance the OECD Background Paper which does not appear to (seriously) question the paradigm of an adverserial manufacturer-retailer relationship).[35] True, the manufacturer and the retailer each aspire to best achieve their individual interests. However, it is conceivable that those individual interests can better be achieved through a co-operative structure. Some authors have implicitly raised this sensitive point. In particular, one US author carefully noticed that big manufacturers seem not to fight against practices like slotting allowances (see below for a deeper analysis):

> [W]hy is it only the small and regional grocery manufacturers who are complaining to Congress and petitioning the FTC for action? Where are the large manufacturers [...] Or, much more plausibly, the explanation may be: (3) Because the big manufacturers believe (but are reluctant to admit in public) that they do better in a world with slotting allowances than they would in a world without slotting allowances. And why might that be? The only obvious answer is that slotting allowances may have at least some marginal impact in reinforcing the dominance of major brands. Thus it seems reasonable to take as a working hypothesis that

---

[35] See the OECD Report, above note 3, at 20.

many manufacturers may be acting opportunistically, taking advantage of retailer demands to achieve some exclusionary effect.'[36]

In view of the notion of the 'dynamics of the manufacturer-retailer relationship', this tenderly worded 'working hypothesis' will be further examined in the next paragraphs. If we look back at the phenomenon of supranational superstore chains, we should – and this makes the case of superstore chains so interesting – to the abovementioned evolution starting around the 1950s add the information technology innovations that have been implemented over the last decades. In particular, these information technology innovations provided sophisticated retail stores with a cost-efficient capability to obtain *and* use an enormous mass of customer behavior data and information. By means of the contemporary information technology, vast amounts of information generated each split second can easily and at a relatively low cost be targeted, processed, monitored and transmitted.

It is conceivable that in certain sectors this ready access to information, to which are added the know-how and resources to effectively exploit the information, may serve as leverage for the bargaining power of the large and sophisticated retail stores, not only in their downward relation with consumers (i.e. their 'selling power'[37] which may be leveraged compared with that of their smaller competitors), but also in their upward relation with wholesalers, distributors or manufacturers (i.e. their 'buying power').

The importance of this ready access to information and how this influences the dynamics of the relationship between retailers and manufacturers should not be underestimated. Let us illustrate this briefly with three examples which we believe are indicative of the shift in power towards large and sophisticated retailers and exemplify the impact of their 'buying power' on the upward distribution chain: (i) the use of 'loyalty schemes', (ii) the deployment of 'category management' and (iii) the occurrence of 'slotting allowances'. For the purposes of this text, we do not attempt to analyze these three arrangements, nor do we consider other instances – such as the increased use of private labels – which could serve as additional illustrations.

The information that can be derived from loyalty schemes may serve as powerful tool for the purposes of targeted marketing or category management

---

[36] See R. Davis, 'A Mystery Wrapped in an Enigma: Slotting Allowances and Antitrust', (2001) 15 *Antitrust*, Spring , 69, 75.
[37] See also references above note 15.

(see further below). The use of such customer data will often be unobtrusive for customers since, after having signed the initial documentation and after having received their membership card, they will barely notice that their behavior is taped, analyzed, and processed. Even if they grasp this, they may not perceive it as harmful to themselves. Participation in a loyalty scheme is (in most of the cases) voluntary and in many cases even involves a certain degree of enthusiasm since discounts or vouchers come into sight. Manufacturers,[38] on the other hand, are confronted with the fact that the information advantage (see further below), once held by them,[39] has shifted away to the retailers.[40]

A second example illustrating the increased shift of power to retailers is the occurrence of 'slotting allowances' or 'slotting fees'. We mention this phenomenon briefly as an illustration of the dynamics of the manufacturer-retailer relationship, but refer for a detailed analysis to the Report on the Federal Trade Commission Workshop on Slotting Allowances and Other Marketing Practices in the Grocery Industry of February 2001.[41] Many definitions exist, some of which are contested, some of which are technical, some of which are restricted. We use the term in the sense 'slotting allowances' have been defined by Ronald Davis, namely as 'payments by product manufacturers to retailers in exchange for access to shelf space', although we are aware that many types of 'slotting allowance' can be distinguished in practice.[42] Generally, 'slotting allowances' involve a kind of a payment (in cash or by other means) by a manufacturer, supplier or wholesaler to a retailer in exchange for which the retailer commits himself, for instance, to carry a supplier's product in the store or to provide a fixed amount of shelf space or to provide preferential display space for a new product or to make a visible product introduction, and so on.[43] In the cited 1999 economic study, retailers

---

[38] To a lesser extent wholesalers or distributors. For the purposes of the clarity and succinctness of this text we will focus on the relationship between retailers and manufacturers.

[39] Although manufacturers in a competitive market also face uncertain demand. For a general analysis on this subject see D. Butz, "Vertical Price Controls with Uncertain Demand (1997) 40 *Journal of Law and Economics* 433.

[40] Kahn and McAlister, above note 15, 36.

[41] See in general the Report on the Federal Trade Commission Workshop on Slotting Allowances and Other Marketing Practices in the Grocery Industry of February 2001, available on the website of the FTC.

[42] Davis, above note 36.

[43] E. Larose and P. Poff, 'Slotting Allowances and the Emerging Antitrust Enforcement Debate", (1990) 74-NOV *Florida Bar Jo*urnal, 1990 42, 42-3 and 46.

and manufacturers were surveyed to ascertain the existence of such slotting fees. The study found a certain degree of consensus amongst both groups on the following three assertions. First, slotting allowances are associated with a higher degree of retail influence. Second, slotting allowances have led to changes in the relative influence of the manufacturers and retailers towards one another. Third, larger and arguably more powerful retailers are more likely to require slotting allowances and benefit from them.[44]

A last illustration of the increased shift in power are various types of 'category management'. Category management can have many forms and the term is often misused. It can most accurately be described as a vertical partnership in which confidential data and information is shared between retailers and manufacturers to cut costs and to increase the margins of both parties.[45] The retailer will provide the manufacturer with information on the customers' behavior, on the basis whereof the manufacturer can get a better understanding of the wishes and needs of the customer (and/or the retailer). To this end, the traditional adversarial relationship between manufacturers and retailers is to be replaced by a co-operative one, based on mutual trust.[46] In principle, category management involves a vertical arrangement, often but not necessarily between a retailer and a manufacturer,[47] which might entail – to a greater or lesser extent – behavioral restrictions in respect of both the manufacturer (such as the obligation to obtain consent of a consultant designated by the retailer) and the retailer (for instance as a result of a slotting allowance in the form of shelf space granted to a particular manufacturer).[48]

---

[44] See P. Bloom, G. Gundlach and J. Cannon, *Slotting Allowances and Fees : Schools of Thought and the Views of Practicing Managers* (Marketing Science Institute, Working Paper, Report number 99-106, 1999) 22-3.

[45] R. Steiner, Category Management – A Pervasive, New Vertical/Horizontal Format', (2001) 15 *Antitrust*, Spring 77.

[46] *Idem*, at 78.

[47] Provided that they dispose of enough know-how, resources and provided that they have ready access to product development, distributors or wholesalers may also act as category managers.

[48] An accurate analysis of slotting allowances is even more subtle, since slotting allowances may in fact be evidence of the buying power of certain large retailers: in the cited 1999 survey, manufacturers as well as retailers responded that slotting fees shift the risk of product innovations away from the retailers and back to the manufacturers: Bloom, Gundlach and Cannon, above note 44, 20-1.

3. The Resulting Notion of a 'Vertical Cooperative Information-based Structure'

We are of the view that the importance of the information advantage resulting from the data and information generated and controlled by a large retailer should not be underestimated.[49] From a general economic point of view, the large retailer who 'owns' such information, holds one of the keys on a door that normally would remain locked in a market economy,[50] since the data and information might contain relevant indications of how large demand can be expected to be, and consequently might answer questions on product output, quality perceptions, and consumer wishes and expectations.[51] The manufacturer who is able to obtain such information and then appropriately combine it with its own capabilities and skills may increase, among other things, its probability to develop a product that better meets market demand from which, goes the argument, both the retailer, the manufacturer and arguably the consumer shall profit.[52]

At this point we would like to introduce a second notion – the notion of a *'vertical cooperative information-based structure'* – which results from an initial analysis based on the dynamism of the particular relationship between manufacturers and large and sophisticated retailers. In a vertical cooperative information-based structure, two or more vertical market players exploit a comparative advantage based on (upwards and downwards) communication

---

49   Compare the Guidelines, at para. 119(8): 'The more the vertical restraint is linked to the transfer of know-how, the more reason there may be to expect efficiencies to arise and the more a vertical restraint may be necessary to protect the know-how transferred or the investment costs incurred.'

50   Another way to open the door (or more precisely to control and influence the mechanism of the doorframe) arguably would involve the existence of horizontal (information exchange) arrangements. Please note the restrictive EC competition law in this respect. See R. Whish, *Competition Law* 4th edn (London: Butterworths, 2001) 441-450 and 469-470.

51   Consider the following: 'The role that uncertainty plays in influencing the decisions of firms to integrate vertically is both diverse and pervasive [...] The major significance of uncertainty in explaining vertical integration has long been recognized.'. See R. Blair and D. Kaserman, *Law and Economics of Vertical Integration and Control* (New York: Academic Press, 1983) 83.

52   On the importance of information in evolving environments and its relation with vertical restraints see I. de Leon, 'A Neo-institutional Analysis of Vertical Integration and Its Implications for Antitrust Enforcement in Developing Countries', (2000) 26 *Brooklyn Journal of International Law* 251, 278-80. See also B. Klein and K. Murphy, 'Vertical Restraints as Contract Enforcement Mechanisms', (1988) 31 *Journal of Law and Economics* 265.

and use of information.[53] Together they form kind of a 'value-added partnership', in which, theoretically,[54] the coordination and scale efficiencies associated with large integrated companies can be combined with the flexibility, creativity and low overhead usually found in small companies.[55,56]

Equally important is the presence of mutual trust and cooperation between vertical market players.[57] The mutual trust and cooperation are based on a perception that neither a manufacturer nor a retailer alone can compete most successfully for the consumer's cash.[58] It will be the 'Gestallt' of their combined knowledge and abilities added to their coordinated efforts that will enable not only a more accurate estimation of market and product demand, but also a more adequate supply of the resulting products and services, as well as a more targeted communication and marketing strategy.[59]

The resulting *'vertical cooperative information-based structure'*, as reflected in category management or slotting allowances arrangements, is not

---

[53] Such cooperation may be a fine alternative to vertical integration to reduce demand uncertainty. On the means to reduce market demand, see D. Butz, 'Vertical Price Controls with Uncertain Demand' (1997) 40 *Journal of Law and Economics* 433, in particular 437-449.

[54] For this purpose, vertical integration can be a viable alternative, since it is often used as a device for reducing costs under competitive conditions (See e.g. I. Stelzer and R. Schmalensee, 'Potential Costs and Benefits of Vertical Integration, (1983) 52 *Antitrust Law Journal* 249, 249-250) whereby transaction costs stemming from negotiating and drafting the contractual framework between two companies can be avoided, as well as risks allocated to one or the other party pursuant to particular contractual provisions.

[55] R. Johnston and P. Lawrence, 'Beyond Vertical Integration – The Rise of the Value-Adding Partnership', *Harvard Business Review* (July-Aug., 1988), 94, 99.

[56] Arguably such cooperative vertical agreement may be able to avoid one of the major disadvantages of vertical integration, i.e. the risk of reduction of flexibility to respond to qualitative demand shifts, that is believed to operate to the advantage of smaller retailers. On this topic, see M. Pitt and G. Johnson, 'Managing Strategic Change: A Chief Executive's Perspective', in G. Johnson (ed), *Business Strategy and Retailing* (John Wiley & Sons: 1987) 197.

[57] It can be noted that mutual trust and cooperation may ultimately depend on the combination of contractual arrangements and the (potential) use of power between wholesalers and retailers. On the interdependency between contracts, power as well as the reciprocal processes of fairness and trust, see S. Hyvönen, *Integration in Vertical Marketing Systems – A Study on Power and Contractual Relationships between Wholesalers and Retailers*, The Helsinki School of Economics and Business Administration, Series A:72 (Helsinki: 1990)191-3.

[58] L. Wortzel and M. Venkatraman, *Manufacturer and Retailer Relationships*, Marketing Science Institute, Working Paper, Report number 91-129, (1991), 8.

[59] *Idem.*

146

to be confused with vertical integration. Both entities (at the manufacturer's level as well as on the retailer's level) can remain separate entities and are not merged or otherwise integrated. Instead they have created a structure that lies somewhere[60] on a continuum of transaction governance methods[61] (with spot market exchanges and full ownership as the extremes).[62]

III.   SET OF QUESTIONS INVOLVED

The analysis set out in the previous section, when it is viewed from an EC competition law perspective,[63] leads us to deduce the following set of questions:

1. To what extent does the Block Exemption Regulation (including the Guidelines) correctly take into account the *'dynamics of the changed or changing manufacturer-retailer relationship'*, as this is reflected in buying power?

2. How does the Block Exemption Regulation (including the Guidelines) apply to a vertical cooperative information-based structure, such as category management or slotting allowances?

In addition to these questions, stemming from the changing world of retail business, the following question, stemming from the reality that contract law in this area is (still) national, has to be addressed:

3. What are the contract law consequences, in the light of the nullity sanction of Article 81(2), of a system of a block exemption with a series of exclusions of the benefit of the exemption for certain clauses (or for distribution contracts containing certain clauses)?

---

[60] Depending on the actual legal and economic structure of ties between the two respective legal entities.

[61] See, amongst others, Stelzer and Schmalensee, above note 54, at 250.

[62] See in general Blair and Kaserman, above note 51, 25-7.

[63] Many of the observations made in section II lead to open questions that touch economics rather than law, which this text does not attempt to answer but which may be the subject for a thorough economic research.

In order to be able to come to a reasoned answer, we will first discuss in section IV the particularities and policy underpinning of the Block Exemption Regulation and the Guidelines, which will enable us to answer questions 1 and 2 (in section V) which will lead us to question 3 (in section VI).

IV.   THE BLOCK EXEMPTION REGULATION: ITS POLICIES AND EFFECTS

1.   Analysis of the Block Exemption Regulation in its Entirety

Alexander Schaub identified the presence of four key features in the 1999 Block Exemption Regulation.[64] First, the new rules embody an economic approach. Second, the new rules result in a significant degree of deregulation.[65] Third, the rules contain in Article 4 a hardcore list of forbidden restrictions that lead to the exclusion of the whole vertical restraint from the scope of application of the Block Exemption Regulation. Fourth, the rules present a first, modest step in the direction of decentralization.[66] Those four key features will be further examined in the paragraphs below.

The Block Exemption Regulation clearly reveals an economic approach towards vertical arrangements.[67] It replaces regulations that provided market players with a mechanical white-list approach whereby agreements were to be brought within the formalistic exemptions of Regulations 1983/83,[68] 1984/83[69] 1475/95[70] or 4087/88.[71] Those old Regulations were subject to

---

[64] Discussion Panel, "Vertical Restraints Under EC Law", in Hawk, above note 12 , Chapter 14, 217 at 218.

[65] It may be more appropriate to speak in terms of "liberalization" rather than "deregulation". This prong once more indicates that the whole Block Exemption Regulation and the shift in policy approach underlying it are to be placed in context of the wider modernization debate of EC Competition law.

[66] See on the relation between the White Paper and the Block Exemption Regulation amongst others the recent contribution of J. Folguera, 'The Impact of the Commission's Modernization White Paper and Vertical Restraints Regulation on Member State Antitrust Laws', in Hawk, above note 12, Chapter 11, 151 at 157.

[67] S. Bishop and M. Walker, *The Economics of EC Competition Law: Concepts, Application and Measurement* (London: Sweet & Maxwell, 1999) at 88, 4.26.

[68] OJ 1983 L-173/1.

[69] OJ 1983 L-173/5.

[70] OJ 1995 L-145/25 which is now replaced by the Block Exemption Regulation for the Motor Vehicle Industry, above note 23.

[71] OJ 1988 L-359/46.

heavy criticism, partly because the application of this body of rules resulted in a permanent work overload of the Commission, partly because it produced perverse incentives,[72] partly because lawyers were maneuvering the wording of the agreements to fall artificially within the scope of the exemptions,[73] and therefore too much emphasis was placed on the wording of a clause rather than its economic effect.[74]

The new rules generally can be described as non-formalistic, since they do not very narrowly prescribe – or forbid – the exact details of particular vertical arrangements.[75] Indeed, the Guidelines even literally state that since the standards set forth in the Guidelines are to be applied in circumstances specific to each case,[76] a mechanical application is ruled out.[77] The Commission will apply the Guidelines reasonably and flexibly,[78] and commits itself to 'an economic approach which is based on the effects on the market'.[79] The Commission seems to be willing to reconsider – on the basis of an economic reasoning[80] – certain vertical agreements which once one would have believed to be restrictive of competition.[81]

---

[72] See in this context: B. Hawk, 'System Failure : Vertical Restraints and EC Competition Law', (1995) 32 *Common Market Law Review* 973, and in general the authors of the so-called Chicago school. See further B. M. Audia, P. Tamussino and D. Hull, 'Recent Developments in European Competition Law: Vertical and Horizontal Agreements', 19 No.7, ACCA Docket 52, July/August 2001, 52 at 58: 'Under the old rules, agreements between companies with a combined market share of 80 percent were treated in much the same way as an agreement between two companies with a combined market share of 15 percent.'

[73] In this sense legal 'creativity' was being hurt: I. Verloren van Themaat, 'Een Nieuw Beleid ten aanzien van Verticalen, *Nederlands Tijdschrift voor Europees Recht*, 2000, nr. 1/2, 14, at 15/6.

[74] Bishop and Walker, above note 67, at 77, 4.03.

[75] M. Hughes, C. Foss and K. Ross, 'The Economic Assessment of Vertical Restraints under U.K. and E.C. Competition Law' (2001) 22 *European Competition Law Review*, Issue 10, 424, 430.

[76] Compare with the Green Paper on Vertical Restraints in EC Competition Policy (1997, Com (96) 721) in which the Commission argued that following the heated debate amongst economists vertical restraints are no longer regarded as *per se* suspicious or *per se* pro-competitive but should rather be analyzed on the facts of the case in question. (at p. iii)

[77] Guidelines, at para. 3.

[78] *Idem*. See also paras. 9 and 100-2 of the Guidelines.

[79] Guidelines, at para. 7.

[80] Even the 'additional' goal of the Block Exemption Regulation is perceived as a function of the economic aim: 'Market integration is an additional goal of EC competition policy. Market integration enhances competition in Europe.' Guidelines, at para. 7; see also para. 103.

[81] R. Whish, 'Regulation 2790/99: The Commission's "New Style" Block Exemption

Importantly, the other side of the coin of this de-formalized economic approach is that the benefit of the Block Exemption Regulation may be withdrawn,[82] for instance if a supplier (or a buyer in the case of exclusive supply obligations)[83] which holds a market share not exceeding 30 % enters into a vertical agreement that does not give rise to objective advantages.[84] Another way by which the benefit of the Block Exemption Regulation may not be granted is the procedure of disapplication, which enables the Commission to exclude from the scope of the Block Exemption Regulation, by means of a regulation, 'parallel networks of similar vertical restraints', if they cover more than 50% of a relevant market.[85]

Pursuant to such an economic approach, 'vertical agreements' are now defined as agreements or concerted practices entered into between two or more undertakings each of which operates, for the purposes of the agreement, at a different level of the production or distribution chain, and relating to the conditions under which parties may purchase, sell or resell certain goods or services.[86] Conversely, 'vertical restraints' are circumscribed as vertical agreements that contain restrictions of competition that fall within the scope of Article 81(1) EC Treaty.[87]

Although an in-depth discussion on the application of the Block Exemption Regulation falls beyond the scope of this text, it can be helpful (for a good understanding of how the Block Exemption relates to the changed or changing manufacturer-retailer relationship) to briefly point out the three key elements contained in the definition of vertical agreements. First, agreements with final consumers do not fall under the Block Exemption Regulation, as they do not fall under Article 81(1).[88] Second, the agreement or concerted practice should be between undertakings each operating at a different level of the production or distribution chain.[89] Third, vertical agreements concern

---

for Vertical Agreements' (2000) *Common Market Law Review* 887, 890.

[82] In such case an infringement of Article 81 (1) EC Treaty shall be established. In such case the Commission shall nonetheless bear the burden of proof (Guidelines at para. 72).

[83] Defined narrowly in Article 1 of the Block Exemption Regulation (below, note 105).

[84] See Articles 6-7 of the Block Exemption Regulation.

[85] See Article 8 of the Block Exemption Regulation and the Guidelines at paras. 80 and following.

[86] Article 2.1. of the Block Exemption Regulation.

[87] *Idem.*

[88] Guidelines, at para. 24.

[89] Guidelines, at paras. 24 and 26/7.

the conditions for the purchase, sale or resale of the goods or services[90] supplied by the supplier or concern the conditions for the sale by the buyer of the goods or services which result from those originally supplied and incorporate these goods or services.[91]

It should be stressed that pursuant to Article 2(3) of the Regulation, the exemption also applies to vertical agreements containing provisions which relate to the assignment to the buyer or use by the buyer of intellectual property ("IP") rights, provided that those provisions do not constitute the primary object of such agreements and are directly related to the use, sale or resale of goods or services by the buyer or its customers. In other words provisions on IP rights, which are ancillary to distribution, as in business format franchise agreements, are also covered by the block exemption. Typically, IP rights related obligations are obligations on the franchisee not to compete with the franchisor, not to disclose secret know-how to third parties, only to use the franchisor's know-how for the purpose of the franchise, not to assign the rights and obligations under the franchise agreement without the consent of the franchisor.[92]

This leads us to the not so trivial remark that the Regulation takes into account the fact that distribution agreements are often more than pure agreements on the conditions of sale and resale of the goods which are distributed and can also be based on some kind of co-operation between supplier and reseller (as in franchise systems) (see also further below). Nonetheless, it must in this respect be pointed out that the ancillary provisions referred to in the Regulation are only those based on a downstream assignment or licensing of rights by the supplier in the framework of a distribution system set up by him.

Furthermore, the Commission has stressed in its Guidelines that it considers vertical restraints to be generally less harmful than horizontal restraints.[93] Such view is grounded on some of the insights generated by the Chicago School-Harvard School debate.[94] The argument goes that, in vertical agree-

---

[90] On the precise scope of 'goods or services', Whish, above note 81, 890.

[91] Guidelines, at para. 24.

[92] Guidelines, para. 44.

[93] Guidelines, at para. 100.

[94] See in particular W. Comanor, 'Vertical Arrangements and Antitrust Analysis' (1987) 62 *New York University Law Review* 1153; O. Williamson, 'Assessing Vertical Market Restrictions: Antitrust Ramifications of the Transaction Cost Approach', (1979) 127 *University of Pennsylvania Law Review* 953, and the seminal works: R. Bork, *The Antitrust Paradox* (1978), and R. Posner, *Antitrust Law: An Economic Perspective* (1976).

ments, the exercise of market power usually hurts the company at the other level, which provides the latter with an incentive to prevent the exercise of the market power by the other.[95] The Commission normally should only intervene when a particular vertical restraint might lessen inter-brand — and to a lesser extent intra-brand — competition, and consequently the consumers' welfare is at stake.[96] The effect of the Block Exemption Regulation is in this sense deregulatory, or better, liberalizing.

Nevertheless there are four principal negative effects of vertical restraints that are — according to the Guidelines — worth an intervention.[97] Those involve, first, the occurrence of barriers to entry (with the effect of foreclosing other suppliers or buyers); second, the reduction of inter-brand competition between companies on a market; third, the reduction of intra-brand competition between distributors of the same brand; and finally, the creation of obstacles to market integration.[98] Such negative effects may result from various categories of vertical restraints, which for the purposes of facilitating the analysis can be divided into four groups: single branding arrangements, limited distribution arrangements, resale price maintenance ("RPM") arrangements and market partitioning arrangements (see further below).[99]

Conceptually, such view has led to a dramatic shift in the Commission's policy towards vertical restraints. The operative factor (that renders the Block Exemption Regulation applicable or not) is the degree of 'market power'[100]

---

[95] Guidelines, at para. 100.

[96] Guidelines, at para. 102. Please note that in this paragraph reference is made only to 'competition [...] important to ensure efficiencies and benefits for consumers.' Arguably, the Commission applies a 'consumer welfare standard' rather than an 'aggregate welfare' or 'efficiency' standard. See in this respect S. Salop, 'Analysis of Foreclosure in the EC Guidelines on Vertical Restraints' in Hawk, above note 12, Chapter 12, 177, 179-80.

[97] Guidelines, at para. 103. See in this context also P. Nicolaides, 'An Essay on Economics and the Competition Law of the European Community', (2000) 27 *Legal Issues of Economic Integration* 7, 18. This author welcomes the fact that the Guidelines take into account the potential beneficial effects of vertical agreements but notes that the attachment to the ideals of no impediments to parallel trade and no absolute territorial protection has not been abandoned altogether.

[98] Guidelines, at para. 103.

[99] Guidelines, at paras. 104/5. For an analysis of those four groups, please refer to paras. 106-114.

[100] It has in this respect been argued that the Block Exemption Regulation reflects a "graded" economic approach to competition review: J. Ratliff and A. De Matteis, 'European Commission Adopts Block Exemption on Vertical Restraints' (2000) *International Business Lawyer* 206 at 207.

of a particular market player, as calculated on the basis of such player's market share. For most vertical restraints competition concerns can only arise if there is insufficient inter-brand competition or, in other words, if there is some degree of market power.[101] Such degree of market power has been set – quite arbitrarily?[102] – at 30%:

> It can be presumed that, where the share of the relevant market accounted for by the supplier does not exceed 30%, vertical agreements which do not contain certain types of severely anti-competitive restraints generally lead to an improvement in production or distribution and allow consumers a fair share of the resulting benefits; in the case of vertical agreements containing *exclusive supply obligations, it is the market share of the buyer which is* relevant in determining the overall effects of such vertical agreements on the market."[103] (We do not address the *de minimis* doctrine).[104]

Article 3(1) of the Block Exemption Regulation states that vertical restraints may only be exempted if the market share held by a supplier does not exceed 30% of the relevant market on which it sells the contract goods or services. Article 3(2) adds that in the event of vertical agreements containing 'exclusive supply obligations',[105] it will be the market share of the buyer that may not exceed 30% of the relevant market for the exemption to (possibly) apply. The Guidelines address in Section V market definition and market share calculation issues,[106] but do not override[107] the general guidance on rules, criteria and evidence given by the Commission notice on the definition of the relevant market for the purposes of Community competition law.[108]

---

[101] L. Peeperkorn, 'E.C. Vertical Restraints Guidelines: Effects-Based or Per Se Policy – A Reply' (2002) 23 *European Competition Law Review* 38, 40-1.

[102] Evidently one can argue about the correctness of the 30% cap: Whish, above note 50, 579.

[103] Recital 8 of the Block Exemption Regulation.

[104] See the Notice on agreements of minor importance of 9 December 1997, OJ 1997 C 372, 13. See also the Guidelines, at para. 8 and following.

[105] It should be noted that 'exclusive supply obligation' has a specific meaning under the Block Exemption Regulation : 'any direct or indirect obligation causing the supplier to sell the goods or services specified in the agreement only to one buyer inside the Community for the purposes of a specific use or for resale.' (see Article 1(c) of the Block Exemption Regulation).

[106] Guidelines, at paras. 88 to 99.

[107] Guidelines, at para. 88.

[108] OJ 1997 C-372.

In particular, a vertical restraint will be assessed through application of the following analysis: First, the relevant market share of the supplier or the buyer (in the case of an exclusive supply agreement) must be established. Second, if the relevant market share does not exceed the 30% threshold, the vertical agreement is covered by the Block Exemption Regulation, subject to the hardcore restrictions and further conditions set out in that regulation (see below). On the other hand, if the relevant market share is above the 30 % threshold, it will be necessary to assess whether the vertical agreement falls within Article 81(1) EC Treaty. If that is the case, it will be necessary to examine whether it fulfils the conditions for exemption under Article 81(3) EC Treaty.[109]

Article 3(1) and 3(2) of the Block Exemption Regulation and the related paragraphs of the Guidelines have been subject to criticism.[110] The Guidelines note that the simplified approach of the Block Exemption Regulation which takes only into account the market share of the supplier (Article 3(1)) or the buyer (Article 3(2)) on the market between these two parties facilitates the application of the Block Exemption Regulation and enhances the level of legal certainty.[111] Nonetheless the Block Exemption Regulation is criticized precisely for providing the business world with too low a level of legal certainty, most importantly, because the definition of the relevant market cannot always easily and unambiguously be given.[112] In the current Block Exemption Regulation, the degree of legal certainty seems moreover to be negatively correlated to the degree of sophistication of the enforcement agencies (whether or not they employ a simple or complex analysis of the relevant market).[113]

Article 4 of the Block Exemption Regulation sets out a series of five "hardcore" exclusions. On the other hand, Article 5 of the Block Exemption Regulation sets out a series of three additional restrictions which merely have a 'severable' effect. The precise implication of either the "hardcore"

---

[109] Guidelines, at para. 120.

[110] Luc Peeperkorn attempted to refute some of these critical remarks: Peeperkorn, above note 101, 41.

[111] Guidelines, at para. 22.

[112] See for instance the discussion in the Case T-25/99, *Colin Arthur Roberts and Valerie Ann Roberts v Commission of the European Communities*, (2001) ECR II-1881. See also S. Bishop and D. Ridyard, 'E.C. Vertical Restraints Guidelines: Effects-Based or Per Se Policy, (2002) 23 *European Competition Law Review* 35, 37.

[113] S. Salop, "Analysis of Foreclosure in the EC Guidelines on Vertical Restraints", in Hawk, above note 12, Chapter 12, 177, 199.

exclusion or the 'severable' exclusion may easily be misunderstood. Consequently we cite once more Alexander Schaub who has portrayed the effects of Articles 4 and 5 of the Block Exemption Regulation as follows :

> The [Block Exemption Regulation] contains [...] five hardcore restrictions that lead to the exclusion of the whole vertical agreement from the scope of application of the [Block Exemption Regulation]. Individual exemption of vertical agreements containing such hardcore restrictions is unlikely. Although Article 81 does not contain any per se rules because individual exemptions are never totally excluded, this hardcore list resembles what would be called a per se rule in the United States.[114]
>
> [Article 5] of the [Block Exemption Regulation] excludes three types of restrictions from the coverage of the [Block Exemption Regulation] even though the market threshold is not exceeded. However, the [Block Exemption Regulation] continues to apply to the remaining part of the vertical agreement if that part is severable from the non-exempted restrictions.[115]

For the purposes of the further analysis we do not consider it necessary to give a full restatement of Articles 4 and 5 of the Block Exemption Regulation. In summary, Article 4 of the Block Exemption Regulation, provides five hardcore restrictions. First, a buyer cannot (contractually) be restricted in his freedom to determine a minimum sale price, although the supplier can validly impose a maximum sale price or can recommend a sale price.[116] Second, the territory into which, or the customers to whom, the buyer may sell the contract goods or services cannot be restricted, except (i) in the event of a restriction of *active* sales into the exclusive territory or to an exclusive customer group reserved to the supplier or allocated by the supplier to another buyer, provided that such a restriction does not limit sales by the customers of the buyer, (ii) in the event of a restriction of sales to end users by a buyer operating at the wholesale level of trade, (iii) in the event of a restriction of sales to unauthorized distributors by the members of a selective distribution system, and (iv) in the event of a restriction of the buyer's ability to sell

---

[114] A. Schaub, 'Vertical Restraints : Key Points and Issues under the New EC Block Exemption Regulation', in Hawk, above note 12, Chapter 13, 201, 207.

[115] *Idem*, at 210.

[116] Article 4(a) and paras. 47-48 of the Guidelines. The supplier must pay attention to the fact that imposing a maximum sale price or recommending a sale price may amount to a fixed or minimum sale price as a result of pressure from or incentives offered by any of the parties.

components, supplied for the purposes of incorporation, to customers who would use them to manufacture the same type of goods as those produced by the supplier.[117] Third, *active* or *passive* sales to end users by members of a selective distribution system operating at the retail level of trade cannot be restricted, without prejudice to the possibility of prohibiting a member of the system from operating out of an unauthorized place of establishment.[118] Fourth, cross-supplies between distributors within a selective distribution system (including between distributors operating at different level of trade) may not be restricted.[119] Finally, a supplier of components and a buyer who incorporates those components cannot agree to prevent the supplier from selling the components as spare parts to end-users or to repairers or other service providers not entrusted by the buyer with the repair or servicing of its goods.[120]

On the other hand, the following three clauses will be 'severably' excluded from the application of the Block Exemption Regulation (Article 5), which means that an obligation subject to such restriction will not be covered by the Block Exemption Regulation – even though the market share threshold is not exceeded – while the Block Exemption Regulation continues to apply to the remaining part of the vertical agreement.[121] First, any direct or indirect non-compete obligation, the duration of which is indefinite or exceeds five years, shall be 'severably' excluded from the application of the Block Exemption regulation. A non-compete obligation which is tacitly renewable beyond a period of five years is to be deemed to have been concluded for an indefinite duration. However, as Article 5 of the Block Exemption Regulation furthermore states, the time limitation of five years shall not apply where the contract goods or services are sold by the buyer from premises and land owned by the supplier or leased by the supplier from third parties not connected with the buyer, provided that the duration of the non-compete obligation does not exceed the period of occupancy of the premises and land by the buyer.[122] Second, any (direct or indirect) obligation causing the buyer, after termination of the agreement, not to manufacture, purchase, sell or resell goods or services shall also be 'severably' excluded from the

---

[117] Article 4(b) and paras. 49-52 of the Guidelines.

[118] Article 4(c) and paras. 53-54 of the Guidelines.

[119] Article 4(d) and para. 55 of the Guidelines.

[120] Article 4(e) and para. 56 of the Guidelines.

[121] Guidelines, at para. 57.

[122] Article 5(a) and paras. 58-59 of the Guidelines.

application of the Block Exemption Regulation. There exists nonetheless an exception to this exclusion. The Block Exemption Regulation shall apply in the event such obligation relates to goods or services which compete with the contract goods or services, is limited to the premises and land from which the buyer has operated during the contract period, is indispensable to protect know-how transferred by the supplier to the buyer, and if the duration of such non-compete obligation is limited to a period of one year after termination of the agreement.[123] Finally, any (direct or indirect) obligation causing the members of a selective distribution system not to sell the brands of particular competing suppliers shall also be 'severably' excluded from the application of the Block Exemption Regulation.[124]

2. Analysis of the 'Buying Power' Provisions of the Block Exemption Regulation

While the Block Exemption Regulation does not itself define buying power,[125] the Guidelines contain several paragraphs explicitly dealing with buying power,[126] while other paragraphs deal with instances of buying power without explicitly stating so.

In paragraph 145 of the Guidelines it is stated that, in assessing a supplier's market power, 'countervailing power' is relevant, as powerful buyers will not easily allow themselves to be cut off from the supply of competing goods or services.[127] Foreclosure by suppliers which is not based on efficiency and which has harmful effects on ultimate consumers, the Guidelines continue, is therefore mainly a risk in the case of dispersed buyers (in other words, when no such countervailing power exists).[128] In this respect the question arises

---

[123] Article 5(b) of the Block Exemption Regulation furthermore specifies that this obligation is without prejudice to the possibility of imposing a restriction which is unlimited in time on the use and disclosure of know-how which has not entered the public domain. See also para. 60 of the Guidelines.

[124] Article 5(c) and para. 61 of the Guidelines.

[125] Article 1(c) of the Block Exemption Regulation dealing with exclusive supply can be regarded as implicitly dealing with one of the restrictions that often but not necessarily accompany 'buying power vertical agreements'.

[126] See in this respect also W. Borhesani, P. de la Cruz and D. Berry, 'Food For Thought: The Emergence of Power Buyers and Its Challenge To Competition Analysis, (1998) 4 *Stanford Journal of Law, Business and Finance* 39, 41.

[127] Guidelines, at para. 145.

[128] *Idem.*

whether the Guidelines in their focus on the countervailing effects of buying power incorporate a correct economic approach. This important question will be further addressed below in section V.1.

Conversely, lack of countervailing power causing one party to impose its will on the other (i.e. resulting in a restraint which subjects mainly one party to restrictions or obligations) may further to paragraph 133 of the Guidelines also be caught under the Block Exemption Regulation.[129] Even if both parties accept restrictions or obligations, the resulting restraint (which in that case is said to be 'agreed' instead of 'imposed') can still be caught under the Block Exemption Regulation.[130]

Other paragraphs of the Guidelines also deal with buyer power in express words. The central provision is paragraph 125 (in the context of the general analysis to be applied for the assessment under article 81(1) EC Treaty (see also above, IV.1):

> Buying power derives from the market position of the buyer. The first indicator of buying power is the market share of the buyer on the purchase market. This share reflects the importance of his demand for his possible suppliers. Other indicators focus on the market position of the buyer on his resale market including characteristics such as a wide geographic spread of his outlets, own brands of the buyer/distributor and his image amongst final consumers. The effect of buying power on the likelihood of anti-competitive effects is not the same for the different vertical restraints. Buying power may in particular increase the negative effects in case of restraints from the limited distribution and market partitioning groups such as exclusive supply, exclusive distribution and quantitative selective distribution.[131]

In this paragraph 125 two major indicators of 'buying power' are summed up: the market share of the buyer on the purchase market – which is to be considered a prime indicator, since the market share reflects the importance of his demand for his possible suppliers – while the market position of the buyer on his resale market is also to be considered as an indicator. Importantly, the Guidelines thus state that in the assessment of the market position of the buyer on his resale market (e.g. a supermarket chain vis-à-vis its

---

[129] Guidelines, at para. 133.
[130] *Idem.*
[131] Guidelines, at para. 125.

customers) one must also consider the buyer's characteristics, such as a wide geographic spread of his outlets, own brands of the buyer/distributor and his image amongst final consumers.[132] This implies that, not only the (upward) relation with the suppliers counts, but also the (downward) relation with the final consumers matters (see also below in this section the discussion of paragraph 204).

Further to the wording of paragraph 125, an analysis of the downward relation seems to involve not only the assessment of more or less objective factors (such as the geographic spread of the stores and the availability of own brands), but also the weighing of more "subjective" elements (such as the image final consumers have of it). Again, particular questions may arise in this context (e.g. is it appropriate to put in the definition subjective elements?; is it necessary to look at the downward relationship between retailers and their customers?; How is such downward relationship to be accurately assessed?; etc). These questions further cumulate in the central question whether the test suggested in paragraph 125 differs from the test suggested in paragraph 204 (see further below in this section). All this will be further elaborated below (in section V.1).

Other paragraphs dealing with specific matters are similarly interesting. For instance, paragraph 221 of the Guidelines (in the context of tying) states the following:

> Buying power is relevant, as important buyers will not easily be forced to accept tying without obtaining at least part of the possible efficiencies. Tying not based on efficiency is therefore mainly a risk where buyers do not have significant buying power.[133]

Again, this statement implicitly presumes buying power to be a countervailing power, thus reducing the risks of anti-competitive behavior by a supplier. As we already noted, this presumption may be criticized. Other paragraphs seem to focus more on the potential anti-competitive effects of 'buying power', and concern more particularly the foreclosure of other distributors. According to paragraph 166 of the Guidelines (in the context of exclusive distribution), foreclosure of other distributors may become a problem in instances where buying power co-exists with downstream market power, in

---

[132] *Idem.*
[133] Guidelines, at para. 221.

particular in the case of very large territories where the exclusive distributor becomes the exclusive buyer for a whole market:[134]

> An example would be a supermarket chain which becomes the only distributor of a leading brand on a national food retail market. The foreclosure of other distributors may be aggravated in the case of multiple exclusive dealership. Such a case, covered by the Block Exemption Regulation when the market share of each supplier is below 30 %, may give reason for withdrawal of the block exemption...[135]

The example given in the Guidelines is well chosen since, indeed, from a consumer welfare point of view, it seems difficult (if not impossible) to justify that one supermarket chain can be the sole distributor of a leading brand on a national food market. But also in this respect several questions need to be answered: is the proposition that foreclosure of other distributors may become a problem in instances where buying power co-exists with downstream market power, which admittedly is true in the example given, true in most other fact patterns? Even more importantly, can it be the case that paragraph 166 of the Guidelines misses the underlying essential point? Again, these questions will be considered below (in section V.1).[136]

Besides that, paragraphs 167 (in the context of exclusive distribution) and 191 (in the context of selective distribution) focus on the potential risk for collusion on the buyers' side. More specifically, paragraph 191 states:

> 'Buying power' may also increase the risk of collusion between dealers and thus appreciably change the analysis of possible anti-competitive effects of selective distribution...[137]

---

[134] Guidelines, at para. 166.

[135] *Idem*. Compare also para. 71: 'The presumption of legality conferred by the Block Exemption Regulation may be withdrawn if a vertical agreement, considered either in isolation or in conjunction with similar agreements enforced by competing suppliers or buyers, comes within the scope of Article 81(1) and does not fulfill all the conditions of Article 81(3).'

[136] Please note that the quoted para. 166 may not have general validity (the rationale seems to be applicable to essential goods such as 'food' rather than for luxury goods like 'hi-end stereo equipment').

[137] Guidelines, at para. 191. See also para. 167: 'Buying power' may also increase the risk of collusion on the buyers' side when the exclusive distribution arrangements are imposed by important buyers, possibly located in different territories.

Finally, as we noted in section IV.1, the Block Exemption Regulation and the Guidelines contain specific rules concerning 'exclusive supply obligations' (see e.g. Article 3(2) of the Block Exemption Regulation, which was discussed above). Article 1(c) of the Block Exemption, Regulation defines an 'exclusive supply obligation' as follows:

> any direct or indirect obligation causing the supplier to sell the goods or services specified in the agreement only to one buyer inside the Community for the purposes of a specific use or for resale.[138]

Paragraph 202 of the Guidelines furthermore specifies that exclusive supply is to be considered the extreme form of limited distribution in as far as the limit on the number of buyers is concerned. In the agreement it is specified that there is only one buyer inside the Community to which the supplier may sell a particular final product.[139] The Guidelines identify several competition concerns. Further to paragraph 204, the main competition risk of exclusive supply arrangements is foreclosure of other buyers. It is stated that for the assessment of this competition risk, the following factors are relevant. The first factor is the market share of the buyer on the upstream purchase market.[140] Foreclosure of competing buyers, it is argued, is not very likely where these competitors have similar buying power and can offer the suppliers similar sales possibilities.[141] To this end it must be considered whether entry barriers at the supplier level exist,[142] whether countervailing power of suppliers exists (because important suppliers will not easily allow themselves to be cut off from alternative buyers),[143] and what the level of trade is and what the nature of the product is.[144] The second factor is the importance of the buyer on the downstream market.[145] If the buyer has no market power downstream, then in principle no appreciable negative effects for consumers should be expected. In this context, the Guidelines state that negative

---

[138] Article 1(c) of the Block Exemption Regulation.

[139] Guidelines, at para. 202.

[140] Guidelines, at para. 204.

[141] Guidelines, at para. 206.

[142] Guidelines, at para. 207.

[143] Guidelines, at para. 208 in which is stated that: 'Foreclosure is therefore mainly a risk in case of weak suppliers and strong buyers'.

[144] Guidelines, at para. 209.

[145] Guidelines, at para. 204.

effects can however be expected when the market share of the buyer on the downstream supply market as well as the upstream purchase market exceeds 30% (see also the discussion in section V.1).[146] In other words, where a company is dominant on the downstream market, any obligation to supply the products only or mainly to the dominant buyer may easily have significant anti-competitive effects. A third factor to consider is the extent to and the duration for which the exclusive supply obligation will be applied.[147] The higher the tied supply share and the longer the duration the more significant the foreclosure is likely to be.[148] With regard to the duration, the Guidelines suggest that exclusive supply arrangements shorter than five years entered into by non-dominant buyers usually require a balancing of pro- and anti-competitive effects.[149]

Also in this context a few questions may arise. One important question, which we have already touched upon, is the question how downstream market power is to be assessed. It seems that paragraph 204 offers a rather objective test (i.e. the market share on his downstream market), while we have seen that paragraph 125 refers to several more subjective criteria (see also the discussion above in this section). Do these two tests differ? If so, why are they divergent? Should they be different? etc. These questions will form the subject of the discussion in the next section.

V. ASSESSMENT OF THE FIRST TWO QUESTIONS IN THE LIGHT OF THE PRECEDING SECTION

Having dwelled upon the particularities and policy underpinnings of the Block Exemption Regulation and the Guidelines, we turn again to the questions that were set out in section III, in order to consider whether the framework offered by the current law is appropriate to adequately reflect the notions and economic realities identified.

---

[146] *Idem.*

[147] Guidelines, at para. 205.

[148] *Idem.*

[149] *Idem.*

162

1. To what extent does the Block Exemption Regulation (including the Guidelines) correctly take into account the 'dynamics of the changed or changing manufacturer-retailer relationship', as this is reflected in buying power?

A first important observation is that buying power is not an easy concept, and that neither the Block Exemption Regulation nor the Guidelines really seem to capture the concept.

To a certain extent, of course, every buyer has the basic power to buy or not to buy. Obviously, such power is typical for each potential buyer and (taken on its own) does not imply the existence of the concept 'buying power' as it is used in this text. On the other hand, in some markets – such as many second hand markets – buyers may have – at least to a certain extent – an impact on the price. Again, that is 'negotiation', which is typical behavior for contractual parties, and does not imply the existence of 'buying power'.

The self-evident truth of those propositions notwithstanding, statements like those make it difficult to come up with an accurate universal definition of 'buying power'. The OECD has suggested several definitions. The definition used by the Secretariat of the OECD in its 1999 Background Paper was the following:

> Buyer power is [...] globally defined as the ability of a buyer to influence the terms and conditions on which it purchases goods.[150]

It is to be questioned whether this definition[151] makes much sense. Intuitively, the definition seems to be too generalized, too broad, as the ability to influence the terms and condition of purchase can have many other causes

---

[150] OECD, *Buying Power of Multiproduct Retailers*, DAFFE/CLP(99), 1999, Background Paper at 20. In an earlier draft of its background paper the Secretariat of the OECD had defined the term as follows : "A retailer is defined to have buyer power if, in relation to at least one supplier, it can credibly threaten to impose a long term opportunity cost (i.e. harm or withheld benefit) which, were the threat carried out, would be significantly disproportionate to any resulting long term opportunity cost to itself. By disproportionate, we intend a difference in relative rather than absolute opportunity cost." This definition was cited in the Report produced by Dobson Consulting, above note 31, 25. See in this respect : P. Collins, 'Retailer Buyer Power: Abusive Behaviour and Mergers/Acquisitions, in Hawk, above note 12, Chapter 25, at p. 435-6.

[151] Alternative definitions exist, such as the definition by the OFT Competition Act Guideline: M. Bloom, 'Retailer Buyer Power' in hawk, above note 12, Chapter 23, 396.

than the sheer exercise of buying power (imagine a student getting a better deal just because of sheer sympathy).

Other authors have noticed a series of additional flaws. One commentator, Philip Collins, correctly observed that the intrinsic problem of the definition is that it relies, implicitly or expressly, on some form of discrimination compared to the terms available or obtained by other buyers. Such a comparison would easily become flawed due to the fact that such terms vary depending on the negotiation strength and marketing policies and practices of each particular buyer.[152] We believe that is very much true but would add to this additional factors which might influence the terms of a certain vertical arrangement, such as the negotiation skills – and guts – of both parties, long term strategies of both parties, quality of the legal input obtained, and so on. Another commentator, Joachim Lücking, added that the definition fails to specify whether the influence relates to the buyer's absolute size and market position or the buyer's relative position in the bargaining process with the supplier.[153]

An alternative – and, as opposed to the definition criticized above, less general – way of defining 'buying power' involves the insertion of a reference to some kind of 'force' or 'credible threat'.[154] This way of defining buying power should also be criticized, albeit on other grounds. Envisage for instance a joint venture whereby the superstore exchanges vital information on customer behaviour on the basis of which the manufacturer can develop a product on the condition that the superstore shall be guaranteed a certain profit margin on each product sold and that during a specific period the new product shall be supplied only to the superstore in question. As can be recalled, we labeled such structure as kind of a *vertical cooperative information-based structure* based upon the sharing of information (see section II). Although in this last example the manufacturer is not coerced, and has the freedom not to enter in the joint venture, doubts may exist on the practical reality of this freedom, for instance in the event the manufacturer depends for a substantial part of its output on the demand of this buyer.

Moreover, from an analysis of the dynamics of the manufacturer-retailer relationship, it seems that buying power involves a rather invisible, some-

---

[152] Collins, above note 150, 436.

[153] J. Lücking, "Retailer Power in EC Competition Law", in Hawk, above note 12, Chapter 26, at p. 469.

[154] For instance the 1998 definition of the OECD, as cited by the Report produced by Dobson Consulting, above note 31, 25.

times purely potential power, or even a logical pressure or incentive. Again, if entering a *vertical cooperative information-based structure* is proposed by a large superstore chain, a manufacturer may be pushed in the direction of accepting such arrangement *by pure logic rather than by force*. The information offered to him has a high value and can help him to compete better with his competitors. In some instances rational behavior itself may trigger the impact of buying power, even in the absence of any coercion or threat. The mere logic of a manufacturer as *rational market player* – i.e. why should he refuse to enter into a vertical information-sharing structure if the anticipated benefits for the manufacturer outweigh the anticipated costs? – could be enough for buying power to sort its effects.

Buying power in this sense constitutes a peculiar kind of *'adaptive upstream gravitation'*, which ranges from force and credible threat, to invisible or camouflaged power, to persuasion and temptation rather than force.

On the other hand, buying power itself is under constant (upward) market pressure, since even large retailers can be expected to be subject to market demand.[155] Large retail stores may decide to terminate all relations with a particular manufacturer; but if they do so, they risk losing customers (in this sense the notion 'gatekeeping power' may be misleading, since buyers are not completely free to open or close the gate – see in this context section II.1). Therefore, an analysis of 'buying power' should take into account not just the terms and conditions of a particular vertical arrangement, but also, as Patrick Rey suggested, 'what happens if they cannot reach an agreement – that is, what happens if consumers do not find a particular brand in a particular store?'[156]

As was already noted in section IV.2, this idea has been reflected in paragraph 125 as well as paragraphs 204-205 of the Guidelines. Paragraph 204 of the Guidelines. It sets out as one of the three factors for assessing the competition the risk of exclusive supply obligations, the market position of the buyer not only on the upstream market (i.e. its suppliers), but also on the downstream market (i.e. its customers). In addition, paragraph 204 accurately takes into account the fact that upstream and downstream power may influence and interact with each other:

Negative effects can however be expected when the market share of the buyer on the downstream supply market as well as the upstream pur-

---

155 Farris and Ailawadi, above note 21.

156 Rey, 'Retailer Buying Power and Competition Policy, in Hawk, above note 12, Chapter 27, at p. 490.

chase market exceeds 30 %. Where the market share of the buyer on the upstream market does not exceed 30 %, significant foreclosure effects may still result, especially when the market share of the buyer on his downstream market exceeds 30 %. In such cases withdrawal of the block exemption may be required. Where a company is dominant on the downstream market, any obligation to supply the products only or mainly to the dominant buyer may easily have significant anti-competitive effects.[157]

On the other hand, In paragraph 125 it is stated that :

> Other indicators [of buying power] focus on the market position of the buyer on his resale market including characteristics such as a wide geographic spread of his outlets, own brands of the buyer/distributor and his image amongst final consumers.

This paragraph 125, taken on its own as well as read together with paragraph 204, is to be criticized. It can be questioned whether the indicators of downstream market power are adequate to establish in practice that a particular chain has buying power and that another has not. Is the 'image amongst final consumers' not too vague a criterion? How is it determined? Is the image to be assessed on a EU wide basis (in the hypothesis that the chain operates throughout the EU)? If so, it must be considered that, possibly, the image of a superstore chain may vary from Member State to Member State (or even more locally) – taking into account that many of the supra-national chains have emerged through mergers with and acquisitions of already existing stores. Also, the geographic spread of the outlets is difficult to employ as an indicator: a large retailer offering massively discounted electronic equipment may have only one store located in the suburbs of a major city, while its (smaller) competitors have much more locations.[158] Consider also e-commerce stores, which are at the same time everywhere and nowhere. Or in the case that a few large chains cooperate in a buying alliance, is the image, geographic spread and/or private label brands of all participants to such alliance to be counted together or should each such characteristic be subject to a separate analysis? etc.

Admittedly, some of these questions could readily be answered by someone confident in taking competition policy decisions. However, even in that

---

¹⁵⁷ See para. 204 of the Guidelines.
¹⁵⁸ See section II above, and Chapter 2; see also Stern and El-Ansary, above note 8, 444.

166

case, it can be anticipated that such answers would most probably lead to other questions, which *regardless of one's vision on competition policy* in the end would lead to the troubling fact that, although downstream buying power in many instances can intuitively be 'felt' to exist, no conclusive evidence yet exists on the true reason and functioning of the kind of downstream magnetic force of large chains (and therefore no precise calculation of the downstream market strength can be given): is it "image", "geographic spread", "habit", "ease and comfort", "lower prices", or the "product range", or is it a result of the fact that competitors disappear or change (i.e. in the case of consumer goods retail, as Paul Dobson has convincingly argued, the consolidation of powerful retail chains have led to a marginalisation of independent retailers, restricted to acting as convenience stores),[159] or other factors, or a melange of all such elements?

Paragraph 204, on the other hand, subjects downstream buying power to a market share test (of 30%). Hence (and irrespective of the question whether a different test would be applied in practice), it can be argued, based on the wording of this paragraph 204, that the characteristics referred to in paragraph 125 do not really matter except to the extent that they are relevant to determine the market share. Does this imply that the test suggested in paragraph 204 should be preferred over the test in paragraph 125? In our opinion, this question is to be answered negatively.

In the context of buying power, the sole calculation of buyer market share may lead to incorrect conclusions. Consider for instance markets where not only very few buyers but also very few consumers exist (leading to a high market share of the buyer, who has no buying power at all when confronted with a manufacturer who also delivers goods to other markets); consider distributors with a high downstream market share in the automobile industry,[160] and so on. Conversely, consider for instance a buyer with a presently relatively low market share, but who bears a strategic long term potential for the manufacturer, so that the buyer knowing this potential may be able to influence the price of the supply.[161]

The foregoing shows that both tests seem to fail to recognize the true dynamism in the manufacturer-retailer relationship, which is a criticism that

---

[159] P. Dobson, 'Competition and Mergers in Consumer Goods Industries: The Case of Pet Foods', (2001) *European Competition Law Review* 443. 446.

[160] As noted before in section II, this situation might change upon the entry of force of the Block Exemption for the Motor Vehicle Industry.

[161] Reference may be made to section II, and in particular to the views expressed in Stern and El-Ansary, above note 8, 444.

also applies to the other buying power related provisions discussed in section IV.2. In assessing buying power, a two or three step process (i.e. step 1: examination of the supplier's position; step 2: examination of the buyer's position; step 3: examination of the restraint) risks leading to inaccurate conclusions. Such a simple assessment process misses the point that the buyer's position and the supplier's position may be interrelated and may interact with each other. The relationship is, as we called it, dynamic rather than static. The Guidelines in this sense reflect a static and, more specifically, a static *manufacturer-centric* approach. Hence, the buying power provisions set out in section IV.2 seem to be corrective nuances to such manufacturer-centric approach rather than a useful analysis. We will elaborate further on this in our assessment of vertical co-operative structures in section V.2.

By way of a preliminary conclusion, we can summarize that the Guidelines fail correctly to appreciate buying power in its complex meaning, which we described as a peculiar kind of adaptive upstream gravitation, the actual substance of which will depend on the particulars of a dynamic manufacturer-retailer relationship. Or as one commentator has stated: 'Buyer power is not just about getting better terms and conditions. It concerns every aspect of the relationship between supplier and retailer and, indeed, the retailer's own commercial and marketing strategy.'[162]

2. How does the Block Exemption Regulation (including the Guidelines) apply to 'vertical cooperative information-based structures', such as category management or slotting allowances?

As it appears from the general discussion of section IV.1, most of the hardcore and severable restrictions concern a typical fact pattern whereby a manufacturer imposes on its distributors several duties. This is explained by the fact that the whole analysis of vertical agreements, as it is provided by the Block Exemption Regulation, mostly presupposes a manufacturer drawing on a mechanism of vertical arrangements in an attempt to take control of or steer the behaviour and underlying incentives of its distributors or its retailers, thus constituting a 'manufacturer-centric' approach.[163]

---

[162] Collins, above note 150, 436.

[163] See Articles 4 and 5 of the Block Exemption Regulation and the analysis provided in Chapter 4.

Let's take for instance the hardcore restrictions, which clearly represent a manufacturer-centric approach. Essentially – irrespective of the exceptions to the rules – a manufacturer is blocked from contractually restricting the buyer to determine its minimum sale price,[164] from imposing some kinds of territorial restrictions (Article 4(b)),[165] imposing restrictions on active or passive sales to end users by retailers of a selective distribution system,[166] restricting cross-supplies between distributors within a selective distribution system,[167] and under certain conditions limiting the supplier to selling the components as spare parts to end-users or to repairers or other service providers.[168]

As we have already noted, taking into account the apparent 'manufacturer-centric' approach, it appears that the paragraphs on buying power constitute corrective nuances rather than rules.

Imagine the functioning of a *vertical cooperative information-based structure'*.[169] One party is a large retailer who has the know-how and resources to collect and process the data and information on its customers' behavior. This data might contain relevant indications of how large demand can be expected to be, and consequently might answer by how much the output must be increased or how the product characteristics must be qualitatively altered to meet customers' wishes. The other party is a manufacturer or wholesaler who knows the value of this information, and thus expects that exactly this information may and will provide him with a cost-efficient opportunity to develop or redesign a product that better meets market demand. In consideration for the provision of information and data, the retailer may be given several benefits such as price reductions (as the case may be combined with the arrangement to charge higher prices to other distributors), a high shelf fee (the costs of which may be borne by other retailers to whom the higher prices are charged), a thorough category management and marketing which better adjusts customers' incentives to buy a particular product, and constant adjustment of the output, etc.

As we indicated in section II, such a vertical agreement is based on co-operation rather than on unilateral force or countervailing forces – we referred to it as a 'value-added partnership'. It seems that the Block Exemp-

---

[164] See Article 4(a).

[165] See Article 4(b).

[166] See Article 4(c).

[167] See Article 4(d).

[168] See Article 4(e).

[169] As it has been described in section II.

tion Regulation does not really take into account this possibility in that it adds to its manufacturer-centric approach the assumption that forces are unilateral, or at best, countervailing. Only paragraph 133 of the Guidelines seems to refer a restraint, which is 'agreed' and can still be caught under the Block Exemption Regulation.[170] Indeed, it is conceivable that many of such co-operative vertical arrangements can be structured in such way that they fall within the scope of the exemption of the Block Exemption Regulation (within the limits that are described in section IV,1. and 2., and subject to paragraph 133 of the Guidelines).

Nonetheless, we believe that, even if exempted under the Block Exemption Regulation, certain of these vertical cooperative information-based structures may still have a potentially distorting effect on competition. For instance, it can be perceived that a potential *horizontal effect*[171] may affect the manufacturer's competitors. It may be contended that on the retailers' level the ready access to information on customers' behaviour is relevant mainly for marketing purposes and that it has no horizontal effect on the other retailers whatsoever. However, once the information is communicated to the manufacturer in the context of a co-operative vertical arrangement, this information becomes a potentially powerful tool in enabling the manufacturer to use the advantage of such information to hurt its competitors, especially when, on the basis of the information, successful new products are developed (and patented), which are then given to the retailer as an exclusive distributor.

We do not on the basis of economic theory know under which circumstances a similar vertical structure should be permitted or not. At least theoretically, we believe that, apart from the potential benefits, several competition risks may also be involved, not the least the risk of foreclosure of other buyers (or manufacturers). Taking into account the analysis of the foregoing paragraphs, we would like to suggest that in that context further economic research is required.

VI. 'PRIVATE ENFORCEMENT' OF VERTICAL RESTRAINTS THAT ARE NOT EXEMPT UNDER THE BLOCK EXEMPTION REGULATION

In addition to the questions tentatively answered in section V, stemming from the changing world of retail business, the following question, originat-

---

[170] *Idem.*
[171] We do not imply that this necessarily is an anti-competitive effect.

ing from the reality that contract law in this area is (still) national, has to be addressed: what are the contract law consequences, in the light of the nullity sanction of Article 81(2), of a system of a block exemption with a series of exclusions of the benefit of the exemption for certain clauses (or for distribution contracts containing certain clauses)?

1.   General Background

(a)   Article 81(1) is directly effective

Article 81(1) EC is directly effective. As the Court of Justice of the European Communities (the "European Court of Justice" or "ECJ") noted in the landmark *BRT* case, Article 81(1) EC creates direct legal rights in respect of the individuals concerned.[172] The national courts must safeguard those rights.[173] In addition, Article 81 EC bears in itself the capability of being 'privately enforced' – and therefore supports the system of competition enforcement that is favored by the Commission, as a result of which national courts,[174] as well as national competition authorities,[175] would become more involved in the enforcement of EC competition rules:[176,177]

The national court may have to reach a decision on the application of Articles [81] and [82] in several procedural situations. In the case of civil law proceedings, two types of action are particularly frequent: actions relating to contracts and actions for damages. Under the former, the defen-

---

[172] Case 127/73, *Belgische Radio en Televisie et société belge des auteurs, compositeurs et éditeurs v SABAM et Fonior ("BRT/SABAM I")*, 30 January 1974, 1974 ECR 51 at para 16.

[173] *Idem.*

[174] See the view of the Commission of private enforcement in its *Notice on Cooperation between National Courts and the Commission in Applying Articles [81] and [82] of the EC Treaty* [renumbered by the authors], published in OJ 1993, C 39/6.

[175] See the *Notice on Cooperation between National Competition Authorities and the Commission in Handling Cases Falling within the Scope of Articles [81] and [82] of the EC Treaty* [renumbered], published in OJ 1997, C 313/3.

[176] See also the White Paper on *Modernization of the Rules Implementing Articles [81] and [82] of the EC Treaty*, OJ 1999, C 132/1 and the ensuing *Proposal for a Regulation implementing Articles 81 and 82 (and replacing regulation 17).*, OJ, N° C 365E, p. 284.

[177] This shift in policy has not been uncontested. See for instance the critical viewpoint of M. Hutchings and M. Levitt, 'Concurrent Jurisdiction' (editiorial), (1994) 3 *European Competition Law Review* 119.

dant usually relies on Article [81 (2)] to dispute the contractual obligations invoked by the plaintiff. Under the latter, the prohibitions contained in Articles [81] and [82] are generally relevant in determining whether the conduct which has given rise to the alleged injury is illegal. 18. In such situations, the direct effect of Article [81 (1)] and Article [82] gives national courts sufficient powers to comply with their obligation to hand down judgment.[178]

(b)　Article 81(2): nullity sanction

An agreement that infringes Article 81 (1) EC and that is not exempt because of Article 81 (3) EC shall be void in application of Article 81 (2) EC. Companies as well as individuals can therefore use Article 81 EC as a defense in a civil action for enforcement of such agreement, or they can use it as a cause of action themselves. In addition, even if the individuals don't, since Article 81 EC is a measure of public policy, national courts are obliged on their own motion to declare agreements void if they find them in breach of Article 81 EC.[179]

With regard to the possibility for a judge to invoke the unfair character – as provided by the Directive – on his/her own motion, it may be recalled that in *Van Schijndel*[180] the Court held that Community law does not require national courts to raise of their own motion an issue concerning the breach of provisions of Community law where this would oblige them to abandon the passive role assigned to them by going beyond the ambit of the dispute defined by the parties.

With regard to the nullity sanction of Article 81(2) the ECJ has made a difference between agreements in existence at the time of entry into force of Regulation 17 (13 March 1962), or, in case of agreements between undertakings in new Member States, at the time of entry into force of the relevant accession Treaty ('old agreements), on the one hand, and agreements which were not in existence at such time ('new agreements'). Old agreements benefit from a 'provisional validity'. This means that, subject to their timely notification (unless they are dispensed from notification), the national courts have

---

[178] *Notice on Cooperation*, above note 174, paras. 17 and 18.

[179] Joined Cases C-430/93 and C-431/93, *Jeroen van Schijndel and Johannes Nicolaas Cornelis van Veen v Stichting Pensioenfonds voor Fysiotherapeuten*, [1995] ECR I-4705.

[180] *Idem.*

to hold them valid for so long as the Commission has not taken any decision on their compatibility with Article 81(1). By contrast, new agreements do not benefit from such a provisional validity. Within the limits which result from the lack of power of national courts to apply Article 81(3) (limits which will disappear if and when the Commission proposal for a new implementing Regulation is adopted), national courts can apply Article 81(1) and 81(2) to their full extent. If a national court finds that an agreement undoubtedly falls within the prohibition of Article 81(1) and can obviously not benefit from an exemption, it should declare such agreement null and void. Such a decree of nullity is capable of having a bearing on all effects of the agreement, either in the past or in the future, and is therefore of retroactive effect.[181] However, the decree of automatic nullity only applies to those parts of the agreement affected by the prohibition or to the agreements as a whole if those parts are not severable from the agreement.[182] Whether that is the case depends on the national law applicable to the agreement (which takes into account the will of the parties). The consequences of the decree of nullity for the other parts of the agreement and for any contracts and rights and obligations based on it are also governed by the national law applicable to the agreement.[183]

(c) Article 81(3), which is not (presently) directly effective, as a handicap

In the absence of an individual or block exemption, national courts have no jurisdiction, for the time being, to determine that an agreement falling within Article 81 EC is eligible for exemption. By contrast, they can apply Article 81(1) and the nullity sanction of Article 81(2) to an agreement which, while not being dispensed from notification,[184] has not been notified to the Commission and can therefore not benefit (with retroactive effect) from an exemption, even though it fulfills (or might fulfill) the substantive conditions of Article 81(3).[185]

---

[181] Case 48/72, *SA Brasserie de Haecht v Wilkin-Janssen ("Haecht II")*, [1973] ECR 77, at points 26-27.

[182] Case 56/65, *Société Technique Minière v Maschinenbau Ulm*, [1966] ECR 235.

[183] Case 319/82, *Société de vente de Ciments v Kerpen and Kerpen*, [1983] ECR 4173; Case 10/86, *VAG France v Magne*, [1986] ECR 4071.

[184] All vertical agreements are, since 1999, dispensed from notification pursuant to the Article 4 (2) of Regulation 17, as amended by Regulation 1216/99.

[185] See Case C-234/89, *Stergios Delimitis v Henninger Bräu AG*, [1991] ECR I-935.

(d) Article 81(1) not containing a 'rule of reason' as a further handicap

When applying Article 81 national courts are not allowed to take into account, for instance, that the pro-competitive effects of a particular agreement outweigh its anticompetitive effects.[186] As several commentators have argued, the absence of jurisdiction by national courts to apply a certain kind of 'rule of reason', as the US courts do with certain types of vertical restraints, may be perceived as a handicap to 'private enforcement' in the courts when applying Article 81 EC.[187]

However, arguably, the ECJ has recently abandoned its reluctance to read a "rule of reason" in Article 81 EC. Indeed in its famous *Wouters* Judgment,[188] the Court considered (at point 97 of the Judgment):

> However, not every agreement between undertakings or any decision of an association of undertakings which restricts the freedom of action of the parties or of one of them necessarily falls within the prohibition laid down in Article 85(1) of the Treaty. For the purposes of application of that provision to a particular case, account must first of all be taken of the overall context in which the decision of the association of undertakings was taken or produces its effects. More particularly, account must be taken of its objectives, which are here connected with the need to make rules relating to organisation, qualifications, professional ethics, supervision and liability, in order to ensure that the ultimate consumers of legal services and the sound administration of justice are provided with the necessary guarantees in relation to integrity and experience (see, to that effect, Case C-3/95 Reisebüro Broede [1996] ECR I-6511, paragraph 38). It has then to be considered whether the consequential effects restrictive of competition are inherent in the pursuit of those objectives.

---

[186] Case 28/67, *Brasserie de Haecht v Wilkin-Janssen*, [1973] ECR 77 ("Haecht II"). See also Case C-234/89, *Stergios Delimitis v Henninger Bräu AG*, [1991] ECR I-935.

[187] L. Ritter, W. D. Braun and F. Rawlinson, *European Competition Law: A Practitioner's Guide* 2nd edn, (The Hague/London/Boston: Kluwer Law International, 2000) 930. Those authors nevertheless believe that the effects of this 'handicap' are reduced by the power of national courts to apply Article 81 (3) EC Treaty negatively and because of the existence of block exemptions.

[188] Case C-309/99; *Wouters et al. v Algemene Raad van de Nederlandse Orde van Advocaten*, Judgment of 19 February 2002, not yet reported.

Scholars have already engaged in passionate discussions on whether this remark embodies the application of a kind of 'rule of reason' similar to the rule applied in US antitrust law (or one of its variants, such as the 'ancillary restraints doctrine'). This debate notwithstanding, *Wouters* has reactivated another debate which may be called the "Monster of Loch Ness" of EC competition law. For the appraisal of distribution contracts (and vertical restrictions in general) under EC competition law, this debate is probably less important, since these contracts (and restrictions) are largely exempted, and since the hard core black listed clauses which are not exempted would hardly qualify for an appraisal under a rule of reason.

*(e)   Intermediate Conclusion: private enforcement is still largely
       a matter of National law*

Even though the legal nature of Article 81 EC (i.e. having a direct effect and the automatic voidance pursuant to Article 81 (2) EC Treaty) and the obligations of the national courts regarding to the enforcement of Article 81 are a matter of Community law,[189] the remedies that may be granted by a national court (principally) are still a matter of national law:

> The application of Articles [81] and [82] of the Treaty by the national authorities is, in principle, governed by national procedural rules. Subject to the observance of Community law, and in particular its fundamental principles, it is therefore a matter for national law to define the appropriate procedural rules in order to guarantee the rights of the defense of the persons concerned. Such guarantees may differ from those which apply in Community proceedings.[190]

(f)   'Modernization' enhances the role of the national courts

Following the 'Modernization' idea, set out in its 'White Paper on modernization of the rules implementing Articles 81 and 82 of the EC Treaty', the Commission has recently proposed to amend Regulation 17 (Regulation

---

[189] Ritter, Braun and Rawlinson, above note 187, 926.

[190] Case C-60/92, *Otto BV v Postbank NV,* [1993] ECR I-5683.

[191] See in this context J. Stuyck, H. Gilliams (eds.) and E. Ballon (ass. ed.), *Modernisation of*

implementing Articles 81 and 82), in order to give more powers to national courts and authorities to apply Article 81.[191] The Commission proposes to abandon its exclusive power to grant exemptions (now enshrined in Article 9(1) of Regulation 17). Article 81 would become a 'unitary' norm which, taken as a whole, would become directly effective.[192] National authorities and national courts would be enabled (and obliged) to verify whether an agreement is restrictive within the meaning of Article 81(1) and if so, whether it fulfills the conditions of Article 81(3), the latter provision becoming a 'legal exception' to the prohibition in Article 81(1), rather than a basis for an 'exemption'.

(g) But National Courts remain under an Obligation to avoid Decisions that Conflict with Decisions of the Community Institutions

Pursuant to the judgments of the ECJ in *Delimitis*,[193] and *Masterfoods*,[194] national courts are under a duty to avoid giving judgments which would either conflict with a decision which the Commission might take under Article 81 or 82 EC or a decision which the Commission has already taken but the legality of which is still under review before the Community courts. This duty seems to be very general and to imply that a national court, which is confronted with an agreement which has been declared contrary to Article 81 (or 82) by the Commission, has to suspend any decision regarding either an action for enforcement or nullity of the agreement or a claim for damages founded on an alleged violation of Article 81 or 82, until the Community courts have decided on the validity of the challenged decision (this may be the ECJ after appeal against a judgment of the CFI), or until the ECJ has answered a preliminary question on the validity of the Commission decision, a question which the national court may refer at any time to the ECJ. In the meantime the national court should, however, consider whether it is necessary to order interim measures in order to safeguard the interests of the parties pending final judgment.

European Competition Law – The Commission's proposal for a New Regulation Implementing Articles 81 and 82 EC (Antwerp/Oxford/New York: Intersentia, 2002).

[192] OJ N° C 365E, p. 284.

[193] See Case C-234/89, *De Limitis v Henninger Bräu*, [1991] ECR I-935, at point 47.

[194] Case C-344/98, *Masterfoods Ltd v HB Ice Cream Ltd*, Judgment of 14 December 2000, not yet reported.

*(h) It may be argued that there is a Community Law basis for Actions
      for damages in case of infringements of Articles 81 and 82*

Recently the ECJ rendered its judgment in the long awaited *Courage* case[195]
concerning the possibility of seeking compensation for loss caused by a contract or by conduct liable to restrict or distort competition. The ECJ reminded
us first that, in accordance with settled case-law, the national courts whose
task it is to apply the provisions of Community law in areas within their
jurisdiction must ensure that those rules take full effect and must protect the
rights which they confer on individuals.[196] The effectiveness of Article 81
and, in particular, the practical effect of Article 81(1) would be put at risk if
it were not open to any individual to claim damages for loss caused to him
by a contract or by conduct liable to restrict or distort competition. [197]

From that point of view, actions for damages before the national courts
can make a significant contribution to the maintenance of effective competition in the Community.[198] There should therefore not be any absolute bar to
such an action being brought by a party to a contract that would be held to
violate the competition rules.[199]

However, *in the absence of Community rules governing the matter*, it is
for the domestic legal system of each Member State to designate the courts
and tribunals having jurisdiction and to lay down the detailed procedural rules
governing actions for safeguarding *rights which individuals derive directly
from Community law*, provided that such rules are not less favourable than
those governing similar domestic actions (as will further be elaborated, the
so-called 'principle of equivalence'), and that they do not render practically
impossible or excessively difficult the exercise of rights conferred by Community law (the 'principle of effectiveness').[200]

Community law does not prevent national courts from taking steps to
ensure that the protection of the rights guaranteed by Community law does
not entail the unjust enrichment of those who enjoy them.[201]

---

[195] Case C-453/99, *Courage Ltd v Bernard Crehan and Bernard Crehan v Courage Ltd and
Others*, [2001] ECR I-6297.

[196] Case 106/77, *Amministrazione delle Finanze dello Stato v Simmenthal SpA*, [1978] ECR
629, para. 16; Case C-213/89 *Factortame* [1990] ECR I-2433, para. 19.

[197] Case C-453/99, above note 195, at para. 26.

[198] *Idem*, at para. 27.

[199] *Idem*, at para. 28.

[200] *Idem*, at para. 29.

[201] *Idem*, at para. 30 with reference to Case 238/78 *Ireks-Arkady v Council and Commission*

Similarly, provided that the principles of equivalence and effectiveness are respected, [202] Community law does not preclude national law from denying a party who is found to bear significant responsibility for the distortion of competition the right to obtain damages from the other contracting party. Under a principle which is recognized in most of the legal systems of the Member States and which the Court has applied in the past,[203] a litigant should not profit from his own unlawful conduct, where this is proven.[204]

To the extent that 'the rights which individuals derive directly from *Community* law' in paragraph 29 of *Courage* include the right to damages, the judgment means that this right is been given a Community law foundation (which may co-exist with a national law foundation), as opposed to a mere obligation to shape national laws on damages in such a way as to guarantee the full effectiveness of Community law. The ruling by the Court that national law cannot bar a party to the agreement to bring an action for damages militates in favor of such a reading of the judgment. If this interpretation is correct, the ECJ will probably be called upon further to define in more detail the conditions for such a Community law action (as it did for actions for liability of member states for infringements of Community law).

In that regard, the matters to be taken into account by the competent national court include the economic and legal context in which the parties find themselves and the respective bargaining power and conduct of the two parties to the contract.[205]

2. Set of Questions

In this context, a further set of particular questions may arise. This set of questions deals with the problem of the nature of the sanction contained in Article 81 (2) EC.[206]

[1979] ECR 2955, para 14, Case 68/79 *Just* [1980] ECR 501, para 26, and Joined Cases C-441/98 and C-442/98 *Michaïlidis* [2000] ECR I-7145, para. 31.

[202] See Case C-261/95, *Rosalba Palmisani v Istituto Nazionale della Previdenza Sociale (INPS),* [1997] ECR I-4025, para. 27

[203] See Case 39/72 *Commission v Italy* [1973] ECR 101, para. 10

[204] Case C-453/99, above note 195, para. 31.

[205] *Idem*, at para. 32.

[206] The assumption behind the formulation of this set of questions is that the national court, applying the basic reasoning set out in the paragraphs above, would have considered a particular vertical restraint to be conflicting with Article 81 EC Treaty.

Generally – in the absence of Community rules governing the matter[207] – the remedies and the procedural rules for obtaining remedies for violations of Article 81 EC may not less be favorable than the remedies (and the procedural rules) for violations of similar national competition law (i.e. the principle of equivalence).[208] Moreover the national rules may not render practically ineffective the internal market rules (i.e. the principle of effectiveness).[209]

This twofold obligation may be perceived as going beyond requiring from national courts a simple declaration that a particular vertical restraint (or a particular clause of a vertical agreement) is void because it is incompatible with Article 81 EC Treaty, since at least from a theoretical viewpoint it cannot be excluded that an effective private enforcement of Article 81 EC requires the existence of an adequate arsenal of injunctions, restitutions and damages, even if such arsenal were not to exist in the legal order of the particular member state. However, notwithstanding this remark, it is – as a matter of *hard law* – unclear to what extent national courts are bound to apply, to amend or even to 'invent' particular remedies.

For instance, in the event of a vertical restraint, the distinction must be made between the hardcore restrictions of the Block Exemption Regulation on the one hand and the 'severable' restrictions on the other (see supra). Suppose a national court is requested to judge on a particular clause which falls under a 'severable' restriction of the Block Exemption Regulation. Normally, (only) this clause will not be exempted under Article 81 (3) EC Treaty, and would therefore fall within the scope of Article 81 (2) EC Treaty. In other words, the national court will have the obligation to declare that particular clause void, while the rest of the agreement can be left unaltered. Nonetheless, a problem potentially arises if national law embodies the rule that, if a clause is essential (or determinative) to the conclusion of the contract, and if such clause falls away (e.g. because it was not exempted under Article 5 of the Block Exemption Regulation), the contract as a whole is to be declared void since the parties would never have consented to an agreement lacking the clause that is fallen away. Alternatively, a reduction of the obligation or right in question may be proper under the national law instead of an avoidance of the particular clause.

---

[207] Case C-453/99, above note 195, para. 29.
[208] Case 199/82, *Amministrazione delle Finanze dello Stato v SpA San Giorgio*, [1983] ECR 3595, at para. 14.
[209] *Idem.*

The legal orders of the Member States seem to have developed a body of law dealing with such intrinsic conflict between their state-made national laws and this national spill-over of EC law.[210] However, the exact 'thin red line' between the sanction of avoidance of Article 81 (2) EC Treaty (which is for the purposes of this text to be read together with the Block Exemption Regulation), on the one hand, and the particular remedies provided for under the respective national laws of the Member States, on the other, is in most cases difficult to predict. Moreover, as will be often the case with vertical restraints, one of the parties may not be acquainted with the legal order of the other party. It is therefore not surprising that in this context an ongoing quest has commenced as to what is or should be the (national) level of effectiveness of the enforcement of EC competition law, and therefore also the (national) availability of appropriate remedies.

The landmark Opinion of Advocate General van Gerven in the *Banks* case[211] – besides being an exceptional illustration of legal refinement[212] – bears particular relevance for any discussion on this topic. The relevant part of the Opinion turned on the question whether a national court has the power and/or the obligation under EC law to award damages in respect of breach of the EC Treaty (or the ECSC Treaty – which ended on 23 July 2002)[213] for a loss sustained as a result of such breach?[214] In answering this question, the Advocate General referred to the settled case law, affirming that directly applicable Treaty provisions merely offer a minimum guarantee and strict compliance with such provisions is not to be equated with a full implementation:

---

[210] Ritter, Braun and Rawlinson, above note 187, 926 et seq.

[211] Opinion of the Advocate General van Gerven in Case C-128/92, *H. J. Banks & Company Ltd v British Coal Corporation,* [1994] ECR I-1212. For the purposes of this text the most interesting paragraphs can be found between pages I-1243 and I-1255.

[212] It should be noted that the European Court of Justice avoided going into such an analysis. It more specifically stated that, since the Commission has sole jurisdiction to find that the provisions of Articles 65 and 66(7) ECSC Treaty have been infringed, the national courts may not entertain an action for damages in the absence of a Commission decision adopted in the exercise of that jurisdiction. Note that, even though the apparent broad wording of Advocate General van Gerven's Opinion, this case ultimately did not turn around an interpretation of the competition provisions of the EC Treaty. See Case C-128/92, above note 211, para. 21.

[213] The Treaty establishing the European Coal and Steel Community (ECSC), which was signed on 18 April 1951, and entered into force on 23 July 1952, has terminated on 23 July 2002.

[214] Above note 211, para. 36.

> [T]he right of individuals to rely on the directly applicable provisions of the Treaty before national courts is only a minimum guarantee and is not sufficient in itself to ensure the full and complete implementation of the Treaty."[215]

From this case law the Advocate General deduced that the direct effect of a Treaty provision constituted 'a point of departure' for legal protection,[216] and did not preclude EC law from setting a higher standard for national courts to comply with, as was exemplified by the cases *Factortame,*[217] *Francovich,*[218] and *Simmenthal.*[219] The Advocate General on this basis stated that:

> In my view it follows from the terms in which the Court in paragraphs 31 and 32 of its judgment elicits, as a matter of principle, the rule of State liability from "the general system of the Treaty and its fundamental principles" that the ruling in Francovich also serves as a precedent for this case.[220]

It was further stressed, with a reference to the *Simmenthal* judgement, that the full effect of Community law would be impaired if one does not have the possibility of obtaining reparation from the party who can be held responsible for the breach of Community law,[221] which lead to the conclusion that:

> The only effective method whereby the national court can in those circumstances fully safeguard the directly effective provisions of Community law which have been infringed is by restoring the rights of the injured party by the award of damages. Even a declaration that the legal relationship

---

[215] Case C-120/88, *Commission v Italy*, [1991] ECR I-621, at para 10; Reference was also made to, amongst others, the cases Case C-119/89 *Commission v Spain* [1991] ECR I-641 and Case C-159/89 *Commission v Greece* [1991] ECR I-691.

[216] Above note 211, para. 37.

[217] Case C-213/89, *The Queen v Secretary of State for Transport, ex parte: Factortame Ltd and others*, 1990 ECR 2433.

[218] Joined Cases C-6/90 and 9/90, *Andrea Francovich and Danila Bonifaci and others v Italian Republic*, [1991] ECR I-5357.

[219] Case 106/77, *Amministrazione delle Finanze dello Stato v Simmenthal SpA*, [1978] ECR 629.

[220] Above note 211, para. 42.

[221] *Idem*, at para. 43.

between the parties is void [...] is not capable of making good the loss and damage (already) suffered by a third party.[222]

Parts of the Advocate General's reasoning in *Banks* may have inspired the Court of Justice in its 2001 *Courage* decision,[223] which was referred to the European Court of Justice because, first, the English Court of Appeal had held earlier that Article 81(1) EC Treaty was designed to protect third-party competitors and not parties to the prohibited agreement and, second, English law did not allow a party to an illegal agreement to claim damages from the other party. In other words, even if the applicant's claim that his lease infringed Article 81 EC were upheld, English law would bar his claim for damages.[224]

The Court in this case stated that no 'absolute bar'[225] can exist to block a claim for damages for loss caused to any individual by a contract or by conduct liable to restrict or distort competition. The imposition of such bar would hamper the full effectiveness of Article 81 EC Treaty and the working of the Community competition rules in general.[226] However, the Court continued that, in the absence of Community rules governing the matter, it is for the domestic legal system of each Member State to designate the courts and tribunals having jurisdiction and to lay down the detailed procedural rules governing actions for safeguarding rights which individuals derive directly from Community law, provided that such rules are not less favorable than those governing similar domestic actions (i.e. the principle of equivalence), and that they do not render practically impossible or excessively difficult the exercise of rights conferred by Community law (i.e. the principle of effectiveness).[227] The Court then went on as follows :

In that regard, the matters to be taken into account by the competent national court include the economic and legal context in which the parties find themselves and [...] the respective bargaining power and conduct of the two parties to the contract. In particular, it is for the national court

---

[222] Notice on Cooperation, above note 174, para. 19.

[223] Case C-453/99, above note 211.

[224] Opinion of Advocate General Mischo, 22 March 2001, above note 211.

[225] Case C-453/99, above note 211, para. 28.

[226] *Idem*, at para. 27.

[227] *Idem*, at para. 28/9. See also Case C-261/95, *Rosalba Palmisani v Istituto Nazionale della Previdenza Sociale (INPS)*, [1997] ECR I-4025, para. 27

to ascertain whether the party who claims to have suffered loss through concluding a contract that is liable to restrict or distort competition found himself in a markedly weaker position than the other party, such as seriously to compromise or even eliminate his freedom to negotiate the terms of the contract and his capacity to avoid the loss or reduce its extent, in particular by availing himself in good time of all the legal remedies available to him.[228]

The latter observation, though giving deference to the national courts, may be interpreted as a reference to Advocate General Mischo's Opinion in this case, in which he argued that the protection conferred by Article 81 EC Treaty ceases if the party that is to be protected bears significant responsibility for the distortion of competition, for instance if the latter party is equally responsible for the distortion of competition:[229]

In particular it should be ascertained whether one party was in a markedly weaker position than the other. That weaker position must be such that it seriously calls into question the freedom of that party to choose the terms of the contract. [... I]t must be added that the fact that a party bears negligible responsibility does not preclude its being required to provide evidence of reasonable diligence to limit the extent of its loss.[230]

Evidently, Advocate General Mischo's words, as well as the reasoning developed by the European Court of Justice, bring us back to the information exchange vertical restraints, with their particular mix of cooperation and differences in bargaining power (see supra).

3.   Tentative Answers

The civil consequences of the fact that a clause in a distribution agreement is not exempted under Regulation 2790/99 will be different depending on whether the clause is listed in Article 4 or in Article 5 of the Regulation.

Since clauses listed in Article 4 bring the whole of the agreement outside the scope of Article 81(3), the case law of the ECJ (*Haecht, Société de Vente de Cimenteries*) on the (civil) severability of the clause would still seem to

---

[228] Above note 211, paras. 32-3.
[229] Above note 224, paras. 70-1.
[230] *Idem*, paras. 74-5.

apply. Only the clauses which are contrary to Article 81(1) are null and void. This will be the case for the black listed clause itself, except, in the unlikely hypothesis, that the clause would qualify for an individual exemption.[231] All the other clauses in the agreement which are restrictive are automatically void (unless individually exempted pursuant to the proper notification of the agreement), since they cannot benefit from the group exemption.

Whether the agreement as such is valid depends on national law. The case law of the ECJ, as described here above, fully applies to this situation. In this respect the judge will have to take into account that under the presently applicable rules (Regulation 17/62, as amended in 1999) the parties can still notify the agreement pending a dispute before him and that the Commission might possibly exempt such an agreement with retro-active effect. Under the proposed new rules, where the possibility of notification will disappear and the national courts will have the power to apply Article 81 as a unitary norm, i.e. including the 'legal exception' of Article 81(3), the judge will not be faced with this problem anymore.

If the non-exempted clause is null and void, and if it is, according to the law applicable, not severable from the entire agreement, then the entire agreement is null and void as well.

An Article 5 clause by contrast does not, according to the very wording of that provision, affect the appraisal of the agreement as such in the light of Article 81. The agreement remains exempted and can therefore not be declared null and void in any of its parts, except for the clause which is not exempted. It is submitted that this is even so where, according to the national law applicable, the nullity of the clause would affect the validity of the whole contract. The latter clause would, again only be null and void to the extent that it would not benefit from an individual exemption which, contrary to what is the case for the hard core restrictions of Article 4, is not at all unlikely to occur.

Finally, as to actions for damages, it results form *Courage* that not only third parties, but also a party to a vertical agreement containing a black listed clause, has the right to claim damages if it has suffered a loss as a consequence of the application of said clause.

---

[231] For vertical restrictions the possibility to obtain an exemption does not require anymore, since 1999, the prior notification of the agreement. The Commission can, even after an *a posteriori* notification, still grant an exemption with retroactive effect.

184

VII. Concluding Remarks

Irrespective of the doctrinal issues underlying vertical restraints competition policy and, in general, competition law analysis of the economic realities, it appears from the text above that such economic realities should not too quickly be assumed as being "static". In the discussion above, we have tried to show that relationships between vertical market players may rather be seen as 'dynamic, and thus require an economic and a legal analysis which, amongst other things, should take into account the dynamism (in space, in time).

Based on such approach we identified a set of interesting questions which we analyzed in section IV-VI. The analysis led us to the conclusion that the Guidelines seem to fail correctly to appreciate buying power in its complex meaning, the actual substance of which will depend on the particulars of a dynamic manufacturer-retailer relationship. Moreover, it seems that the Block Exemption Regulation embodies a static 'manufacturer-centric' approach to which is added, perhaps incorrectly, the assumption that forces are unilateral, or at best, countervailing. The manufacturer-retailer relationship is, as we called it, perceived as dynamic rather than static. Hence, the buying power provisions set out in section IV.2 seem to be corrective nuances to such manufacturer-centric approach rather than a useful analysis.

It was further argued that this could lead in turn to an inaccurate appreciation of potentially anti-competitive effects of so-called 'co-operative vertical arrangements', which can be structured in such way that they fall within the scope of the exemption of the Block Exemption Regulation (within the limits that are described in sections IV.1 and 2, and subject to paragraph 133 of the Guidelines).

Nonetheless, we feel that empirical economic research may be appropriate to measure the extent of the changed and changing relationship between that type of large retailers and manufacturers and the extent of the impact thereof on the current economic view on vertical restraints.

The last section can be seen as a further elaboration on particular aspects of the Block Exemption Regulation raised in the preceding sections. If one must approach vertical restraint analysis from a realistic standpoint on the changing world of retail business, one must adopt the same realistic viewpoint on the reality that contract law in this area is (still) national, and that there might be a challenging tension between national law and the nullity sanction of Article 81(2) surrounded by a system of a block exemption with a series of exclusions of the benefit of the exemption for certain clauses (or for distribution contracts containing certain clauses). Again, it must be underlined that the tentative answers given in respect of this last set of questions may also form the subject of interesting follow-up legal analysis.

7. EC Consumer Protection Law and EC Competition Law: How Related are They? A Law and Economics Perspective

Fernando Gomez

I.   INTRODUCTION

Consumer Protection Law and Competition Law count as some of the major branches of the Law dealing with the legal regulation of markets. Their relationship in terms of goals, main issues and structures has not been extensively considered, however, especially in relation to their role in EC policy and Law. In this paper I will try to offer an analysis of this relationship between consumer protection law and competition law from the perspective of Law and Economics. Even though neither subject can be understood and operated irrespective of each other, I will attempt to underline how the apparent similarities substantially disappear when one looks at the substantive market imperfections that each of them faces. The emphasis I will place on informational failures as the major rationale for legal activism in consumer markets is fully consistent with the findings of several recent commentators, with a more or less explicit economic propensity in their approach.[1] I will also stress what I take to be important lessons for the design and operative functioning of EC Consumer Law.

In section II, I will deal with the common goal in consumer protection law and competition law of promoting the benefit of consumers. In section III, I present what I deem to be the key factor for enabling a deeper understanding of the proper role of both areas of legal regulation: the economic problem

---

[1]   See G. K. Hadfield, R. Howse, and M. J. Trebilcock, 'Information-Based Principles for Rethinking Consumer Protection Policy', (1988) 21 *Journal of Consumer Policy* 131; S. Grundmann, W. Kerber, and S. Weatherill, 'Party Autonomy and the Role of Information in the Internal Market – an Overview', in S. Grundmann, W. Kerber, and S. Weatherill (Eds.), *Party Autonomy and the Role of Information in the Internal Market*, (Berlin/New York: Walter de Gruyter, 2001) 7; S. Grundmann, 'Verbraucherrecht, Unternehmensrecht, Privatrecht – warum sind sich UN-Kaufrecht und EU-Kaufrechts-Richtllinie so ähnlich?', (2002) 202 *AcP* 40, 61.

H. Collins (ed.) The Forthcoming EC Directive on Unfair and Commercial Practices, 187-208.
©2004. Kluwer Law International. Printed in the Netherlands.

that each of them needs to address adequately. In section IV, I discuss why consumer protection law is not an efficient instrument for dealing with the issues of monopoly and related practices, and how a focus on market power would be misleading and, ultimately, counterproductive for the operation of EC consumer Law. In section V, I propose a more restricted but, I think, more effective type of approach to consumer protection law, that permits an increased understanding of its economic strengths and weaknesses. In section VI, I provide a brief and simple example of circumstances in which joint consideration of competition and consumer protection issues seems advisable, and I also conclude.

II. The Essential Alignment in Goals of Consumer Protection and Competition Law

At first glance, of all possible pairings of sectors or areas within a legal system, only a few can claim to be as well aligned in terms of goals and underlying foundations and structural components as consumer protection law and competition law. Both areas of the law, as I will attempt to demonstrate in this section, seem to share, in a fundamental way, a core purpose behind their corresponding legal rules, doctrines, and enforcement mechanisms.[2]

To say that the goal of consumer protection Law is to promote the benefit and the interests of consumers is almost tautological. It is true, however, that what constitutes the benefit of consumers is not something that everyone would agree upon, and that it can be understood in different forms and with various emphasis: as economic efficiency and social welfare in consumers' markets, as a re-distributive policy objective favoring consumers, or even as a paternalistic view of what the legal and economic rights of the consumer

---

[2] Of course, for those who believe in the coherence and purpose of a legal system, all areas of the law share a common goal, be it justice, equality, happiness, efficiency, wealth maximization, social welfare, or other imaginable goal. Even though I do think that the whole theoretical and human machinery of the legal system is not a blind enterprise, and that there is a fundamental common purpose in it – albeit instrumental and not self-defined –, what I am referring to in my claim, is narrower than the fundamental ends of the legal system: it is the presence of a more specific and operational affinity in goals, that is not to be found in other areas of the Law – say, Tort Law, or Intellectual Property Law – despite the possible overall encompassing existence of a common goal in the legal system. For an excellent review of fairness or justice-based and human welfare-based conceptions of the goal of a legal system (with a strong bias and forceful arguments in favor of the latter), see L. Kaplow and S. Shavell, *Fairness versus Welfare*, (Cambridge, Mass.: Harvard University Press, 2002).

population should look like.[3] Probably, the reasons behind all real-world consumer protection legislation in all real-world legal systems combine to a greater or lesser extent, welfare, redistribution, and paternalist threads,[4] rightly or wrongly understood, and EC consumer protection Law is no exception to this pattern. Additionally, the qualifying element of building an effective internal market also for all consumers' goods and services looms large in EC consumer policy and Law. This feature comes as no surprise, given the nature and constraints (particularly the legal constraints posed by articles 153 and 95 EC Treaty) concerning the role of the EC in this field and its law-making powers. But this emphasis on the cross-border and harmonization dimension does not undermine the central purpose of the legislative effort as being one directed to the promotion of the benefit of consumers.

The purpose of competition law is evidently to preserve and enhance the competitive structure of markets for goods and services. As simple economic theory shows, the big winners from competitive market structures are precisely the consumers of the goods and services. Perfect competition ensures that all consumers who value a certain good or service at more than what it would cost for the society to produce the good or provide the service, will obtain it at the price that reflects the exact social cost. Allocative and productive efficiency are simultaneously achieved. Moreover, the surplus generated by the production and provision of goods through the competitive market

---

[3] For instance, in the Commission's new consumer policy strategy for the period 2002-2006, adopted on 7 May 2002, the bold statement that '...*all consumers (across the EU) should benefit from the same high level of protection...*', in line with the provisions of articles 95.3 and 153.1 of the EC Treaty, could (although not necessarily 'should') be interpreted as an open admission of the fact that achieving a homogeneous high amount of consumer protection is a proper and valuable goal in itself, no matter how much or how diversely different consumers might value the level of protection, and how willing they would be to pay for it. In other terms, that a high level of consumer protection is a 'merit good' (one which the political power has decided should be consumed by citizens in a certain amount, no matter how the real demand for it may be) that helps and benefits consumers, even if they themselves do not recognize it. I am not implying by this that EC consumer policy has to be understood largely as a paternalistic policy, just that some of its formulations are not inconsistent with this view, and that some amount of it is an ingredient of EC policy.

[4] See I. Ramsay, 'Consumer Protection', in P. Newman (ed), *The New Palgrave Dictionary of Economics and the Law*, vol. I, (London: MacMillan, 1998) 410, emphasizing the combined presence of those three rationales, and expressing an overall positive judgement on this plurality of motivations. For reasons that will become clear in section V below, I am somewhat sceptical about the appeal of the re-distributive and paternalistic motives in consumer protection law.

accrue entirely to consumers, so their position cannot be improved by Government policy or legal rules.

As is widely understood among economists, lawyers, and policy-makers, however, the attempt to replicate the conditions for perfect competition in all markets for goods and services is doomed to failure, and it can even be counterproductive. The standard assumptions in economic theory for a perfectly competitive market are the following: atomicity of producers (the number of producers is so large that no single producer has an impact on what others do); product homogeneity (the products by all different producers are perfect substitutes); perfect information (both producers and consumers have perfect knowledge of all relevant variables); equality of producers (all producers have the same technology and cost functions); free and unlimited entry (any producer may enter or exit the market as it wishes). Of course, this set of assumptions clearly shows that perfect competition is a theoretical construct, and that it is not something that we can derive by induction or observation from real-world markets. Still, it is an extremely useful benchmark to evaluate the performance and the possible corrective measures in real life markets.

The desire to bring all markets as close as possible to these ideal conditions with the use of legal rules and policies will be futile in many cases, because of unavoidable constraints on the number of producers, the level of information, entry costs, and so on. Moreover, it may be overtly inefficient and, therefore, harmful to consumers under several circumstances: when there are increasing returns to scale, a small number of producing firms, even just one firm, might be required for productive efficiency, that is, for producing the good or service at the lowest available cost for society; when informational goods are involved, the need for an incentive to produce the good in the first place may require the award of a temporary monopoly in the distribution of the product.[5]

So, more realistically, the proper economic role of competition law, and of competition policy more generally, is to avoid the negative efficiency

---

[5] The use of patents and copyrights as exclusive rights on the production and distribution of a given informational good (invention, work of literature or art, computer program, etc.) conferring some monopoly power on the right-holder is explained in economic terms by the need to provide dynamic incentives for the creation of informational goods: if these were sold from the start under conditions of perfect competition, and given that the marginal cost of providing an additional access to the informational good (an additional viewer of the film, an additional user of the computer program, for instance) is close to zero, the expected

consequences of those market structures that most openly depart, without good reason, from competition, notably those arising from the presence of a single producer or a group of producers acting like a single producer, that is, monopoly and collusive behavior. Still, this relatively more restricted scope of competition Law does not alter the fact that consumers remain the beneficiaries of curtailing monopoly and collusive behavior of firms.

When a monopolist, or a group of firms behaving like one, restricts output to maximize profit, it causes a rise in price above the competitive level. This rise will bring about a shift in the ultimate beneficiary of the surplus of the market exchange. A fraction of this surplus (even the whole surplus, under certain conditions) will be transferred from consumers to producers, making the former worse-off and the latter better-off. More importantly in economic terms, the restriction in output will determine that some consumers who value the good or service above the social cost of its provision – but less than the monopoly price- will be deprived of the possibility of purchasing it, and will be forced either to do without it, or else to turn to less-preferred -or more costly to produce in social terms- alternative goods. This is the most characteristic economic deadweight loss caused by monopoly and collusion.[6] Its elimination or weakening by competition law serves primarily the interest of consumers, and benefits them, in very much the same way as consumer protection law, albeit perhaps in a more indirect and less easily observable

---

profit for the original producer of the good also approaches zero, so the inventor or creator will not be able to recover the fixed costs of creating the invention or work in the first place. To provide incentives to overcome this problem, the legal system grants temporary exclusive rights, leading to market structures departing, in some cases widely, from the conditions of perfect competition. Needless to say, these exclusive rights pose problems of their own, even some that are of great interest to competition Law (under-dissemination of existing works, abuse of patent and copyright, monopoly leverage). These disadvantages are the reasons used by some to advocate, on economic grounds, the use of other alternatives to provide incentives for the production of new intellectual goods: See T. van Ypersele and S. Shavell, 'Rewards versus Intellectual Property Rights' (2001) 44 *Journal of Law and Economics* 525. Nevertheless, the economic case for making an exception, at least to some extent, to the conditions of perfect competition, in order to induce a more desirable level of production of informational goods, has firm grounds in economic theory.

6 Other economic inefficiencies have been claimed as arising out of monopoly. One is the wasteful rent-seeking that will be encouraged by the desire to acquire or to maintain the monopoly rents, rent-seeking process that in the extreme would eat up all supra-competitive profits, transforming the shift in consumers' to producers surplus in a net loss. This claim is associated particularly with the Chicago Law and Economics School, most notably, with R. Posner, 'The Social Costs of Monopoly and Regulation' (1978) 83 *Journal of Political*

manner. Competition law, however, might pursue, by means of legal rules against monopolistic and collusive behavior, other goals that differ from the elimination of those efficiency losses that monopoly creates to the detriment of consumers. Some of these alternative goals might also be inspired by the intention to benefit consumers directly (redistribution of market surplus or income, more generally, in favor of consumers), or might be largely independent of consumers' welfare (the promotion and advance of small and medium-sized enterprises instead of large firms,[7] the desire to block the leverage and concentration of the political power of economic interests and groups). I am highly doubtful about the aptitude of any competition law system to achieve these other 'non-economic goals', but the likelihood of its past, present, or future adoption as goals by a given legal system cannot be entirely disregarded, although it is uncertain whether some of these purposes do play a role in the operation of EC competition Law.

III. The Different Underlying Economic Problems in Consumer Protection and Competition Law

From this community of goals and intended beneficiaries, it would be easy to jump to the conclusion that the fundamental economic questions involved, and an adequate theoretical approach are also the same in both branches of the law. I will try to show that this view is misleading, and, moreover, that it can prove notably harmful for a proper design and understanding of consumer protection generally, and at the EC level more specifically.

Economy 807. There is also relatively widespread sharing of the idea that monopolistic market structures might be less friendly to innovation and to the development and introduction of new technologies. Although there is sound theoretical support for this claim, at least since Arrow's classic article [K. Arrow, 'Economic Welfare and the Allocation of Resources for Inventions', in R. Nelson (ed), *The Rate and Direction of Inventive Activity*, (Princeton, NJ: Princeton University Press, Princeton, 1962)], it is not unlikely that other strategic factors might counteract the disadvantage of monopolistic firms in terms of the pure incentives to innovate, so that the actual relevance of this inefficiency remains unclear: J. Tirole, *The Theory of Industrial Organization*, (Cambridge, Mass.: MIT Press, 1988) 392 et seq.. Less well-grounded still is the claim that monopoly would lead necessarily to a decrease in the quality of goods and services offered to consumers: Neither in economic theory nor in empirical evidence is there sufficiently strong support for this view. See O. Shy, *Industrial Organization. Theory and Applications*, (Cambridge, Mass.: MIT Press, 1995) 315 et seq., and infra, p. 7-8.

[7] A motivation that might not be totally absent from Directive 2000/35/EC, of 29 June 2000 on combating late payment in commercial transactions.

Despite the fact that promoting consumers' welfare can be justly considered the governing purpose of both competition law and consumer protection law, the divergence between the economic problems that both sets of legal rules are supposed to address is very substantial. I will argue that consumer protection law is apt – and, consequently, should be used primarily for this purpose – at redressing the inefficiencies in consumer markets arising from a family of market failures, namely imperfect information, and particularly, at least for the more 'contractual' portion of consumer protection law, asymmetric information between producers and consumers. Competition law, in turn, is – and should be -, as argued in the previous section, primarily concerned about the inefficiencies derived from monopolistic market structures and related issues (collusive and exclusionary practices).[8] Using consumer protection law to deal with issues of monopoly power to the detriment of consumers is not only futile in most instances, but will lead us astray in the appropriate design and implementation of consumer protection law, and can result in unintended harmful consequences for consumers' welfare.

Let me first illustrate the idea that the negative consequences for consumers of monopolistic structures and practices are typically those that competition law is precisely supposed to tackle.

As is well known, and was briefly examined in the previous section, when there is only one producing firm (or several firms acting as a cartel) output is restricted and the price of the goods or services increases to the detriment of consumers' and society's well-being.[9] But no matter how large the market power or the monopoly power of the firm, it usually has no incentive to engage in other types of contractual behavior that are unfair or detrimental to consumers' welfare.[10] If consumers can observe the relevant variable of the transaction (quality of the goods, fairness and adequacy of the rights and obligations from the contract, accuracy of advertising statements, and so forth), the monopolist will generally have the appropriate incentives to offer

---

[8] As Hadfield, Howse, and Trebilcock, above note 1, 150 very aptly state it: Antitrust policy focuses on the structure of markets, and consumer protection policy focuses on the structure of consumer transactions.

[9] One should keep in mind the qualifications mentioned in text corresponding to note 5 above.

[10] This proposition is true under conditions of perfect information. With imperfect information it does not necessarily hold, and for a monopolistic firm (a competitive firm too, as we will see) market incentives might fail in ways that prove harmful for consumers, but the real issue is, then, the informational problem, and not the monopolistic structure of the market.

the level of quality in the relevant variable that consumers desire.[11] If the firm offered a level of quality, say in the rights and obligations in case of breach of contract, lower than the one that consumers would prefer, this would mean that the value of increased quality to consumers would exceed the cost to the firm of providing the additional quality to reach the level preferred by consumers. By definition, the monopolist would not be maximizing profit in this situation, because the firm could raise quality to the consumers' desired level, and raise the contract price an amount that would more than compensate the firm for the increased costs of providing the additional quality. Cheating consumers in quality in order to save production costs will only result in a lower willingness on the part of consumers to buy the goods or services, and thus, would lead to lower prices and lower profits for the monopolist.

IV. THE SUBSTANTIAL IRRELEVANCE OF MONOPOLY POWER – AND INEQUALITY OF BARGAINING POWER- FOR CONSUMER PROTECTION LAW

In the ordinary understanding of consumer protection legislation, particularly with respect to the contractual sphere, inequality of bargaining power between firms and consumers appears to be one of the bigger, if not the biggest, source of concern and failure in the contracting process, requiring the corrective intervention of legal measures directed to redress the imbalance in contractual power.[12] This is, for instance, the view of the ECJ who, in regard to the Directive on Unfair Terms in Consumer Contracts stated that:

---

[11] In more technical terms, this conclusion that the monopolist will offer the socially optimal level of quality in all observable contract variables holds only for a homogeneous population of consumers. When consumers differ in their valuations and preferences for quality (some would be willing to pay a high price for fair contractual rights and obligations, but others largely disregard this aspect), the monopolistic firm would care for the quality preferences of the marginal consumer, and if these are lower or higher than the ones of infra-marginal consumers, quality would be too low or too high: A. M. Spence, 'Monopoly, Quality and Regulation', (1975) 6 *Bell Journal of Economics* 417. A presentation of these results in a more lawyer-friendly way, in R. Craswell, 'Passing on the Costs of Legal Rules: Efficiency and Distribution in Buyer-Seller Relationships' (1991) 43 *Stanford Law Review* 361.

[12] The idea that the exercise of economic power over consumers is the major traditional rationale behind consumer protection policy is also present in Hadfield, Howse, and Trebilcock, above n 1, 133; P. Rekaiti and R. van den Bergh, 'Cooling-Off Periods in the Consumer

…the system of protection introduced by the Directive is based on the idea that the consumer is in a weak position vis-à-vis the seller or supplier, as regards both the bargaining power and his level of knowledge.[13]

It is also the view expressed by many legal commentators on contractual consumer protection Law.[14] According to the economic substance of the interaction under perfect information, though, this view is largely unfounded, as it equates the issue of quantity restriction (which is, justifiably, associated with monopoly) with that of reduction in quality of the relevant transaction variables, including contractual rights and obligations. The fact that we have a large monopolistic firm contracting with a minuscule (in economic terms) consumer, does not by itself raise concerns and suspicions about the terms of the transaction that consumer protection law is well-placed to address and eventually to improve upon. Improvements, if such is the case, might come from the side of competition law, but these will affect price paid and quantity transacted by all consumers, and not the terms of the individual contract.

It is true, though, that there are instances in which a link between monopoly and imperfect information can be traced. Firms enjoying monopoly power might have incentives to exploit, or even to create, imperfections in the information available to consumers, especially with the goal of price discrimination between groups of consumers which differ in their ability to obtain or

---

Laws of the EC Member States: A Comparative Law and Economics Aproach', (2000) 23 *Journal of Consumer Policy* 371, 373.

[13] Joined Cases C-240/98 to C-244/98 ECJ, *Océano Grupo Editorial SA v. Rocío Murciano Quintero and others.*

[14] See H. Beale, 'Inequality of Bargaining Power' (1986) 6 *Oxford J. Legal Studies.* 123; M. Wolf, 'Party Autonomy and Information in the Unfair Contract Term Directive', in Grundmann, Kerber, and Weatherill, above n 1, 313, 323; Remiert Tjittes, in Beale, Hartkamp, Kötz, Tallon (eds), *Cases, Materials and Text on Contract Law*, (Oxford and Portland, Or.: Hart Publishing, 2002) 527. S. Grundmann, above n 1, at p. 65 is more dubious about the strength of the belief of European lawyers in the inequality of bargaining power theory. To be fair to lawyers, it must be said that faith in that theory was shared by most economists before the development of the economics of information. Moreover, apart from the issues discussed in this same section, it is true that private information is not unrelated to bargaining power in a bargaining situation or game. Indeed, private information is a big source of bargaining power. Private information, however, is far from being perfectly correlated with size or economic dimension (firm *vis-à-vis* consumer) and, in fact, in many transactions between consumers (used houses or second-hand vehicles) it is indeed pervasive.

process the relevant information.[15] This and other related problems do not call for consumer protection measures specifically addressed to monopoly power issues. They can be more fruitfully understood and tackled within the overall setting of the provision of information to consumers in the market, in which the efficiency condition of equality between marginal social benefits and marginal social costs of providing information to consumers are very rarely met, and this regardless of the competitive or monopolistic structure of the underlying product or service market (although inefficiencies arise for different reasons).

There are also circumstances in which an existing imperfection in the available information might induce a monopolistic firm to alter the preferred level of quality in the contract in order to maximize profits. It is not consumers' ignorance about a relevant variable of the transaction that drives this result, but rather the producer's lack of information.

If consumers differ in their valuation of the goods or services, the monopolist would maximize profits by sorting them into groups according to their willingness to pay and charging them a different price (price discrimination). If the monopolist could readily observe the type of a given consumer, no changes will be required in the most efficient level of quality of the contract terms. But if the monopolist ignores the type of a given consumer, and if willingness to pay is correlated with some dimension or element in the contract terms (say, a term contemplating liquidated damages for breach of the contract), the producer will be inclined to introduce[16] a menu of contracts to divide consumers into groups corresponding to their willingness to pay for the good or service: for instance, one contract will include a high damage term together with high price, and the other would include an inefficiently low damage term (the inefficiency is introduced on purpose to prevent high-valuation consumers from choosing the cheap contract) together with a low price.[17]

---

[15] S. Salop, 'The Noisy Monopolist: Imperfect Information, Price Dispersion and Price Discrimination' (1977) 44 *Review of Economic Studies* 393; H. Beales, R. Craswell, and S. Salop, 'The Efficient Regulation of Consumer Information' (1981) 24 *Journal of Law and Economics* 507.

[16] In technical terms, the fact that the initiative is on the side of the uninformed party (the producer, in this case), makes the interaction one of screening and not of signaling. See on this, E. Rasmusen, *Games and Information. An Introduction to Game Theory*, 3rd edn, (Oxford: Blackwell, 2001) 161-162, and 277.

[17] This is a well-established result of the economic theory of imperfect information: See I.

One might think that, if we were able to identify the existence of monopoly power in a setting of heterogeneous consumers and monopolist ignorance of consumers' types, consumer protection legislation should enter the picture by imposing a minimum level of quality in the contractual terms, so that no inefficient terms are introduced in the contracts offered by the monopolist with the purpose of price discriminating among different types of consumers. The problem with this demand for consumer protection law to redress the evils of monopoly is that the impact of its rule in this setting is largely indeterminate, and, eventually, might act to the detriment of consumers, for three reasons. Firstly, because if not all the relevant terms that might be used by the producer for screening purposes are covered by the minimum standards imposed by consumer legislation, we would simply get a shift in the distortions towards those terms not regulated under the consumer protection measures.[18] Second, because it is hard for legislators, regulators or Courts to collect and elaborate all the information required to reasonably determine the optimum floor for all relevant contract terms. Finally, and more importantly, because the legal imposition of levels of quality and contract terms for consumer transactions involving a monopolistic seller might induce not a better serving of all types of consumers but simply a price rise that would leave those groups with a lower willingness to pay excluded from getting access to the product or service.[19]

Macho-Stadler and D. Pérez-Castrillo, *An Introduction to the Economics of Information. Incentives and Contracts*, (Oxford: Oxford University Press, 1997) 106 *et seq*. For applications in the law of contract damages and default terms in the legal regulation and interpretation of contracts, see J. S. Johnston, 'Strategic Bargaining and the Economic Theory of Contract Default Rules' (1990) 100 *Yale Law Journal*; I. Ayres and R. Gertner, 'Filling Gaps in Incomplete Contracts: An Economic Theory of Default Rules' (1989) 99 *Yale Law Journal* 87; I. Ayres and R. Gertner, 'Strategic Contractual Inefficiency and the Optimal Choice of Legal Rules' (1992) 101 *Yale Law Journal* 729; and a recent survey of all this literature, in F. Gómez, *Previsión del daño, incumplimiento e indemnización*, (Madrid: Civitas, 2002).

[18] A. Schwartz, 'An Examination of Nonsubstantive Unconscionability' (1977) 63 *Virginia Law Review* 1053.

[19] In more technical economic terms, that the legal regulation of terms might not only lead from the original and less efficient separating equilibrium (separating because each consumer type gets a different thing, in this case, each signs a contract with different terms, some of which, as we have seen, are inefficient) to a more efficient pooling equilibrium (pooling because there is no discrimination and all consumers get the same contract terms). The imposed terms might imply that the profit-maximizing strategy for the monopolist is one leading to a separating equilibrium, but one in which separation occurs because the

In summary, there do not seem to be any good reasons to engage the machinery of consumer protection law to directly combat the negative effects of monopoly and monopolistic practices. This should be primarily left to competition law, or other relevant branches of the Law, such as public regulation of the market.[20] Consumer protection legislation has a comparative advantage, however, in addressing (some of) the deficiencies in the operation of consumer markets arising from a broad and complex range of market failures that can be loosely grouped together under the heading of imperfect information.

V.   Consumer Protection Law as a Set of Instruments to Reduce Information Imperfections in Consumer Markets

In this section I will argue that the economic understanding of imperfections in the information available in consumer market transactions offers the best guide for the definition, scope, boundaries, and instruments, but also the inherent limitations of consumer protection law. Other alternative principles do not allow for the theoretical coherence and the empirical testability that imperfect information brings to this area of the law, and, moreover, they result ultimately in a lower level of consumers' preferences, satisfaction and social welfare than the economic understanding makes possible. I will not deal extensively with these alternatives, but, once the monopoly power rationale has been discarded, I will say a few words about re-distributive and paternalistic motivations in consumer Law.

Distributional concerns are of great importance for social welfare and, thus, a legitimate concern of the legal system as a whole. But there are, I think, convincing reasons that allow us to think that a strong re-distributional concern in favour of consumers and away from firms has no good claim to a proper place in a well-functioning consumer law. The argument is twofold. First, the re-distributional concern will largely be moot due to changes in contract prices: given that typically consumers and producers are in a contractual relationship, the attempt to redistribute through substantive rules favoring

---

price is so high that only consumers with high willingness to pay get the good or service and the rest do not buy. On this result, see F. Gómez, above note 17.

[20] In the same sense, in addition to authors cited in note 1 above, C. Kirchner, 'Justifying Limits to Party Autonomy in the Internal Market – Mainly Consumer Protection', in Grundmann, Kerber, and Weatherill, above note 1, 165, 168.

consumers will be to a large extent defeated by adjustments in price and other terms that will offset the intended redistribution.[21]

Second, even when the re-distributive effort is not counteracted by contractual rearrangements, substantive legal rules are a more haphazard and less effective way to achieve this end than the tax and public transfers system.[22]

The case for paternalism in consumer protection Law is, at first glance, and somewhat paradoxically, not as unconvincing in economic terms as the one favoring redistribution. Consumer protection law, and the legal system more generally, can influence individuals' preferences and, thus, can change them in a way that is in the long-term interest of the individuals affected by the preference change. For instance, by imposing a certain level of consumers' information, rights, and protections, EC consumer Law could instill in European consumers a new preference for extended rights and, say, healthier consuming environments that might positively affect the well-being of those consumers in the long run, even if most of them did not have the preference in the beginning and were not willing to pay a price for the rights and protections afforded by the legal rules. From an economic standpoint this paternalistic legal intervention would be viewed favorably, as long as, as we had assumed for the sake of the argument, it increases social welfare. This is, of course, a purely theoretical possibility. Quite a different matter is how likely it is that the paternalistic motivation behind legislators, regulators and Courts in the field of consumer protection will actually be converted into

---

[21] See Craswell, above note 11; D. Weisbach, *Taxes and Torts in the Redistribution of Income*, University of Chicago Law School, John M. Olin Program in Law & Economics, Working Paper No. 148 (2002). Not everyone agrees on this, of course: Ramsay, above note 4, 413.

[22] L. Kaplow and S. Shavell, 'Why the Legal System is Less Efficient Than the Income Tax in Redistributing Income' (1994) 23 *Journal of Legal Studies* 667; L. Kaplow and S. Shavell, 'Should Legal Rules Favor the Poor? Clarifying the Role of Legal Rules and the Income Tax in Redistributing Income' (2000) 29 *Journal of Legal Studies* 821. The core of the argument is as follows: the use of taxes and transfers as re-distributional mechanisms just creates a distortion, namely in the work-leisure trade-off. Substantive legal rules generate a double distortion: one, the same we have just described for taxes, the other, the inefficiency generated by a legal rule chosen not on its efficiency merits, but on its re-distributional effectiveness. Again, some disagree with this gloomy view of legal rules as re-distributive instruments: C. Jolls, 'Behavioral Analysis of Redistributive Legal Rules', in C. Sunstein (ed), *Behavioral Law and Economics*, (Cambridge: Cambridge University Press, 2000), 288. Su, *Economics*, (Cambridge: Cambridge University Press, 2000), 288; C. W. Sanchirico, ' Taxes versus Legal Rules as Instruments for Equity: A More Equitable View' (2000) 29 *J. Legal Studies.* 797.

consumers' welfare-enhancing policies and rules. In this respect, the affirmative is much more uncertain.

I am doubtful whether re-distributive and paternalistic motivations can be traced in EC consumer protection law. The grouping together in art. 95.3 EC Treaty of consumers' and workers' rights might be a hint towards the former motivation, and some wording in Directives' preambles and Community programs can also be interpreted as a hint towards the latter. In any case, from an economic perspective none of them provide a sound basis for EC consumer Law.

Imperfect information, on the contrary, constitutes a type of market failure able to provide a reasonable starting point for organizing our knowledge about the optimal role and likely effects of consumer protection legislation. Of course, we should not think that consumers' markets are the only markets in which informational imperfections are likely to loom large. Corporate law, insurance law and even general contract law are areas in which economic models of imperfect information play a crucial role in understanding legal institutions and rules and predicting their relative performance in real-world markets.

On the other hand, we should not think that consumer markets are entirely dominated by imperfect information. Even if we abstract from legal constraints and requirements to this effect, the level of information provided by and at the disposal of market participants in consumers' markets is by no means negligible.[23]

Consumers acquire information about relevant characteristics and variables affecting the transactions on goods and services by several means; in some cases, by direct observation;[24] in others, by learning through repeat purchase and consumption.[25] They can also get information about relevant aspects from third parties, be they people known to them, or independent private and public sources.

Producers themselves are major providers of information in consumers'

---

[23] A recent review of instruments increasng information available to consumers in T. Wein, "Consumer Information Problems – Causes and Consequences", in Grundmann, Kerber, and Weatherill, above note 1, 80.

[24] In these cases, economists speak of search goods or search characteristics, given that search can make consumers informed about them.

[25] In these cases, economists speak of experience goods or characteristics, because consumers will become informed after consuming the good. When even after consumption the relevant variables are not ascertainable by the consumer, economists speak of credence goods.

200

markets. Through labels, product descriptions, and contract information firms communicate significant amounts of information to consumers on goods and services. Of course, advertising plays a key role in transmitting information on the existence, characteristics, prices and other determinants of market transactions. And not only so-called 'informative' advertising has this positive informational role. Even advertising apparently devoid of any significant informational content (like celebrity endorsement of a product, say), is able to convey to consumers valuable signals about the level of quality or other important features of the transaction: advertising, and the reputation that is usually associated with it, are extremely powerful market mechanisms to effectively signal consistent levels of quality to consumers, particularly in markets for experience goods.[26]

More surprisingly, market forces can, under some conditions, induce producers to disclose even unfavorable information to consumers or, more generally, to the other party in a prospective transaction. In what is one of the more striking results of the economics of information, it can be shown that, when the private information in possession of the seller is verifiable (that is, *ex post* it can be determined if disclosure of information was truthful), and the consumer knows that the seller has private information (though not its content, or else it would not be private information of the seller), the seller will voluntarily reveal the information even if it is unfavorable (for instance, that the quality of her product is below average). This unraveling result stems from the fact that, given the two assumptions just mentioned, consumers expect from all silent sellers the worst possible news concerning the content of the private information. Sellers whose private information is best would voluntarily disclose it, and so would set in motion a continuous process of revelation by the decreasingly good-news sellers, until only that with the worst private information (say, the worst quality) is left alone without disclosure. And consumers would actually observe that their expectations are met: only the worst private information remains undisclosed, and the rest is voluntarily revealed.[27]

---

[26] On this warranty function of advertising, see F. Gomez, 'The European Directive on Consumer Sales: An Economic Perspective', in S. Grundmann and C. M. Bianca (eds), *EU Sales Directive Commentary*, (Oxford and Portland, Or.: Hart Publishing, 2002) 53 and literature cited therein.

[27] The unravelling result was developed by S. Grossman and O. Hart, 'Disclosure Laws and Takeover Bids', (1980) 35 *Journal of Finance* 323; P. Milgrom, 'Good News and Bad News: Representation Theorems and Applications' (1981) 12 *Bell Journal of Economics*

But even if the amount of information provided to consumers through market mechanisms is considerable, it is undeniable that in many circumstances and for many transactions in consumer markets the level of information is far from perfect, and that there is room for improvement in this lack of information through legal rules suitable for the correction of informational market failures.

These informational market failures arise out of a broad range of factors: First, some market participants might engage in fraudulent and deceptive practices, thereby inducing inaccurate impressions in consumers that cause distortions in their decisions and behavior. Perhaps due to the uncontroversial characterization of fraud, misrepresentation and deception as undesirable phenomena, the fact is that the role of consumer protection law in deterring such inefficient market practices has not been fully appreciated. Probably the unscrupulous fly-by-night producer is the major source of consumers' misinformation and overall harm, and the efforts to deter this type of seller are among the most valuable in the whole enterprise of consumer protection policy.[28] This explains and justifies the existence of rules against misleading advertising,[29] as well as strict information and contract formation require-

---

380; and S. Grossman, 'The Informational Role of Warranties and Private Disclosure of Product Quality' (1981) 24 *Journal of Law and Economics* 461. A less technical presentation with applications to various fields of the law, in D. Baird, R. Gertner and R. Picker, *Game Theory and the Law*, (Cambridge, Mass.: Harvard University Press, 1994) 89 et seq.; R. Gertner, 'Disclosure and unravelling' in Newman, above note 21, 605. Empirical studies have found clear evidence of voluntary disclosure and unraveling: for instance, A. Mathios, 'The Impact of Mandatory Disclosure Laws on Product Choices: An Analysis of the Salad Dressing Market', (2000) 43 *Journal of Law and Economics* 658-660, shows how the unobservable information (fat content) concerning salad dressings is subject (albeit not completely) to the unraveling effect, by which almost all of the low-fat producers voluntarily disclose the fat content whereas the high-fat ones remain silent.

[28] By the way, here we can observe some discrepancy between the conditions and outcomes of competitive market and those of adequate consumer protection: Rogue sellers are more likely to be operating in a market when there are low – or virtually none – barriers to entry, when there are many sellers, and when the rate of entry and exit in the market from the producer's side is high. All these conditions are typical features of a competitive market structure. See Hadfield, Howse, and Trebilcock, above note 1, 153, 155.

[29] Directive 84/450/EEC of 10 September 1984 on misleading advertisements, and Directive 97/55/EC of 6 October 1997, concerning misleading advertising so as to include comparative advertising. Needless to say, this does not make the determination of when an advertisement is deceptive or misleading an easy task. Issues such as context, implied claims, heterogeneity of consumers, and existence of more informative alternatives are relevant to this

ments in those consumers' markets and contractual practices more likely to have a high proportion of small and quickly exiting firms, such as door-to-door sales, distance sales, and electronic sales.[30]

Consumers' lack of information can be the result of well-documented phenomena[31] in consumers' behaviour, such as bounded rationality (limited capacity to acquire and process information),[32] over-optimism, use of cognitive heuristics (hindsight bias, excessive reliance on easily available data, excessive representativeness of small samples, too little weight attributed to future and uncertain events, etc), and rational ignorance (if acquiring information is – even minimally – costly for the consumer, but having the information would not change either the terms of the transaction or future use, the consumer may rationally forgo the acquisition of information and prefer to remain ignorant on a relevant variable).[33]

Consumers' ignorance due to all these factors is hard to ameliorate. Firms do have some incentives to educate and inform consumers, so that those problems are less acute in many cases. But the market incentives for firms do not reach the level of the socially appropriate incentives to educate and inform consumers. Each single firm would not be able to internalize all the gain from the increased consumers' information, so its incentive to bring it about will be insufficient compared to the social gains from the increase in

---

sort of inquiry. A detailed analysis of these and other issues for advertising regulation, in R. Craswell, 'Interpreting Deceptive Advertising' (1985) 65 *Boston University Law Review* 658; R. Craswell, 'Regulating Deceptive Advertising: The Role of Cost-benefit Analysis' (1991) 64 *Southern California Law Review* 549.

30 Directive 85/577/EEC of 20 December 1985, on contracts negotiated away from business premises; Directive 97/7/EC of 20 May 1997, on the protection of consumers in respect of distance contracts; Directive 2000/31/EC of 8 June 2000, on electronic commerce.

31 See M. A. Eisenberg, 'Cognition and contract', in Newman, above note 21, (editor), 282; Sunstein, above note 22.

32 Moreover, bounded rationality makes the appeal of deceptive and misleading advertising higher for some producers: see M. Nagler, 'Rather Bait than Switch: Deceptive Advertising with Bounded Consumer Rationality' (1993) 51 *Journal of Public Economics* 359. And surveys of advertisers show that legal constraints are the most important factor influencing decision-making about advertising content and policy: J. Davis, 'Ethics in Advertising Decisionmaking: Implications for Reducing the Incidence of Deceptive Advertising', (1994) 28 *Journal of Consumer Affairs* 380.

33 The most notable example of this problem in consumer contracts arises in the context of standard form contracts: reading and understanding the standard terms is costly for the consumer – in time and effort –, and given that the terms are not subject to negotiation, the consumer will usually opt for not even starting to read the forms.

consumers' information. So the market[34] will not by itself provide the optimal amount of education and information to overcome those factors affecting consumers' ignorance.

Consumer law can to an extent provide a partial remedy in some contexts, particularly through disclosure requirements and the creation and imposition of a standardized system of measuring and expressing one or more of the variables relevant to the transaction. Probably the best example of this kind of legal intervention is the standardized annual percentage rate that Directive 87/102/EEC of 22 December 1986 on consumer credit (modified by Directives 90/88 and 98/7) imposes as a disclosure requirement for consumer credit contracts. Here, the most (but not the only) relevant element of the transaction needs to be expressly and noticeably communicated in a homogenous and – at least relatively – easily computable and user-friendly way for consumers, so that consumers will be more aware of the relevant variable, and so that the possibility of shopping around for more attractive credit terms is significantly enhanced.[35] Mandatory and standardized labeling and information disclosure are also common concerning health and safety factors, and experimental and empirical studies have shown them to have had a positive impact on welfare-enhancing consumer choices in the relevant markets.[36] Additionally, cooling-

---

[34] By the way, here again a monopoly market structure will arguably approximate better than a competitive one to the optimal provision of information, given that the monopolist can internalize more in terms of profits the gains from increased information. The same applies to rational ignorance: competitive firms are more likely to exploit consumers' rational ignorance than monopolists, because competitive pressures can unleash a 'race to the bottom' for those variables that the typical consumer rationally decides to ignore.

[35] Standardized disclosure obligations might pose some problems of its own, that might have an economic impact: they can induce producers to concentrate quality efforts on the variables included in the standard, at the expense of others left out of it, that may be also important to consumers, and the required disclosure may displace other information that the producer would have conveyed, and might also have been informative to consumers. See, Beales, Craswell, and Salop, above note 15, 523 et seq. Regarding the specific standardized disclosure requirement in consumer credit contracts, some have criticized this from an economic perspective, stressing the increase in compliance and litigation costs, the negative effects on credit collection terms and customer service (variables not included in the standard disclosure), and the fact that only already well-informed and wealthy borrowers are likely to benefit from it. See R. Posner, *Economic Analysis of Law*, 5th edition, (New York: Aspen Publishers, 1998) 408; R. Hynes and E. Posner, 'The Law and Economics of Consumer Finance' (2002) 4 *American Law and Economics Review* 194-195. Standardized information on contract terms, however, can also be efficient on account of network externalities (the addition of new users increases the utility derived by existing users).

[36] C. Moorman, "A Quasi Experiment to Assess the Consumer and Informational Determ-

off periods allowing the consumer to cancel the transaction during a limited period after it was agreed,[37] can be understood as a way of reducing the impact of bounded rationality and cognitive deficiencies in those consumer transactions in which these problems might seem more serious.[38]

This leads to another source of consumers' lack of information, namely search costs. If search costs are relatively high, consumers will not be informed and so the terms of the transaction (including price, even when the market is competitive) might not be optimal.[39] Disclosure requirements and standardized informative messages, such as the one referred to in the previous paragraph, serve also to reduce search costs in various consumer markets and, thus, to improve the functioning of these markets.

The preceding considerations should not induce us to think that the imperfect information rationale sets an insurmountable boundary to the kind of rules that an economically oriented consumer protection law would be allowed to use. In particular, the tools of consumer law can include not

---

    inants of Nutrition Information Processing Activities: The Case of the Nutrition Labeling and Education Act' (1996) 15 *Journal of Public Policy and Marketing* 28; Mathios, above note 27, 660.

[37] Directive 85/577/EEC of 20 December 1985, on contracts negotiated away from business premises; Directive 94/47/EC of 26 October 1994, on time-sharing; Directive 97/7/EC of 20 May 1997, on the protection of consumers in respect of distance contracts.

[38] Rekaiti and van den Bergh, above notes 12, 371, 374 and following, and 385 and following, argue that cooling-off periods, particularly those introduced by EC consumer protection legislation, are potential remedies for irrational behavior, situational monopoly and informational asymmetries. Some, however, doubt the effective impact of those measures, the reason lying in the prediction that few consumers would exercise a right of cancellation that requires them to admit to themselves that they acted as suckers by signing the contract in the first place: See Ramsay, above note 21, 412. Others do not only consider them irrelevant, but criticize those provisions as important sources of *ex post* opportunism by consumers: H-P. Schwintowski, 'Contractual Rules Concerning the Marketing of Goods and Services – Requirements of Form and Content versus Private Autonomy', in Grundmann, Kerber, and Weatherill, above note 1, 331, 346.

[39] For optimality in markets with positive search costs, however, it is not necessary that all buyers shop around. When producers cannot distinguish consumers who have searched for contract terms from those who haven't, and when the proportion of searchers is large enough (but not 100%), the terms will be optimal, because producers would prefer to sell to all consumers rather than only to non-searchers. See A. Schwartz and L. Wilde, 'Intervening in Markets on the Basis of Imperfect Information: A Legal and Economic Analysis', (1979) 127 *University of Pennsylvania Law Review* 630; A. Schwartz and L. Wilde, 'Imperfect Information in Markets for Contract Terms: The Examples of Warranties and Security Interests (1983) 69 *Virginia Law Review* 1387.

only information-enhancing measures, but also disclosure and standardization requirements, and the prevention of deception and fraud. Additionally, the characteristics of some informational problems may (but only "may") suggest that mandatory regulation of some contractual terms is the best cure for such informational market failures. We have mentioned the case of rational ignorance regarding standard form contracts. Information disclosure and facilitating rules might be insufficient, given the very nature of the lack of information (even a minuscule information cost would make consumers rationally and intelligently decide not to read the fine print). And the race to the bottom in the quality of contract terms that can ensue from this set of conditions might call for legal regulation of a minimum level of quality or bundle of consumer rights. That is precisely what Directive 93/13/EEC of 5 April 1993 on unfair terms in consumer contracts does in Article 3 and the Annex. Of course, it is debatable whether the Directive has achieved an optimal balance in the determination of the required quality of contract terms, even if any legislator or court can realistically aspire to it, but economic theory does not in itself exclude the use of mandatory regulation in this type of setting.

Moreover, if the legally required disclosure would lead to complex revelation of information by producers, and this complexity would significantly raise information-processing costs for consumers, an outright ban on a certain product or service may (but only "may") be preferable on efficiency grounds. This outcome would be the case, if the reduction in informational costs outweighs the costs that both producers (loss of profit) and consumers (loss of enhanced product choice or variety) incur as a consequence of the prohibition.[40]

Similarly, in circumstances in which the asymmetry in information does not affect the consumer, but the seller, a case for mandatory intervention may (but only "may") be made on pure efficiency grounds. Here, it is the consumer who has some piece of private information that the producer cannot observe. This is particularly likely in credit markets, in which the professional creditor cannot usually observe the likelihood or the willingness of the consumer to pay back the credit. Imperfect information may give rise here to the use of harsh contract terms or securities that act as signal of belonging to the 'good' credit-worthy type of consumer, and not to the bad type. Even if

---

[40] See Hadfield, Howse, and Trebilcock, above note 1, 159.

some of these signals are too crude and undesirable for the joint welfare of market participants, they may persist over time. Legal rules setting limits to those terms (for instance, personal bankruptcy protection, limits to repossession, assets excluded from forfeiture, and the like) may (but only "may") be efficient under some of these circumstances.[41]

All these matters, however, have been – wisely, in my view – left outside the scope of the Directive on consumer credit (with the partial exception of limits to third-party rights and assignment, which is theoretically akin to the other limits), and referred to the laws of the Member States. In fact, the set of substantive (that is, not pertaining to increased levels of information) consumer rights under this Directive allows for extensive freedom of the Member States to implement the quite general principles sketched to that effect, in contrast with the detailed regulation of the disclosure requirements that the same Directive contains.

VI. THE WEIGHING OF COMPETITIVE GAINS IN CONSUMER PROTECTION LAW

The arguments presented in the previous sections lend support to the substantial independence of the economic function of consumer protection law from that of competition law, and to the need to keep distinct the approach of each of these fields of the law. Despite this, there are cases in which the competitive consequences of consumer protection issues are significant and should receive their due amount of attention. I will now provide an example of what I mean by this joint balance of consumer protection and competitive issues.

The area of advertising is particularly likely to give rise to issues of barriers to entry established by dominant firms in order to deter entry by potential new entrant firms. Heavy advertising expenditures, especially if associated with strong trademarks, serve as goodwill and brand loyalty multipliers, and can constitute barriers that entrants will have difficulty in overcoming. One way in which this may happen is through aggressive advertising campaigns that make use of comparison with the established firm, or stress the advantages of the entrants (in price or in other relevant dimension) over the incumbent. In the enforcement of consumer protection rules in advertising

---

[41] A full economic discussion of these measures can be found in Hynes and Posner, above note 35, 168.

one should take into account that, in order to surmount the advertising barriers erected by the incumbent firm, the entrants might need some greater leeway as to the aggressiveness of comparative advertising and to the level of substantiation of the claims contained in their advertisement. In the end, entry by new firms would benefit consumers through increased output and reduced prices, so it is efficient that in the enforcement of consumer protection rules on advertising, regulators and courts take into account the future competitive gains of the advertising campaign – especially when it is the incumbent who challenges it on charges of being misleading.

Other examples are possible (for instance, some contract terms like exclusivity clauses and contractual damage clauses might also eventually serve to raise barriers against potential competitors),[42] but the point is clear. Competitive gains are real social gains, and they should be given weight when one is designing, interpreting and implementing consumer protection law. But this should not mean that in this process we take a side road and forget what I believe is the proper role and economic rationale for consumer law, and especially EC consumer protection law, which is to address the problems of imperfect information in consumer markets. The challenges that EC consumer protection legislation faces in building a consistent framework that would serve to increase efficiency in consumer markets that are still largely (though certainly not always to the same extent) fragmented by national, cultural, and linguistic barriers, are, to be sure, enormous. To burden EC consumer policy with the extra task of increasing the amount of competition in European consumer markets does not seem to me a sound policy prescription. It is a task which this branch of EC Law (in fact, the private and public laws of the Member States also) is ill-suited to accomplish successfully.

---

[42] P. Aghion and P. Bolton, 'Contracts as Barriers to Entry' (1987) 77 *American Economic Review* 388.

8. EC Consumer and EC Competition Law: How Related are they? Examining the Existing EC Contract Law Sources

Stefan Grundmann

The paper shares the basic assumptions of Prof. Gomez' paper, which are taken up which are discussed in section I. They are that competition law (here antitrust law), just like consumer law, is aimed at consumer welfare; that consumer law should not be guided by the paradigm of inequality of bargaining power between professional and consumer, but by that of information asymmetries and more generally information problems which consumers face; that restricting both competition and information asymmetries are different types of market failure, and that therefore they should also be distinguished. In this paper I stress that in reality both phenomena are not restricted to consumers, but are important for all players in the markets. Therefore, it is argued that competition law is general market regulation (a statement which nobody would contest) and that consumer law is really about informing markets, often more generally, and therefore it is general contract or private law and should not be separated from it (a statement which certainly many would question).

Prof. Gomez' paper seems highly convincing to me in its general thrust. Modifications are, however, possible if one steps from the general thrust of his paper to the existing body of law and competition law is considered in its entirety. In section II it is argued that in EC competition law (here antitrust law) one can find important cases that are really concerned with information problems. The Commission – on the basis of a competence which excludes the Parliament from legislation – really regulates consumer, or more generally client, information problems. In these instances, there is a better argument for integration into consumer law – or more correctly: general business to consumers contract law. In section III, the scope of discussion is widened. Besides antitrust competition law, there is the law against unfair competition. This is a much older body of law and is concerned with a conglomerate of types of market failure: partly information problems, partly abuse

H. Collins (ed.) The Forthcoming EC Directive on Unfair and Commercial Practices, 209-222.
©2004. Kluwer Law International. Printed in the Netherlands.

of dominant positions, partly situations resembling theft or more generally external effects. Here, Prof. Gomez' plea for clarity would speak in favour of dismantling these controls. In the case of the directive on misleading and comparative advertising, the most important EC law measure in this area, this argument would support its integration into the general information regime of consumer contracts (and indeed all contracts and general EC contract law) concerned with marketing and distribution.

I.   THE COMMON SCOPE OF EC CONSUMER AND EC COMPETITION LAW AND THE DIFFERENCES

Commenting on Professor Gomez' paper is a pleasure for many reasons.

The first is that I cannot disagree and indeed would firmly endorse the basic assumptions of Gomez' line of arguments. It should be stressed, however, from the outset: Gomez speaks almost exclusively about the branch of competition law which is concerned with combating restriction of competition via cartelisation and abuse of dominant positions, i.e. the part which found its way into the Treaty itself and which is often called antitrust law (today articles 81 and 82 Treaty of the European Community). He only briefly touches upon the second branch, which indeed is much weaker in EC Law, but which exists in virtually all national legal systems of the Union (see below in section III), and which is the one the Commission had first in mind when proposing a merging of competition law and consumer law.[1] This is the law against unfair competition which term, for the sake of clarity, I will use in the following way.[2] I find it helpful that Gomez concentrates on the part which probably is more important today and was more important at least in the mind of the founding fathers of the Community. I also find it very helpful because competition law (antitrust law) is a much clearer category with a much clearer scope and theory. Any discussion should therefore start with clarifying the relationship between consumer law and antitrust competition law. In a second step, I will nevertheless (and I think one should) include also the other branch of competition law.

Gomez' first core argument is that EC competition law is aimed at protect-

---

[1]   Green Paper on European Union Consumer Protection, COM(2001) 531 final, p. 6, 13 *et passim*.

[2]   In some countries this branch is called competition law in the narrow sense, often because it is the much older branch. This is the case, for instance, in Germany.

210

ing consumers. This is generally accepted in economic competition theory, i.e. it is true for any competition law. One can even generalise and say that it potentially protects all players in the market not participating in the practice: any player on the other market side, not only consumers, but also professional clients; and also the competitors, i.e. players on the same market side. It therefore is general market regulation, and therefore regulation of markets, in which consumers transact. It is general regulation, protecting consumers. That consumers are among those whom competition law seeks to protect can be clearly deduced from the economic constitution of the Community itself. Art. 81 (3) EC allows deviations if they further the interests of consumers and part of the gain is passed over to consumers. The idea behind this clause is that unlimited competition may always be the optimum in theory, but not in the real world, and that whenever gains can be derived from a restriction of competition, for instance when there are increasing economies of scale they should be shared with consumers or, more generally, clients. The other side of the market that normally enjoys the full benefits of competition must at least have a share in them. The gains may not be completely transferred to the suppliers which participate in the restrictive practice. Moreover, Art. 2 of the EC Treaty holds that via the measures named in Art. 3 EC, a 'high level of ... social protection' should be achieved. Among the measures named in Art. 3 EC, 'competition ... not distorted' in the sense of Art. 81 and 82 EC is one of the most outstanding.[3] Consumer protection is also an important part of 'social protection' in the sense of Art. 2 EC.

I would not disagree with Gomez' second core argument either, and indeed put much emphasis on it myself.[4] This argument is that consumer law should not be guided by the paradigm of inequality of bargaining power between professional and consumer, but by that of information problems and asymmetries which consumers face. The conclusion can even be more radical: the paradigm is not only preferable in theory, existing EC Consumer law *is* indeed mainly guided by the paradigm of information problems and asymmetries which consumers face and not by that of inequality of bargain-

---

[3] For this understanding and connection already the leading case of ECJ 21 February 1973, Case 6/72, *Continental Can* [1973] ECR 215, 244-246.

[4] See S. Grundmann, 'Verbraucherrecht, Unternehmensrecht, Privatrecht – warum sind sich UN-Kaufrecht und EU-Kaufrechts-Richtlinie so ähnlich?', *Archiv für civilistische Praxis* 202 (2002) 40-71 = 'Consumer Law, Commercial Law, Private Law – how can the Sales Directive and the Sales Convention be so similar?', working paper SECOLA (www.secola.org, Rome Conference 2001).

ing power between professional and consumer.[5] The latter has often been proposed during the legislative process, but has always been rebutted by the Council. This was so in the case of the Consumer Credit Directive of 1987,[6] the first important legal measure of European substantive contract law, and in the case of the Sales Law Directive, the most recent important legal measure of European contract law.[7] And the conclusion can be more radical in that it completely departs from the idea that the consumer is the core player and that we are dealing with a restricted part of contract law. Consumer law really is about informing markets, often more generally (and indeed in EC law in the majority of cases more generally),[8] and therefore is general contract or private law.

Prof. Gomez' final conclusion seems to flow quite naturally from these two ideas: (1) Consumer and competition law share a common scope, they both protect consumers (and more radically or generally market transactions, i.e. contracts, in general). (2) They concern, however, different types of market failure and should therefore be kept separate. Otherwise there is a risk that the paradigm of unequal bargaining power unjustifiably dominates consumer contract rules. Both parts of the conclusion are important and have to be emphasised. I would even stress that European contract law is special

---

[5] See more extensively the contributions in S. Grundmann W. Kerber, and S. Weatherill (eds.), *Party Autonomy and the Role of Information in the Internal Market*, (Berlin: de Gruyter, 2001).

[6] Council Directive 87/102/EEC of 22 Dec. 1986 for the approximation of the laws, regulations and administrative provisions of the Member States concerning consumer credit, EC OJ 1987 L 42/48; amended in EC OJ 1990 L 61/14 and 1998 L 101/17. Paternalistic restrictions of consumer credits had been considered, but finally regulation was largely restricted to information rules only.

[7] European Parliament and Council Directive 1999/44/EC of 25 Mai 1999 on certain aspects of the sale of consumer goods and associated guarantees, EC OJ 1999 L 171/12; see COM(95) 520 final and S. Grundmann, 'Introduction', in M. Bianca and S. Grundmann (eds.), *EU Sales Directive – Commentary*, (The Hague: Intersentia,, 2002), para. 13-15 and art. 2 para. 9.

[8] This is so even though competence of the Community is much more difficult to justify if clients in general are protected, not consumers. Private international law restricts the freedom of choice of law only in the second case, and the European Court of Justice does not see any violation of fundamental freedoms whenever the freedom of choice of law is left to the parties: ECJ 24 January 1991, Case C-339/89, *Alsthom Atlantique* [1991] ECR I-107, 124. Therefore in business to business relationships, it can be argued that there is no EC competence given that the functioning of the internal market is not at stake and given that the fundamental freedoms are fully carried through.

in one further sense which is connected to them: European contract law is not so much concerned with what is the traditional core of contract law, i.e. default rules that serve as facilitative (enabling) law without curing market deficiencies, just providing a set of rules in case parties do not draft their own rules. It is rather concerned with market order and regulation, i.e. with curing different types of market failure, namely that of restriction of competition and that of information asymmetries and other information problems.[9] Therefore the two paradigms of market failure, which Prof. Gomez distinguishes and discusses, are really what European contract law is mainly about. The second part of the conclusion is sound in theory. The risk mentioned should in any case be kept in mind. However, existing EC competition law does contain quite a few rules that are devoted to the supply of information and not really, at least not primarily, about restricting competition. Here clarification would mean reintegration into consumer contract – or more precisely general contract – law.

II. Some Examples for a Mixing of Antitrust Rules and Information Rules

In this section, it is argued that one can find in EC competition law (here antitrust law) important cases which are really concerned with information problems. Prof. Gomez' himself thinks that in some cases the effect of a rule on competition (antitrust) may be important also when interpreting rules about information, i.e. that one paradigm may at times influence the other. The cases seem to be rather unimportant in his eyes. And indeed it is difficult to imagine what would really change under the directive on misleading and comparative advertising[10] in the example he gives. An aggressive compari-

---

9   S. Grundmann, 'Europäisches Handelsrecht – vom Handelsrecht des laissez faire im Kodex des 19. Jahrhunderts zum Handelsrecht der sozialen Verantwortung', *Zeitschrift für das gesamte Handelsrecht* 163 (1999) 635, 665-676; S. Grundmann, 'The Structure of European Contract Law', (2001) 4 *European Review of Private Law* 505, passim; see more generally also H. Collins, *Regulating Contracts*, (Oxford: Oxford University Press, 2000).

10   Council Directive 84/450/EEC of 10 Sept. 1984 relating to the approximation of the laws, regulations and administrative provisions of the Member States concerning misleading advertising, EC OJ 1984 L 250/17; amended in EC OJ 1997 L 290/18 (now including comparative advertising). For a comparative law survey (including transposition) see P. Schotthöfer (ed.), *Handbuch des Werberechts in den EU-Staaten einschließlich Norwegen, Schweiz, Liechtenstein und USA*, 2nd. edn. (Cologne: Schmidt, 1997).

son is allowed under the directive if the data is correct and this is so for any competitor, not just for the newcomer. And it should be allowed, because it furthers the interests of participants in the market in acquiring information (clients and consumers). This means the rule is already fully justified under the rationale of supplying accurate information in order to aid a competitive market. Conversely, a comparison not supported by data is, and should not be, allowed for the same reason and again this rule is already justified under principles governing the supply of inaccurate information.

These are, however, only marginal examples in existing competition law of the EC. The examples which seem to be less marginal are contained in block exemptions. These block exemptions are based on Art. 81(3) EC and contain an exception to the automatic nullity of cartels to be found in Art. 81(2) EC. They contain a list of clauses which are allowed and a list of clauses which must always be avoided if the cartel is to be validated under the block exemption. Moreover, some block exemptions contain a series of conditions, i.e. clauses which have to be included in order to bring the cartel under the block exemption. In this sense the block exemptions function like a set of standard terms some of which have to be included, some of which may be included (and are included in order to profit from the advantages the exemption brings) and some of which must be left out.

This is important in two respects. First, these rules are applicable only in cases where competition is restricted, although they might well equally be supported as sensible principles for the general law of contract. Second, the competence is quite different. It is true that the Commission bases its block exemptions on a general enabling directive issued by the Council, but the European Parliament does not have a say in this process, and the delegation is very general. The consequence is that the Commission largely decides on these matters, and in practice it is decided within part of the Commission – the Directorate General on Competition (formerly DG IV), i.e. a restricted body. This is perhaps sensible under an approach where block exemptions are largely competition related only, i.e. technical in the sense that the scope (full competition) is fixed and that particular ('non-political') expertise is paramount. Such a competence is, however, potentially less advisable where rules are at stake that should be characterized as general contract law. In these instances, their proper integration into consumer law – or more correctly general EC contract law – seems advisable.

Two examples may be illustrative of the problem. The first is taken from the block exemption on agreements, decisions and concerted practices in the insurance sector, currently under discussion again.[11] Title III contains an

____

[11] Commission Regulation (EC) No 3932/92 of 21 Dec. 1992 on the application of Article 85 (3) of the Treaty to certain categories of agreements, decisions and concerted practices in the insurance sector, EC OJ 1992 L 398/7; amended in EC OJ 1994 C 241/60 and 1995 L 1/21.
Title III

Standard policy conditions for direct insurance

Art. 5
(1) The exemption provided for in Article 1(b) shall apply to agreements, decisions and concerted practices which have as their object the establishment and distribution of standard policy conditions for direct insurance.
(2) The exemption shall also apply to agreements, decisions and concerted practices which have as their object the establishment and distribution of common models illustrating the profits to be realized from an insurance policy involving an element of capitalization.

Art. 6
(1) The exemption shall apply on condition that the standard policy conditions referred to in Article 5(1):
a) are established and distributed with an explicit statement that they are purely illustrative; and
b) expressly mention the possibility that different conditions may be agreed; and
c) are accessible to any interested person and provided simply upon request.
(2) referring to Art. 5(2)

Art. 7
The exemption shall not apply where the standard policy conditions referred to in Article 5(1) contain clauses which:
a) exclude from the cover losses normally relating to the class of insurance concerned, without indicating explicitly that each insurer remains free to extend the cover to such events;
b) make the cover of certain risks subject to specific conditions, without indicating explicitly that each insurer remains free to waive them;
c) impose comprehensive cover including risks to which a significant number of policyholders is not simultaneously exposed, without indicating explicitly that each insurer remains free to propose separate cover;
d) indicate the amount of cover or the part which the policyholder must pay himself (the 'excess');
e) allow the insurer to maintain the policy in the event that he cancels part of the cover, increases the premium without the risk or the scope of the cover being changed (without prejudice to indexation clauses), or otherwise alters the policy conditions without the express consent of the policyholder;
f) allow the insurer to modify the term of the policy without the express consent of the policyholder;

exemption for standard policy conditions for direct insurance, i.e. for sets of standard terms which in most Member States are drafted for the whole insurance sector by the professional association of insurance undertakings and which the association communicates to its members as a model. Title III also contains a block exemption for model calculations, which I will not discuss. The model set of standard terms, even though it is not binding, is clearly restricting competition with respect to conditions. The block exemption was justified, however, as a measure that enhances the supply of information to the consumer (or client). As this measure leads to standardisation, policy conditions typically resemble each other, and deviations can be recognized more easily. The information situation is enhanced if anybody can have the model at hand at any time (see Art. 6(1) lit. c). This policy of promoting the supply of information is combined with a freedom of drafting policy which is shaped in as efficient a way as possible: The freedom has to be explicitly stated and it is fully guaranteed: The model must not be binding in any of its parts and this has to be stressed (Art. 6(1) lit. a and b and also Art. 7(2)).[12]

---

g) impose on the policyholder in the non-life assurance sector a contract period of more than three years;

h) impose a renewal period of more than one year where the policy is automatically renewed unless notice is given upon the expiry of a given period;

i) require the policyholder to agree to the reinstatement of a policy which has been suspended on the account of the disappearance of the insured risk, if he is once again exposed to a risk of the same nature;

j) require the policyholder to obtain cover from the same insurer for different risks;

k) require the policyholder, in the event of disposal of the object of the insurance, to make the acquirer take over the insurance policy.

(2) The exemption shall not benefit undertakings or associations of undertakings which concert or undertake among themselves, or oblige other undertakings not to apply conditions other than those referred to in Article 5(1).

Art. 8

Without prejudice to the establishment of specific insurance conditions for particular social or occupational categories of the population, the exemption shall not apply to agreements, decisions and concerted practices which exclude the coverage of certain risk categories because of the characteristics associated with the policyholder.

Art. 9

Referring to Art. 5(2)

[12] Forbidding the use of other standard terms is equivalent to imposing the ones proposed without any possibility of deviation. This is so because forbidding the use of other standard terms would mean that insurance policies which might deviate would have to be drafted as individual contracts – an alternative which is absurd in practice.

In clauses which are perhaps less obviously justified by the matter itself, the freedom to deviate has to be stressed explicitly for the particular clause (Art. 7(1) lit. a-c); and prices may not be included in the model, not even as a recommendation (Art.7(1) lit. d), because information problems do not exist here anyway. The question arises whether all these rules are really concerned only with antitrust policies. Telling clients that any insurance undertaking is free to draft its own policy even if there are model policies published by the professional association of insurance undertakings seems to cure information problems as well. And more importantly, one may ask whether a set of standard terms should not be less deeply scrutinized when made public, and when perhaps they are even drafted with the consent or approval of an organized body of the other market side. Therefore, the level of regulation to be found in the block exemption may even be too high. All these questions are questions of unfair standard contract terms, of information problems, not particularly of antitrust competition law.

The remainder of Art. 7(1) (lit. e-k) is even more consumer or contract law related. These provisions can clearly be explained as striking down standard terms which put the client at a unjustified disadvantage. They cause a 'significant imbalance in the parties' rights and obligations' in the words of Art. 3(1) of the Unfair Contract Terms Directive,[13] and they are regarded as being 'unfair' for this reason.

The second example is taken from the block exemption regime for motor vehicle distribution and servicing agreements. The old regulation[14] spelt out expressly in its Art. 3 that the dealer can be bound by contract (cartel):

(4) not to permit a third party to benefit unduly, through any after-sales service performed in a common workshop, from investments made by a supplier, notably in equipment or the training of personnel
(5) neither to sell spare parts which compete with contract goods without matching them in quality nor to use them for repair or maintenance of contract goods or corresponding goods.

These measures are concerned with marketing and distribution methods and

---

13 Council Directive 93/13/EEC of 5 April 1993 on unfair terms in consumer contracts, EC OJ 1993 L 95/29.

14 Commission Regulation (EC) No 1475/95 of 28 June 1995 on the application of Article 85 (3) of the Treaty to certain categories of motor vehicle distribution and servicing agreements, EC OJ 1995 L 145/25.

contracts in the narrow sense. Although the new regulation[15] is not explicit, it flows from Art. 4 lit. k *e contrario* (restrictions forbidden only for 'spare parts of matching qualifity'), and from the fact that clauses which protect the manufacturer from having his particular know-how exploited are not included in the black list of Art. 4 either, that the same cartels are still possible under the new regime. This means that all over Europe manufacturers may protect themselves from having inferior spare parts from competitors used in workshops which give the impression of being in line with their high standard of quality. And this also means that all over Europe manufacturers may protect themselves from having their particular know-how exploited for the use of competitors. What, however, the regulations fail to achieve is a clarification that using such parts etc. is a misleading practice if the client is not clearly told this. This result could be achieved, however, (and potentially should be achieved) by including such a rule in a general contract law rule about the supply of accurate information, for instance in the directive on advertising or another directive on unfair competition. And again, as most manufacturers in the motor vehicle sector are forced to use the block exemption, the rule is one which is almost generally applied without, however, having the consent of the legislative bodies to whom general contract law is entrusted.

This example brings us to the third section regarding the law of unfair competition.

III. DISMANTLING THE LAW AGAINST UNFAIR COMPETITION AND REALLOCATING DIFFERENT TYPES OF MARKET FAILURE

Unfair competition law is mainly national law. Therefore EC competition law can easily be seen as not really comprising this body of law.

The models in the national laws vary not only in content but also in legislative technique.[16] In Italy, competition law is to be found in the general Civil Code, in articles 2598-2601 *Codice Civile*. In France, where the law against unfair competition originated and unfair competition is called 'con-

---

[15] Commission Regulation (EC) No. 1400/2002 of 31 July 2002 on the application of Article 81 (3) of the Treaty to categories of vertical agreements and concerted practices in the motor vehicle sector, EC OJ 2002 L 203/30.

[16] For a survey see the country reports in Ekey, Klippe, Kotthoff, Meckel, Plaß, *Wettbewerbsrecht*, (2000), by Chouchena and Ehlers (France), Alexander (Great Britain), Preussler (Italy), Heidkamp (Belgium), Mascaray-Marti and K.Schmidt (Spain); Kampermann and Sanden, *Unfair Competition Law*, (Oxford: 1997).

currence déloyale', parts of unfair competition law are integrated into the *Code de la Consommation*. In Germany, there is a special Act, the *Gesetz gegen unlauteren Wettbewerb*, which has always been considered to attain a particularly high level of regulation, most say too high. There is a special Act also in Belgium and Spain, however, which at least in the latter case is much more liberal. In Great Britain, the courts did not develop a general clause, but basically restricted themselves to interventions in cases of misleading indications (passing-off). Later, they stepped in with respect to cases where competitors had been denigrated. Acts of Parliament are to be found mainly in connection with consumer law and trademark law.

Unfair competition law is not as important in EC law as antitrust competition law. It is, however, not non-existent either. For a long time it was one of the most important – if not the most important – area of private law[17] for scrutiny of laws by reference to the fundamental economic freedoms of the EC Treaty.[18] All these decisions were about allegedly misleading practices (price cuts in promotional sales, comparative advertising, the use of trademarks etc.), occasionally also about allegedly obstructive behaviour with respect to distribution channels of competitors. There is the directive on misleading and comparative advertising. And unfair competition law is the main area for which Art. 3 of the Directive on e-commerce prescribes a home country principle.[19] There are also some other practices – like cold-calling – which are regulated (or left to the regulation by the Member States) in various other measures of European Contract Law, namely the Directive on e-commerce and distance selling.[20]

---

[17] In most Member States unfair competition law contains only or primarily remedies for private parties – which is different from the remedial system for antitrust competition law.

[18] ECJ 7 March 1990, Case C-362/88, *GB-Inno-BM* [1991] ECR I-667, 689; ECJ 18 May 1993, Case C-126/91, *Yves Rocher* [1993] ECR I-2361, 2386-2391; ECJ 13 December 1990, Case C-238/89, *Pall / Dahlhausen* [1990] ECR I-4827, 4847-4850; and intitiating a new line of cases, with less intensive scrutiny of national law: ECJ 24 November 1993, Joint Cases C-267/91 and C-268/91, *Keck & Mithouard* [1993] ECR 1993, I-6097, 6130-6132; ECJ 15 Decembre 1993, Case C-292/92, *Hünermund* [1993] ECR I-6787, 6822 et seq.; and, restricting again the area of reduced scrutiny: ECJ 6 July 1995, Case C-470/93, *Mars* [1991] ECR I-1923, 1941; ECJ 10 May 1995, Case C-384/94, *Alpine Investment* [1991] ECR I-1141, 1176-1178.

[19] Directive 2000/31/EC of the European Parliament and of the Council of 8.6.2000 on certain legal aspects of information society services, in particular electronic commerce, in the Internal Market ('Directive on electronic commerce'), EC OJ 2000 L 178/1.

[20] Council Directive 97/7/EC of 20 Mai 1997 on the protection of consumers in respect of

In national laws, this area of unfair competition law could already be found late in the 19th and early in the 20th centuries. It thus is much older than antitrust competition law, which in the Community is basically a post World War II phenomenon – under the influence of ordoliberal thinking. At the same time, unfair competition law reflects much more a conglomerate of ideas, not based on one uniform economic phenomenon with basically one coherent theory. It is a conglomerate of different types of market failure, partly information problems, partly abuse of dominant positions (related to antitrust competition law), partly situations resembling theft or more generally external effects. And this heterogeneous character is also reflected in European law.

It is not surprising that national laws treat this area in many different ways – not only with respect to substantive content, but also in the way they codify or perceive this area of law. Some states include parts of the law of unfair competition in a Code on consumer protection, some in a Code against unfair competition, and Italy integrates it into the general Civil Code.

Gomez' plea for clarity would speak in favour of dismantling these distinctions. In the case of the directive on misleading and comparative advertising, the most important EC law measure in this area, this proposal would speak in favour of an integration into the general information regime of consumer contracts and indeed all contracts and general EC contract law concerned with marketing and distribution. And indeed, Gomez includes this most outstanding example of an information-related rule of unfair competition in his section on consumer protection – without even raising the question of category. At least on the European level, this approach is certainly preferable. The decision to treat information problems partly in a Code on unfair competition, and partly in contract or consumer contract law, is related to the question of who should have the right to enforce the information standard (the giving of information or the clarity or truth of the information given). In the one case, these enforcers are the competitors or a public agency, in the other case they are the parties to the contractual relationship. If, however, on the European level this question is typically left open,[21] or different alternatives

---

distance contracts, EC OJ 1997 L 144/19. There is now a separate directive for the area of financial services so far excluded. See Directive 2002/65/EC of the European Parliament and of the Council of 23 September 2002 concerning the distance marketing of consumer financial services and amending Council Directive 90/619/EEC and directives 97/7/EC and 98/27/EC, OJ 2002 L 271/16.

[21] The typical standard is that of primary EC law, i.e. Art. 10 EC which is interpreted as

are imposed in principle,[22] it is pointless to segregate information standards on the basis of these criteria. In European law, typically the primary duty is fixed, not the sanctions (except for the general efficiency standard named). Therefore the similarity of the primary duty, the information standard, would have to be the guiding principle also for answering questions about codification and categorisation

So far, the other two categories – antitrust situations and situations resembling theft or, more generally, external effects – are largely theoretical on the European level. There is no substantial harmonization in these areas. There is only case law affecting situations of these two categories. The antitrust situations certainly would best be taken care of by antitrust law. The situations resembling theft or external effects could probably well be fitted into a Code on marketing and fair dealing, which concentrates on the problems of the supply of information. It would nevertheless be a legal measure which would be mainly concerned with information problems. The risk that is raised by combining antitrust competition law and information/consumer law does not seem to play a major role here. This is the risk that one paradigm – that of unequal bargaining power – is transposed to another situation in which it has adverse effects. The Italian solution – of dealing with these questions as questions of general private and contract law – seems to be most advisable.

IV. Summary

Consumer Law is basically about information problems and asymmetries of information, which in turn are general market problems. Consumer law should therefore be conceived as part of general contract and private law. Competition law is about restrictions of competition. These are two types

---

imposing two standards: Under this Article, sanctions have to be 'effective, proportionate and dissuasive': ECJ 21 September 1989, Case 68/88, *Commission / Greece* [1989] ECR 2965, 2985; 10 July 1990, Case C-326/88, *Hansen* [1990] ECR I-2911, 2935. This may mean, among other things, strict liability and no fixing of lump sum damages below the average award: ECJ 10 April 1984, Case 14/83, *von Colson and Kamann* [1984] ECR 1891, 1908; 10 April 1984, Case 79/83, *Harz* [1984] ECR 1921, 1941 et seq.; and ECJ 2 August 1993, Case C-271/91, *Marshall II* [1993] ECR I-4367, 4409; 22 April 1997, Case C-180/95, *Draempaehl* [1997] ECR I-2195, 2219-2225. Moreover, sanctions imposed for the violation of comparable national laws may not be stricter than those imposed for the violation of rules based on European harmonisation.

[22] This is so only in exceptional cases, one of which is the directive on misleading and comparative advertising (see above note 11): See Art. 4 of this Directive.

of market failure, which are distinct in economic theory, and which should be kept distinct also in legislation – although they certainly can form two parts of the regulation of one particular phenomenon, such as marketing and distribution chains. They are the two core features of existing European contract law.

If one wants to keep both types of market failure and their regulation distinct, this calls for one small step and one larger one. The small step is to integrate those parts of antitrust competition law into general contract law (or 'consumer' contract law), which are really about information problems, and are not concerned only with situations of restricted competition. In these situations, the Commission should not profit from a competence not designed for this purpose. The larger step is that of dismantling the law against unfair competition. It is a conglomerate of different types of market failure, partly information problems, partly abuse of dominant positions, partly situations resembling theft or more generally external effects. The parts on information problems (today the most important parts, especially on the European level) should be integrated into general contract law (or 'consumer' contract law); those related to dominant positions should be seen as antitrust competition law. The rules on situations resembling theft or more generally external effects can go without harm into a general Code on marketing and fair dealing. They are, however, not harmonized so far, and therefore the question is still today a theoretical one on the European level.

9. Contract Law Enforcement of Provisions on Marketing: The Solution of the Consumer Sales Directive

Thomas Wilhelmsson

I. INTRODUCTION

The *Green Paper on European Union Consumer Protection*[1] brings onto the agenda many interesting basic questions related to the future development of European Community consumer law. In a context which mainly focuses on the future regulation of marketing and good market behaviour the Green paper asks whether a framework directive or more specific rules would be preferable on a European level. It also seems to press for a development of EC consumer law in this area from minimum harmonisation measures towards a more fully harmonised approach, which from a consumer point of view cannot be applauded.[2]

A main part of the Green Paper discusses enforcement, which clearly is one of the key issues with regard to the regulation of marketing. As the Green Paper notes, '(a)ny regulatory measures must be linked to adequate enforcement structures that ensure their consistent application.'[3] Since supervision measures and injunctions traditionally have been used as the main remedies against unlawful marketing in Europe, it is quite natural that the Green Paper in this context analyses these kinds of enforcement measures. It submits for consultation only questions concerning a possible legal framework for improving co-operation between consumer protection enforcement authorities.[4]

---

[1] COM(2001) 531 final: 'Green paper'.

[2] For a criticism of the maximalist approach, see G.Howells & T.Wilhelmsson, 'EC consumer law – has it come of age?' (2003) *European Law Review*, 370. In the recently adopted Consumer Policy Strategy 2002-2006, COM(2002) 208 final, this policy is unfortunately reinforced (p. 12).

[3] Green paper, 16.

[4] At p. 19. In the Consumer Policy Strategy 2002-2006 the Commission announces its inten-

H. Collins (ed.) The Forthcoming EC Directive on Unfair and Commercial Practices, 223-240.
©2004. Kluwer Law International. Printed in the Netherlands.

In the enforcement palette of the Green paper there is no hint at the possible role of private law. The question of consumer redress – of individual remedies of consumers – is not addressed. However, there are private law rules which can have some – certainly relatively small – relevance in this context. Private law remedies may be attached to some such marketing behaviour which is considered unlawful in a regulatory perspective. Although the private law remedies usually are not directly attached to the breach of public law duties, as the particulars of the relevant duties usually are fixed independently in private law, these remedies nevertheless should be taken into account when discussing the general picture of enforcing rules on marketing.

The most obvious examples to be mentioned here are various kinds of rules on liability in contract for information given in marketing. In addition, general clauses on unfair contract terms can also in some cases provide solutions to problems connected with unfair marketing. Besides contract law, tort law may also have a role to play here. Consumers who have not yet entered into contractual relations with the business performing the unlawful marketing may nevertheless have a claim in tort for (usually, however, rather small) damages to compensate for losses which have arisen because of the marketing. Competitors may also have tort claims related to comparative advertising or other marketing directly violating their rights.

In this paper, I will not analyse the use of tort law, but restrict myself to discuss the role of contractual claims related to marketing information in the enforcement of regulation of marketing. Furthermore, I will look at the issue mainly in relation to consumer contracts. In other words, my paper concerns certain consumer contract law claims as a method of enforcing rules on marketing: what rules do we have and how should they be applied? And furthermore: how should these rules be developed in order to facilitate as much as possible the role of the consumers as private law enforcers of rules on marketing?

Already at this stage I should underline, that I do not see such contract law enforcement as an alternative to the administrative enforcement procedures described and discussed in the Green Paper. As I make clear in the next section of the paper, I certainly prefer the traditional European – and especially the Nordic – 'model of regulation and administration' rather than the American 'model of information and litigation'. However, even in a system

---

tion to propose a legislative framework for enforcement co-operation, COM(2002) 208 final, p. 17.

(rightly) dominated by public law enforcement, private law may have some minor role to play. I will here analyse this type of enforcement, not as an alternative to, but only as a complement to the primary means of administrative enforcement.

At a meeting of the Society of European Contract Law (SECOLA), I find it especially worthwhile to discuss the role of contract law as a means of addressing problems in marketing. The discussion may add a little piece to our views on how European contract law(s) should look like. The issue offers a good example of a situation in which European contract law has facilitated and can further promote the movement of experiences from some Member States to others.

II. THE ROLE OF CONTRACT LAW ENFORCEMENT

The role and relative weight of private law measures in the enforcement palette of consumer protection regulation in general can be more clearly grasped, if one compares the general approaches in Europe with those in use in the USA. Especially in the latter country, private law litigation has traditionally been used as a means for controlling market behaviour. In very general terms one may call the European consumer protection model a 'model of regulation and administration', whilst the American approach could be called a 'model of information and litigation'.[5] In Europe, consumer protection has in many countries been developed from above, by the state, and the supervision of consumer markets has been entrusted to state authorities or heavily state-subsidised organisations. On the other hand, in the US, collective consumer activism – with Naderism as a keyword[6] – has been important and state intervention has relied mostly on information measures. This has also meant an emphasis on private litigation as an important regulatory technique. The responsibility of the consumers themselves and of their organisations in enforcing a liability for the businesses and thereby indirectly creating norms

---

[5] See more in detail G.Howells and T.Wilhelmsson, 'EC and US Approaches to Consumer Protection – Should the Gap Be Bridged?' (1997) *Yearbook of European Law* 207.

[6] See, for example, Y. Gabriel and T. Lang, *The Unmanageable Consumer* (London: SAGE Publications 1995) 159-62. It should be noted that the ideology of the Naderist movement is based on strong individualism, H. Gorey, *Nader and the Power of Everyman* (Grosset and Dunlap, 1975) p. 64 writes, 'Nader genuinely believes in free enterprise. He likewise believes it no longer exists. He supports competition in the marketplace. Where true competition exists, he opposes government regulation.'

to guide their behaviour is underlined. This is, as is well known, encouraged through various incentives for the consumers, like mimimum damages, multiple damages and punitive damages, and it is also closely connected with the contingency fee system as well as with the possibility of class action.

Even though the US information and litigation model has some influence today on thinking in Europe, especially at the EU level, one should not see it as a possible alternative in the European context. Both the cultural/ideological, the private law, and the procedural law prerequisites are lacking in Europe. The strong individualist ideology, the private law incentives, and the claimant-favourable system of justice simply are not there. Therefore a change of the European state-centred model towards an American model of the 'information and litigation'-type would easily end up in the regulation falling between both stools, with no efficient enforcement at all.[7] Although I am here discussing a private law measure I therefore want to repeat that such a measure cannot be more than an addition to the public law regulatory measures which should dominate also in the future when developing the European regulation of marketing.

However, supervision and other kinds of administrative measures are primarily used at national level. This should be the case also in the future, as national authorities are closest to the problems and have the best insight in the culture in which they are operating. What is misleading or otherwise problematic in one cultural setting may not be so in another. The European perspective in the area of administrative enforcement therefore mainly has to focus on co-operation between national authorities and organisations, as the Green Paper on European Union Consumer Protection quite wisely does.[8] In view of the rather wide differences between the supervision systems in the various Member States, it is therefore difficult to discuss the issue of supervision more comprehensively as a European matter. On the other hand, as the huge variations partially are a result of different administrative and supervision traditions, they are less relevant when discussing contract law. Even though contract law measures may be of small practical importance

---

[7] I may here cite a sentence in our above-mentioned paper Howells and Wilhelmsson, above n 5, 266, as it is written by my co-author: 'Of course a switch from regulation to information combined with a lack of litigation may appeal to business leaders, but then policy-makers should be aware that they would be adopting only half of the US package.' It goes without saying that our conclusion in the paper recommends sticking to the European solution.

[8] Green paper, 16-19. The thought of a European Consumer Ombudsman now seems to be buried, and I think there are few mourners.

from a general regulatory point of view, they may be the only ones concerning which one may really discuss the possibility of more or less common European solutions. Such solutions can also be flexible enough to cater for the cultural differences mentioned above.

Contract law, as with traditional private law in general, is self-implementing in character. Application of the rules is not watched over by any prosecuting or supervising authority. The initiative for the process of applying the rules is left to the parties themselves, in the present case primarily to the consumer. No general European administrative structures are needed to have more common substantive solutions in this area.

This self-implementing character also brings in a necessary degree of flexibility and adaptation to national cultural needs in the enforcement process. A marketing measure which in a certain culture is not regarded as problematic is less likely to become a target of private law proceedings in the first place. And if some person, contrary to the prevailing local view, brings a case to the court, the court can take into account the local cultural expectations in the decision, as the decision is always related to the individual (local) parties. It goes without saying that the private law rules should give sufficient leeway for such adaptation to national expectations.[9]

As private law primarily is there in order to protect the rights of individual parties in individual cases, the value of developing private law rules should not only be assessed on the basis of their overall impact on market behaviour in general. Good private law rules are of course always to be welcomed from the point of view of the individual parties. However, when judging the impact of contract law measures against unlawful marketing one should not overlook the fact that future changes in the procedural setting in Europe may give such measures a somewhat more general importance than they have today. The emergence of various new types of collective procedure for promoting mass interests brings in substantial new possibilities for private law strategies. The introduction in the Nordic countries as well as in the EU of a class action

---

[9] The thought of the principle of consumers' legitimate expectations as a basic principle of EC consumer law is well-founded also in this respect. See on the principle H.-W. Micklitz, Principles of Justice in Private Law within the European Union, in Paasivirta and Rissanen (eds.), Principles of Justice and the Law of the European Union (Brussels: European Commission, DG XIII, Cost A7, 1995) 284 et seq.; H.-W.Micklitz, Legitime Erwartungen als Gerechtigkeitsprinzip des Europäischen Privatrechts, in Krämer, Micklitz and Tonner (eds.), Law and Diffuse Interests in the European Legal Order (Baden-Baden: Nomos, 1997) 245, as well as G.Howells and T.Wilhelmsson, above note 2, 320-323.

in the consumer area is being seriously discussed, and in Sweden the Parliament has very recently adopted a Government Bill on class actions.[10] Such a procedure could conceivably be a useful tool in cases of the type treated here. Some option of collective procedures for damages and other pecuniary claims is certainly needed, be it in the form of a public, an organisational or a 'pure' class action. Classes of consumers who have been misled by marketing measures into acquiring some consumer goods or services could through a class action have much more impact on future behaviour of businesses than through a few (small) individual cases.

Looking at the issue from a more societal point of view one should also not forget the growth of various forms of 'micropolitics'[11] in the postmodern society. In the consumer area, micropolitics has often taken the form of consumer boycotts and similar campaigns.[12] However, in the current media society, litigation can also be used as a tool for bringing consumer concerns onto the public agenda. Litigation can form one aspect of the strategies by which consumers practice their micropolitics. For example contract law liability can be used as a part of multi-measured collective campaigns. Consumer boycotts and similar measures could be supplemented with campaigns to get consumers who had already bought the product to lodge claims and demand cancellation of the purchase. Such legal strategies might be used also against unlawful marketing, if the private law rules in this area adequately sanction such marketing.

---

[10] The new legislation will enter into force 1.1.2003. See more closely the Swedish Government Bill 2001/02:107. For the discussion in the Nordic countries, see NEK-rapport 1990: 7 as well as the proposals SOU 1994:151 (in Sweden), OLJ 1/1995 (in Finland) and NOU 2001:32 (in Norway). A good overview of the 'world situation' is given by P.H.Lindblom, *Progressiv process* (Uppsala: Iustus, 2000) 427 et seq.

[11] The term is used by F.Jameson, *Postmodernism or, the cultural logic of late capitalism* (London-New York, Verso, 1991) 318 et seq.; U.Beck, 'The Reinvention of Politics: Towards a Theory of Reflexive Modernization', in Beck, Giddens & Lash (eds.), *Reflexive Modernization* (Cambridge, Polity Press, 1994) 16, 18, speaks about 'sub-politics' as an characteristic feature of our time. These terms refers to the fact that various kinds of small groups, minorities and social movements are taking new places on the social scene. The development of the information society seems to have strengthened this tendency. It is not surprising that the leading 'guru' of the information society Manuel Castells, *The Power of Identity* (Oxford: Blackwell, 1997), for example at pp. 354 et seq., both emphasises new forms of grass root activism as one of the important features of the new society as well as connects his hope for change to this kind of activism.

[12] A good overview of various forms of consumer boycotts is given by M.Friedman, *Consumer Boycotts: Effecting Change Through the Marketplace and the Media* (London, Routledge, 1999).

228

III. Misleading Advertising and Non-Conformity of Goods

So, even though rules on contract law liability for marketing are of secondary importance, they may in certain situations and under certain preconditions get a more general practical relevance. What rules of this kind do we have?

Provisions connecting remedies against non-conformity of goods sold by means of misleading information given in marketing are the perhaps most obvious example of contract law remedies against problematic marketing. Such provisions have existed in some EU jurisdictions and have now been introduced also in the others.

For a long time, Nordic sales law, first for consumer sales and nowadays also for commercial sales, has made the seller liable for non-conformity, if the goods do not conform with information given in marketing. The product is deemed to be defective, if it does not correspond with particulars given during its marketing or otherwise before purchase and that may be assumed to have influenced the purchase.[13] Also, according to the Dutch civil code, the seller is bound by public statements, with very narrow exceptions.[14] In the comparative overview made in the Green paper on guarantees for consumer goods and after-sales services the very general conclusion is drawn that in the determining whether there is a defect 'there seems to be a move from the obligation concerning conformity with normal use towards an obligation to conformity with the information provided...'[15]

Prepared on the basis of the Green Paper, the Consumer Sales Directive[16] now requires a kind of marketing liability to be included in the national legislation. For several Member States this requirement probably means an extension of existing seller's liability. A marketing liability of the kind prescribed in the Directive improves the protection of consumers, in comparison with the previous law, for example in England,[17] Ireland,[18] Germany,[19] Austria[20] and Greece.[21]

---

[13] See Sec. 18 of the new Nordic Sale of Goods Acts, Sec. 19 of the Swedish Consumer Sales Act and Chap. 5 Sec. 13 of the Finnish Consumer Protection Act.

[14] BW 7:18. E.Hondius and H.Schelhaas, 'In conformity with the Consumer Sales Directive? Some remarks on transposition into Dutch law', (2001) European Review of Private Law 327, 331 note that the Dutch rule is more consumer-friendly than the provision of the Consumer Sales Directive.

[15] COM(93) 509 final, p. 28.

[16] Directive 1999/44/EC of the European Parliament and of the Council on certain aspects of the sale of consumer goods and associated guarantees.

[17] See G.Howells, 'Implementation of the EC Consumer Sales Directive in the United King-

In the Consumer Sales Directive the provision concerning a marketing liability of the seller is not spelled out very clearly, but rather in a more indirect form. It is hidden in the normal quality rule in Art. 2(2)(d). According to this rule consumer goods are presumed to be in conformity with the contract if they 'show the quality and performance which are normal in goods of the same type and which the consumer can reasonably expect, given the nature of the goods and taking into account any public statements on the specific characteristics of the goods made about them by the seller, the producer or his representative, particularly in advertising or on labelling.' The last part of the rule indicates that also according to the Directive remedies for non-conformity may at least as a main rule be applied, if the goods do not correspond to the information given in marketing. A similar binding effect of advertising is also reflected in the provision on guarantees, in Art. 6(1), according to which a guarantee shall be binding 'under the conditions laid down in the guarantee statement and the associated advertising.'

Of special importance is the fact that the provision in Art. 2(2)(d) does not only cover marketing information given by the seller, which relatively easily could be interpreted as a part of the contract even with the help of traditional contract principles, but also marketing by persons without any contractual relation to the consumer. The Directive expressly mentions 'the producer or his representative'. By such a broad liability rule, the Directive

---

dom,' in: Grundmann, Medicus & Rolland (eds.), *Europäisches Kaufgewährleistungsrecht* (Köln, 2000) pp. 161, 177, as well as S.Watterson, 'Consumer Sales Directive 1999/44/EC – The impact on English law' (2001) *European Review of Private Law* 197, 208.

[18] T.C.Bird, 'Directive 99/44/EC on certain aspects of the sale of consumer goods and associated guarantees: its impact on existing Irish sale of goods law', (2001) *European Review of Private Law* 279, 287-288.

[19] T.Zerres, 'Das neue Sachmängelrecht beim Kauf,' *Verbraucher und Recht* 1/2002, 3, 6. Compare, however, G.Rieger, 'Die Richtlinie zu bestimmten Aspekten des Verbrauchsgüterkaufs und der Garantien für Verbrauchsgüter vor dem Hintergrund des geltenden Rechts', *Verbraucher und Recht* 1999, 287, 289, who claims that the rule more or less corresponds to prevailing court practice in Germany. As S.Grundmann, 'Verbraucherrecht, Unternehmensrecht, Privatrecht – warum sind sich UN-Kaufrecht und EU-Kaufrechtsrichtlinie so ähnlich?' AcP 2002, pp. 40, 47, notes, the really new thing is the liability of the seller for information given by others.

[20] C.Jeloschek, 'The Transposition of Directive 99/44/EC into Austrian Law'(2001) *European Review of Private Law* 163, 169.

[21] G.I.Arnokouros, 'The transposition of the Consumer Sales Directive into the Greek legal system' (2001) *European Review of Private Law* 259, 269.

acknowledges that marketing today is often made by others than the seller, and that this should be recognised in contract law as well.

Remedies for non-conformity can usually be applied only if the marketing information has influenced the purchase or such an influence at least can be assumed. According to the Consumer Sales Directive, Art. 2(4), the seller is not bound by public statements, if he shows that the decision to buy the consumer goods could not have been influenced by the statement,[22] or that the statement had been corrected by the time of the conclusion of the contract. The same paragraph of the Directive also provides – concerning public statements made by others than the seller – that the seller is not bound by such statements, if he shows that he was not, and could not reasonably have been, aware of the statement in question.

The Consumer Sales Directive, and the national legislation which is based on it, offer a legal basis for using the contract law remedies connected with non-conformity (repair, replacement, price reduction, rescission and/or damages,[23] as the case may be) against misleading information in marketing, if it has affected the decision to purchase the goods. This provision in the Directive is a hook on which one can hang contract law enforcement of rules against misleading advertising. The impact of the provision is, however, to some extent dependent on its interpretation and implementation. I will in the following first discuss a few problems in this respect, and then turn to the question, whether the rule in the Consumer Sales Directive should be generalised to cover other types of contracts as well.

IV.   EXTENSIVE INTERPRETATION OF THE CONSUMER SALES DIRECTIVE

The rule on marketing liability in the Consumer Sales Directive is, as I noted earlier, not very clear and precise. In this context, I will discuss three important problems of interpretation in practice. With the aim of achieving as efficient contract law enforcement of the rule against misleading market-

---

[22] As the burden of proof here lies on the seller, and advertising usually affects our conduct, the seller can probably make use of this exemption only in rare cases.

[23] Strictly speaking, the Directive does not require the remedy of damages to be attached to this rule, as it does not contain any provisions on this remedy, K.Riesenhuber, 'Party Autonomy and Information in the Sales Directive', in S. Grundmann, W. Kerber, and S. Weatherill (eds.), *Party Autonomy and the Role of Information in the Internal Market* (Berlin: de Gruyter, 2001) 348, 356. However, in the implementation of the Directive, it would seem rather odd to have different standards of non-conformity in relation to different remedies.

ing as possible, one should not resort to a very narrow interpretation and implementation of the rule in these respects.

Firstly, the rule on marketing liability is only expressed indirectly in the Directive. It is only a kind of presumption.[24] 'Public statements ... particularly in advertising' should be 'taken into account' when assessing what the consumer can reasonably expect of the goods. The connection between the advertising and the remedies is therefore not clearcut, and one may at least in theory envisage a case in which a court, in spite of the fact that certain particulars concerning the goods were presented in advertising, nevertheless considers that a consumer should not have reasonably expected the goods to correspond to the information. In jurisdictions where a contractual liability for marketing was less well known before the Directive, there is a special risk that some courts may resort to such a narrow application of the rule.

However, a more natural and certainly more efficient reading of the Directive would start from the assumption that concrete statements about the goods always give the consumer legitimate reasons to expect them to be fulfilled, and that only very general statements which are rather to be considered mere sales talk[25] do not have such automatic consequences. In other words, concrete information should as a rule be considered part of the contract and binding on the seller in the assessment of non-conformity, if the explicit exceptions mentioned in the Directive are not applicable. This more clearcut interpretation – which is in line e.g. with Nordic law as well as with the Principles of European Contract Law, to be mentioned later – seems to have some support also in the wording of the Directive: as the exception rule in 2(4) enumerates those cases in which the seller 'shall not be bound by public statements', it seems that he should be regarded as 'bound' in other cases. The less general clause-like and the more rule-like the provision is understood to be, the better it works from a general enforcement perspective.

Secondly, because in many cases the relevant advertising and other marketing measures is performed not by the seller(s) but by businesses forming earlier links in the distribution chain, it is very important that the seller's liability for marketing information should also cover such marketing. As I mentioned above, the Directive acknowledges this by speaking about 'public

---

[24] D. Staudenmayer, 'Die EG-Richtlinie über den Verbrauchsgüterkauf', NJW 1999, 2393, 2394, uses the word 'Vermutung''.

[25] Mere advertising puffery is not intended to be relevant, see D.Staudenmayer, 'The Directive on the Sale of Consumer Goods and Associated Guarantees – a Milestone in the European Consumer and Private Law', (2000) *European Review of Private Law* 547, 552.

statements ... by the seller, the producer or his representative'. However, there are also other parties in the distribution chain than the producer and those who strictly speaking can be regarded as 'representatives' of the producer, whose marketing should be considered relevant in this context. As examples one could mention importers and wholesale dealers who do not 'represent' the producer.

In other words, the description of those for whom the seller is responsible should not be read too literally. In the implementation of the Directive, Member States in fact have made some extensions: for example in Germany it seems that the importer to the common market has been included.[26] As mentioned above, a more general and covering description is used for example in Nordic law. The Principles of European Contract Law also uses a more general expression: 'a person in earlier links of the business chain'.[27] Such an expression seems more appropriate in this respect. It reflects more accurately the ways in which marketing in today's consumer markets work. The marketing of the whole chain should be taken into account – the consumer cannot be expected to know who acts as the 'representative' of the producer.

Thirdly, it is also important that one does not adopt too narrow an interpretation of the words 'quality and performance' and 'specific characteristics of the goods' in the Directive, and of similar expressions in the implementing legislation. These words should not only cover descriptions of the goods and its performance as such, but also information concerning its environmental impact, on how it was produced, and on similar issues.

I have elsewhere tried to show that misleading environmental claims given in marketing can lead to non-conformity according to the Directive.[28] This is in fact as a starting point quite natural, considering that the liability for marketing information is based on a notion that the information forms part of the contract in the same way as explicit particulars of that contract do. If particulars concerning the environmental impact of the goods had been explicitly agreed upon, they would without doubt imply sales law liability for environmental harmfulness.

The main possible counterargument to such a contract law liability for

---

[26] See the amended BGB § 434(1), with reference to the Produkthaftungsgesetz § 4(1) and (2).

[27] Art. 6:101(3), see O.Lando & H.Beale (eds.), *Principles of European Contract Law*, (The Hague: Kluwer, 2000) 300, mentioning e.g. advertising by wholesale dealers.

[28] See Bidrag till en grön köprätt, in Blume & Petersen (eds.), *Retlig polycentri* (Copenhagen: Akademisk forlag, 1993) 19.

environmental claims marketing is the rule, mentioned above, according to which only marketing information that can be presumed to have influenced the purchase is relevant in this context. However, as I have analysed more in detail in the above-mentioned paper, both empirical and normative reasons can be offered against such a line of reasoning. Empirically it seems obvious that a significant group of consumers, when purchasing products, considers the possible harm they may cause to the environment.[29] The presumption therefore ought to be the reverse: incorrect particulars of environmentally relevant characteristics may be assumed to have affected the purchase, unless otherwise is shown in the individual case. This conclusion is reinforced by the normative argument that in other parts of the legal order considerable importance has been accorded to marketing information on products' environmental properties. Since the influence of environmental information on consumers' purchasing behaviour, as well as other behaviour, has been stressed within marketing law, it would be inconsistent if sales law were to deny the existence of such influence.

Similar reasoning may be employed when assessing marketing information relating to other kinds of socially relevant 'characteristics' of the goods. If a marketing claim is made that the product has not been produced by using child labour,[30] or that it has been produced in factories where fundamental workers' rights are respected, one should understand it as a case of non-conformity of the goods, if the claim is not true.

Environmental and other similar claims obviously constitute a very small proportion of all statements made in marketing. I nevertheless here wanted to use some space in this paper in order to mention the interpretative problems related to such claims, because of their obvious connection to what I earlier called 'micropolitics'. Many actors in micropolitics are especially interested in claims of this nature. One could easily imagine such an actor – for example an environmental organisation – wanting to sponsor a contract law case as a

---

[29] See on the research available e.g. T.Wilhelmsson, 'Consumer Law and the Environment: From Consumer to Citizen', (1998) *Journal of Consumer Policy* 45, 53. Today the interest for such information seems to be growing again, for example, in Germany, see H.Imkamp, 'The Interest of Consumers in Ecological Product Information is Growing – Evidence from two German Surveys' (2000) *Journal of Consumer Policy* 193

[30] J.Kihlman, *Fel* (Stockholm: MercurIUS, 1999) 109 proposes that, in the application of the Swedish Sales Act, a reasonable expectation test might in some cases lead one to consider production by child labour as a situation of non-conformity, even when this question has not been touched upon in the marketing of the goods.

234

way of bringing about a debate on the behaviour of businesses in relation to environmental claims onto the public agenda.

V.   BROADENING TO OTHER TYPES OF CONTRACT

The Consumer Sales Directive only deals with marketing concerning consumer goods. However, the same kinds of problems arise in connection with marketing concerning consumer services as well. There is no obvious reason to treat marketing of services differently than marketing of goods in this respect. In both cases the consumer should have the right to trust the information given in marketing and should be able to use contract law means to defend his rights.

From an enforcement perspective there is also no point in making a sharp distinction between goods and services in this respect. The administrative enforcement rules usually do not make this distinction. The Green Paper discusses the enforcement of the rules on marketing in general terms. Why should then the contract law rules vary depending on the type of contract?

In the Principles of European Contract Law a general solution is adopted. The Principles contain a provision on liability for marketing, which is not limited to certain types of contract.[31] According to this provision, if a professional supplier 'gives information about the quality or use of services or goods or other property when marketing or advertising them or otherwise before the contract is concluded, the statement is to be treated as giving rise to a contractual obligation unless it is shown that the other party knew or could not have been unaware that the statement was incorrect.' Similar information given by a person in earlier links of the business chain also binds the supplier, unless 'it did not know and had no reason to know of the information or undertaking.' These rules in the Principles cover all types of contracts, both sale of goods and contracts for delivery of services as well as other types of contracts. They also cover both business and consumer contracts, as long as the supplier is professional.

In EC law and the law of Member States, some general proposals in this direction have also been made.[32] However, in existing law the need for a

---

[31]   Art. 6:101. See Lando & Beale, above note 27, 299 et seq.

[32]   During the preparation of the Unfair Contract Terms Directive, the proposal was made in the European Parliament to include a provision on the binding nature of advertising in this Directive, see European Parliament, Session documents A3-0091/91, Report of the Committee on Legal Affairs and Citizens' Rights p. 10. In Finland there is also a proposal for

general rule on contractual liability for statements in marketing is primarily demonstrated by the growth of rules on such liability for particular contract types. For example, in both Finnish and Swedish law the legislation on consumer services contains a similar provision on liability for marketing as the law on sales.[33] In addition, one may mention a special Finnish insurance contract law provision, which prescribes that if the insurer or its representative has given false or misleading information in marketing – or even has failed to give necessary information! – the insurance contract is deemed to have the content that the insured had reason to believe on the basis of the information given.[34] As this fairly radical rule has not lead to difficulties in practice it has now been proposed that it should also be included in the legislation on credit institutes.[35]

As another practical example one could mention marketing materials on package tours.[36] According to the Package Tour Directive,[37] Art. 3, particulars contained in a broschure are binding on the organiser or retailer of the tour. However, other marketing material should also be taken into account in specifying the obligations of the organiser or retailer. If the organiser or retailer, for example, gives to the consumer a broschure concerning the place of destination which, to its knowledge, contains false information on relevant issues, liability should arise.[38] Such a solution would clearly be in line both with the ideology of the Package Tour Directive as well as with the general principle of contractual liability for marketing information sketched here. The explicit rule in the Package Tour Directive can be seen as an expression of the broader general principle.[39]

---

adding a general rule of this kind to the Contracts Act, see Komiteanmietintö 1990:20, proposal Sec. 1c. The proposal was a part of a proposal for a general revision of the Contracts Act, which has not been carried out.

[33] The Finnish Consumer Protection Act, Chap. 8 Sec. 13, the Swedish Consumer Services Act, Sec. 10.

[34] The Finnish Insurance Contract Act of 1994, Sec. 9.

[35] Kuluttajavirasto & kuluttaja-asiamies, Vuosikertomus 2001, p. 19.

[36] The practical value of a liability rule is here enhanced by the recent ruling of the European Court of Justice, according to which breach of a contract of package travel should entitle the consumer also to compensation for non-material damage, *Simone Leitner v. TUI Deutschland*, Case C-168/00.

[37] Council Directive 90/314/EEC on package travel, package holidays and package tours.

[38] This was the solution of the Finnish Consumer Complaint Board in the case 84/35/3365.

[39] I have defended this idea in T. Wilhelmsson, *Social Contract Law and European Integration* (Aldershot: Dartmouth, 1995) 130.

Sales law is often understood as paradigmatic for contract law in general. One could therefore see the rule on liability for marketing information in the Consumer Sales Directive as an expression of an evolving general principle of European contract law. If one were to construct more general principles out of the *acquis*,[40] the contractual liability for marketing is certainly a good candidate. The rule on liability for marketing information in the Directive should therefore be implemented to be applicable to and/or be applied by analogy to other contracts as consumer sales as well.

As the need of consumers for correct information is the same irrespective of the type of contract, it is relatively obvious that such a broadening of the rule to other consumer contracts than consumer sales is well-founded. However, as both the Principles of European Contract Law as well as some national examples[41] show, one may even go further and use this legal experience also on business-to-business contracts. One may see the the liability for marketing information not only as a protective measure, as such to be confined to the realm of consumer law, but also as a natural adaptation of contract law to the realities of the present marketing and media landscape.[42]

VI. CONCLUSIONS

I have tried to show here that, although the Green Paper on European Union Consumer Protection does not mention it, there is some space for contract law remedies as a part of the machinery for enforcing rules against problematic marketing. Admittedly, the practical role of contract law remedies in this context cannot be very important, but they can have some effect in certain circumstances and under certain procedural preconditions. However, the self-implementing mechanism of private law can suit the European enforcement level. At least ideologically a common European rule on contract law liability for information given in marketing seems valuable.

As much marketing is cross-border activity, this is one of those issues where one may defend European harmonisation, even when one views the idea of a general harmonisation of contract law with great scepticism.

---

[40] The establishment of an Acquis Group, with the task of analysing 'Principles of Existing EC Private Law' was recently made public.

[41] As mentioned earlier, the marketing liability of Nordic sales law covers both consumer and commercial contracts. In German law the new BGB § 434 is applicable to all kinds of sales as well.

[42] In this direction Grundmann, above note 19, 47.

It seems possible to implement such a common detail in various national contract law environments without any general harmonisation of contract law. This is a context where a free movement of legal ideas and doctrines in Europe should result in a learning process where jurisdictions for which a contract law liability for marketing is more unfamiliar could take over solutions from others which already have made use of the rule.

The Consumer Sales Directive offers the European basis for such 'a new departure in most of the existing civil laws'.[43] As shown above, however, in order to become as useful as possible as an enforcement mechanism the provision on liability for marketing in this Directive should not be given a narrow interpretation. The liability rule should also be extended to other types of contracts than sales, as there is no good reason to distinguish between different types of contracts in this respect. It should become a recognised piece of general European contract law.

A general rule on contract law liability for marketing information might be achieved through analogy and principle-oriented reasoning in jurisdictions where a general rule of this kind is not yet expressly codified. As the distinction between private law and public law measures is rather alien for much of EC law, it is also not impossible to imagine a provision on such a contract law liability to be included in the possible framework directive on misleading and deceptive practices which is offered as one of the options in the Green Paper on European Union Consumer Protection.[44] Admittedly, such a solution would seem very strange for many civil lawyers, still used to a relatively sharp distinction between the main areas of law. Nothing would, however, preclude the implementation of such a provision of a framework directive through amendments of national contract laws.

Anyway, a rule on contract law liability for information, in other words a liability for false and misleading marketing, covers only a part of the whole area of unlawful marketing, of marketing in breach of what in the Green paper is described as 'fair commercial practices' or 'good market behaviour'.[45] Even though the concept of 'misleading' can and should be given a broad interpretation, there are still many types of unlawful marketing which are not connected with information in the way that it would seem possible to create a liability through using the contract law concept of non-conformity. A relatively streight-forward rule, like the described rule

---

[43] Staudenmayer, above note 25, 552.
[44] At pp. 13-14.
[45] Green paper, 13.

238

on liability for false and misleading marketing, within contract law liability for other forms of unlawful marketing is not easy to imagine. This does not mean, however, that there are no contract law remedies available in this case. Most certainly the requirement of good faith in the fairness test of the Unfair Contract Terms Directive[46] allows, and even obliges, the court also to take into account the marketing leading to the contract in assessing the fairness of its provisions. As the Directive states, 'all the circumstances attending the conclusion of the contract' should be taken into account in the assessment. However, even though this Directive creates a basis for reaching fair results in individual cases, its flexibility especially with regard to the issue of procedural fairness probably makes it very unsignificant as a mechanism to have a general impact on unlawful marketing. When speaking about contract law enforcement of provisions on marketing the best contract law can offer is the liability for non-conformity which I have discussed in this paper – and that is certainly not very much.

---

[46] Directive 93/13/EEC on unfair terms in consumer contracts.

10. Consumer Protection, Fair Dealing in Marketing Contracts and European Contract Law – A Uniform Law?

Luisa Antoniolli

I.   INTRODUCTION

Taking as a starting point the Green Paper on EU Consumer Protection, the aim of this paper is to set it in the wider context of the efforts currently going on at the European level in order to achieve greater uniformity in contract law. In fact, The Green Paper, issued by the Commission in October 2001,[1] must be analysed in a wider framework of documents and initiatives, both official and unofficial, in order to assess its relevance and possible future impact.

The purpose of this document, as in generally the case for Green Papers, is to launch an extensive public consultation on several issues related to consumer protection, the most important being whether differences in national regulations on fair commercial practices are such as to constitute significant barriers to the working of the internal market; secondly, should such barriers be proven, the question becomes which is the most desirable strategy to achieve greater harmonisation at the Community level as between the so-called specific approach, based on a number of legal instruments tackling specific problems, and the so-called mixed approach, i.e. a framework directive containing a general clause concerning the fairness/unfairness of commercial practices, coupled with several other specific legal instruments.

---

[1]   Commission of the European Communities, Green Paper *on European Union Consumer Protection*, 2 October 2001, COM (2001) 531 final: 'Green paper'

H. Collins (ed.) The Forthcoming EC Directive on Unfair and Commercial Practices, 241-294.
©2004. Kluwer Law International. Printed in the Netherlands.

II.   THE GREEN PAPER ON CONSUMER PROTECTION, THE INTERNAL MARKET AND COMPETITEVENESS

The Green Paper takes as a starting point the idea that the cross-border movement of goods and services is a necessary condition for consumer protection, since the competitive pressure at the Community level produces a more efficient and competitively priced supply of goods and services. The document terms this a 'virtuous circle,[2] which needs to be established through a suitable regulatory framework that stimulates cross-border trade both on the consumers and businesses side.

Although the existence of a link between a working market of goods and services and the possibility of consumers to take advantage of it cannot be seriously challenged, the choice of the Commission to base its analysis and proposals on the competitiveness of the internal market is highly significant, because it moves the issue of consumer protection from the forefront of the scene to a kind of beneficial side-effect.[3] In other words, it seems that competitiveness is the predominant and ultimate goal of intervention, whose establishment is capable also of producing positive results for consumers, mainly in terms of access to greater choice and better prices. This is in fact no novelty in itself: EC intervention in the field of consumer law is historically a result of the evolution of the policies concerning the internal market, and the close link existing between the working of the internal market and consumer protection is constantly repeated in every legal measure affecting consumers.[4] Still, this element must not be forgotten, because of its potential impact on future developments in EC consumer protection law. As it has been pointed out, the strategy of the Green Paper is to link the market to the 'confident consumer', who can act as a catalyst for competitiveness; yet, 'there must remain a doubt whether the measures required by the confident consumer are equal to the measures required by the protected consumer'.[5]

---

[2]   Green paper, 3.

[3]   Cf. H. Collins, 'EC Regulation of Unfair Commercial Practices', in this volume.

[4]   This characteristic has been defined as 'the Janus faced nature of EC consumer policy': G. Howells, 'European Consumer Law – The minimal and maximal harmonisation debate and pro Independent Consumer Law', in S. Grundmann, J.Stuyck (eds.), *An Academic* Green Paper *on European Contract Law*, (The Hague: Kluwer, 2002) 73, who observes that the internal market ideology can sustain both high or low level of consumer protection, which therefore cannot be defined *a priori*.

[5]   H. Collins, above note 3.

242

The rationale of EC consumer protection will be analysed later in this paper, but the existence of potential tensions and ambiguity must be borne in mind from the outset.

According to some, the main reason for the Commission's emphasis on competitiveness is not the need to find a suitable legal basis for action (which is certainly a relevant element), but rather the belief that this seems to be the best strategy in order to convince European citizens that they too, and not only businesses and professionals, have something to benefit from the strengthening of the internal market, by enhancing their living standards. Still, although there is clearly a need to convince consumers, and more generally citizens, that the European Community is taking care of their interests,[6] it is far from clear that this can be achieved merely by enhancing the economic performance of the market: "Unless the Commission is prepared to act as the champion of the consumer, it seems likely that some national legislators will insist upon keeping the higher standards of domestic law, so that EC regulation will have to remain a minimum standards form of harmonisation, with the consequence that regulatory diversity is preserved and this possible obstruction to cross-border trade left partially in place".[7]

Moreover, the Commission is rather transparent in emphasising that EC action is not targeted exclusively to the consumers, since businesses as well can profit from it, particularly small and medium enterprises: 'The internal market's main asset is that it has the largest pool of consumer demand in the world – and this asset is not being fully exploited. Enabling businesses, especially SMEs, to access this potential, as easily as domestic markets, would be a powerful stimulus to competitiveness'. [8]

III. DIFFERENCES IN NATIONAL LAWS AS AN OBSTACLE TO THE INTERNAL MARKET

The other basic tenet upon which the analysis of the Green Paper is based is that differences in national laws can hinder the cross-border trade between consumers and businesses and thereby the correct working of the internal

---

6   Green paper, 3-4: 'If it [the opportunity to develop the consumer internal market through the circulation of the Euro] is not taken, citizens will be left with the impression that the EU's core project – the internal market – is an irrelevance to their daily lives and simply a project designed to serve the interests of business'.

7   H. Collins, above note 3.

8   Green Paper, 9.

market. Consequently these barriers of national laws need somehow to be removed: 'Where cross-border restrictions to business-to-consumer trade exist, a greater degree of harmonisation of the rules that regulate business-consumer commercial practices is essential to the development of a fully functioning internal market'.[9] In fact, this issue has a rather ambiguous status, since it is simultaneously considered as a working hypothesis, and therefore considered as existing, and as a probable (but not certain) situation to be established through analysis and external information: the Commission takes for granted that a fragmented set of regulations and a fragmented system of enforcement hampers the working of the internal market, but at the same time the first question on which it invites comments from all stakeholders concerns what are the main barriers resulting from differences in national regulations.

The existence of significant differences among national laws in the field of fair commercial practices has been established, as has been demonstrated by three extensive expert studies undertaken on the request of the Commission.[10] Most Member States have a general principle regulating business to consumer commercial practices, although its content can vary significantly (*bonos mores*, fair commercial practices, good marketing practices, fair commercial practices, etc.). These general principles are further specified by specific legislation or pertinent case law. Although some common trends can be detected, the scope and application of national legislation varies widely in practice and, according to the Commission, this divergence 'can act as a barrier to trade and distort competition'.[11]

The Green Paper also underlines the fact that further divergence stems from EC law itself, since EC consumer protection law does not constitute

---

[9] Green Paper, 10. See also *Follow-up Communication to the* Green Paper, below note 23, 3: 'The central argument of the Green Paper was that the fragmentation of EU and national rules on consumer protection means that the internal market does not work properly for business to consumer transactions'.

[10] V.I.E.W., *Study on the feasibility of a general legislative framework on fair trading*, November 2000 (three volumes, comprising an analysis of national laws and a final proposal); Price Waterhouse Coopers, *Study on consumer law and the information society*; Lex Fori, *Study to identify best practice in the use of soft law and to analyse how this best practice can be made to work for consumers in the EU* ; the papaers are available at http://europa.eu.int/comm/consumers (the first is the document on which most of the proposals contained in the Green Paper are based, although with significant modifications).

[11] The Green Paper lists several issues where this happens, such as advertising, marketing practices (sales promotions etc.), pre-contractual, contractual and after sale relationships, self-regulation: pp. 2, 7.

a comprehensive regulatory framework, and moreover it generally allows Member States to keep stricter or more detailed measures. Paradoxically, therefore, existing EC law, although it harmonises some selected issues, at the same time produces a higher level of discrepancies between national laws.[12]

Moreover, EC consumer law suffers from several drawbacks, because Directives are often very detailed, and after some time prove to be inflexible and obsolescent, particularly in relation to an area such as marketing practices, which are constantly and rapidly evolving. At the same time, changing these Directives is cumbersome and time-consuming, and therefore traditional EU law-making instruments may be inefficient, if not flanked by other regulatory strategies.

IV. The Specific and the Mixed Approach

As a consequence of the existence of significant barriers to the working of the internal market deriving from legal divergence, the Commission proposes two alternative strategies: the first is to continue along the existing pattern, enacting a series of directives tackling specific problems (the so-called specific approach); the second, termed the 'mixed approach', consists of a system based on a comprehensive framework directive on commercial practices establishing a general clause (centred either on fair commercial practices or on misleading practices),[13] supplemented and completed by specific directives where needed. According to the Green Paper, the first strategy has the advantage of having a narrower focus, and therefore it should be easier to reach agreement among the Member States. Yet, it is clearly not the way preferred by the Commission: 'there are clearly some doubts as to the effectiveness of relying exclusively on this approach in delivering a genuine internal market'.[14]

---

[12] Green Paper, 5 and 7: 'The interaction between the EU consumer protection rules and the other measures cited has created a regulatory framework which is complicated and difficult to understand for business and consumers'.

[13] On the structure and content of the framework directive see H. Micklitz, 'A General Framework Directive on Fair Trading', (The author headed the team of scholars who produced the *Study on the feasibility of a general legislative framework on fair trading*, above note 10, which also contains an analysis of national laws on fair trading and the general standards emplyed: see vol. III). The general legislative framework would work as an 'umbrella' or "safety net", which would cover all issues that are not subject to special rules.

[14] Green Paper, 11; among the drawbacks cited in the document, the first is that minimum

The mixed approach would, on the other hand, have the considerable advantage that 'its comprehensive nature reduces the need for further detailed consumer protection regulation',[15] thereby achieving greater flexibility. Besides, the existence of a general legal framework would reduce (although not eliminate completely) the need for specific regulation concerning individual issues.

General clauses are a mechanism that is well known in all national systems, even though their use and scope varies significantly. They are particularly useful because their generality allows flexibility, i.e. adaptation in their application according to the changing circumstances of the legal environment to be regulated. At the same time, this characteristic constitutes an important limit: being general, their content cannot be established *ex ante*; therefore they leave great discretion to the interpreter, thereby creating a risk of divergent and idiosyncratic application, and impairing legal certainty.[16] The Commission is aware of this risk, but seems to be convinced that it can be avoided: 'To provide the required certainty and prevent differing legal interpretations by national courts, the framework directive would have to be more than simply a general principle regulating business-consumer commercial practices. It would address the main differences in national rules on commercial practices which affected the operation of the internal market, through establishing clear EU-wide rules through harmonisation'.[17] Still, this is exactly the problem: if *ex hypothesi* there are significant divergences among national laws, the question is to devise a general principle sufficiently specific to avoid divergent application, and at the same time sufficiently general not to generate the same problems produced by specific directives.

---

protection clauses contained in consumer protection directives produce divergences and therefore obstacles to trade; moreover, the more specific the directives are, the greater the effort needed in order to keep them up-to-date.

[15] Green Paper, 11.

[16] See Collins, above note 3, 'general clauses tell us nothing useful. (…) A general clause merely delegates the law-making power to the decision-maker, with no guarantee that the objective will be pursued'. But cf. J.B. Gloeckner, *Think Big! Some remarks on the European Commission's* Green Paper *on consumer protection against unfair trade practices and the proposal for a regulation concerning sales promotions in the internal market*, paper available on the Commission's Internet site, p. 14: 'If European law is to remain practicable in the future, if it is to keep its inherent legitimation, there is no other way left than to turn to comprehensive legislation relying heavily on general clauses. Only general clauses are adequate instruments for compensating for protection gaps, which are created automatically with each act of punctual, sector-specific harmonisation'.

[17] Green Paper, 11.

In other words, what is required is a sort of squaring of the circle, no easy task – even for EC institutions.

According to the Commission, this result could be achieved by devising a combined strategy, which complements the general standard of the framework directive with other mechanisms: the first is the already known method of specific directives; along with it, greater use should be made of EU-wide self-regulation (involving greater stakeholder participation),[18] and non-binding practical guidance, either through Commission Recommendations or an indicative list of general and sector-specific examples of commercial practices, which could be updated by a regulatory committee at the Community level ensuring transparency and consultation.[19]

A further problem that concerns the issue of consumer protection is the standard that should be employed as the core concept of the general clause. Theoretically, two alternatives are possible: the standard of 'fair commercial practices' (or 'good market behaviour') and that of 'misleading (or deceptive) practices', the second having a narrower focus. The Commission clearly favours the more general concept of fair commercial practices, although it recognises that it might be easier to reach agreement on the concept of misleading practices, which is a kind of 'common core of unfair trading concepts across the EU'.[20] Significantly, the Commission underlines that in

---

[18] According to the Commission, self-regulation could solve several problems that are not suited for regulatory action, but at the same time it recognises that at the moment "there is no means of ensuring effective EU-wide self-regulation in the field of consumer protection" (Green Paper, 14). A proposed solution is to promote a common European code of conduct to which business could voluntarily adhere; non compliance with its rules should be considered as a misleading or unfair trading practice, thereby guaranteeing effective enforcement. This proposal has provoked mixed reactions: according to some, particularly consumers' associations, strict enforcement mechanisms such as the ones envisaged in the Green Paper are required before self-regulation is granted a more relevant role in consumer protection issues. Others, among which several business and trade associations, observe that external enforcement of standard set through self-regulation would impinge on the self-regulatory character of the rules, and would therefore be in contrast with the idea of voluntary commitment: see. ICC (International Chamber of Commerce), *ICC Comments on the European Commission's* Green Paper *on EU Consumer Protection,* 3: 'Self-regulation is not linked to law and proceeds on a voluntary basis'.

[19] Green Paper, 15; the Commission cites the example of the unfair contract terms directive (dir. 93/13/EC, OJ L95, 21/4/93, p. 29), where an indicative list is annexed to the text of the directive; the main advantage of this mechanism is that it formally links the guidance to the legislative text.

[20] Green Paper, 13; the main drawback of the misleading practices approach is that it does

both approaches a central element would be the existence of general obligations on information disclosure, implying a duty to 'disclose all material information to consumers in a timely and clear manner'.[21] In order to avoid national discrepancies, the general clause would have to be complemented with general tests of fairness and specific rules on commercial practices, such as information disclosure, misleading and deceptive practices, marketing and commercial practices in the contractual and after-sale phases.

The last crucial issue of the Green Paper concerns enforcement mechanisms: the Commission recognises that 'any regulatory measures must be linked to adequate enforcement structures that ensure their consistent application', otherwise they run the risk of a remaining dead letter. Still, enforcement is currently mainly left to the Member State level, although some co-operation and co-ordination has developed.[22] This situation seems unsatisfactory, particularly in the perspective of the enactment of a wider EC regulatory framework. First of all, systematic information exchange through mutual assistance of national enforcement bodies is crucial, because 'extensive information exchange is the keystone of effective market surveillance'.[23] This requires a EU framework for co-operation between national authorities, where the EC Commission would act as a monitor through the use of systematic feedback information.[24] According to the Green Paper, this strategy

---

    not cover all commercial practices, and therefore would not eliminate completely national divergences.

[21] Green Paper, 14; a fair commercial practices standard could also ban practices such as deliberate information overload, excessive use of fine prints, deliberate omission of relevant information. See also H. Micklitz, above note 13, according to whom there should be a general information duty related to the general clause on fair trading based on the legitimate expectations of consumers (since a detailed listing would be too complex and possibily overloaded), relating to the contents of the contract, the communication means used, as well as health, safety and environmental aspects.

[22] See for example the injunctions directive (dir. 98/27 on injunctions for the protection of consumers' interests, OJ L166 of 11 June 1998, pp. 51-56), which empowers national consumer enforcement bodies and consumer associations to seek injunctions in other member States in order to protect consumer rights deriving from several EC directives.

[23] Green Paper, 17.

[24] The crucial role of effective enforcement is stressed also by the U.S. Federal Trade Commission, the powerful governmental agency whose task is (among various others) to protect consumers from unfair methods of competition and unfair practices: 'cross-border enforcement of consumer protection laws could be greatly imporved with European-level coordination. The European Commission can play a unique role in this regard' (FTC, *Staff Comments on EU* Green Paper, 8).

should be based both on regulatory and non-regulatory measures (such as exchange of best practices, information and education initiatives),[25] and should be based not only on *ex post* control (such as the one performed by courts), but on preventive control as well.

V.   THE FOLLOW-UP COMMUNICATION TO THE GREEN PAPER

The Green Paper has launched an extensive debate among stakeholders, and in June 2002 the Commission has published a Follow-up communication,[26] in which the Commission recognises that not all the proposals of the Green Paper are supported by all respondents, but nevertheless underlines the fact that broad support exists on a number of crucial issues, among which is approval for the proposal for a framework directive, and therefore that further action is required.[27]

Of those who support reform through a framework directive,[28] most agree

---

[25] Among the possible mechanisms to be used, the Green Paper, at 19, proposes: the nomination of competent national authorities co-ordinating enforcement and acting as a single contact point; reciprocal mutual assistance rights and obligations among the States involving information exchange and investigation powers; monitoring and evaluation of enforcement at the national level by the Commission; information and communication networks; joint enforcement actions among States; co-operation with third countries and international organisations (such as the IMSN, International Marketing Supervision Network, which has a EU sub-group); establishment of a committee comprising the Commission and the member States with the task of implementing co-operation, although with no legislative powers.

[26] *Communication from the Commission – Follow-up Communication to the* Green Paper *on EU Consumer Protection*, 11 June 2002, COM (2002) 289 final: '*Follow-up Communication*'. The Green Paper has received 169 responses, mainly from business and consumer organisations, with an uneven geographical distribution (but all Member States have responded), which can ben consulted at http://europa.eu.int/comm/consumers/ policy/developments/fair_comm_pract/responses/responses_en.html. See also *Follow-up Communication*, 4 and ff., and Annex II. Moreover, a public hearing on the Green Paper was held on December 7, 2001 in Brussels (http://europa.eu.int/comm/consumers/policy/ developments/fair_comm_pract/hearing_greenpap_en.html).

[27] 'The response to the consultation is more than sufficiently clear to justify further steps towards reform': *Follow-up Communication,* 7. The need for action is demonstrated also by an express request by the Council to work on a follow-up to the Green Paper as a priority. The Commission recognises that there is a need to continue developing research work through surveys, as well as developing impact assessment and list of relevant obstacles to cross-border trade for every legislative proposal.

[28] One member State opposes any reform, and two more States only support reform of existing directives. Several business associations argue that the analysis according to which differ-

that the most suitable standard would be that of fair commercial practices. The main elements of such a directive (on which the Commission intends to have further consultation) should be: maximum harmonisation with a high level consumer protection; simplification and deregulation of existing provisions; application of the principle of mutual recognition and control by the country of origin; balance between legal certainty and adaptability to market circumstances; a general clause based on the standard of fair commercial practices comprising two core elements (unfairness of the practice and consumer detriment test) and supplemented by specific rules;[29] and focus on unfair practices that cause detriment to the interests of consumers as a whole.[30]

These elements should be debated within an expert group established and chaired by the Commission, comprising experts nominated by national governments that should exchange views and identify, through the comparison of common and divergent concepts and rules, the level and content of any harmonising measure.[31] Moreover, the Commission is also planning to set up an academic group that should work on a comprehensive comparative law study dealing with the notion of fairness, in order to distinguish common features and elements that are specific to one or more national legal systems.

The Commission repeatedly underlines the fact that any regulatory measure concerning fair commercial practices would not deal with contract law and contractual remedies,[32] since these issues should be dealt with in the Follow-up to the Communication on European contract law, which is due before the end of 2002. Even though the choice to keep contractual aspects

---

ences in national laws create barriers to trade, is unproven and therefore further evidence is required. Most consumer organisations agree that there is a need for reform through a mixed approach.

[29] *Follow-up Communication,* 9, and annex I. According to the 'consumer detriment test', a practice would be considered unfair if it causes or is likely to cause direct detriment to the consumer, determined on the standard of an 'average consumer'. Specific rules giving content to the general clause should cover all stages of the consumer/business relationship, such as misleading practices, failure to provide all material information (duty to disclose) prior to the purchase, use of force, harassment, coercion and undue influence, failure to provide after-sale assistance and complaint handling.

[30] *Follow-up Communication,* 8-9, annex I.

[31] *Follow-up Communication* 13-14. Consumer and business associations, together with other interested stakeholders, will be invited to present their position to the expert group, which will meet on a regular basis and prepare working papers and documents.

[32] *Follow-up Communication* 10, 14 and 15. Other aspects that would be left outside this area of intervention relate to health and safety.

250

together with the general issues of contract law seems reasonable, it would have been useful if the Commission could have provided some clues on how it intends to relate consumer contract problems to general contract law, since this seems to be a very controversial and yet crucial issue, particularly because a significant portion of existing EC contract law relates to consumer protection.[33]

The Follow-up Communication sticks to the idea that codes of conduct voluntary entered by business could be a very helpful complement to the framework directive, and that in order to protect legitimate expectations of consumers, non-compliance with the rules of the code would be considered unfair under the framework directive.[34]

A further issue where the Commission deems that further elaboration is required is stakeholder participation, an element which is of great importance to ensure proper commercial practices, but for which adequate mechanisms are lacking. According to the Commission, the framework directive should set general criteria for the selection of the relevant stakeholders, in order to ensure fair representation. Finally, further consultation is required also for defining the best mechanisms for producing non-binding guidance: this is surely needed in order to supply a point of reference for businesses, consumers and judicial and enforcement authorities, and to ensure legal certainty and coherent application of the general standard, but there is not sufficient agreement on whether this can be better achieved through Recommendations

---

[33] As a mere example, one could mention the issue of the duty of disclosure: this is expressly defined as a founding element of the general clause of fair commercial practices, but at the same time it is surely one of the cornerstones of general contract law (also related to general clauses such as good faith), which consequently need somehow to be co-ordinated.

[34] The Commission, after having noted their usefulness, nevertheless warns that "Codes of conduct are not a panacea: . The can be abused either to mislead consumers or for anti-competitive reasons. Codes do not have the same legal status as legislation. The ultimate fallback of sectoral legislation will always remain": *Follow-up Communication* 11. Another possibility would be to use the regulatory technique of "safe harbours", i.e. of rendering immune from legal challenge traders' behaviour that comply with approved codes of conduct. This mechanism has been used in some legal systems, such as the United Kingdom. According to this document, a "code owner", defined as the body responsible for the development of the code (business or business association) should be responsible for ensuring conformity of the rules of the code with the framework directive, but not for compliance of members with the code. The Commission is aware that endorsement of codes by public authorities might give rise to problems of compatibility with competition rules, and therefore proposes further consultation on this point.

issued by the Commission or through guidelines established by a regulatory committee.[35]

The Follow-up Communication stresses that the largest support from all stakeholders involved was given to the proposal concerning the creation of mechanisms for enforcement co-operation (judicial, administrative and informal), to the extent that the Commission intends to adopt a proposal on this matter by the end of 2002.[36]

An issue, which is only briefly sketched, but is nevertheless extremely important, concerns the role of mutual recognition and the principle of country of origin. According to the Commission 'The combination of an adequate level of harmonisation and the principles of mutual recognition and country of origin (which should be enshrined in the framework directive) will have as a consequence that divergent interpretations in jurisprudence at national level will not result in the fragmentation of the internal market'.[37] This point is related to the question of selecting the proper level of harmonisation between minimum and maximum, a problem that has been often debated.[38] Recent documents of the Commission seem to point to a strategic shift from minimum harmonisation, which is a widespread feature of existing EC consumer law, to maximum harmonisation, which seems to be a preferable alternative, because it avoids problems of divergence in national transposing rules.[39] Yet, as we will see, the shift from minimum to maximum harmonisation is not merely a technical choice, but on the contrary has crucial policy implica-

---

[35] *Follow-up Communication* 6, 11-12,

[36] *Follow-up Communication* 3. The document sets a date for further reactions to the proposals at the end of September 2002.

[37] *Follow-up Communication* 8 and 19.

[38] According to Micklitz, above note 13, 'Both concepts [harmonisation and mutual recognition], however, trust in mandatory regulation alone. They do not consider the combination of mandatory and voluntary regulation, which might be of particular importance in the field of marketing practices. This is likewise true for the idea to combine harmonisation and the country of origin principle, which has remained in academic writing so far.'. He consequently argues in favour of a new approach on technical standards and regulations in marketing practices regulation, combining mandatory legislation with new forms of self-regulation, involving business and consumer associations as well as national enforcement authorities (in fact a new hybrid between self- and co-regulation, since it contains binding standards.

[39] A similar trend can be detected in the debate about the possibility of shifting from directives to regulations as a standard regulatory technique in the field of private law: W. van Gerven, 'Codifying European Private Law: Top Down and Bottom Up', in Grundmann and Stuyck, above note 4, 405.

252

tions, which can be rather controversial. The Commission itself seems to acknowledge this problem when it affirms 'it is not politically realistic to expect Member States to abandon the minimum clauses in existing consumer protection directives without addressing these underlying differences [i.e. differences of approach to consumer protection in Member States]'.[40]

VI.   THE CONSUMER POLICY STRATEGY 2002-2006

The Commission has issued another important document in the field of consumer protection in May 2002, containing the Consumer Policy Strategy for the years 2002-2006.[41] The Commission, noting that 'EU Consumer Policy is at a critical juncture', and that 'consumers should reap tangible benefits from the single market',[42] sets three mid-term objectives: a high common level of consumer protection, which requires 'the establishment of common consumer protection rules and practices across Europe';[43] effective enforcement of consumer rights, guaranteed through better co-ordination of public national authorities;[44] greater involvement of consumer organisations in EU policies through consultation requirements, participation in consultation bodies and working groups, and information and education initiatives. Once again, the aim of consumer protection in the EC is linked to the internal market: 'The development of consumer policy at EU level has been the essential corollary of the progressive establishment of the internal market',[45] and 'Barriers to

---

[40]   *Follow-up Communication* 10. The statement relates to the prospects of reform of existing EC consumer protection law, but the argument applies equally to future regulatory action.

[41]   *Communication from the Commission to the European Parliament, the Council, the Economic and Social Committee and the Committee of the Regions – Consumer Policy Strategy 2002-2006,* 7 May 2002, COM(2002)208final, OJ C137/2, 8 June 2002.

[42]   *Ibid* 24.

[43]   *Ibid* 11.

[44]   This is in line with the priority given to effective enforcement through co-operation of national authorities (together with the strengthening of ADR mechanisms) in the Green Paper *on Consumer Protection.*

[45]   *Consumer Policy Strategy,* above note 41, 6; emphasis is given to the protection of consumer interests through rules ensuring an autonomous and informed choice, but it is recognised that "in some situations, providing a basis for informed choice and legal redress has been regarded as insufficient, notably as regards protection of physical health and safety. In such situations, harmonised rules are considered necessary to guarantee an adequate level of protection to all consumers quite independently of their ability to protect themselves by making informed choices. The decision to adopt such a measure depends to a large extent

cross-border trade should therefore be overcome in order that the consumer dimension of the internal market can develop in parallel with its business dimension'[46] Again, a source of obstacles to cross-border trade is found in the different consumer protection rules that apply in the Member States, which hampers both consumers and businesses, creating uncertainty and increasing costs.[47] For consumers what is required is harmonisation (besides safety issues) of 'those aspects of consumer economic interests that give consumers the confidence necessary to conduct transactions anywhere in the internal market'.[48] According to the Commission, 'It could mean setting in place a common set of simple and clear EU rules and safety requirements, on commercial practices and on consumer contractual rights. It could also mean filling gaps between existing EU rules, which will require reform of existing directives'.[49] To this end the document recalls the Green Paper on Consumer Protection, and its strategy to reform existing EU consumer protection directives by adapting them from minimum to full harmonisation, since a sufficient degree of harmonisation would be needed before the principle of mutual recognition could be applied for the remaining questions.[50]

---

on a political assessment of the importance of the interest to be protected and the feasibility of consumers being able to protect themselves by informed choices in practice.'

[46] *Ibid* 7.

[47] *Ibid* 9: "This implies simpler and more common rules, a similar level of enforcement across the EU, more accessible consumer information and education and effective redress mechanisms". The *Strategy* also underlines the fact that legal heterogeneity will significantly increase after enlargement, not only because of the sheer increase in the number of States involved, but even more because of the significant differences in the characters of the new legal systems.

[48] *Ibid* 11.

[49] *Ibid* 11-12; nevertheless, this "does not mean regulating all consumer protection in detail at European level. That would be neither desirable nor practical". According to the Strategy, business and consumer responsibility should be increased through a combined use of alternative forms of regulation, such as self-regulation, co-regulation and standardisation.

[50] The document also refers to the *Communication on European Contract Law*, and emphasises the mix of regulatory and non-regulatory measures (such as the elaboration of common principles and terminology) proposed in the various options. According to the Commission the working programme ensuing from the consultation process should comprise a review of existing consumer contract law 'in order to remove existing inconsistencies, to fill gaps and to simplify' (such as e.g. the harmonisation of the cooling-off periods of several directives): p. 13.

VII. THE COMMUNICATION ON EUROPEAN CONTRACT LAW

The documents related to consumer protection must be evaluated in the light of another important document issued by the Commission in July 2001, the Communication on European Contract Law,[51] which has started a wide debate among all legal actors involved in European law, – institutions, businesses, practitioners and academics. This fundamental document shares with the Green Paper the basic premise: further harmonisation is required at the European level because divergent national laws create significant obstacles to the working of the internal market. Of course, there are significant differences between the two documents, the main one being that the Communication deals with the whole of contract law (which is, moreover, understood in an extremely wide sense), rather than with a special area such as consumer protection in the field of commercial practices; this larger focus, as we will see, raises a much larger and complex number of issues (such as legislative competence).

The context in which the Communication has been drafted[52] is characterised by a renewed interest by EC institutions for a large scale harmonising intervention in the area of private law, after the debate started by two Resolutions of the European Parliament in the late 1980s and beginning of the 1990s had remained almost dead letter.[53] This change is remarkable, because it does not just come from the European Parliament (which has reaffirmed its position in a Resolution of 2000 concerning the working programme of the Commission for the year 2000[54]), but also from the European Council,

---

[51] *Communication of the Commission to the Council and European Parliament on European Contract Law*, 11 July 2001, COM(2001) fin, in OJ C 255, 13 September 2001, p. 1.

[52] See D. Staudenmayer, 'The Commission Communication on European Contract Law: What Future for European Contract Law?' (2002) *Eur. Rev. Priv. Law* 249 (published also as 'Die Mitteilung der Kommission zum Europaeischen Vertragsrecht' i(2001) *EuZW* 485). The author, who chaired the Commission which prepared the Communication, states that 'Whatever the results of the debate and whatever the approaches selected, it is obvious that the present Commission Communication is a major step in the development of European private law' (p. 260). See also Editorial Comments, 'On the way to a European Civil Code?' (2002) *Comm. Market L. Rev.* 219.

[53] See European Parliament Resolution A2-157/89, in OJ C 158 of 26 June 1989, p. 400 and Resolution A3-0329/94 in OJ C 205 of 25 July 1994, p. 504. Both resolutions called for intervention by the EC institutions in order to achieve greater harmonisation in the field of private law, albeit in a rather general and vague manner.

[54] European Parliament Resolution B5-0228,0229-0230/2000, No. 28, in OJ C377 of 29 De-

an institution which, as it represents the sum of the individual interests of the Member States, has been traditionally reluctant to endorse a policy of systematic regulatory intervention at the Community level, but preferring rather to intervene on specific problems that require common solutions. In the conclusions of the important meeting of Tampere in October 1999,[55] the European Council has mandated a global study concerning the necessity to harmonise national legislation of Member States in the field of private law; the emphasis is laid especially on civil procedure,[56] but substantive law is considered as well.

The Communication also mentions important developments which have taken place in the academic world, where several common projects have been set up in the field of contract law and have produced scientific results that in various ways can serve as a basis for harmonisation at the European level.[57] Of the many projects currently going on, the Commission mentions the so-called "Pavia Group" (the Academy of European Private Lawyers), a team of scholars led by Prof. Gandolfi of the University of Pavia, which published in 2001 a Preliminary draft for a European Contract Code;[58] the

---

cember 2000. The Directorate-General for Research of the European Parliament has also commissioned a broad expert comparative study, published under the title (defined by Von Bar as "heterogeneous sounding and in any case breathtaking") *The private law systems in the EU: discrimination on grounds of nationality and the need for a European Civil Code* (von Bar (ed.), Barendrecht, Basedow, Drobnig, van Gerven, Hondius, Kerameus, Koussoulis, Lando, Tilmann), Working Paper, Legal Affairs Series, JURI 103 EN (Brussels, 1999).

[55] Conclusions of the Presidency of the European Council of Tampere, 15 and 16 October 1999. SI (1999) 800. para. 39.

[56] On the evolution of a European civil procedure see G. Tarzia, *Nozioni comuni per un processo civile europeo*, paper presented at the conference on the European Civil Code in Rome, 12 July 2002; G. Tarzia, 'L'ordine europeo del processo civile' (2001) *Riv. dir. civ.* 902.

[57] The literature on European contract law is constantly growing; among the many: H. Koetz, A. Flessner, *European Contract Law* (English translation by T. Weir), (Oxford: Clarendon, 1997); Weyers (ed.), *Europaeisches Vertragsrecht*, (Baden-Baden: Nomos, 1997); C. Quigley, *European Community Contract Law*, (Kluwer, 1997); S. Grundmann, 'The Structure of European Contract Law' (2001) *Eur. Rev. Priv. L.* 505 ff.; S. Grundmann *Europaeisches Schuldvertragsrecht – das Europaeische Recht der Unternehmengeschaefte*, (Berlin: de Gruyter, 1999); A. Tizzano (cur.), *Il diritto privato della Comunità europea*, (Torino: Giappichelli, 2000); A. Hartkamp et al (eds.), *Towards a European Civil Code*, 2 rev. ed., (The Hague, Kluwer, 1998), ch. 12-24; H. Beale et al. (gen. eds.), *Contract Law, Casebooks on the Common Law of Europe*, (Oxford: Hart 2002).

[58] G. Gandolfi (gen. ed.), *Code européen des contrats – Avant-projet, Livre I*, Milano, 2001;

so-called Lando Commission (the Commission for European Contract Law), a commission composed of scholars and practitioners, who have worked for almost two decades, and who published in 1995 (part I) and 2000 (parts I and II) the Principles of European Contract Law,[59] a body of rules which cover issues such as formation, validity, construction and contents of contracts, agency, performance, non-performance, remedies; the Study Group for a European Civil Code, a large group of academics, led by professors Von Bar and Lando, who are working on an all-encompassing project concerning European private law,[60] which should produce in the future a number of Restatements covering the whole of European private patrimonial law that could serve as a basis for codification (which, nevertheless, is only a secondary and possible target). Several other projects not mentioned in the Communication are currently going on, such as the Trento project on the Common Core of European Private Law,[61] chaired by professors Mattei and

---

see also G. Gandolfi, *Communication from the Commission on European Contract Law (Harmonisation, Code, Optional Code) – Mitteilung szum Europaeischen Vertragsrecht*, in Grundmann and Stuyck , above note 4, 193.

[59] O. Lando, H. Beale (eds*.), Principles of European Contract Law – Part I: Performance, Non-performance and Remedies*, (Dordrecht, Nijhoff, 1995); O. Lando, H. Beale (eds*.), Principles of European Contract Law – Part I and II*, (The Hague, Kluwer, 2000). The third and final volume of the Principles deals with conditions, illegality, plurality of debtors and creditors, assignment, substitution of debtors and creditors, set-off, prescription; the results should be published within a short time. An Italian edition (C. Castronovo (ed.), *Principi di diritto europeo dei contratti*, Milano, 2001) and a German edition (C. von Bar, R. Zimmermann (eds.), *Grundregeln des Europaeischen Vertragsrecht, Teile I und II, Kommission fuer Europaeisches Vertragsrecht*, Muenchen, 2002) have been published.

[60] The group was constituted in 1998; work is divided among several teams that are based in different Member States, and there is also a co-ordinating group; currently the areas under investigation cover sales, service contracts, long-term contracts, securities, non contractual obligations, transfer of property of movables, negotiorum gestio, and in the future possibly also land law and registration systems. See C. von Bar, *From Principles to Codification: Prospects for European Private Law*, paper presented at the conference held in Rome in July 2002, pp. 11-13.

[61] M. Bussani, U. Mattei, 'The Common Core Approach to European Private Law' (1997/8) 3 *Col. J. Eur.* L. 339; U. Mattei, M. Bussani (eds.), *Making European Law – Essays on the "Common core" Project*, (Trento, Dipartimento di Scienze giuridiche, 2000); M. Bussani, U. Mattei (eds.), *The Common Core of European Private Law – Essays on the Project*, (Kluwer, forthcoming 2003). The project is described as aiming at producing 'a reliable geographical "map" of the law of Europe. This task is conceived as part of building a common European legal culture, in which cultural diversity is an asset but not a dogma, and of creating a suitable basis for a discussion about unification of the law. Although the project seeks to analyse the present situation without trying in any way to force uniform

Bussani, and the Casebooks for the Common Law of Europe, led by professor Van Gerven,[62] which form a very lively basis for the study and elaboration of European private law.[63]

All these elements compose a new scenario, where prospects for future action on a large scale seem definitely more plausible (if not probable) than in the past, although at this stage it is impossible to tell how long it will take, and what the final outcome will be.[64]

As in the Green Paper, there is an ambiguity in the Commission's position on general contract law, since the existence of obstacles to the internal market due to differences in national law is at the same time the underlying leitmotiv of the document and an issue to be proven through evidence assembled by the Commission and through the information provided by stakeholders.[65]

According to the Commission, the scope of analysis and possible intervention comprises sales and service contracts, performance, non performance, remedies, formation, validity and construction of contracts; other elements outside contract law that might come under consideration, because they are strictly connected, include guarantees on movables and unjust enrichment, as well as some aspects of tort law related to contracts.[66]

---

solutions, it is not hostile towards codification (...)': A. Hartkamp, 'Perspectives for the Develoment of a European Civil Code', in Mattei and Bussani, above note 61, 57; for a critical evaluation see M. Shapiro, *The Common Core: Some Outside Comments*, in *ibid*, 123. See also J.R. Gordley, *Mapping Private Law*, in *ibid*, 27; H. Koetz, *The Trento Project and its Contribution to the Europeanization of Private Law*, in *ibid.*, 115.

62 W. Van Gerven, J. Lever, P. Larouche, *Cases, Materials and Text on National, Supranational and International Tort Law* (Oxford: Hart, 2000); H. Beale, et al, above note 57; another volume deals with unjust enrichment (E. Schrage, J. Beatson eds.).

63 See Hartkamp, above note 61, 39. G. Alpa, N. Buccico (eds.), *Il codice civile europeo. Materiali dei seminari 1999-2000*, (Milano, Giuffrè, 2001); G. Alpa, N. Buccico (eds.), *La riforma dei codici in Europa e il progetto di Codice civile europeo. Materiali dei seminari 2001*, (Milano, Giuffrè, 2002).

64 von Bar, above note 60, 14-15: "No one today can foresee how things will develop if Europe will have progressed so far. (...) We can wait for all of that serenely. "We must walk before we can run"". See also van Gerven, above note 39, 'All this, codification in two stages (...) will take much time and, in order to succeed, must be done with moderation and without obstination. *Festina lente* should be the device. Just like Rome was not built in one day, it will take time and patience for a common law of Europe to emerge'.

65 In the *Communication of the Commission on European Contract Law,* above note 51, 2, the Commission seems to take as proven only the existence of obstacles to the internal market (mainly in the form of greater costs discouraging trade), and seems to be seeking information on whether these can be due to divergences in national contract laws.

66 *Ibid,* 6-7. The Commission explicitly leaves out aspects related to labour law and family law.

In the first part, the Communication focuses the analysis on existing contract law in the international environment:[67] besides the *acquis commmunautaire*, the most important international legal instruments are the Rome Convention on the law applicable to contractual obligations of 1980,[68] and the UN Convention on international sales of goods (CISG) of 1980.[69]

As for EC law in the field of contract law, the Commission observes that, in spite of the increasing number of legal instruments that have a bearing on contract law, their scope remains limited and fragmented, and therefore it is necessary to assess whether there is a need to shift to a new kind of regulatory technique, focused on intervention of a more general and systematic character,[70] since 'the case-by-case approach might not be able to solve all problems'.[71]

The policy of the Commission is made clear when it focuses on the consequences for the internal market of this plurality of legal sources: 'The Commission is seeking information as to whether problems result from diver-

---

[67] *Ibid,* Annex II, containing a list of international conventions and other international documents elaborated by the UN, Unidroit, the Council of Europe.

[68] OJ C 27 of 26/1/1998, p. 34. Although the Convention is an instrument of international law, it belongs to the framework of the European Community, being signed and in force in all member States. The main principle of the convention, which harmonises rules of private international law related to contracts, is that parties are free to chose the law applicable to their contracts; exceptions are foreseen for contracts where one of the parties is considered to be structurally weaker, as in consumer and labour contracts.

[69] The Convention, which goes beyond the European context, has been ratified by all Community member States except the United Kingdom, Ireland and Portugal. It contains default rules, i.e. rules that apply unless the parties decide otherwise; contracts concluded for personal purposes (i.e., according to EC concepts, consumer contracts) are outside the scope of the convention. The rules cover the formation of contracts and the obligations of the parties, but not the validity of the contracts and the passing of title on the goods, which are left to national laws.

[70] *Communication of the Commission on European Contract Law,* above note 51, 8. Annex I contains a list of the *acquis communitaire* relevant for private law, comprising a list of directives based on what seems to be rather casual (and possibly confused) criteria: see N. Reich, *Some Critical comments on the Commission Communication of 11 July 2001, Com(2001)398 final "On European Contract Law"*, in Grundmann and Stuyck, above note 4, 283. Annex III, on the other hand, is a reasoned analysis of the *acquis*, structured on the impact on offer and acceptance, form, discharge, pre-contractual and contractual obligations of the parties (information duties and warranties), performance, non-performance and legal remedies (rescission, termination, damages), tort rules related to contracts (product liability and protection of privacy).

[71] *Communication of the Commission on European Contract Law,* above note 51, 2.

gences of contract law between Member States and if so, what. In particular, the Communication asks whether the proper functioning of the Internal Market maybe hindered by problems in relation to the conclusion, interpretation and application of cross-border contracts. Also the Commission is interested in whether different national contract laws discourage or increase the costs of cross-border transactions'.[72] This way of posing the problem of European contract law is mainly due to the compelling need for the Commission to find a suitable legal basis for legislative action, which is necessarily linked to the most important and general policy of the EC, the internal market.[73] Yet, although the link is clear and understandable, it is far less clear how this relates to crucial limits to EC legislative competence, such as subsidiarity and enumerated powers.[74]

The Communication lists several of these obstacles, such as mandatory rules, which differ in every national legal system (e.g. those on *ordre public*), and standard contracts, which are subject to different rules, and many others. Ignorance of foreign legal rules can render parties reluctant to conclude trans-border contracts, particularly small enterprises (SME) and consumers, and in any case, the need to gather the necessary information increases transaction and litigation costs (such as costs related to the need to get legal advice).

Another issue analysed by the Commission concerns the fact that even where contract rules are harmonised through EC legislation, there is a risk of uneven and contrasting transposition and application in national legal systems, which multiplies the obstacles. This problem is particularly acute in the

---

[72] According to the Commission, two elements that will have a strong stimulating effects on the working of the internal market are the introduction of Euro as a single currency, and the possibility offered by Internet to trade across the borders. Still, it must be remembered that not all member States have opted in the Euro, and that today the use of Internet for concluding contracts is still very limited.

[73] See H. Collins, 'Transaction Costs and Subsidiarity in European Contract Law', in Grundmann and Stuyck, above note 4, 269. C. von Bar, above note 60, 'The Commission's Communication is also quite plainly directed towards the economic requirements of the common market; the symbolic force of a uniform European private law does not come in for a mention'.

[74] The *Communication*, above note 51, 2-13 refers to the fact that the EC has limited powers, and that its intervention must respect fundamental principles of competences, such as subsidiarity and proportionality, but does not point to any overwhelming difficulty in reconciling those principle with the possible strategies of intervention in the field of contract law. See S. Weatherill, 'The European Commission's Green Paper on European Contract Law: Context, Content and Constitutionality' (2001) *J. Cons. Policy* 339 ff.

field of contract law, where there is a multiplicity of (sometimes overlapping) instruments dealing with very specific legal problems.[75] Moreover, the use of legal terms that have often different meanings in various legal systems, which in turn lead to different legal consequences and application, adds to the difficulty of ensuring a homogeneous application of Community law.[76]

1. The Options for Intervention

The Commission envisages four possible strategies of intervention, in order to tackle problems of legal divergence that hinder the common market: the so-called market option, i.e. leaving the possibility of finding solutions to the initiative of private stakeholders; promoting the development of non-binding common principles of contract law that could assist legal actors, both private and public, in finding common solutions; revising existing EC law in order to guarantee greater coherence and systematicity; adopting a common Community instrument concerning the law of contract.[77] The options are of a

---

[75] *Communication of the Commission on European Contract Law,* above note 51, 10-11. The Commission mentions the fact that the intervention of the European Court of justice, which must ensure consisting interpretation and application of EC rules, is not enough to dispel this risk.

[76] *Ibid,* 11, which gives as an example the problem of finding a common definition of "damage" (see footnote 18 and the recent case decided by the ECJ in *Leitner v TUI Deutschland GmbH,* C-168/00). The Communication refers to the use of "abstract terms", which is rather misleading, because the problem is not that terms are not sufficiently specific; rather, it derives from the fact that legal terms do not refer to objects physically existing in the world, but they are intellectual concepts created in order to sort and regulate social phenomena. Therefore, the solution to the problem does not lie in finding "concrete" concepts, but rather in developing a common legal terminology and therefore a common legal culture throughout Europe.

[77] The fourth option is generally termed the "Code option", since the idea of a comprehensive binding legal instrument comes close to the idea of codification; yet, the Commission is very careful in avoiding to use the terms "code" and "codification", probably because they are heavily loaded with policy implications that could prove controversial. See Collins, above note 73, 'The great European Codes were ostensibly introduced not just to reduce transaction costs, but rather as a political statement of the values of a liberal society and as a technique or affirmation of nation-building. (...) Personally I regret the absence of any broader political discussion. I see a parallel between the introduction of a single currency and a single contract law. They have equal symbolic political significance in my mind, representing the transition from nation states towards a transnational political and economic order'.

very heterogeneous character, ranging from no intervention at all,[78] to a mere restructuring of existing EC law, to an intervention of a general and systematic character, either binding or not. The Commission itself deems that the list is not exhaustive, and that the various options could be combined in different ways. Clearly, the consequences of adopting one or the other strategy are extremely different. Although this paper will not delve in detail into such an analysis, some of the fundamental issues need to be discussed in order to develop our reasoning concerning the relationship between the Commission strategy in the fields of contract law and consumer protection.

Option I, concerning the possibility of developing new rules merely through the intervention of market forces, is a strategy that the Commission is probably not proposing as autonomous, but rather as a complement to other regulatory activities at the EC level. The underlying idea is that since the internal market is a free market steered by competition among economic actors, these can autonomously develop rules that suit their needs: 'As a result of competitive behaviour, many of the problems created by the market may be solved automatically by the pressure exercised by interest groups involved (consumers, NGOs, enterprises). Public authorities can enhance this coincidence of self-interest and the public interest'.[79] This hypothesis, coming close to the well-known idea of the 'invisible hand of the market', and to its modern legal off-shoot, which favours the use of soft law as a kind of panacea, does not seem entirely convincing, because, leaving aside all policy considerations (which are ultimately based on subjective value considerations), it runs against the basic strategy that the European Community has actively pursued from the '60s onwards: that of intervening actively in the market with regulatory strategies.[80] This possible return to *laissez-faire* strategies has provoked opposite reactions, ranging from enthusiastic approval to complete rejection. It can be generally said, though, that lawyers do not favour it as an independent option; what varies among them is the degree of importance and

---

[78] This in fact can hardly said to be an option, since it presupposes activities that are outside EC control. It could be an option only if it would imply not only a passive reaction to change, but positively a strategy of removing existing EC law, a strategy which today seems hardly feasible.

[79] *Communication of the Commission on European Contract Law*, above note 51, 13-14.

[80] The fact that EC intervention has sometimes deregulated the market, by banning national rules and practices that hindered trade, does not change the fact that it was a regulatory intervention: the crucial issue was that the elaboration of rules was not in the hand of the market itself.

autonomy that is left to soft law as opposed to binding law.[81]

Option II concerns the elaboration of common principles of contract law that would foster legal convergence among national legal systems. Actually, the Communication uses the term 'promotion', which means not only that the principles would not be binding, but also that they should not be elaborated directly by the Commission; rather, it should have a co-ordinating and invigorating role. In fact, the document refers to initiatives aimed at promoting legal research among academics and practitioners,[82] which should produce a body of principles that could be useful for a series of different purposes: they could be used by parties when drafting contracts (particularly standard contracts); by judges and arbitrators when deciding trans-border litigation; by national legislators when drafting new legal rules or amending existing ones. The main feature of this strategy seems to be the non-binding character of the principles: their use would depend ultimately on their substantive quality, which should convince legal actors that their application would lead to better results as compared with national rules (which is also linked to an effective spread of knowledge of them, which requires careful education and information initiatives). From this perspective, this option is closely related to several academic and private initiatives that are currently going on at the European and international level, such as the Principles of European contract law and the Unidroit principles on international contracts,[83] and would point to the possibility of building up synergetic activities between the EC institutions and other legal actors on the European scene.[84]

Option III concerns the qualitative improvement of existing EC legislation

---

[81] For a strong critique of the increasing role of laissez- faire conception in EC law see U. Mattei, 'Hard Code Now! A Critique of "Softness" and a Plea for Responsibility in the European debate over Codification', in Grundmann and Stuyck, above note 4, 215. A. Somma, 'Tutte le strade portano a Fiume. L'involuzione liberista del diritto comunitario' (2002) *Riv. crit. dir. priv.* 263.

[82] *Communication of the Commission on European Contract Law,* above note 51, 14-15.

[83] Unidroit, *Principles of International Commercial Contracts*, Unidroit, Rome, 1994; see J. Bonell, *An International Restatement of Contract Law: the Unidroit Principles of International Commercial Contracts*, 2 enl. edn., (Irvington (N.Y.): Transnational Publishers, 1997).

[84] Although the strategy of keeping the common principles as non-binding law refers back to the idea of soft law, this is a very different choice than the so-called "market option", because the elaboration of the content of the principles would not be left to the market as such. On the influence exercised by legal academics on the elaboration of European soft law and the impact of their interests as a class see U. Mattei, above note 81; M.W. Hesselink, 'The

in the field of contract law. This seems to be the least controversial option, since there is today widespread agreement among both institutional and private stakeholders that the existing legal framework needs to be simplified, updated and rendered more coherent and workable: the limits and defects of a fragmentary and case-by-case approach have become a veritable leitmotiv in the debate on EC law, not only in academic circles, and do not require any lengthy discussion to be accepted.[85] In fact, several commentators think that option III is no real option,[86] as they consider that there is already a determined will to take such action, even though its character is not yet completely defined.[87]

Option IV is the real challenge to the existing *status quo*: adopting what is termed 'new and exhaustive legislation' concerning general contract law and specific contracts at the Community level. The Commission is careful to

---

Politics of European Contract Law: Who has an Interest in What Kind of Contract Law for Europe', in Grundmann and Stuyck, above note 4, 181; T. Wihelmsson, 'Private Law in the EU: Harmonised or Fragmented Europeanisation?', (2002) *Eur. Rev. Priv. L.*,77, 83-84: 'the process of harmonisation of private law offers one (but not the only) way for an academic community, which sees its power and influence decreasing in favour of judges and bureaucrats, to try to regain its lost status' (p. 78).

[85] See for example C. von Bar, above note 60, 'All European jurists sense that matters cannot stay as they are with the present approach to law making in the institutions of the European Union. Many directives are only harmonisation success story from the perspective of Brussels: from the perspective of the national legal systems they lead to new fault lines. (...) The current sectoral and "piecemeal" approach of directives, exclusively conceived from the perspective of consumer protection law, is already placing the quality and the systematic coherence of our national systems of private law in permanent danger'. But for a different opinion concerning European contract law in general see S. Grundmann, 'The Structure of European Contract Law' (2001) *Eur. Rev. Priv. L.* 527: 'European contract law as the EC legal framework for contract making in the internal market is not fragmentary. Empirically it has proven to be highly successful. Is not fragmentary as long as regulation that is internationally enforced is seen as the only real restriction to cross border commerce. This area has been harmonized thoroughly. To consider only this area, means to regulate only market failure.'

[86] See for example Reich, above note 70, who is very critical of the entire document: "Der Berg kreiste ein Maeuschen".

[87] The Communication lists several initiatives at the EC level that concern the improvement of EC law, such as the request by the European Council of Lisbon to the Commission in order to define a strategy for regulatory simplification, the Interinstitutional agreement on the quality of legal drafting of 1999 for the Council, the Commission and the European Parliament, and several projects launched in order to simplify existing legal instruments, such as SLIM (Simplifying Legislation for the Internal Market), started in 1996, and the task force BEST, created in 1997 for simplifying law related to trade. See *Communication of the Commission on European Contract Law,* above note 51, 15-16.

avoid the terms 'code' and 'codification', terms which are loaded with policy and ideological meanings.[88] Moreover, the Communication does not discuss in any depth the basic characters and consequences of such a choice. Rather, it concentrates on issues such as the legal instrument to be used (regulation, directive, recommendation) and whether it is preferable to have an opt-in, opt-out, or mandatory model of application.[89] Important as these elements are and the many others that may arise (it is sufficient to contemplate the problem of whether the common legislation should coexist or substitute for national laws), the lack of discussion of the main substantive elements of the proposed common legal instrument is very significant. As is often the case, omissions are sometimes more telling than affirmations. A possible explanation of this approach is that the proposal is so new, that little more can be done than to launch the debate on whether such an instrument is desirable and feasible. Alternatively, the omission can signal the desire of the Commission to keep a neutral position towards the possible contents of such an instrument, leaving it to the confrontation of the position of all stakeholders involved, before taking any positive step. Being mere speculations, these arguments must stop at this. Nevertheless, they must be kept in mind as a background to the debate that meanwhile has developed in legal, economic and political circles.[90]

---

[88] Cfr. C. von Bar, above note 60, 'it all depends ultimately on what one understands by the notion of a European Civil Code – whether it is conceived as a wide-ranging act of conventional type for the purpose of crowning the birth of a state or the triumph of a revolution or rather as an intellectually sound model with the potential, progressively and bit-by-bit, to grow in legal authority and binding force" (a statement which clearly favours the non-political aspects of producing a code exclusively through scholarly work; still, it is clear that at some point a political choice is necessary, since a common European code is not a mere technical instrument, but has important political implications). See also C.von Bar, 'Paving the way Forward with Principles of European Private Law', in Grundmann and Stuyck, above note 4, 137.

[89] In the opt-in model the common rules apply only if the parties so choose, whereas in the opt-out model common rules apply as default rules unless parties decide otherwise. A number of mandatory rules can be foreseen in both models (i.e., some rules cannot be avoided by the parties if the body of common rules applies).

[90] A European Civil code would have significant consequences not only for European states, but could also serve as a relevant model that could be used for legal transplants in all the world: see. U. Mattei, *Hard Code Now!,* above note 81, pp. 11-12, 14; von Bar, above note 60, 11: 'Europe also needs a "single currency" in law, a further symbol of its cohesion, not least with one eye on its growing role in the world'.

2. The Reactions to the Communication

The Communication on European contract law has stimulated numerous and various reactions by all stakeholders.[91]

(a) The European Council

The European Council has adopted on 16 November 2001 a report on the need to approximate Member States' legislation in civil matters.[92] The document, described by the Commission as 'fairly balanced", recalls the mandate by the European Council of Tampere to develop an area of freedom, security and justice, of which greater convergence of civil law is considered to be an important part,[93] and consequently requires an overall study on the need to approximate substantive as well as procedural law in civil matters.[94] According to the report, the Tampere mandate is broad enough to encompass all of private law, therefore the focus of the Commission on contract law should be enlarged in order to cover issues of non-contractual liability, property law, and, rather surprisingly, family law as well.[95] This approach is a very

---

[91] The responses can be found on the Commission website: http://www.europa.eu.int/comm/consumers/policy/developments/contract_law/comments/index_en.html. A summary of the responses to the Communication can be found in a document issued by the Commission, *Reactions to the Communication on European Contract Law*. Geographically the highest number of contributions comes from Germany and the UK, and "professionally" from academic and business communities. Remarkably, no or few contributions have been received from some member States (none from Ireland and Luxembourg, one from Portugal, two from Greece). The geographical "concentration" of the debate is an element which is little discussed, but which could have important consequences, since it focuses the discussion and attention on some "leading" legal systems, marginalising the contribution of different experiences. A selection of responses by academics is contained in in Grundmann and Stuyck, above note 4; others will be published in the *European Review of Private Law* and in Schulte-Noelke, Schulze, Bernaredau, *Europaeisches Vertragsrecht im Gemeinschaftsrecht*, (Berlin: 2002).

[92] 12735/01 justiciv 124, 18 October 2001 (23.10) (http://register.consilium.eu.int/pdf/en/01/st12/12735en1.pdf).

[93] "in a genuine European area of justice individuals and businesses should not be prevented or discouraged from exercising their rights but the incompatibility or complexity of legal and administrative systems in the Member States": para. 28 of the Tampere Council conclusions. On greater convergence of civil law see ch. VII of the conclusions.

[94] On the whole, the Tampere Council conclusions lay greater emphasis on civil procedure than on substantive law: see ch. VII of the conclusions.

[95] In fact, a large part of the Report is devoted to the analysis of family law, which is generally considered to be a field remaining in the sphere of national law, since it is very sensitive

significant step: the European Council is the Community institution which represents the political will of all the member States, and the fact that it not only endorse the interventionist strategy of the Commission in the field of private law, but it even proposes to give it a wider focus, is a symptom of a dramatic change in the political landscape surrounding the debate on European private law,[96] as is recognised by the Commission: 'for the first time the Council indicates that the necessary degree of confidence could be attained in the future if the convergence of substantive law is enhanced'.[97]

(b) The European Parliament

The European Parliament, too, has a very positive attitude towards the proposal of the Commission. This is rather less surprising, since Parliament was historically the first Community institution to propose a general legal intervention in the area of European private law. In a Resolution of 15 November

---

to cultural, social and religious values that are related to local specificities. Yet, according to the European Council, the principle of freedom of movement of persons and the aim of creating an area of freedom, security and justice is a legal basis on which the Community could take legal action: see para. I.2 and 3; para. IV.

[96] The European Council Report sets legal approximation of national private laws in a wider legal context: better compatibility among legal systems should be achieved also thorough other instruments, such as private international law, mutual recognition of judicial decisions, international conventions. Besides, the Report acknowledges that the *acquis communautaire* "has (…) been accused of lacking in consistency and structure" due to the "step-by-step" approach, and that consequently "Community legislation must be founded on principles which guarantee that Community rules are consistent and ensure proper transposition into national law"; finally, the Report stresses the importance of ensuring consistency between instruments governing consumer contracts, and of the use of a uniform legal terminology, an analysis close to option II of the Commission Communication on Contract law: para. III.9 of the Conclusions.

According to the Report, a solution to the problem of legal divergences could be based on a "vertical" harmonisation, or instead on a "horizontal" approach "aiming at the creation of a European "common core" of private law". This observation is concluded by the statement that "If it is revealed that there is a need for harmonisation, priority could be given to a more "horizontal" approach so as to find a more consistent and more convincing solution" (Conclusions, para. III.9c), which could be read to favour the third option proposed in the Commission Communication on Contract law.

In the conclusions (para. VI), the European Council invites the Commission to submit to the other EC institutions the results of the study, together with observations and recommendations (possibly in a Green or White Paper) before the end of 2002 (but for analysis concerning family law the deadline is set in June 2003).

[97] Commission report, *Reactions to the Communication on European Contract Law*, above note 91, 2.

2001 (one day before the European Council Report) concerning the approximation of the civil and commercial law of the Member States,[98] the European Parliament 'advocates a body of law which is close to citizens, accessible, respects established traditions and at the same time takes into account the requirements of the internal market'.[99] The basis for such action is the same as the one proposed by the Commission, i.e. the obstacles to the functioning of the internal market determined by different national laws where mutual recognition cannot be applied.[100] On the Commission Communication, Parliament states that it 'Regrets the fact that the Commission has surprisingly restricted its communication to private contract law',[101] since the Tampere mandate was much broader, and 'Notes that current problems concerning the conclusion, performance and termination of contracts cannot be solved unless issues relating to general formal provisions, non-contractual liability, the law of restitution and property law are also addressed'.[102] Parliament is therefore more specific than the European Council in defining the links of contract law with bordering areas of private law, and leaves out other fields exceeding private patrimonial law, such as family law. Moreover, it goes into the detail of proposing the instrument through which greater harmonisation of European contract law should be pursued: it should be a regulation, 'a European instrument available for use on an optional basis under private international law in legal relationships'.[103] Although the definition is not very

---

[98] A5-0384/2001, (COM(2001)398 – C50471/2001 – 2001/2187 (COS). The Resolution is opened by the statement that "similarities between the legal traditions of the peoples of Europe ultimately outweigh the differences between them" (lett. A), but immediately after acknowledges that "the discussion of large-scale harmonisation of Member States' core civil law is a politically charged and sensitive issue" (lett. C). The document recognises that some "directives give rise to problems when implemented in conjunction with national civil codes" (No. 3), and that "in an enlarged Union of 500 million inhabitants it will become more and more difficult to guarantee the uniform application of European law" (No. 4). Although only at the end of the document (No. 17), Parliament states that progress should be made first of all in harmonisation of civil procedure (jurisdiction and enforcement) and recognition of judgements, in line with the emphasis given by the EC Council to the link between procedural and substantive law.

[99] EP Resolution, No. 8.

[100] In fact, the Resolution (No. 18) proposes as a suitable legal basis art. 95 of the EC Treaty, i.e. the internal market provision.

[101] EP Resolution, No. 9.

[102] EP Resolution, No. 13.

[103] EP Resolution, No. 11 and No. 20 (where the use of a regulation is proposed as a "more effective and reasonable" instrument for future internal market legislation). Understand-

specific, it seems to point to option IV of the Commission's Communication on Contract Law (i.e. a comprehensive legal instrument), in its opt-in version. Besides, the European Parliament explicitly acknowledges the link between general contract law and consumer protection, and 'urges the Commission to present proposals to revise the existing consumer protection directives relating to contract law, in particular to remove minimal harmonisation clauses which have prevented the establishment of uniform law at the EU level to the detriment of the protection of consumers and the smooth functioning of the internal market'.[104] We have already touched on the issue of the advantages and drawbacks of minimum harmonisation clauses when analysing the Green Paper, and we will later see that the problem becomes even more entangled if it is analysed in the wider framework of general contract law.[105]

A remarkable feature of the Resolution is that it sets a very detailed and tight timetable: by the end of 2004 the Commission should compile a database of national legislation and case law in the field of contract law and promote comparative legal research aimed at finding 'common legal concepts and solutions', as well as a common legal terminology, which should be used on a voluntary basis[106] The same deadline is foreseen also for legislative proposals concerning the consolidation of existing Community law. From 2005 onwards the use of the common legal concepts and solutions should be promoted in academic training and in the syllabuses of the legal professions, and all EU institutions should use them. From 2006 this body of rules should be transfused in European legislation 'for cross-border or national contractual relations', whose application should be reviewed in 2008. Finally, in 2010 a 'body of rules on contract law in the European Union that takes account of

---

ably, Parliament stresses that the codecision procedure should be used (No. 21), where its input in the law-making procedure is most significant.

[104] EP Resolution, No. 12.

[105] See *infra* para. 9.

[106] EP Resolution, No. 14. According to the Resolution, common concepts, solutions and terminology should cover the following issues: general contract law, sales, service contracts (including financial services and insurance contracts), personal securities, non-contractual obligations (comprising tort law and the law of restitution), transfer of ownership of movables, credit guarantees and movables, trust law. As is apparent from the list, the scope is much wider than mere contract law. The results should be publicised in 2005.

von Bar, above note 60, p. 11 stresses the fact that in its latest Resolution Parliament has shifted from a "top down" approach to a "bottom up" approach, based 'on the growing acceptance of bodies of legal rules gradually maturing from within the field of European expertise in private law'.

the common legal concepts and solutions' should be adopted. These developments should be backed by the creation before the end of 2002 of a European Legal Institute, which should work out the scientific basis for action.[107] This is clearly a very ambitious and daring schedule, which presupposes a very strong political will and a significant speeding up of EC action in this field.

(c) Other stakeholders

As far as other stakeholders are concerned, the first reactions to be mentioned are those of national governments. Despite significant variations, most of them accept that there are significant obstacles to Community trade due to differences in national legislation, and that therefore they are in favour of some kind of legal intervention.[108] This attitude is shared by many consumer associations and by academic lawyers, while businesses and legal practitioners are divided on this issue. Going into the details of the options proposed by the Commission, the market option is opposed by most Member States (except the UK), consumer associations, practising lawyers and academics, while the business community shows mixed opinions. The 'Restatement' option (i.e. general principles) has received substantial support, but is considered as insufficient by itself in many replies (particularly those from consumer organisations), though it is supported as a complementary strategy to options III or IV.[109] The option of improving, streamlining and simplifying existing EC law has also been widely endorsed by all stakeholders, again not surprisingly, since there is widespread agreement that the current fragmented regulatory approach has severe flaws.[110] Option IV, i.e. a comprehensive legal instrument on contract law, has not surprisingly proven to be the most controversial proposal: most national governments deem it an unrealistic target in the short term, and several judge it negatively even in the long run,

---

[107] According to the Resolution, the European Legal Institute should comprise policy-makers, administrative authorities, judiciary and "those responsible for applying the law". Academics are only mentioned as a partner for cooperation with the Commission's Scientific Council, where it is explicitly said that the results must maintain "a balance between the civil law and common law traditions".

[108] The two significant, but on the whole not surprising, given their traditional scepticism of strong regulatory activism of the EC, are the United Kingdom and Denmark.

[109] Not surprisingly, most academics favour this option, where their input could be substantial and probably crucial, as the experience of existing groups working on elaboration of principles through comparative analysis shows.

[110] Still, there are significant differences on how this should be achieved: shift from minimum to maximum harmonisation, use of framework directives instead of detailed measures, etc.

raising arguments related to subsidiarity and the lack of a sufficient legal basis. A negative attitude prevails also among businesses, while consumer associations and legal practitioners are split. On the contrary, most legal academics are in favour of a comprehensive legal instrument, although most of them believe that, in order to guarantee the necessary substantive quality, the work must be done gradually and conceived as a long-term objective.[111]

After having collected a significant number of responses, the Commission intends to present observations and recommendations before the end of 2002 in the form of a Green or White Paper, which should point out the areas where national laws undermine the proper functioning of the internal market and the uniform application of Community law, define in greater detail the options for action (which will surely include the improvement of existing EC legislation), and set a detailed action plan with chronological implementation schedule.

(d) Academics

Of the replies to the Communication on European Contract Law coming from academics,[112] two are analysed here for the paradigmatic arguments that they raise: the issue of legal competence of the European Community and the relationship of contract law with private patrimonial law.

In his response to the Communication, van Gerven,[113] a leading scholar in EC law who, besides his academic role, has a long experience as an Advocate General at the European Court of Justice (and therefore combines an 'external' and 'internal' view of the EC legal process), advocates European

---

[111] According to the Commission report, *Reactions to the Communication on European Contract Law*, above note 91, 20, most academics are in favour of an opt-in or opt-out model, which would keep the European instrument side by side with national contract laws; this option "would combine the advantages of centralised and decentralised rule-making", since "European codification would lead to rigidity or stagnation in the law".

[112] All replies to the Communication can be found on the Internet site of the Commission at this address: http://europa.eu.int/comm/consumers/policy/developments/contract_law/comments.

[113] van Gerven, above note 39. In his paper he approves the strategy to combine comprehensive legislation with the improvement and consolidation of existing EC legislation (i.e. option III of the Communication of the Commission), and proposes to replace the current directives by regulations, in order to unify national rules and avoid the possibility of diverging national implementing rules. According to him, the existing sectoral approach could be usefully supplemented by non-binding general principles which, being soft law, do not raise the problems of democratic legitimacy of a code.

codification, i.e. comprehensive legislation, of areas of private patrimonial law, but stresses forcefully that currently the legal system of the European Communities does not possess a suitable legal basis for action,[114] and consequently either an amendment of the existing Treaties, or an ad hoc Treaty is needed. Van Gerven poses the issue of legislative competence for private law in a wider framework of democratic legitimacy,[115] and he underlines that art. 95 of the EC Treaty, referring to the internal market as a basis for regulatory action, is not a suitable basis, no matter how broadly it is read.[116] A politically sensitive and important measure such as a contract (or civil) code, as history shows, requires not only detailed and careful preparatory technical work, but also a strong political will that must involve public opinion and the democratically elected representatives of European citizens. Van Gerven consequently proposes to devise an ad hoc procedure in order to ensure legitimacy and acceptability:

---

[114] *Ibid.*, 'there is no jurisdiction within the Community that is broad enough to enact a Civil Code (…). This limitation of Community jurisdiction constitutes a crucial point which cannot be disregarded in the discussion about codification at EC level'; this implies that 'in the field of contract law, none of the Community institutions has the authority to bring some unity into the various sets of rules which regulate, in varying degree, the different "categories" contract'.

[115] On the widely discussed issue of the democratic deficit in the European Union see P. Craig. G. de Burca, *EU Law*, 2 ed., (Oxford: Oxford University Press, 1998) 155-161.

[116] van Gerven, above note 39, notes that using art. 95 would permit to reach a vote by a qualified majority in the Council, which could lead to the paradoxical result that a code could be enacted against the will of a number of States (e.g., it could "impose codification of core provisions of private law on all of the (supposedly) "non codification minded" Member States", i.e. UK, Ireland, Denmark, Finland, Sweden). The same negative assessment goes for art. 94 EC, which provides for approximation of national laws which directly affect the establishment or functioning of the common market. Art. 94 EC is wider than art. 95 EC but, differently than the latter, it only allows the enactment of directives and does not require the co-decision procedure, the law-making procedure that guarantees a significant role for the European Parliament, the only democratically elected body of the EC. Finally, not even art. 308 EC, providing residual powers, is sufficient to establish legislative competence. See also W. Van Gerven, 'Coherence of Community and national laws. Is there a legal basis for a European Civil Code?' (1997) *Eur. Rev. Priv. L.* 465, and the paper delivered at the VIII Common Core meeting held in Trento on July 6, 2002 (video available at http://www.jus.unitn.it/services/arc/2002/0704/home.html). Van Gerven recalls the very important recent judgement of the Court of justice in the so-called Tobacco case of October 2000 (*Germany v. Parliament and Council*, C-376/98, [2000] ECR I-8419), on which see below.

Under that procedure codification could be prepared by experts designated by the Member States who, at an early stage, would take the advice from parliamentary commissions in the European Parliament and the national parliaments (...). draft bills could be prepared (...) by committees of experts, and then made public to invite comments from all segments of society. After such broad consultation and ensuing amendments, the draft bills would be submitted to final deliberation in a "Convention" (...) and finally adopted, in view of submission to approval by the Member States, by the Council and the European Parliament (...) After it has been approved by all Member States, the agreement would come into force.[117]

Whether this is or is not the way that is going to be chosen, the proposal underlines an important reality: the Code is not merely a body of technical rules, and deciding whether Europe should or should not have a common code simply cannot be decided merely on the basis of the existence of obstacles to trade. Something more is required, and this is the realm of political choices, which should be openly acknowledged and discussed.[118]

Another important issue contained in Van Gerven's article is that even if a Code should prove feasible, that would not by itself be enough, because in order not only to have common rules, but common results as well, a common legal culture is needed,[119] and this can only be built through a slow and pervasive education of legal actors (students, scholars, lawyers, judges, civil

---

[117] Van Gerven, above note 39; the model for this procedure is the special method devised for the European Charter of Fundamental Rights, solemny declared in the Council of Nice of December 2001, which underlines the political relevance of the choice for a European Civil code. Van Gerven also recalls the long and time-consuming process that has led to the approval of the Dutch Civil Code, where all private and public stakeholders were involved in the debate leading to its approval.

[118] "At the end of the day the desirability issue turns around the question of how much fragmentation a legal system is able to support or, in other words, how coherent a legal system must be. That is a question not only of efficiency (...) but also of fairness and justice" Ibid.. See also Mattei, above note 81, 'the deficit of democracy that is plaguing Europe should not be seized by influential professional guilds to claim privileges and powers that clearly do not belong to them. (...) The Code should not be the decision of lawyers'.

[119] The importance of gradually forming a common legal culture is also stressed in the *Communication on European Contract Law – Joint Response of the Commission on European Contract Law and the Study Group on a European Civil Code*. See also M. Eisenberg, *The Unification of Law*, in Mattei and Bussani, above note 61, 15-26.

servants, etc.). Since 'European codification may not start from scratch',[120] a programme of flanking measures is proposed, which ranges from planning new academic curricula, developing a new kind of legal literature (textbooks, journals and so on), common research projects,[121] and other initiatives that will create a new class of lawyers capable of truly working with a European common law.[122] In other words, the bottom up approach to the creation of a code must necessarily be combined with the top down approach to a new legal system, if this is not to be a 'mission impossible'.[123]

Another fundamental aspect concerns the role of contract law as part of a larger framework of private law, and it is analysed in the joint response of the Commission on European Contract Law (i.e. the so-called Lando Commission) and the Study Group on a European Civil Code,[124] containing a detailed and lengthy reply to the proposals of the Commission, which not only represents the position of a large group of comparative legal scholars, but also of two among the most influential academic projects going on concerning European private law. The response agrees that diversity in national contract laws creates obstacles for the internal market, which are due to several kind of difficulties, such as the impossibility of having uniform sales strategies for business, deficient estimation of the risk of liability, need to get costly legal information and advice,[125] greater risks of subsequent litigation, etc. As a consequence, there is a need of further harmonisation in order to over-

---

[120] van Gerven, above note 39.

[121] The paper mentions several projects currently going on, among which the initiative for the preparation of a series of *Casebooks for the common law of Europe*, the Trento group on the *Common core of European private law*, and the Vienna/Tilburg group (ed. J. Spier et al., ii): p. 28.

[122] Van Gerven also stresses the importance of ensuring a common application of the Code, and proposes the creation of a preliminary ruling procedure before a Community court; in order to avoid paralysis due to overload, either a new court should be created, or the existing one should be extended: Ibid..

[123] "Without flanking measures (…), European codification would be an enterprise that is carried out in the abstract, *i.e.* with no past and probably no future": *Id.*, p. 31.

[124] *Communication on European Contract Law – Joint Response of the Commission on European Contract Law and the Study Group on a European Civil Code*. As already mentioned, the two groups partly overlap, since approximately two thirds of the members of the Commission on European Contract law also belong to the larger group of scholars active in the Study Group.

[125] The reply significantly points out that 'costs arises even if the relevant foreign contract law is identical with the internal national law' (p. 11), since the existence of equivalent outcomes is an information that requires complex and sometimes uncertain legal analysis.

come this 'multitudinous European legal jungle',[126] which should not limit its attention to contract law, because this area is closely linked to other sectors of private patrimonial law,[127] such as the whole of the law of obligations and some parts of property law, particularly those pertaining to movables. Indeed, this seems to be a widespread position among European academics, who are generally very concerned about systematic arguments. This does not mean that initially the focus could not be concentrated on contract law, but rather that the general plan should envisage an instrument covering also related areas, in order to create a systematic and coherent body of law. The whole reply insists on the creation of a European private law as a progressive enterprise that requires time and the synergetic intervention of all legal actors (national and European law-makers, practising and academic lawyers, businesses and consumer associations, etc.). The document consequently sees the two options of a "Restatement" and a "Civil code" not as opposite strategies, but rather as connected phases;[128] first of all, work should continue on the elaboration of common principles and a common legal terminology,[129] and only after these have been tested, their content has been made widely

---

[126] P. 11.

[127] "We (...) recommend concentrating on contract law, taking this, however, in as wide a sense as possible and keeping always in view the fact that contract law forms an organic whole with all economically relevant branches of private law which must be developed in tandem" (p. 4), because "the law of contract is integrated into a seamless legal web" (p. 20). The reply lists as relevant areas (pp. 19-20): law of obligations, comprising general contract law, law of particular contracts, precontractual liability, tort law, unjustified enrichment, negotiorum gestio; parts of the law of property, in particular credit securities in movables and trusts. In this respect the position is close to that expressed, although with some differences, by the EC Council and Parliament. See also Mattei, above note 81, who proposes to insert in the code rules on contract, torts, property, restitution and corporations, and underlines the need to avoid to be captured in taxonomies (which vary significantly across the national legal systems), which are useful tools for organizing legal rules, but must not be considered as determinant of substantive solutions.

[128] The reply considers that leaving further harmonisation to market forces would not be a sufficient strategy (pp. 21-27, where a critical evaluation is given also concerning the possibility of achieving greater harmonisation through private international law), and that the improvement of existing EC legislation, desirable as it is, is a strategy that works on a different plane from options II and IV, and consequently should be pursued simultaneously with the others, profiting from the elaboration of a uniform legal terminology and of common principles (pp. 34-36).

[129] The reply uses strong words in favour of the Restatement: "It would be perfectly inappropriate to pursue any other method" (p. 27). The necessary preparatory work should be backed by "an organisational framework and institutionalised funding", and should be

known to all legal actors, and the required political will formed, could they be transfused in a binding and comprehensive legal instrument.[130] The end goal of a European Civil Code, however, is a mere possibility, not a logical or political necessity, whose feasibility cannot be assessed today, since the evolutionary process is still in an early stage.[131]

VIII. EC LEGISLATIVE COMPETENCE AND THE RELATIONSHIP BETWEEN COMMUNITY AND NATIONAL LAW: THE MINIMUM/MAXIMUM HARMONISATION DEBATE

One the most frequent criticisms of EC law, not only with respect to consumer law, is that its piecemeal, incremental and sectorial approach inevitably causes gaps, overlaps, and inconsistencies. True as this surely is, it must not be forgotten that there are compelling reasons for this situation. One of the basic tenets of the relationship between the EC (and more generally the EU) and the Member States is that Community competences are enumerated, i.e. limited. If a legal measure is not supported by a specific legal basis in the Treaty, it is not valid, because it unlawfully impinges on national compe-

---

conducted by "panels of independent experts" (p. 33). The work of the Commission and the Study group should be used as a starting point ("at present they may well still be the only trans-European working groups which command at their disposal the network of academic expertise and labour power necessary for the enterprise", p. IV), and in fact one of its leader, Von Bar, explicitly proposes the Study group as the core on which to build a European Law Institute and a European Law Academy, above note 60, 13.

[130] The reply proposes an action plan (pp. 40-42) according to which the Restatement should be firstly used in academic education and as a persuasive instrument by courts and by EC institutions (stage I); only later it could be transformed in a binding legal instrument, first on an opt-in basis (stage II), and then on a opt-out basis (stage III). Finally, if these phases should bear positive results, the principles should be inserted in a European Civil code (stage IV), which would finally completely substitute national civil codes (stage V) : "The question whether any further measures should be adopted and, if so, what sort is essentially a political one. (...) an immediate and complete codification in the form of a regulation is not called for, but equally matters cannot be left on their present non-binding footing. (...) There are good reasons in favour of fashioning a phased plan for the further legislative measure" (p. V).

[131] Cf. von Bar, above note 60, 10: 'in the immediately foreseeable future there will neither be a body of rules embracing the entirety of private law nor probably a civil code of the type of codification conventionally found in continental Europe. At first it is much more likely to be a multifunctional compression of the bases of European patrimonial law'.

tences, which are general and residual.[132] This position is true also for consumer law and even more for private law, and it is probably the main reason for the strong and recurring emphasis in all the official EC documents on the relationship between the internal market and the possible legislative actions envisaged at the Community level.[133]

Moreover, the EC law-making process has a very specific character, which strengthens the tendency to work through sectoral interventions. The need to find a workable compromise among member States in the Council (which was stronger when unanimous votes prevailed, but it is very important even today in majority voting) makes it easier to work on narrow issues. Besides, the sectoral approach is favoured by the variable composition of the Council itself, whose members change according to the policies involved. Finally, the Commission too (which plays a crucial role, since it is the only EC institutions that can start the law-making process by formalising a proposal) is split in its work into several Directorates General, whose positions and objectives do not always coincide.[134]

---

[132] But see G. De Burca, *Setting Constitutional Limits to EU Competence?*, Working Paper 2001/02, Faculdade de Direito da Universidade Nova de Lisboa, Francisco Lucas Pires Working Papers Series on European Constitutionalism. for a discussion of how the division of competences between the EC and member States actually works: "the evolving and dynamic nature of the EU legal and political entity (...) undermines or marginalises attempts to impose a strict kind of constitutional formalism in so far as the limits of competence are concerned. (...) the focus on positivistic legal solutions – on a list of competences, or the drawing of exclusionary lines in the Treaty – is misconceived, and fundamentally important issues are ones which can get only limited help from law: those are the issues of instutional design on the one hand, and political culture on the other" (p. 2).

[133] See European Consumer Law Group, *Response to the Communication on European Contract Law*, p. 2: "one should not forget that the constitutional structure of the European Community allows for a problem-oriented approach only".

[134] See the illuminating example of the Green Paper *on Consumer Protection* and the *Communication on Sales Promotions* (COM(2001)546fin): both documents have been issued by the Commission on the same day (2 October 2001), but they are the work of two different DG: the first has been elaborated by DG SANCO (DG XXIV, dealing with consumer protection), while the second is a product of DG XV, competent for the Internal Market. In spite of the large degree of overlap between the topics of the two documents (fair trading and sales promotions), the approach is significantly different. The *Communication on Sales Promotions* proposes a draft regulation of an important part of marketing practices, strongly based on transparency and information as instruments to guarantee a working market both for businesses and consumers. The choice of the form of a regulation instead of a directive is explicitly based on the need to increase legal certainty and overcome national diversities, leaving the remaining area to the working of the principle of mutual recognition. See J.B.

From the point of view of competence, the situation of consumer law is rather different than general contract law. While for the former there is a rather solid legal ground, referring not only to art. 95 EC (harmonisation linked to the internal market) but also to art. 153 EC (competence related to consumer protection), the same cannot be said for general contract law, and even more for private patrimonial law. As we have already pointed out, the point has often and convincingly been argued that currently there is no legal basis for a comprehensive legislative intervention in the field of private law, since the competence related to the working of the internal market is linked to specific legal problems, and therefore all that can be currently done is to lay the ground through comprehensive and reliable preparatory work, which will be used when (if ever) such a competence may be established.[135] This position was been strengthened by the European Court of Justice: in the Tobacco judgement of October 2000.[136] The Court held that mere disparity between national law and an abstract risk of obstacles to fundamental freedoms and the internal market is not sufficient to justify the choice of art. 95 EC as a legal basis. According to the ECJ, the distortion must be concrete and significant in order to justify regulatory action. The official documents issued by the Commission (and by the Council and European Parliament as well) that we have analysed hardly mention this very important development concerning Community legal competence. Again, an open discussion of the

---

Gloeckner, *Think Big! Some remarks on the European Commission's* Green Paper *on consumer protection against unfair trade practices and the proposal for a regulation concerning sales promotions in the internal market*, paper available on the Commission's Internet site, pp. 4-8. For a critique of the divergences in the strategies of the two documents see European Consumer Law Group, *Position Paper on the* Green Paper *on Consumer Protection under due consideration of the Commission's Communication on Sales Promotion in the Internal Market*, ECLG/011/2002, which underlines that in the case of the *Communication* consumer associations were not consulted, nor were consumers' interests duly taken into account.

[135] See especially Van Gerven, above note 39. See also European Consumer Law Group, *Response to the Communication on European Contract Law*, p. 4: "What is really needed is the political will of the Member States, the European Community and citizens to install a common legal frame on contract law. (…) There is a clear need for democratic voting in Europe for such an important matter as the replacement of 15 national civil legal orders by a European Code on Contract Law".

[136] *Germany v Parliament and Council*, C-376/98, [2000] ECR I-8419. The directive was prompted mainly by concerns about the dangers of smoking, but the EU Treaty does not provide for a sufficient legal basis concerning health (cfr. art. 129 EC). For a discussion of problems of competence and adequate legal basis see De Burca, above note 132, 4-7.

problems of competence would surely have been preferable, and silence is probably due to the reluctance to raise sensitive political questions. Yet, it is clear that further action concerning general legislative intervention in the field of contract law would need to be clear and convincing in establishing a compelling link between the obstacles to the working of the internal market and the measures proposed.

The different approach to legal intervention and competence in the EC and the Member States is not merely a technical issue, but also has important policy implications, which are particularly evident in the field of consumer protection. In fact, consumer protection has historically developed as a sort of by-product of market integration, and this 'imprinting' remains today, even when consumer protection has become an autonomous EC policy. This is not the case with national laws: no matter how paternalistic or market-oriented they are, they have been usually developed as a form of protection for a group systematically considered as weak.

This difference of approach has produced numerous frictions between the EC and national legal systems, which become more aggravated the more developed and protective the body of consumer protection law is at the national level (as for example in Nordic countries). Yet, up to now these frictions have been absorbed, because to a very large extent EC consumer law requires only minimum harmonisation, and permits Member States to keep more protective standards. If the move from minimum to maximum harmonisation, envisaged by several EC institutions (Commission, Parliament, Council) and other legal actors, should come true, this accommodation would no longer be possible.[137] Again, this is not merely a technical choice; it requires important and sensitive policy choices:

> European consumer law is and might remain in the years to come marketing behaviour law (...) first and foremost meant to complete the Internal Market. (...) European market behaviour law differs from national consumer protection law in that the latter puts emphasis on the protection of the weaker party in contractual relations whereas the former intends to strengthen consumer confidence in the proper functioning of the Internal Market. As long as the European Community is no "state", the conceptual differences between national and European consumer protection law

---

[137] G. Howells, 'European Consumer Law – The minimal and maximal harmonisation debate', in Grundmann and Stuyck, above note 4, 73.

will subsist. That is precisely where the deeper justification for minimum harmonisation as the appropriate regulatory technique to tie both concepts together may be found.[138]

The crucial issue, therefore, seems to be that the rationale for consumer protection does not coincide in EC and national laws.[139] As long as partial divergence (through minimum harmonisation) between the two is allowed, it is possible to keep them together. Once it is decided that the standard must be one and only one (which is inevitable if maximum harmonisation is chosen), the decision must be taken which one is the right one, and this is clearly and plainly a political choice.[140] Unfortunately, it must be doubted that today there is a sufficient consensus among the Member States and the EC institutions on which is the best standard. Divergence in the application of EC consumer law in national laws is a matter of regret, but it seems (at least partially)[141] to be an inevitable consequence of the flexibility and discretion that must be granted in order to maintain the possibility of harmonising legal rules in a field where national specificities still seem to be overwhelming.

Moreover, 'Member States can act as laboratories, experimenting with practices which if successful can be integrated into EU policy'.[142] The pres-

---

[138] European Consumer Law Group, *Response to the Communication on European Contract Law*, p. 7.

[139] According to some experts of consumer law, it can even be doubted that EC consumer law has one single and coherent concept of consumer protection: see Howells, above note 137, 'EC consumer law has no settled philosophy (...) it is impossible to say what the deeper values of EC consumer policy are, how strong they are and whether they can be viewed as independent of internal market policy. Undoubtedly, however, by their very nature they tend towards a one solution fits all solution and this downplays the local traditions, circumstances and needs'.

[140] Howells, above note 137, 'there is a world of difference between a highly harmonised level of EU consumer law and maximal harmonisation'.

[141] In fact, many problems in the application of EC consumer law stem from bad drafting of the rules themselves (inconsistent terminology, overlaps, gaps and inconsistencies among different directives, etc.), rather that from difficulties deriving from national implementation measures. These could be avoided by improving the quality of EC legal drafting; see *infra* footnote.

[142] Howells, above note 137. See also Wilhelmsson, above note 84, 78: "fragmented Europeanisation (and internationalisation) (...) allows legal experimentalism, the free movement of new legal ideas"; T. Wilhelmsson, 'The Design of an Optional Restatement of European Contract Law – Real Life Instead of Dead Concepts', in Grundmann and Stuyck, above note 4, 353.

ervation of national diversities therefore can serve several different purposes: it permits reflection in legal rules relevant differences in social, economic and cultural patterns, thereby guaranteeing a sufficient degree of correspondence between legal rules and the social phenomena that they regulate. Secondly, it can offer to the EC law-making bodies a variety of solutions which can be flexibly adapted and adopted once a need of harmonisation is established. Finally, competition among legal orders is considered by many[143] to be an alternative to complete direct regulation at the EC level, which has the advantage of working 'bottom-up', instead of 'top down', avoiding many of the drawbacks (such as the need to find compromise solutions and the difficulties in amending and updating rules once adopted) typical of centralized regulatory intervention.[144]

The same reasoning applies to the question of whether there should be a shift of regulatory technique from harmonisation through directives to unification through regulations, a move which has been suggested both by the EC institutions,[145] and by scholars,[146] as a possible solution to the problems

---

[143] On competition among legal orders see N. Reich, 'Competition between legal orders: a new paradigm of EC law?' (1992) *Comm. Market L. Rev.*861; M. Dreher, 'Wettbewerb oder Vereinheitlichung der Rechtsordnungen in Europa?' (1999) *JZ* 108; Sun, Pelkmans, 'Regulatory competition in the Single Market' (1995) 33 *J. Comm. Market Stud.*67; A. Ogus, 'Competition between national legal systems- a contribution of economic analysis to comparative law' (1999) 48 *Int. Comp. L. Quart.* 48; L. Antoniolli Deflorian, *La struttura istituzionale del nuovo diritto europeo – Competizione e circolazione dei modelli giuridici*, Trento, Dipartimento di Scienze giuridiche, 1996.

[144] Of course, the risk of resorting to competition of legal rules is that can lead to a rush to the bottom, i.e. the rules that are selected are not the best ones, but rather the ones that pose the less stringent limits to the stronger players in the market. For a critique of the combined strategy at the EC level of minimum harmonisation together with mutual recognition see Somma, above note 81, 263, who sees this development as a consequence of the influence of the American legal model and its emphasis on market values, rather than as a way of preserving national peculiarities.

[145] Commission, Parliament, Council.

[146] See Van Gerven, above note 39; Howells, above note 137, notes that currently there is a tendency to structure directives in a way similar to regulations, particularly by giving them such a detailed content as to leave little room for national transposition measures. Moreover, the need to guarantee timely implementation and to avoid possible liability for misimplementation often leads national legislators simply to transpose literally the text of the directive, without adapting it to the internal system. In this case, the shift from directives to regulations would in fact produce some beneficial effects, since it would not change much in the substance, and would avoid the need of lengthy and cumbersome (and sometimes useless) transposition procedures. Yet, most stakeholders are convinced that the current practice concerning directives must be changed, and that there should be a return to their original

involved in the transposition process in national legal systems, such as delay, inconsistencies, and divergences. In fact, although using regulations might solve some of these problems (albeit not all, since divergences in application might well happen even once the rule is uniform throughout Europe), it is clear that this aim cannot be isolated from the surrounding context: harmonisation through directives instead of regulations was and is due exactly to the desire of the EC and the Member States to keep a degree of autonomy and flexibility even in areas which have been harmonized. Shifting to regulations might end up in throwing away the baby with the bath water: it may well solve some uncertainties and discrepancies, but it has the major drawback of stifling the manoeuvring margin for national legal systems. This is clearly an issue where there is no clear-cut right answer, being a matter of balancing contrasting interests. It may well be that the advantages of guaranteeing greater uniformity are greater than the disadvantages of limiting national legal systems' flexibility, but this is a choice that again involves, besides merely technical elements, important policy judgements, and these must be openly acknowledged and discussed.

IX. The Relationship Between Consumer Contract Law and General Contract Law

The analysis of the Community documents related to consumer protection and contract law shows that there are many common elements, which suggest a combined approach. The most important commonality is surely the fact that in both areas the rationale for further Community regulatory intervention is the same, namely the need to overcome obstacles to trade and distortions of competition in the internal market created by divergence in national laws. Secondly, both for consumer law and contract law (which in existing EC law overlap on many points) emphasis is laid on the need to streamline and improve existing EC law, in order to eliminate inconsistencies and gaps.

For this reason, it is rather surprising that the Green Paper on EU consumer protection does not even mention the Communication on European Contract Law[147] (although they have both been issued by the Commission

---

character, i.e. of a legislative measures setting aims to be attained, but leaving significant discretion to States in the means to be used.

[147] von Bar, above note 60, p. 8, who terms as "peculiar" the "splendid isolation" of the Green Paper *on Consumer law* from the *Communication on European contract law*.

within a very short period), and the Consumer Policy Strategy 2002-2006 only briefly refers to it, stating that follow-up actions to the Communication 'could suggest a mix of regulatory and non-regulatory' measures, and, among the latter, co-ordination of research activities could lead to the

> elaboration of a general frame of reference, establishing common principles and terminology. Furthermore, it could explain which measures would be taken to ensure coherence of the existing and future acquis (...) In this context, a review of existing consumer contract law in order to remove existing inconsistencies, to fill gaps and to simplify could be envisaged.[148]

The focus is rather narrow, and does not discuss the possible relevance for consumer law of comprehensive action (binding or not) in the field of contract law.

Although it is clearly impossible to tell exactly what are the reasons of this reticence, two hypotheses seem plausible. The decision to focus narrowly on consumer protection in the documents relating to this subject could be due to political expediency; in other words, the Commission may have considered that at this stage consumer protection is a less controversial issue than general contract law, and that therefore it was more prudent and sound to stick to the 'narrow' topic. Alternatively, the reticence could be a matter of pragmatism, since it is easier to deal separately with consumer law issues, rather than having to co-ordinate them with a complex network of rules and interests.[149] Be that as it may, the fact remains that currently the strategy of the Commission seems to be oriented towards keeping consumer law and contract law on separate tracks, and consequently to devise separate action plans. This 'legal schizophrenia' implies that the proposals at the Community level referring to contract law stick to the traditional approach of a body of rules generally considered as default rules, i.e. that can freely be modified by the parties, while for consumer law the high level of protection required is often reached through mandatory rules.[150] Only time will tell whether this

---

[148] *Consumer Policy Strategy 2002-2006*, p. 13. See also supra pp. x-y.

[149] Of course, while the first reading seems prudent, the second one is rather myopic, since sooner or later (and even today at the national level, if not at the EC level) these questions will have to be addressed.

[150] See European Consumer Law Group, *Response to the Communication on European Contract Law*, ECLG/339/2001, p. 2: "Those who favour the development of a unique set of

is a winning strategy, but from a scholarly point of view this choice is to be regretted, because handling the two areas separately will surely create inconsistencies and frictions, while this could have been a unique opportunity to tackle and handle in a systematic ways legal problems that are closely linked, with beneficial effects both for EC and national laws.[151]

Up to now, consumer law has been developed as an isolated area of law. Even within EC consumer law itself discrepancies, overlaps and inconsistencies can be detected, which is one of the main sources of criticism against EC regulatory intervention. Yet, up to now EC private law is structurally a fragmentary law, i.e. it intervenes only in the interstices of national private laws, which still keep the role of building up a coherent system of private law. Inconsistencies and frictions have consequently to be ironed out at the national level, with significantly different results, having in common most of the time only that they prove to be difficult and problematic.[152] If there is

---

common principles on contract law intend to allow the contracting parties to voluntary opt for their application. Whilst such an approach might be useful and feasible for business contracts, it might not be appropriate to deal with the consumer concern. Consumer law is regulatory law, mandatory law meant to intervene into the freedom of contracts to guarantee minimum protection of the weaker parties. (...) Inherent to a restatement on common principles of contract law is the idea of revitalising freedom of contract. This does not exclude the introduction of mandatory rules in the restatement; the question is, however, whether these rules will ever be chosen".

[151] Cfr. European Consumer Law Group, *Response to the Communication on European Contract Law*, p. 6: "consumer law only supplement national civil law rules. Without the national fundament in civil law, consumer law would just hang in the air. That is why consumer law too is inevitably bound to and interwoven with national legal cultures and traditions". Cfr. also the reply to the Green Paper *on Consumer Protection* by the Study Group on a European Civil Code, which states (p. 4): "To a great extent, consumer protection within the EU has been treated as an area of law that could or does stand on its own. This approach has in itself caused some of the problems with the existing system. (...) There is a close link and an interdependency between general private law and consumer protection law. As long as the link is not properly taken into consideration, consumers will to a great extent be treated in different ways in different Member States, without any real foundation in an analysis of differing need or commercial practices (...)".

[152] In fact, it has been often pointed out that EC consumer legislation, although aimed at harmonising legal rules, has often a contrary disintegrative effects, since it may disrupt the balance established at the national level between consumer protection and private law: see Wilhelmsson, above note 84, 79-82, who writes of a "Jack-in-the-Box" effect, referring to the increasing level of indeterminacy of national law due to the introduction of EC law, which lacks a systematic structure. See also C. Joerges, 'Desintegrative Folgen legislativer Harmonisierung: ein komplexes Problem und ein unscheinbares Exempel', in H. Schulte-

any prospect of developing a common European private law, this is bound to change dramatically: it can no longer be ignored that EC consumer law is part of a wider legal framework, relating to contract as well to other areas of law (tort law, property, competition,[153] etc.). Ignoring this fact will simply postpone the moment where workable solutions will have to be found (the later it will come, the more difficult it will be to elaborate them), and possibly even doom the whole enterprise to failure: There can be no separate self-sufficient consumer law. It will always remain anchored in the general private law system. Without progress in harmonising that general sphere there can be no long-term prospect of coherent and workable legislation for consumer protection which is free of internal contradictions.

This link between consumer law and general contract law is crucial no matter what strategy the Community will chose of the ones proposed in the Communication. It is immediately visible if, as a minimum, only the option of improving and streamlining existing EC law will be pursued, and it will be even more unavoidable if comprehensive work on contract law is undertaken.[154] In particular, should the prospect of a European comprehensive legislative intervention on contract law (or even of a 'full' European Civil code) come true, the need would be unavoidable to relate the relevant parts of EC consumer protection law to the general legal framework. The same goes for the relationship with a body of general principles (the Restatement), although the risk of contrasts would have less clear legal consequences.

In the discussion concerning the possibility of enacting comprehensive legislation, two alternatives can be envisaged, i.e. a common codification containing both consumer and contract law, or two parallel and self-consis-

---

Noelke, R. Schulze (Hrsg.), *Europaeische Rechtsangleichung und nationale Privatrechte,* (Baden-Baden: Nomos,1999) p. 205; L. Antoniolli Deflorian, 'consumer contracts in Italian and Community Law – Pattern of Integration and Disintegration', in *ibid,* 119.

[153] On the relationship between consumer law and competition law see S. Grundmann, 'EC Consumer and EC Competition Law: How Related Are They? Examining the exististing EC Contract Law Sources', and F. Gomez, 'EC Consumer and EC Competition Law: How Related Are They? A Law and Economics Perspective', in this volume. The Authors argue that both consumer law and competition law are aimed at consumer welfare, but focus on different market failures: the first concentrates on information asymmetries, the latter on monopoly power. But cf. G. Alpa, *Rules on Competition and Fair Trading,* paper presented at the conference on the European Civil Code in Rome, 12 July 2002, who is critical of the ability of current competition law to take duly into account consumer interests.

[154] The only option that could possibly leave untouched the isolation of consumer law would be option I, i.e. leaving all initiative to market forces.

tent codifications, one having a general and the other a focused scope.[155] In fact, at the national level several Member States have opted for keeping consumer contract law separate from the Civil code (France is an example). This separation may be chosen for several reasons: the desire to leave untouched the systematic structure of the code, the difficulty of coping with a constantly increasing and heterogeneous body of rules in order to insert it in the existing code structure in a timely and fitting manner, and sometimes the implicit or even explicit awareness that the underlying principles of consumer law are not completely in harmony with the fundamental structure of the code.[156]

The issue of compatibility of consumer law with general contract law, and more generally with private law, is therefore a significant problem for all legal systems. In fact, in most of them consumer law is considered as an exception to the general body of private law, characterised by more stringent limits to freedom of contract, a high proportion of rules of a mandatory character, prescriptions of content and clauses, a special range of remedies, all of which move away from the traditional general paradigm of private law, whether contained in a code or in case law. The more this body of 'exceptional' consumer law expands, the more difficult it is to keep it isolated from the general legal framework, both in terms of systematic consistency and of practical application.

Moreover, modern consumer law tends to be built up of a combination of private and public law elements (e.g. via regulation and control by agencies),[157] which further complicates the legal landscape to which it must be related.

---

[155] European Consumer Law Group, *Response to the Communication on European Contract Law*, pp. 6-9, which proposes two separate codes for contract and consumer law. As for consumer law, it should stick to the existing model of minimum harmonisation, because this is the only way to preserve legal and cultural diversity of national legal systems: "the true challenge of today is to strike the correct balance between harmonisation as a means to build up uniform cultures and traditions in order to keep European integration going and fragmentation as a means to safeguard different national legal cultures and traditions" (p. 6).

[156] In this case, obviously, the problem of clash does not disappear, but it is simply removed from the legislative area to the application stage, by judges, agencies or other bodies.

[157] See for example the application of dir. 93/13 on unfair contract terms in consumer contracts in the United Kingdom, where a most relevant role is played by the Office of Fair Trading, a non-governmental agency; cf. Antoniolli Deflorian, *I contratti dei consumatori nel diritto inglese fra common law e diritto comunitario: legal process e forme di tutela*, forthcoming in *Riv. dir. civ.*, 2003.

X.   Political Stakes And Technical Aspects In Contract Law

A significant part of existing EC law concerning consumer contracts deals with mandatory information rules, a policy which is in line with the archetype of the 'active consumer': if the law compels the professional to disclose all relevant information for the contract, the consumer will be able to make a valid choice and conclude an efficient contract.[158] Therefore, these rules have a kind of hybrid content: they are protective insofar they are mandatory, i.e. they cannot be contracted out by the parties, but at the same time they are market-oriented, since they do not impose a specific content upon the contract, but only special means and procedures through which this content has to be established.[159] This seems to be in line with the close link existing at the EC level between consumer protection and the working of the internal market, which views consumer policy as having twins aims, protection for consumers, and stimulation for the market.

The approach is often different in national legal systems, which display a variety of purposes and techniques in consumer protection rules, but are generally based on the idea of the need of protecting the weaker party, and therefore often resort to mandatory substantive protective rules, i.e. rules that prescribe parts of the content of the contract. Even in national contract law, usually a very relevant portion of rules is traditionally not of a mandatory

---

[158] Economic analysis, however, shows that market failures are not only due to asymmetric information, but also to bounded rationality; simply stated, it is not just a matter of giving the consumer the relevant information, but also to make sure that he/she is capable of understanding and processing it, which is often not the case (especially for what economists term "credence goods", whose characteristics cannot be ascertained completely even after repeated purchase): in these cases mandatory information burdens the professional party, but does not provide any further protection to the consumer. See G. Hadfield, Howse, M. Trebilcock, Informatin-Based Principles for Rethinking Consumer Protection Policy, (1998) *J. Cons. Pol.*131; Meyerson, 'The Efficient Consumer Form Contract: Law and Economics Meets the Real World' (1990) *Georgia L. Rev.* 583; T. Rakoff, 'Contract of Adhesion: An Essay in Reconstruction' (1983) 96 *Harv. L. Rev.* 1174.

[159] On the role of mandatory information rules in EC law see S. Grundmann, Information, Party Autonomy and Economic Agents in European Contract Law, in (2002) 39 *Comm. Market L. Rev.*269, who emphasizes the fact that, on the contrary of substantive mandatory protective rules, they are designed to foster party autonomy, not to restrict it. See also S. Grundmann, W. Kerber, S. Weatherill (eds.), *Party Autonomy and the Role of Information in the Internal Market*, (Berlin: de Gruyter, 2001). There are of course also instances of substantive protective rules, such as most of those contained in the directive on unfair terms in consumer contracts (dir. 93/13).

and protective character, but rather aims at affording parties with a reliable system of default rules, which can be changed insofar they do not suit their needs.[160] Yet, the largely default character of the law of contract must not be exaggerated, particularly in the light of recent developments, which show that even in a traditionally 'liberal' area such as contract law there is an increasing tendency to introduce mandatory protective rules. In fact, the 20th century has witnessed a continuing and increasing erosion of the basic tenets of 'classical' contract law, freedom (sanctity) of contract and party autonomy,[161] not only through the development of consumer law, but also a variety of other sectors (such as labour and housing contracts, etc.). This phenomenon is so pervasive, that it may well be necessary to abandon the analysis in terms of rule and exceptions (i.e.viewing protective legal rules as a mere exception to the established framework, which consequently remains virtually unaltered) and try and reconstruct the system. In fact, some scholars have proposed a new paradigm of contract law, based on the category of the contract with asymmetric contractual power,[162] characterised by systematic imbalance in the parties' position, which is reflected in an asymmetric division of duties, powers, and remedies available, and an increased level of external policing of the contract.[163] Others oppose such a move, since it involves a paternalistic evaluation of what is best for individuals, and runs the risk of devising solutions whose results can prove worse than the problems they intend to solve.

Currently these two opposed visions of the role of contract law coexist side by side. A symptomatic mechanism, which is particularly strong in EC contract law, but is often found also in national legal systems, is the division

---

[160] This "liberal" character of traditional private law is one reason why some scholars oppose to a general European codification, preferring rather to stick to the current "patchwork" model: T. Wilhelmsson, above note 84, 84-86: "I claim that the idea of a European Civil Code requires a committment to traditional (liberalist, in American: conservative) values. (…) One may namely doubt whether it is possible to draft a general civil code in which intervening, protective, social, welfarist, consumerist – the label is not important – provisions play an important role.,,As a result, a unification process based on the ideology of the traditional codifications must obiviously be an anachronism'.

[161] See P.S. Atiyah, *The Rise and Fall of Freedom of Contract*, (Oxford: Clarendon, 1979).

[162] See V. Roppo, *Il contratto del duemila*, (Torino, Giappichelli, 2002); V. Roppo, *Il contratto*, Milano, Giuffrè, 2001; H. Beale, 'Inequality of Bargaining Power', (1986) 6 *Oxford J. Leg. Stud.* 123 ff.; J. Cartwright, *Unequal bargaining – A Study of Vitiating Factors in the Formation of Contracts* (Oxford: Clarendon, 1991).

[163] This can be done through the intervention of courts, public agencies, ADR mechanisms, both at the initiative of individuals and associations.

288

between consumer contracts and business contracts.[164] In fact, most protective EC contract rules are limited to consumer contracts, i.e. they do not apply when only professionals are involved. The rationale of the choice is clear: professionals are supposed to have comparable contractual power, and therefore do not need to be protected through special rules. Understandable as this may be, it is not so clear that the distinction consumer/professional is the most suitable one. In fact, the definition of consumer, rather generic and residual (a natural person contracting for reasons external to his/her professional activity), is used as a proxy for weakness, but from a socio-economic point of view it is questionable whether this category is sufficiently homogeneous and well defined. It may be both too wide or too narrow: too wide, because in some cases consumers may have equal expertise and contractual power as their professional counterparts; too narrow, because often professionals too can be in a weak position.[165] Again, the fact that often EC law provides only for minimum harmonisation permits the adjustment of national legal systems, so as to cover other situations deemed worthy of protection. But the problem is merely shifted from the EC to the national level: how do we draw the line between parties that need special protection and those that do not? In fact, no system seems has found a fully satisfactory solution, and most of the time legal intervention seems to be aimed at tackling specific problems considered to be urgent, leaving systematic considerations aside.

There is a very lively debate on whether the use of mandatory protective rules should be extended to European contract law as a whole. According to Mattei, a European civil code should consist exactly of mandatory rules: 'The new European Code should be hard, minimal, not limited to contracts, and process-oriented'[166] This is because a body of default rules (or, even

---

[164] See V. Zeno-Zencovich, 'Il diritto europeo dei contratti (verso la distinzione fra "contratti commerciali" e "contratti dei consumatori' (1993) IV *Giur. It.* 57.

[165] Such as in the case, for example of subcontractors; in fact, an Italian law of 1998 (Act No. 192 of 1998, in G.U., 22 June 1998, No. 143) contains several protective rules aimed at remedying the structural disparity of contractual powers of the parties. See also Dir. 2000/35/EC on late payments in commercial transactions (OJ L 200, 8 August 2000). In the UK, a working paper of the Law Commission dealing with the possibility of merging the *Unfair Contract Terms Act 1977* with the *Unfair Contract Terms in Consumer Contract Regulations 1999*, proposes to extend the protection in some cases from consumers to businesses as well: see *Law Commission Consultation Paper No. 166*, August 2002 (available at http://www.lawcom.gov.uk).

[166] See Mattei, above note 81. According to Mattei, the enthusiasm for the use of soft law derives from the influence on legal scholarship of postmodernism, which has been trans

more, soft rules, as in the case of a Restatement) can work properly only if the limits to individual freedom have been previously firmly settled: 'parties should be left free to make their options only once the legal system has been able to establish, by binding effective law, its control against opportunistic behaviour'.[167] What is needed in order to create a working European internal market, therefore, is harmonisation of mandatory rules, leaving then the possibility of establishing common default rules to a truly competitive process, which in this way can produce efficient results.[168]

In order to assess whether a European contract (or civil) code would contribute to the reduction of transaction costs for interested parties, it is necessary to evaluate whether it succeeds in reducing legal risks linked to contracting, which are determined by the possibility that legal rules and their effects will prove different than what expected by the parties. According to Collins, transaction costs are mainly due to ignorance, i.e. lack of knowledge of relevant rules, and to uncertainty, i.e. the difficulty in assessing the outcome of applicable rules.[169] Theoretically, harmonised European contract rules could reduce the risks connected to ignorance (provided that they would substitute, and not coexist with national rules, otherwise this risk would increase), but it cannot be established *ex ante* that they would reduce uncertainty of application, since a common set of rules does not automatically imply common results.[170] The crucial issue therefore becomes whether there are sufficient

---

planted from American legal thought to Europe: see U. Mattei, A. di Robilant, *The Art and Science of Critical Scholarship: Postmodernism and International Styule in the Legal Architecture of Europe*, (2002) *Eur. Rev. Priv. L*.29.

[167] Mattei, above note 81, 'If the law is soft with aggressive and opportunistic market actors that under the shield of soft legality succeed in transferring costs to society rather than facing the real social cost of their market activity, it is much better to have it hard.'

[168] See U. Mattei, 'A Transaction Costs Approach to the European Code', (1997) *Eur. Rev. Priv. L.* 537; U. Mattei, 'Efficiency and Equal Protection in the New European Contract Law. Mandatory, Default and Enforcement Rules', (1999) *Virginia J. Int.'l L.*, 607-641. Grundmann, above note 150. 292, underlines the importance of information mechanisms for systems competition; see also S. Grundmann, 'The Structure of European Contract Law' (2001) *Eur. Rev. Priv. L.*505.

[169] Collins, above note 73, who underlines that law is only one among several factors that affect trust of stakeholders in cross-border trade. A transaction costs approach is advocated also by W. Van Gerven, above note 39.

[170] The wider the scope of the uniform rules (which is maximum in the case of a Civil code), the greater the risk of uneven application. This has led some scholars, particularly those from common law countries, to prefer an incremental, trial and error approach: see Collins, above note 73; H. Beale, 'Finding the remaining Traps instead of Unifying Contract Law',

mechanisms for ensuring that common rules are evenly applied throughout Europe, and in fact it can be doubted whether a fragmented legal environment such as the current European one, with different legal cultures and traditions and different institutional settings, will be able to meet the challenge.[171]

This is a major difference with the situation existing in the United States, which is very often taken as a model for European legal integration.[172] The fragmentation of the legislative framework (most areas of private law are state law, since the federal level has only enumerated competences) and the diffusion of 'soft' legal instrument such as Restatements and model laws is counterbalanced by a strong common legal culture and by a powerful judiciary that is in charge of the application of law. Moreover, the role of what Eisenberg terms 'aspirational elements' should not be underestimated:

> If the only objective of unification is the promotion of commerce, mandatory unification from the top down might be the most desirable way to proceed. If, on the other hand, the objective of unification is to fulfil an aspiration of a European culture and an aspiration to make the best possible legal rules, then a more gradual, voluntary process of unification, beginning from the bottom up, might be more desirable.[173]

---

in Grundmann and Stuyck, above note 4. For a general analysis of the relationship between "black letter" law and applied law see R. Sacco, *Legal Formants, A Dynamic Approach to Comparative Law*, (I and II), (1991) 39 *Am. J. Comp. L.* 1, 343.

[171] Mattei, above note 81, underlines that this is one of the major differences existing between the European and the American situation. The importance of judicial application for European law is emphasized also by van Gerven, above note 39, whose analysis is limited to the need for strengthening the preliminary ruling in front of the European Court of Justice, and does not deal with national judiciary bodies. See also Collins, above note 73, 'The problem will be to secure a uniform interpretation of the law in each Member State. Common uniform rules will not on their own guarantee such a result. The normal legal technique for ensuring such a result is to establish a hierarchy of courts (...)'; see also H. Collins, 'Transnational Private Law Regulation of Markets', (1998) *Europa e diritto privato* 967.

[172] For an anlysis of the factors that contribute to the unformity of the American legal system, and a comparison with the European situation, see M. Eisenberg, The Unification of Law, in Mattei and Bussani, above note 61, 15, who lists several unifying factors, such as legal education, legal doctrine, a common historical and economic background.

[173] Eisenberg, ibid, 24-25; as for American law, he observes that "national law is the product of aspiration to be an American nation with an American culture and an American law" (p. 22).

Again, we are brought back to the fact that a Code does not stand in isolation, and consequently it can work only if is inserted in a 'legal fabric', based on a common legal culture, a target which (even supposing the will to abandon parochial attitudes by lawyers) will require generations before becoming a reality in Europe. The puzzle is a kind of 'chicken-and-egg' problem: should we start from the creation of a European legal culture, and only once this is firmly established, move to the elaboration of a Code, or should we rather work on the Code, and then back it with the progressive establishment of a common legal culture? Pragmatically, it seems that there is no way to keep these two questions apart: a workable Code can be produced only by comparing thoroughly all European legal systems, and in order to do that, the basis for a common legal culture needs to be developed. Whether emphasis should be laid mostly on the first or the second issue is not only a legal problem, but is linked to complex and partly unforeseeable (at least from a legal point of view) political factors.[174]

The technical debate is consequently inextricably linked to the political one: there are strong technical legal arguments both against and in favour of general harmonisation of private law, and none of them seems to be decisive. The only available option, therefore is to discuss openly all advantages and drawbacks, and then move the final decision back to the political arena, which is ultimately the level where such a decision must be taken.[175]

Scholarly work, therefore, should consciously strive to combine a strictly technical debate on which rules should be inserted in a future code, because they are the most suitable and efficient ones, with an open acknowledgement that even technical choices have ideological basis.[176] This is not only because

---

[174] See A. Hartkamp, *Perspectives for the Develoment of a European Civil Code*, in Mattei and Bussani, above note 61, 59: 'much in Europe has occurred which was not believed to be possible only a few decades ago. A call for codification might all of a sudden become a reality, e.g. when for political reasons a success is necessary'. That legal factors are not the only relevant elements in this process is demonstrated by the fact that the many legal (mainly scholarly) projects on European private law have gone on in splendid isolation for decades, before they were caught in the midst of action once political momentum was gained. See Staudenmayer, above note 52.

[175] See Hesselink, above note 84, "the future of European contract law will depend on political choices".

[176] See M. Hesselink, *Editorial, Special Issue on Critical Legal Theory and European Private Law*, (2000) *Eur. Rev. Priv. L.*, 3; M. Hesselink, *The New European Legal Culture,* (Deventer: Kluwer, 2001), ch. 4 and 5; M. Hesseling, 'The Principles of European Contract Law: Some Choices made by the Lando Commission', in M.W. Hesselink, G.J.P. De Vries,

private patrimonial law rules do perform distributive and social functions,[177] beside facilitating economic exchanges, but also because, as Duncan Kennedy has argued, there is an inherent ideological and rhetorical dimension in these rules, linked to the choice between the two opposite poles of altruism and individualism,[178] i.e. even in the case of situations which do not pose distributive problems, a choice must be made among several alternatives that are all technically feasible but bear different results.

Moreover, technical aspects, fundamental as they are, should not overshadow the importance of the task of building a European private law:

> Just as the single currency seems to be a necessary ingredient for a Single Market, so too greater uniformity in the rules of the marketplace appears to be an essential element in building the largest market on earth. But unlike money, where either you have the same currency or you don't, with the regulation of markets there are many degrees of harmonisation and approximation that could be attempted and that might serve the purpose without the imposition of absolute uniformity. This task has never before been attempted. It involves the re-regulation of national markets with a view to the removal of obstacles to cross-border trade. It is not merely a technical problem, but the task raises profound political questions both about the kind of market order we wish to create, and, more deeply about the identity of European citizenship'.[179]

This demanding task requires us to keep our feet firmly on the ground, but at the same time to be able to look far ahead.

Principles of European Contract Law; Preadviezen uitgebracht voor de Vereining voor Brugerlijk Recht, (Deventer, 2001).

[177] See T. Wilhelmsson, *Social Contract Law and European Integration*, (Aldershot: Dartmouth, 1995).

[178] See D. Kennedy, 'The Political Stakes in "Merely Technical" Issues of Contract Law' (2001) *Eur. Rev. Priv. L.* 7, who analyses several default rules applicable between businessmen of equal bargaining power in a competitive market, i.e. a situation with no politically controversial issues. The distinction individualistic/altruistic is based on an evaluation of whether rules "impose more or less intense duties of sacrifice vis-à-vis vulnerable parties and more or less intense duties of sharing vis-à-vis misfortunate parties" (p. 13). This conception of private law determines also a shift in the boundaries with public law. See also D. Kennedy, Form and Substance in Private Law Adjudication, 89 *Harv. L. Rev.* 1685, and D. Kennedy, *A Critique of Adjudication (Fin de siècle)*, (Cambridge (Ma.), 1997).

[179] Collins, in this volume.